VALUES AND SOCIAL CHANGE IN BRITAIN

STUDIES IN THE
CONTEMPORARY VALUES OF MODERN SOCIETY

The series is based on the large-scale social research programme initiated by the European Value Systems Study Group, Amsterdam, in the late 1970s and developed by a number of universities and research centres in different parts of the world. The series will explore the moral and social values of contemporary society preparing individual national reports, intercontinental and intercultural comparative studies and thematic reviews of major topics including the family and marriage; religion and personal morality; work attitudes and political participation. Extensive use will be made of the unique 27 nation data set possessed by collaborating centres supplemented by newly commissioned follow-up studies where appropriate and relevant research materials made available from other sources.

Already published

Mark Abrams, David Gerard and Noel Timms (*editors*)
VALUES AND SOCIAL CHANGE IN BRITAIN

Stephen Harding and David Phillips (with Michael Fogarty)
CONTRASTING VALUES IN WESTERN EUROPE (*forthcoming*)

Further titles in preparation

VALUES AND SOCIAL CHANGE IN BRITAIN

Edited by

Mark Abrams, David Gerard and
Noel Timms

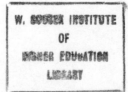

in association with the
European Value Systems Study Group

First published 1985

Published by
THE MACMILLAN PRESS LTD
Houndmills, Basingstoke, Hampshire RG21 2XS
and London
Companies and representatives
throughout the world

Printed in Hong Kong

British Library Cataloguing in Publication Data
Values and social change in Britain.
1. Social values   2. Great Britain—
Social conditions—1945–
I.   Abrams, Marks II. Gerard, David, *1940–*
III.   Timms, Noel   IV.European Value Systems Study Group
303.3'72   HN385.5
ISBN 0–333–38676–0
ISBN 0–333–38677–9 Pbk

This book is dedicated to the families of our contributors and to the sponsors of the British Study: private individuals, charitable trusts and foundations, church organisations and companies. Without their patience and generosity it would not have been possible.

Contents

List of Figures

List of Tables

Acknowledgements

The editors wish to acknowledge their debt to the British sponsors of the Values Study and to thank Ruud de Moor, Jan Kerkhofs, Jacques-René Rabier, the members of the EVSSG Steering Committee and its Technical Group for their support and cooperation throughout. Special thanks are also due to Gordon Heald and Meril James for Gallup's enthusiastic contribution to the design and execution of the Study in the UK and elsewhere, for the provision of basic tabulations of the data and their good-natured willingness to meet authors' subsequent demands for additional output to varying specifications. The contribution of John Hall and Jim Ring of the Survey Research Unit at the Polytechnic of North London at the data-analysis stage was invaluable and the Study team are indebted to them for the Unit's sustained involvement in the research.

The editors also wish to express their gratitude to the individual contributors to the British volume for their work and to Tony Waters and Joan Wilkins Associates for the helpful and efficient way in which they helped to turn our barely legible chapter drafts into final typescript form.

Finally, individual authors wish gratefully to acknowledge the help, advice, encouragement and criticisms they received from: Michael Banton, Ronald Brech, Joan Brothers, Karel Dobbelaere, Gwynn Davies, Jack Dominian, Brian Evans, Chris Harris, Mike Hornsby-Smith, Rev. Gerry Hughes, Rev. Kevin Kelly, Dorothy Lanier, Nicholas Lash, Rev. Vincent Nichols, James O'Connell, Richard Rose, Jean Sparks, Rita Tait, Bob Towler, Rev. Hans Wijngaards.

Membership of the European Value Systems Study Group

STEERING COMMITTEE

Dr M. Abrams	London, UK
Professor P. Delooz	Mons, Belgium
Professor D. J. Kerkofs	Louvain, Belgium
Professor K. Forster	Augsburg, West Germany (died 1981)
Professor H. Maier-Leibnitz	President der Deutschen Forschungsgemeinschaft (until 1980)
Professor R. de Moor	Tilburg, Netherlands
Dr J-R. Rabier	Special Counsellor, EEC Commission Brussels

TECHNICAL GROUP

Institut für Demoskopie, Allensbach, West Germany
Ms R. Kocher
Professor E. Noelle-Neuman   Co-ordinator – Phase 1
Faits et Opinions, France
Madame H. Riffault   Co-ordinator – Phase 2
Professor J. Stoetzel
Gallup, UK
Mr G. Heald   Co-ordinator – Phase 3
Ms M. James
Data, Spain
Professor J. Linz
Dr F. Orizo

Notes on the Contributors

Mark Abrams is Joint Head of the Research Unit of Age Concern, England. His publications include *The Condition of the British People. Social Surveys and Social Action* and *Must Labour Lose?*.

Jennifer Brown is Research Fellow in the Department of Psychology, University of Surrey. She is co-editor of *Uses of the Research Interview* (with M. Brenner and D. Canter).

Miriam Comber is a postgraduate student in the Department of Psychology at the University of Surrey.

Michael Fogarty is Director of the Institute for Family and Environmental Research and also works for the Policy Studies Institute. His recent publications include *Irish Values and Attitudes* (with L. Ryan and J. Lee).

David Gerard is an adviser to a number of trusts and foundations. His publications include *Charities in Britain*.

Karen Gibson is a research student in the Department of Sociology at the University of Surrey.

A. H. Halsey is Professor of Social and Administrative Studies at the University of Oxford. His publications include *Trends in British Society since 1900* (editor), *Power and Ideology in Education* (ed. with J. Karabel), *Heredity and Environment*, and *Change in British Society*.

Stephen Harding is Lecturer in Psychology at Nene College. He was closely involved in the planning of the Values Project. He is currently completing a book on the European results of the survey (in collaboration with David Phillips), also to be published by Macmillan.

Susan Howard is a clinical psychologist at Ealing Hospital with a particular interest in marital therapy.

Father John Mahoney, S.J., is former Principal of Heythrop College, University of London, where he still lectures in Moral and Pastoral Theology. His publications include *Seeking the Spirit* and *Bio-ethics and Belief*.

David Phillips is Research Fellow in the Survey Research Unit of the Department of Applied Social Studies at the Polytechnic of North London. He is co-author with Stephen Harding of a forthcoming volume on the European results of the Values Study, also to be published by Macmillan.

Noel Timms is Professor of Social Work and Director of the School of Social Work at the University of Leicester. His publications include *Social Work Values*.

David Watson is Lecturer in Social Administration at the University of Bristol. His publications in philosophy and public policy include *Caring for Strangers*.

Introduction

This study had its origin in a large-scale programme of social research initiated by the European Value Systems Study Group in Amsterdam. Initially an informal group, consisting of European academics (including theologians) and opinion researchers, the EVSSG was formally established as a foundation in 1978 to design and conduct a major empirical study of the moral and social values underlying European social and public institutions and governing conduct. Originally confined to Western Europe, knowledge of the study excited interest in North and South America, the Middle and Far East, Australia and South Africa. Affiliated groups were set up in these countries, independently financed and controlled, but adopting similar methods and administering the same questionnaire. Agreements were negotiated relating to the exchange of data for the purpose of intercontinental and intercultural comparisons. More recently the survey has extended into Eastern Europe. As a result of these initiatives the EVSSG has access to an unique data set of high quality.

Reports of the overall European results are available in French (Stoetzel, 1983) and English (Harding and Phillips, 1985). This volume is concerned primarily with the British results. The objective is not the simple description of the outcome of administering a lengthy and complex questionnaire (see General Appendix) but rather the presentation of work in progress on the data from a range of analytical perspectives. The fundamental concerns of the EVSSG with the unity or the diversity of a European system of values and with the possibility of fundamental value changes have been pursued through the study of a number of key questions. People were asked about what was important to them, about their likes and dislikes, their emotional states, their beliefs and satisfactions, their attitudes and behaviour, their experiences of guilt and of spirituality, their view of the world and the norms governing their behaviour and that of others. At an exploratory phase such an inclusive approach is justified, corresponding as it does to the common usage of values, where the important logical distinctions between preferences, moral judgements, plans-for-life, motives and cognitions are rarely noted.

The essays in this volume represent the pursuit of these and other questions by a number of specialists who were asked, under conditions of severe space constraint, to consider the abundance of the EVSSG data in relation to Britain from the perspective of their own discipline and interest. No attempt was made to specify a unifying analytical model. Rather, each author was left free to determine how best to treat the material within limited editorial guidelines.

In addition to the studies of selected topics it was considered important to present a number of general commentaries, partly to address the wider significance of the study as a whole and partly through criticisms to indicate at least some directions for future work. Prof A. H. Halsey has provided an opening commentary, whilst the Rev. Dr Mahoney S. J. and Mr David Watson offer respectively theological and philosophical comment.

A multi-disciplinary approach is an essential requirement for any study of values. It is against the background of the established study of social and moral values – in socio-political work, in moral and social philosophy, in social psychology and so on – that the EVSSG research should be illuminated and criticised. Questions concerning the meaning, organisation and permanence of values are not in any sense new, but empirical evidence on the scale of the EVSSG study is. The study is also significant in raising, implicitly or explicitly, a number of major questions of substance and methodology.

Future work will not only make extensive use of the international comparative material but will, it is hoped, begin to unpack the portmanteau 'values' and establish and refine differences within what may presently be treated somewhat generally. Two further questions require systematic attention. First, the EVSSG offers an abundance of detailed material resulting from the administration of a question-naire, but the responses do not enable us to explore in depth the reasons and the reasoning behind the answers. Indeed speaking of what lies 'behind' weakens the point. It is not as if the reasons and the reasoning were information additional to the answers: they are an essential part of any answer and in their absence we can treat of the material only in an exploratory fashion. So ways of in-depth study must be found and used. Second, the EVSSG project raises critical questions concerning the extent to which 'values' constitute for any individual a system enduring and/or changing over time and the extent to which 'values' are shared, partly or completely, with others. It is a measure of the significance of the EVSSG project that it both produces an unique set of data on a range of crucial questions and indicates some of the fundamental methodological and substantive issues to be faced.

1 On Methods and Morals

A. H. HALSEY

The authors of the European Values Study have set themselves a
heroic task. They have aspired to describe the moral condition of
contemporary Europe. In this volume they report on Britain. In this
chapter I comment on their achievement, its limitations, and some
possible directions of its further development.

Britain belongs to a civilisation of such great antiquity and such
formidable internal complexity as to yield to no easy analysis.
European culture could reasonably be described from one point of
view as an evolution of the means to understand itself. Such a
description would be a history of the humanities in which the social
scientific study of culture could claim but a modest part. Indeed the
means to the end of cultural understanding are nothing less than the
accumulated methods of all the arts and disciplines. A chronicle of
them might begin with a salute to the prophetic tradition of the Old
Testament Jews, might admire the Greek experience of attempts to
codify human nature, might describe the encyclopaedia of orthodoxy
and heresy in medieval Christendom, would appreciate the secular
prophets of the age of enlightenment, and so put into perspective the
modern rise of a self-conscious sociology.

Only then, and still more recently, would the small corner occupied
by social scientific survey come into view. Many disciplines have
brought many methods to bear on the definition and explanation of
values. None can claim proprietorship or even hegemony: only
marginal contribution can be expected from any particular technique
of enquiry.

A sociologist is habituated by his profession to define values

1

primarily in terms of the maintenance and disruption of social order
and to seek explanations of values in changes of social structure. He
will have read the giants of global interpretation of social transformation – Comte, Spencer, Marx, Weber, Durkheim. He will be familiar
with Marxist theories treating consciousness as epiphenomenal to
social structure. He will probably know L. T. Hobhouse's *Morals in
Evolution* (1906) as an opposing theory in the liberal tradition.
Whatever his theoretical or political leaning, he will be sympathetic
to sociological explanations and suspicious of theories rooted in
individualistic psychology.

I write from a background of sociological training and as one who
has attempted to assess the culture of a nation in a book drawing on
the results of a wide variety of sociological research (Halsey, 1981).
Many, if not most, readers of the present book will come to it
equipped mostly with personal knowledge. It seems appropriate
therefore to begin with this more traditional and more commonly
shared method of cultural understanding.

THE METHOD OF PERSONAL KNOWLEDGE

I do so first to remind the reader of the immense store of information
about a country which is lodged in the minds and memories of its
inhabitants. The collective store, including as it does visual, auditory,
olfactory, and tactile knowledge, is vastly greater than that of any
conceivable data set stored from a survey into a computer file. Any
British native has accordingly acquired by nurture a formidable
battery of, so to say, tests of significance which he or she may readily
apply to the findings of the Values Study.

To elaborate the point I will cite my own version of this accumula-
tion of personal knowledge: for it happens that I recently tried to
sketch the moral condition of Britain by making a series of excursions
out of Oxford and London with the object of preparing a series of
talks for the BBC. Out of these journeys there emerged eight scripts
of 2,700 words. So is the world ordered by the particular demands of
Radio 3 broadcasting – a contrived artefact with different rhythms
and time spans from those of the travels, conversations, and memories on which they were based. But personal experience and cultural
description can, without absurdity, be linked if they are both thought
of as analogous to travel. Journeys in practice slice life into disciplined and recorded intervals. The railway timetable is one possible

metaphor of social consciousness: it imposes coherence on the flux of events and perceptions. Words along the recording tape are of a piece with miles along the track.

The metaphor can be extended. I was the traveller, yet the words on the tape had to represent not my views but the culture of my country. How, then, was I to describe it? I had previously used sociological knowledge to produce a different kind of picture. The idea now was to use personal knowledge. I tried to eschew official statistics, blue books, or analyses of British social structure. I could not be wholly successful, for professional knowledge inevitably becomes personal. Nevertheless, in anyone of middle-age, memory is more than adequate to a mere 160 minutes of talk; and the journeys could easily be contrived to lift the dust from stored recollections. So I planned my excursions to repeat my own biography, and thus to reconstruct one slender strand in British experience from the early 1920s to the early 1980s.

The professional sociologist will shudder at the imperfections of such a method. The encounters of the traveller are not random: a sample cannot be a scientific basis for assertion about a population without specified probabilities of representing it. Indeed, the people to whom I talked were not even a sample in any scientific sense. I did not choose them in relation to the British population. They were chosen for me by my passage through the restricted circumstances of the street, the railway compartment, or the pub, to which the traveller is confined: or if they were private contacts, they were my friends and acquaintances and thus a refraction of public life through the peculiar network of my personal associates.

On the other hand personal knowledge covers, however unsystematically, a vastly larger territory than any specialised professional knowledge. A man may be no architect, but buildings evoke periods and people he has never known. A woman may be no paediatrician yet spend half her life tending children. People may be innocent of theology but can scarcely avoid coming to terms with life and death. In any case I was committed on this occasion to the method of personal encounter and encouraged in it by awareness of my predecessors. The genre is well known and thoroughly understood. Journeying through the island is a tradition. Every child learns the phrase 'from Land's End to John o' Groats'. There is a large library of books where the author has projected his personal knowledge on to the national screen and called it England. Daniel Defoe, William Cobbett, and J. B. Priestley are only a few famous names in a multitude.

George Orwell (Orwell, 1970, p. 76) justified them all – and me – in
the introductory section of his *The Lion and the Unicorn* to which he
gave the sub-title 'England your England'.

> ... above all, it is *your* civilisation, it is *you*. However much you
> hate or laugh at it, you will never be happy away from it for any
> length of time. The suet puddings and the red pillar boxes have
> entered into your soul. Good or evil, it is yours, you belong to it,
> and this side of the grave you will never get away from the marks
> that it has given you.

THE FINDINGS OF PERSONAL KNOWLEDGE

I pondered this passage before setting out on my summer travels,
knowing that I was a patriot and fearing that I was a sentimentalist.
So I asked myself in advance what fragments in my memory would
put a stamp of interpretation on the journeys I was preparing to
make. Slowly the confused recollections ordered themselves into four
themes as personal preconceptions of my country and my compat-
riots. The reader might care to compare them with his or her own as a
prelude to reading the results of the Values Study in the chapters
which follow.

The first is an age-old tension between urban and rural life. I was
born among the dirty brick, the smoky streets, little men in baggy
trousers, and shapeless women with shopping baskets that made up
Kentish Town in the early 1920s. Then I was transported to Lidding-
ton in Rutland. A railway journey from the grandiose grime of gothic
St. Pancras through the more domestic Victorian elegance of Ketter-
ing station with its neat platforms and its decorated iron stanchions,
ended finally with a horse and cart across the Welland Valley into a
rural world of medieval sleepiness. Stone and thatch, huge skies, vast
woods, and unending open fields were my first memories of the
English countryside.

Nonetheless, I retained a cockney snobbishness towards the 'country bumpkin'. When I first read the *Communist Manifesto of 1848* the
phrase which leapt out of that strident pamphlet of vulgarised
Marxism was 'the idiocy of rural life'. Marx gave historical credit to
the bourgeoisie for our escape from rural stagnation. *I* had to give the
credit to the London Midland and Scottish railway, which gave
railway servants periodic free passes to go anywhere in the country.

We always went back to St. Pancras. The tension never ceased, and I came to accept it not only as a private experience but as an integral part of the national psyche. In the end it gave me two patriotisms, the one of the soil, the other of the Cenotaph.

The second theme was a kaleidoscope in memory of continuous variation of colour, sound, and smell. England is a Jacob's coat of a country. The black splendour of Liverpool Town Hall, white hawthorn everywhere in the spring, the red mud of Devon, the golden stone of villages scattered from Banbury to Peterborough, and the innumerable greens encircling and shrouding all human settlements.

The ear of the traveller too is assailed by a great variety of sound if only from what is called common speech. Shaw's *Pygmalion* is not a caricature. A man from Sunderland has only to say 'Good Morning' to distinguish his origins from the Newcastle man twelve miles away. I remember the two languages which I learned in order to survive the day in a grammar school and the evening in the village street. Scents also linger, persistently pervading my recollections. Coal fires, crushed grass, road tarmac, and pig sties. I can still smell the foetid clammy stink of urine and stale vegetables in the kitchens at the wrong end of the street in contrast to the carbolic soap and boot polish of the respectable families.

Third, there was the hierarchy. A sociologist may refine it into abstractions, but no-one could grow up in England without acquiring a deep personal-cum-anthropological knowledge of class and status. Two memories are enough to evoke it. On one occasion in the 1930s the tram from Kentish Town was slow. My mother, the latest baby, my sister, my brother, and I rushed into the vault of St. Pancras station and bundled with our impedimenta into the corridor of a first-class carriage, seconds before the train drew out. A large, florid-faced man in a pin-striped suit flung open a compartment door to demand of my mother whether she had a first-class ticket. Some years later I was youth hostelling through Bath, and idling beside the entrance to a hotel in one of the stately crescents of classical architecture, when I heard the female version of the same arrogant voice demanding coffee at the reception desk. A mumbling, apologetic but stubborn west-country voice replied that the kitchens were closed. The lady stormed out with the disdainful judgement of English metropolitan snobbery, 'these damned provinces'.

Fourth and finally, there is the sense of tension between change and changelessness in English society. The London townscape has been transformed in my lifetime – invaded by the international architecture of Corbusier and modern brutalism. New towns appear and old industrial development falls into decay, but underneath lies the never-defeated countryside, and English sentiment refuses to give up its rural nostalgia. The Victorian hierarchy has virtually collapsed and generations of 'class abatement' have changed poverty from the common experience of the working class into the misfortunes of the old, the sick, and the deprived areas. Yet the House of Lords, the public schools, the phoney farms of the millionaires, and the shabby back streets of Toxteth and Brixton remain.

I feared that my journeys would confirm a new impulse of destructiveness attending the frenzied search of a new government for new private enterprise. Nevertheless, my expectation was also that the hope of progress, a fundamental element in the experience of my generation, could not have disappeared. For me it is bound up with escape from parochialism and provincialism. I remember Amy Johnson's exploits in the early 1930s and my own childish vision of a larger world of opportunity 'out there'. I flew my first Tiger Moth in 1942 over a wintry Wiltshire and felt again the exhilaration of movement in a flimsy aircraft surrounded by towering cumulus clouds and the English panorama below. England is different. As Orwell wrote, 'When you come back to England from any foreign country, you have immediately the sensation of breathing a different air' (Orwell, 1970, p. 75).

THE METHOD OF SOCIOLOGICAL SURVEY

While I had explored Britain by summer excursions (Halsey, 1983 i) the Values Study of the country was being put together out of a quite different collection of data. Would different methods produce incompatible results?

If my travelling commentary was suspect it is also prudent to acknowledge the frailty of the method used in this book. The survey researchers have taken small population samples and asked 'door step' questions. Many readers will quail. Can it be, they will immediately ask, that questions which lie at the heart of the cultural inheritance of several thousand years for millions of people can be answered in minutes by a few hundred interviewees? Is it intellectually respectable to assimilate prognostication of the next world to methods of predicting the outcome of next week's by-election in Huddersfield? Can a person's attitude towards the Ten Commandments be assessed by methods as crudely simple as those used to forecast how he or she will vote? To put the question in such tendentious rhetoric is, of course, to invite negative answers and dismissal of the project. That is not my intention. The point rather is to emphasise the ambition of the Values Study; to recognise what large results are being asked of small numbers. So to address the problem of what might be the reasonably expected result; what valid interpretation might be supported by the findings and, perhaps most important, what directions of further enquiry might usefully be undertaken.

The challenge to the study can be put in another way. The substance of the book is a description of moral values in Britain. But what *are* moral values – what are their origins and explanations? We are again plunged into theology and moral philosophy. Indeed in Chapter 11 David Watson attempts to argue that the Values Study lacks a plausible account of how moral values are to be identified, and goes on to charge the authors with tacit acceptance of subjectivism – a doctrine which omits reasoning from moral judgement and therefore gives both an unsatisfactory explanation of the genesis of moral values as well as faulty guidance to their implications for policy. That an adequate account of the genesis of moral values must involve reasoning can scarcely be disputed, and Watson presents compelling evidence that subjectivism severs the connection between the two. Whether any of the other authors are committed to subjectivism as a causal explanation of social behaviour is much less evident. Moreover, the moral character of an individual cannot plausibly be represented as a conscious recapitulation of the long history of moral reasoning. Attitudes and opinions typically owe less to individual reflection than to the social processes of upbringing, custom, and habituation. Custom and convention are always open to critical analysis but most people, most of the time, take morals as given from their social surroundings. Establishing the connections between social structures and individual attitudes can illuminate without commitment to any particular theory of social causation.

Much depends here on the meaning of the word causal. The crux of the issue for this book is that the material is used to establish correlations between social variables, especially age and class, and attitudes or opinions. Correlations carefully used can produce reliable predictions and in that sense statistical descriptions can constitute limited explanations. The limit is set by the known logic that correlations are not causes. They are precarious bases for predictions

(= explanations) in the absence of an explicit theory and every effort to falsify it by controlled testing. The theory in question would stipulate the path, whether of reasoning or other psychological processes, which connect a social position to an attitude or an action.

No such theory has been explicated as the basis for collecting the data of the Values Study and, even if it had, an interview survey of the type used here would be unlikely fully to satisfy its requirements. Whether the theory postulated processes of cultural transmission or of individual socialisation, its testing would demand data beyond the scope of a single survey. It does not follow, however, that such a survey can make no contribution to the analysis of how attitudes are generated. At the least it provides a map of correlations to guide further search for the more powerful processes. To this point I shall return.

Meanwhile, with respect to implications for policy, if Watson is right, the consequences are serious. For John Mahoney (Chapter 10) begins from the hope, expressed by de Moor and Kerkhof in their preface to Stoetzel's *Europe at the Crossroads* (1983), that the findings of the Values Study will prove of use to Church leaders and others. He is at pains to trace authority for moral judgement by surveys which do not necessarily raise the question of what reasoning and choices lie behind the attitudes expressed.

Useful knowledge may consist in measuring the incidence of opinion and its social distribution. Mahoney points out that the policies of Church leaders need to be guided by knowledge not only of the opinions of the laity but also those of unbelievers who may be presumed to move from different premises and by different routes to their moral positions. The argument, which is mainly a search for authoritative precedent, runs as follows. St. Paul recognised that a 'natural law' morality was accessible to all peoples by virtue of their human constitution. Thomas Aquinas, in the thirteenth century, concluded that 'the moral commands and prohibitions of the Decalogue were also conclusions of ordinary moral reasoning at its best' (Mahoney, ch. 10).

I would add that Thomas More, in the sixteenth century, constructed his *Utopia* (1516) solely on the basis of the four cardinal virtues of the heathen – wisdom, fortitude, temperance, and justice – that is, without the divine revelation of the Christian virtues of faith, hope, and charity. The Utopians created a moral order of society entirely by the light of reason. More deliberately denied them Christian revelation in order to show his contemporaries that virtuous pagans could create a better commonwealth than they had made shift to do as bad Christians. In our own time the 'new humanism' of the Roman Catholic Church, following the Second Vatican Council of 1962–4, also involves continuous discussion with the laity and with purely secular humanistic movements in an attempt to 'theologise from below' towards, as Henri de Lubac phrased it, an 'open humanism' and what Mahoney terms 'the form of human society which alone can do full justice to man who is also the image of God'.

These precedents, to be sure, do not dispose of Watson's central argument about causal and non-causal accounts of moral judgement. True conclusion cannot logically be inferred from false premises. They do however indicate the existence of other theories of the formation of moral opinion to which Church leaders have access and from which the development of empirical research may proceed. Meanwhile, with all its obvious dangers, the search for truth and goodness may reasonably be held to be legitimately conducted in part through the canvassing of popular opinion. This book reports on such a poll and as such has a claim in principle to be taken seriously. At the same time it bears a considerable weight of responsibility. Its descriptive findings must be accurate: its definitions of moral attitudes must be valid and its explanations of their origin and process must pass the most stringent tests of logical and scientific analysis.

Assessment along these lines inevitably questions the adequacy of the design of an enquiry into the moral condition of a nation. Deferring that issue, we can attend first to the chosen method – a national sample survey.

A sample of 1200 adults is the basis of the data in Britain as in the other European countries covered by the Values Study. Before the main survey of 1981 there was a period of designing and testing of a pilot questionnaire which involved 200 one-and-a-half hour interviews in each of France, Germany and Spain, as well as Great Britain. The British survey was undertaken by Gallup Poll – a well-known and experienced firm in survey and market research. Gallup followed standard procedure. First there was random selection of a nationally representative sample of 1000. The sample was selected in two stages with polling districts as the primary sampling units. The sample was stratified by region and by town size within each region. This procedure gives a list of addresses. Then, in order to randomise the selection of individuals within households, a Kish grid was used (see General Appendix).

An elaboration of this approximation to random sampling was then introduced. Value change was expected to manifest itself most among the young. A quota sample of two hundred 18–24 year olds was therefore added, the quotas being set by sex and age of completed education, so as to ensure adequate cell numbers for statistical comparison with the main sample.

Professional social scientists will recognise all this as standard survey procedure with attendant sampling errors which are in principle measurable and acceptable. Readers without statistical knowledge have to take the resulting numbers, averages and percentages on trust, suppressing intuitive doubt that small samples can faithfully represent large populations. Nevertheless, this assurance with respect to sampling error does not exhaust the problem. There is also the difficulty of non-sampling errors which will be present in any such survey, no matter how carefully designed in terms of the requirements of good sampling. Errors arising from the fact that one sample differs from the next one can be estimated by the application of probability theory, but non-sampling errors are errors of measurement. They raise difficult problems of reliability and validity. The lay reader's worry about sample size is rooted in concern about the total error from both sampling and measurement. In this connection Blalock's point is worth repeating (Blalock, 1960, pp. 441–12):

> The total error is thus a function of two independent sources of error and cannot be substantially reduced unless both types are simultaneously controlled. If nonsampling mistakes such as response or interviewing errors are large, there is no point in taking a huge sample in order to reduce the standard error of the estimate. ... Likewise, if one is willing to go to great pains to reduce nonsampling errors to a minimum, it will be foolish for him to make use of a small sample, thereby having a large sample error. A proper balance between sampling and nonsampling errors should therefore be maintained. Research accuracy limits effective sample size and vice versa.

Measurement errors stemming from unreliability and from invalidity are likely to arise in any sample survey. Reliability is greater or less according to the extent of *random* errors in measurement. Errors of this kind have many possible sources including carelessness or incompetence among interviewers, idiosyncrasy or variable understanding among respondents, coding errors, etc. Error can of course be reduced by high standards of interviewer training, extensive piloting of questionnaire items, and efficient checking of coding. These precautions have no doubt been taken. Further reduction of unreliability can be achieved by including two or more measures of the same variable and intercorrelating the measures. For some of the more important variables in the present survey there are multiple measures, but their intercorrelation is not reported. Still further reduction of unreliability may be accomplished by test-retest on the same sample. Attitude surveys are known to be especially vulnerable to instability of measurement so that here clearly is a desirable improvement in the future programme of the Values Study.

Invalidity is a further source of errors which are *non-random*. They may dwarf the significance of random (that is, reliability) errors. Validity is a difficult and ambiguous notion. Complete validity in this context means that what *is* measured is identical with what is *intended* to be measured. Behaviour and ascribed characteristics such as age or occupation may be relatively unequivocally defined and so yield to valid measurement. Variables like class or income may involve greater difficulties of meaning. Attitudes and assessments of sin or satisfaction, happiness or honesty, are intrinsically still more difficult and contestable.

Thus the interview question may fail to measure what is intended for a variety of reasons, including the practical one for a study of European moral attitudes – that the same interview has to be translated into several languages. In the end the problem of valid measurement may remain disputable. Any method of measurement rests on theoretical assumptions, statistical and philosophical, which are open to contest. That, I take it, is the essential point of David Watson's chapter. Methodological doubt therefore remains and suggests directions for the future development of the Values Study. We may now turn to the picture of popular morals and manners in Britain which the present study affords.

THE FINDINGS OF THE VALUES STUDY SURVEY

Mark Abrams, Michael Fogarty, David Phillips, David Gerard, and Stephen Harding set out their descriptions of British attitudes to work, politics, religion and morals in the following chapters. In the light of variations across Europe the broad and unsurprising impression is of a people culturally close to the countries of Northern Europe, diverging generally towards Scandinavia and away from

Latin Europe. Britain occupies this position with respect to satisfaction with life, the perceived trust among the young towards the old, psychological well-being, job satisfaction, contentment with the financial condition of one's household, willingness to fight for one's country in case of war, belief in the first three Commandments and acceptance of the Commandments against stealing and bearing false witness, belief in God and conception of self as a religious person. On all these variables the average scores for values with a conventionally secular connotation descend from Scandinavia through Northern Europe to Latin Europe. The explicitly religiously-phrased values run in the opposite direction, and for all the variables mentioned Britain lies culturally, as it does geographically, between Northern Europe and Scandinavia. Table 1.1 shows these comparisons.

The British do, however, appear to have some distinctive qualities of outlook. They are the most optimistic of the three European zones about the future and about the promise of science and the use of technology in that future. They are more proud of their nationality, think of themselves as having more pride in their work, more satisfied with their personal health, more approving of any future increase in respect for authority, more inclined to see themselves as to the right in politics and, most conspicuously, more likely to choose personal freedom as against social equality if forced to do so. Moreover, with respect to those of the Ten Commandments which have a moral as distinct from a religious reference, their average score is markedly more moralistic. They are in their normal geographical-cum-cultural position with respect to the religious Commandments to worship only one God, not to take His name in vain, and to keep the Sabbath. But with respect to honouring their parents and the injunctions against murder, adultery, theft, envy, and lust they out-do the Scandinavians, Northern Europeans and Latins in virtuous declaration. In short, though by no means outlandish from the European culture to which they belong, the British are to be seen and see themselves as a relatively unchurched, nationalistic, optimistic, satisfied, conservative, and moralistic people.

The picture, I would add, is in no way inconsistent with my personal impressions from journeys through Britain and gains numeracy in the context of parallel surveys of other European countries. If it lacks the historical dimension lent by personal memory, it gains the precise reliability of impersonal representation of a cross-section of opinion.

TABLE 1.1   *Some British attitudes in European perspective*

		(Percentages or mean scores)				
Q	Attitude	Scandin-avia[1]	Great Britain	Northern Europe[2]	Latin Europe[3]	All
129	Satisfied with life now	8.01	7.67	7.48	6.63	7.13
130	Satisfied with life 5 years ago	7.43	7.37	7.21	6.57	6.93
131	Satisfied with life 5 years on	8.00	8.15	7.72	7.26	7.55
121	Self evaluation of personal health	4.00	4.03	3.80	3.57	3.71
127	Feel free to control own life	7.00	6.71	6.73	6.01	6.43
124	Most people can be trusted (score)	50	43	34	26	31
125	The young trust the old	6.46	5.58	5.47	4.60	5.15
126	The old trust the young	5.52	4.64	4.74	4.47	4.68
128	Happy	3.19	3.33	3.18	2.96	3.08
	Psychological well being scale	2.07	1.41	1.42	0.90	1.23
	Pride in work	3.31	3.75	3.19	2.88	3.07
	Satisfaction in work	8.04	7.72	7.46	7.06	7.34
	Pride in country	3.08	3.43	3.08	3.18	3.13
	Would fight for country (score)	74	62	46	39	45
144	Should obey superiors at work	2.18	2.15	1.97	1.79	1.90
140	Satisfied with income	8.04	7.72	7.46	7.06	7.34
308	De-emphasise money and possessions	2.41	2.52	2.44	2.61	2.52
	De-emphasise work	1.41	1.69	1.74	1.93	1.80
	Emphasise technology	2.03	2.50	2.39	2.50	2.41
	Emphasise the individual	2.82	2.67	2.70	2.86	2.78
	Emphasise family life	2.86	2.82	2.81	2.86	2.84
	Emphasise simple life style	2.84	2.73	2.66	2.91	2.79
	Emphasise respect for authority	1.93	2.68	2.41	2.55	2.44
208	The Commandments apply to self					
	1. No other God	2.04	2.19	2.22	2.23	2.21
	2. Name in vain	2.06	2.11	2.25	2.19	2.21
	3. Sabbath	1.72	1.75	1.89	1.97	1.91
	4. Honour father and mother	2.62	2.79	2.74	2.75	2.74
	5. Killing	2.88	2.89	2.87	2.84	2.86
	6. Adultery	2.64	2.71	2.61	2.36	2.50
	7. Theft	2.85	2.84	2.82	2.75	2.79
	8. False witness	2.75	2.74	2.71	2.66	2.69
	9. Covet neighbour's wife	2.70	2.71	2.64	2.42	2.54
	10. Covet neighbour's goods	2.67	2.71	2.69	2.53	2.62
158	Am a religious person (score)	46	58	59	67	72
163	Believe in God (score)	46	76	74	77	73
167	God is important in my life	4.81	5.72	5.75	6.02	5.80

[1] Denmark, Sweden, Finland, Norway.
[2] Northern Ireland, Eire, West Germany, Holland, Belgium, France.
[3] Italy and Spain.

ALTERNATIVE DESCRIPTIONS

Ethnography has its peculiar charms, and the statistical description which I have outlined will appeal to some readers. The choice of genre is not, however, a mere matter of taste. The strength as well as the weakness of a representative sample survey can be appreciated by comparison with an alternative description offered recently by John Bowker (1983) under the subtitle of 'Religious beliefs and practice in Britain today'. Bowker's book and the Values Study together should help us to decide between two well-known and opposite views: the one that religion is moribund, the other that it is reborn.

The first view is obvious. The 'fixed capital' of Christendom – the spires and steeples of parish churches – is an ubiquitous feature of an ancient landscape. Yet we learn from David Gerard in Chapter 8 that on Sunday no more than one in seven of Britons will attend, and they will be mostly old women. The inference therefore appears to be that Christianity is all but dead. Many modern intellectuals concur and deem themselves progressive in doing so. Religion, they affirm, along with ritual and magical belief, was doomed from the dawn of the scientific age. Religious explanations of life and death are the vestigial remains of past, primitive, ignorant and gullible peoples. Robert Currie in his *Church and Churchgoers* (1977) has compiled the arithmetic of decline since 1700. The desertion of the pews, especially in the state churches like the Church of England or the Lutheran Church in Sweden, may be slow, but, in the time span of two millenia of the Christian era, it is spectacular. Secularisation, though learned sociologists dispute its meaning, describes the long post-medieval cycle of human consciousness.

The second view can be taken from my own description of Coventry airport on Whit Sunday 1982 (Halsey, 1983 ii). 'No popery' has been the common religion of the British people since Henry VIII. Yet here an elegant helicopter wafted the Vicar of Rome out of a clear blue sky on to a vast open-air church to preside over the Eucharist before a congregation of nearly half a million. A Catholic mass rode joyfully on an oceanic tide of belief in *Veni Veni Sancte Spiritus*. An alternative thesis of resurgence therefore appears. The religious impulse is indestructible. He who attempts to assassinate the Pope will attract more attention from the mass media than he who tries to kill the President of the United States. Mrs Thatcher entered Number 10 in May 1979 quoting St Francis of Assisi, and the Church was immensely older in the thirteenth century than the United

Kingdom is now. Mr Reagan announces himself as a 'born-again Christian' supported by the 'moral majority'. British church-going is nearer to heathen Sweden than to the American 'moral majority', but the Values Survey tells us that Britons accept the morality of the Ten Commandments more readily than do Frenchmen or Italians. Even discounting for the British tradition of polite hypocrisy towards interviewers, the evidence of tenacious religious belief, albeit unchurched, constantly renews the promise of religious revival. Some sociologists, like Daniel Bell (1980), discern a new age of faith. Human consciousness cannot be human without the supernatural.

So we may read Professor Bowker in anticipation of a definitive opinion based on new evidence. It is, like the Values Study, an empirical enquiry but through a crucially different method of survey. The author and his BBC team accumulated three hundred hours of taped interviews with declared religious devotees who were not priests or theologians or anthropologists of religion but ordinary practising members of their faith. A neatly sequenced selection from the material constitutes the book. It is unsatisfactory for two main reasons: there are no numbers and no history. The result is a misrepresentation of 'religious belief and practice in Britain today'. An arithmetic fault is intrinsic to Bowker's method. Unlike those who designed the Values Study, he deliberately rules out the lapsed and the unbelieving. He seeks those who are committed to religions which have established themselves in Britain, of which he finds six kinds: Jews, Christians, Muslims, Hindus, Buddhists, and Sikhs. He then proceeds to catalogue what they think and do. Thus a sketch emerges of a multi-cultural society, but its proportions are startling. Lacking the discipline of a representative sample, Bowker sketches the six religions with such mechanical even-handedness as to convey the impression, not of a Christian society secularised, but of a territory shared equally between six religious faiths. The result is a caricature of religious impartiality. The innocent reader receives no hint that Catholics, let alone Christians, outnumber all the other five churches put together by at least two to one, or that the majority do not actively belong to any church at all.

The representative sample survey is reasonably proof against such misdescription. Disciplined numbers aid accurate ethnography. On the other hand, the Bowker study at least notices the existence of religions in Britain other than Christianity. The EVSSG sample is so small that the Jews, Muslims, Buddhists, Hindus and Sikhs have cell sizes too minute to be usable. Professor Bowker's book most usefully fills out the picture of how people of different religious persuasion think and feel about body and soul, heaven and hell, evil and suffering. The Christian Trinity, the Sikhs' Four Vows, and the Buddhists' Five Precepts are defined. Karma, Dharma, moksha and sannyasin are explained. From this catalogue of belief and practice it emerges that the six faiths abound in commonalities: the centrality of prayer to religious practice, the significance of individual life as a balance of virtue and vice determining a fate beyond death, the insignificance of individual life in the pages of eternity, the rooted-ness of religious belief in family continuity and the ultimate belief in one God. This last seems capable of translation into a common ethical creed of love, hope and charity binding a nation and extending towards all mankind, even all creation.

Yet in neither study is there the slightest inkling that the existence of the ethnic minorities of Hindus, Sikhs, Buddhists, and Muslims in Britain is itself a facet of the imperial history of Christianity. They are colonial segments drawn into metropolitan capitalism during the final phase of the collapse of empire. None of this essential historical context appears from the angle of vision of either study. Nor is there an answer to my anticipated question. For a moment in the last pages Professor Bowker appears to offer one: 'religions are not going to disappear', but that answer cannot be inferred from the recordings of the sayings of the uncounted faithful. He simply assumes that religions will not disappear because 'they matter far too much to those who believe'. Sceptics will demand more persuasive evidence, including at least the measurement of historical trends.

ALTERNATIVES TO DESCRIPTION

Statistical description of the here and now could be elaborated at considerable length from the data of the 1981 survey. In the following chapters aspects of it are detailed but with a difference. The description I have summarised is relatively atheoretical. Of course, all description is at least proto-theoretical in the sense that its categories already imply some sort of explanation of the ordered data – in this case that nationality or some correlate of it can explain moral attitudes. Abrams, Fogarty and their colleagues have, however, gone further to correlate attitudes with age, class and other social vari-ables, postulating more or less explicit theories of the determination of attitudes by social structure.

The chapters on work, politics, and religion all provide good examples of this type of correlational analysis. Another, not included here but published elsewhere by Professor Richard Rose (1984, p. 379), is the description of patriotism. As we have noted, pride of nation is conspicuous among Britons. As many as 86 per cent are very proud or quite proud to be British, only 8 per cent declare themselves not very proud, and only 3 per cent 'don't know'. Rose correlates this measure of national pride with such variables as age, education, class, religion affiliation, political party, etc., and so establishes the overwhelming normality or consensus of patriotic sentiment. 'Whether one looks at the middle or the working class, among the young or the old, among English, Scots or Welshmen or among Protestants or Catholics, the average person in each group is proud to be British'.

Rose goes on to develop an explanation in terms of the rootedness of patriotism in the concerns and satisfactions of everyday life and is able to check his theory by further correlations with the relevant attitudinal material on family life, confidence in public institutions, and satisfaction at work. The limit is reached, however, when he postulates that national pride may be affected by government action, for at this point the survey is silent.

The adequacy of a description therefore depends on the sophistication of its underlying theory. An ethnography ultimately depends on its ethnology. Yet the relation can also be interactive. The classical experimental method is to hypothesise, draw inferences, and check them by observation. But a rich data set can allow ex-post hypotheses, suggested perhaps by unexpected correlations between variables. The practical difficulty is that an ex-post hypothesis may be baffled by absence of the relevant data. Collection of all the relevant data for testing an unborn hypothesis cannot be guaranteed by the most elaborate of surveys.

The problem becomes acute when the theory in question has a historical character. An important case in point is Inglehart's theory of post-materialism (1977; 1981) with which David Phillips deals briefly at the end of the chapter on politics. Another is the theory of secularisation and moral decline which is central to Gerard's chapter on religion.

Both examples are a challenge to the survey method which cannot in fact be met by a single study of the type used here. Evidence on a historical process may, of course, be available from other sources as in the case of secularisation: and the survey can provide confirmatory evidence, for example, that church attendance is lower than it was known to be at some past point in time. The temptation, however, is to compare age groups and infer that the old tell us about the past. This is dangerous. It can be used to trace *external* experience over time with fair safety: for example, an age-cohort analysis from a single survey can be used to reconstruct the history of type and length of schooling and thus reveal trends in educational opportunity for different classes and for men and women (Halsey *et al.*, 1980). But in respect of *subjective* experience or attitudes and opinions, such a procedure is likely to produce error by conflating three factors of distinct explanatory import. These are life cycle, period and intergenerational effects. To use age-cohort analysis of attitudes is to assume identity of the three factors. To ask for retrospective attitudes is to build unreliable memory into the analysis. The only reliable method is by panel studies (the same sample over time) or repeated surveys at appropriate intervals.

The continuing debate over Inglehart's theory sharply illustrates the problem. Accepting the validity of his measures of post-materialistic attitudes (though they are in fact disputable) an incautious analyst might cross-tabulate age with attitude and confirm the uninteresting commonplace that age and experience lead individuals out of youthful idealism through worldly responsibility towards materialist realism. Tables for all the European countries more or less repeat and further confirm a simple explanation. Unfortunately the theory is false and a more complex one can only be tested by repeated surveys over several generations to determine the relative weights of ageing, cohort effects, and period effects.

A further difficulty, however, is that the laboratory of life is not wholly under the control of the social analyst. Events may change the independent variables. Inglehart's earlier data from Japan and Germany included repeated surveys which showed the important period effect of post-war generations, especially their more educated and affluent segments, adopting a post-materialist outlook contrasted with that of their pre-war predecessors. A single watershed of this kind could then have slowly transformed itself into an intergenerational or cohort effect as older cohorts were replaced by younger ones until the previously-observed correlation between youth and post-materialism was obliterated. In the event, however, a new period of economic recession in the mid-1970s could, and partly did, begin to reverse the whole process at least in some European countries.

In consequence, progress towards definitive testing of a fully elaborated version of Inglehart's theory remains incomplete: only the simplistic ageing theory has so far been eliminated. The inference for survey technique to be drawn from this and other examples of theories aimed at explaining change in the culture of nations is nothing less than that empirical survey has to become a more-or-less permanent research institution.

Yet, even given the establishment of such desirable conditions, the question remains as to how far a survey approach can afford an adequate design for the future research programme. We have noted the considerable advantages of representative sampling. We have also remarked the disadvantages of small samples. Multivariate analysis rapidly exhausts their numbers. For example, the class categories used in the present study are too simple to capture such concepts as 'the new middle class', 'the educated class', or 'the private and public sectors', while simultaneously deploying other social classifications such as age, ethnicity, religious affiliation, etc. so as to represent all the variables of disputed theory. Analysis of theories of shifts in values and political re-alignment, which are at the centre of contemporary debate, entail complex issues with respect to styles of life, social networks, new social bases of political action, new patterns of family life, work and leisure, and indeed the whole culture of rapidly changing societies. These issues call for comparative study of samples, populations, and institutions, each with a design fitted to the theoretical question to be addressed.

Values inhere in institutions as well as individuals, and in behaviour as well as opinion. The Values Study, so far, is heavily inclined towards tacit definition of values as individual opinion. Sample surveys are ready vehicles in that direction, and the direction is dangerous. For example, it is relatively easier to collect attitudinal data than accurate data about the position of individuals in the structure of class, status, and party. A subtle temptation then follows. Crude social classification produces variables which leave large unexplained variance in the dependent variable. A battery of attitude measures gives more accurate prediction. Therefore it may be concluded, attitudes explain, for example, political preference more powerfully than do social positions. But this conclusion may be the erroneous outcome of a multivariate analysis which explained most of the variance by a tautological or verbally-equivalent question in the battery of attitudinal measures combined with inadequate data for classifying by social position.

Attitudes must not be assumed to be a sufficient explanation of other attitudes. Other approaches as well as attitude surveys must be part of a complete research programme. The point may be taken by considering a study like that of Richard Titmuss's *The Gift Relationship* (1970) from which fundamental and dramatic conclusions are drawn about the values of freedom, altruism, and efficiency from an analysis, not of expressed opinion, but of the organised institutions of different countries. Or consider R. H. Tawney's works *The Acquisitive Society* (1921) and *Equality* (1945) which use history and social statistics to mount a searching critique of the capitalist social order. Yet another example would be Stanley Elkins's *Slavery* (1959) using history and Bettleheim's observations of Jewish prisoners in Nazi concentration camps to produce an illuminating interpretation of the moral personality typical among plantation negroes in the Southern United States. The empirical study of the moral consciousness of nations must encompass works of this kind.

The aim set for themselves by the authors of the Values Study is indeed heroic. Attainment of it will take them beyond the limited methods they have hitherto successfully employed. All the more welcome, then, is the stated intention of EVSSG to regard this book as a report on work in progress along a path of further research in which methods of investigation will be developed to match the problems generated by comparative international study of morals and manners. Meanwhile, the reader of the present volume will find a survey description which is enlightening, and analyses which promise further understanding from future study.

2 Demographic Correlates of Values

MARK ABRAMS

INTRODUCTION

This chapter presents the findings of the Values Study from the point of view of age, gender and social class. It outlines one typology of values – traditional, ambivalent and anti-traditional – and discusses the variations which occur throughout the British adult population on the basis of the above demographic indicators.

THE SAMPLE

A total of 1231 people aged 18 years or more of which 47 per cent were men and 53 per cent were women was interviewed in the Values Study. For purposes of analysis it was necessary to group them into comparatively few age bands, viz:

1. Younger adults aged 18–34 years, currently 37 per cent of the adult population
2. Middle band adults aged 35–54 years, currently 31 per cent of the adult population
3. Older adults aged 55 years or more, currently 32 per cent of the adult population.

Respondents were placed in one of four classes depending on the occupation of the head of the household. The four classes and the percentages involved were as follows:

21

AB = professional/managerial   15 per cent

C1 = sales, clerical and other non-manual   23 per cent

C2 = skilled manual workers   33 per cent

DE = semi-skilled, unskilled, unemployed   29 per cent
       or pensioner   100 per cent

The survey also recorded for each respondent, housing tenure, terminal education age, and respondent's estimate of household income.

There is a 'built in' relationship between age and social class as Table 2.1 illustrates. This is due to the fact that social class DE includes all those whose *main* source of income was a statutory old age pension (but not all those of pensionable age). In fact, 26 per cent of all DE's were aged 65 years or over compared with 13 per cent of those in social classes ABC1.

TABLE 2.1   *Age composition of each class*

Age	ABC1 %	C2 %	DE %	All %
18–34	39	39	30	37
35–54	37	31	24	31
55+	24	30	46	32
	100	100	100	100
Weighted N	468	402	362	1231
Unweighted N	527	341	363	1231

In all three age groups slightly under half the respondents were men, and in all three well over 80 per cent of respondents were in households that had a complete house to themselves. There the similarities ended. A comparison of the younger adults with the older adults shows, for example, that among the latter, 80 per cent completed formal education before reaching the age of 16 but only 23 per cent of the younger adults had done so. Over three-quarters of the older adults lived either alone or with only one other person, but less than one-quarter of the younger adults were in this situation. Of those older adults able and willing to rate their household income, 69 per cent chose the description 'lower' – compared to 26 per cent of younger adults.

Similarly, there were considerable class differences in relation to house tenure, terminal education age and income. Thus, the proportion in owner-occupier dwellings ranged from 78 per cent (ABC1) through 60 per cent (C2) to 30 per cent (DE). The proportions with a terminal education age of 18 or more showed an even steeper gradient – from 36 per cent of ABC1's through 8 per cent of C2's to 4 per cent of DE's.

Household incomes before tax (as at March 1981) were divided into three groups: upper, (£10 000 or more), middle (£4800–£9999), and lower (£0–£4799). In each social class one-quarter of respondents was unable or unwilling to select a figure. Among those who were both able and willing to respond there is a marked association between social class and income. Two-thirds of the DE's put themselves in the lower income group, nearly three-fifths of the C2's chose the middle income group, and four-fifths of the ABC1's came into either the middle or upper income groups.

The striking socio-demographic differences between the social classes might well lead one to expect major resulting differences in values. There were, however, two similarities that might help to generate common values: in all three classes a little over 40 per cent of respondents lived in households that contained children under the age of 18, and in all three classes the balance of the sexes was the same. It is also important to bear in mind that the three age groups represent three cohorts who differ substantially in life experience and in the stages they have currently reached in the life cycle. Those aged 18 to 34 at the time of the survey were born during the years 1947 to 1963. Those born in the middle of this period (in the year 1955) came into a world in which World War II had long ended. The last vestiges of rationing had disappeared; commercial television was competing with the BBC; entrepreneurs discovered and pursued the new affluent teenager. In the world of sport the folk heroes included Stirling Moss and Chris Chataway. The Welfare State was fully launched; the number of houses built was consistently above an annual level of 300 000. The advocates of the comprehensive schools were near to success; the number of unemployed persons was little more than 1 per cent of the total working population; the number of days lost through strikes had reached its highest figure for almost 30 years. In the seven years since 1948 the average standard of living had risen by 20 per cent; the consumption of spirits and tobacco had reached new peaks. In the political field the names of Harold Wilson and James Callaghan were just being added to those of an older generation of party leaders.

Sixteen years later (in 1971) when two-thirds of the 1955 babies had left school, the 'good times' seemed set for unending expansion. For the year ending 31 March 1971, public expenditure on social services and housing was more than 50 per cent higher than for the year ending 31 March 1966. British newspapers and television had familiarised their audiences with the battle-cry of the rioting Paris students: 'What do we want? More! When do we want it? Now!' and with the sight of the students pressing home their demands by breaking up pavements to obtain missiles to hurl at the police. Since 1955 the stock of dwellings had increased from little more than 14 million to almost 19 million, so that the number of dwellings exceeded the number of households, and squatters were a familiar part of the urban scene. The number of people unemployed constituted less than 3 per cent of the total working population, and among the 3.7 million young people aged 15 to 19, 3.4 million were either students or else were settled into jobs. Mods and Rockers were a little passé, and Women's Lib was flourishing. In manufacturing industry the average earnings of boys and girls aged 16 and 17 were half those of men and women working full time in manual jobs and the teenage consumer had long been accepted by many producers as an important segment of their market.

Ten years later (in 1981) the average 1955 baby was aged 26 and large numbers of them were trying to cope with conditions that were entirely new to them. A hitherto unbroken diet of rising expectations easily and quickly gratified suddenly came to a halt. 60 per cent of the men and 75 per cent of the women were by then married, and a majority of those married couples had at least one dependent child. By August 1981, 12.2 per cent of the nation's working population were registered as unemployed, and 50 per cent of the nearly 3 million unemployed had been out of work for over six months. The crock at the end of the rainbow turned out to be filled with woodworm.

Those aged 35–54 had all been born between the years 1927 to 1946. Those born in the middle of this period (in the years 1936 and 1937) had survived at a time when the infant mortality rate was almost five times greater than it is today. It was a time when large social surveys carried out in such comparatively prosperous towns as York, Bristol, Birmingham, Southampton and half a dozen others showed that approximately 29 per cent of all children were born into families that could not afford what the British Medical Association decided was 'the minimum weekly expenditure on food which must be incurred if health was to be maintained'. In the average working class home, 40 per cent of all household expenditure went on food and a quarter of this food expenditure was on bread, potatoes, margarine and tea; abstinence and frugality were the unavoidable habits of good parents and were ones that, however unwillingly, they sought to pass on to their children. By the time those born in 1936–1937 were nine years old, World War II had ended; they were in their middle teens before all post-war rationing ceased. However, by the time they married in the late 1950s and early 1960s the Welfare State was fully launched. Between 1962 and 1967 the retail price index rose by 19 per cent but current expenditure on the social services and housing by the central government increased by 65 per cent; expenditure on education, school milk and school meals, and maternity benefits increased by 90 per cent.

At the time of this survey those who had been born in 1936–7 were aged 44 or 45. The great majority were married and living with a spouse and one or two children; their household gross income was 25 per cent above the national average and approximately 60 per cent owned or were in the process of buying a dwelling they occupied. In 1981 they were young enough to enjoy their affluence and to regard it as 'natural', and were old enough to recall their childhood hardships as incomprehensible and sometimes comical adventures.

Those aged 55 or more had all been born between 1894 and 1926. Those born in the middle of this period (1911) were in time to see their fathers going off to the trenches of World War I and their mothers to the munition factories. When they left school in 1925 they had added to these experiences a rapid sequence of depressions, strikes and lockouts that preceded the General Strike of 1926. Then three years later, when they were still in their teens, the Great Depression started. When, in 1932, they reached the age of 21 and became adults, there were 12.8 million work people insured under the Unemployment Insurance Acts and 21 per cent of them were unemployed; 1½ million people were in receipt of Poor Law relief (exclusive of 'casuals', that is homeless vagrants) and of these, a quarter of a million were either in a Work House or in a Poor Law Infirmary. When World War II broke out in 1939, this cohort was aged 28 and available to spend the next six years either in the armed forces or else as civilians manning the factories, repairing air raid damage and coping with rationing. This last had one consequence which throws a dazzling light on pre-war conditions. Throughout the war the government had conducted annual surveys of urban household diets and when its second report was released after the war, the authors pointed out that the administrative structure of food rationing had reached its complete development by the end of 1943 so that, from a nutritional point of view, the working class diet was probably more satisfactory in 1944 than at any time before the war. They also pointed out that in 1944 almost the only foods that were available in unlimited quantities were bread, flour, potatoes and oatmeal.

By the mid-1950s, when the benefits of rationing were all withdrawn and these respondents were into their forties, all the services and payments of the Welfare State were available to them and they perhaps thought themselves four times blessed – receiving State allowances as the parents of young children, benefiting indirectly from the State pensions enjoyed by their ageing parents, living in subsidised dwellings as householders, and receiving free medical services as patients. As they aged they inevitably lost their role and benefits as the parents of young children and tended to regard the latter as competitors in the State-organised redistribution of real income. For example, in 1958 a public opinion survey carried out among 825 women aged 35 to 54 asked respondents to give, in rank order, their preferences for any increase in government expenditure in four areas. Easily at the top came 'larger old age pensions', then 'more modern hospitals', then 'building more houses', and solidly at the bottom came 'improving education' (Abrams, 1983). By the end of the 1970s when a sample of this cohort (then aged around 70) was asked how much extra money they would need to live without any money worries, over half said they required nothing more – although nearly 85 per cent of this sample had as their main source of income the State retirement pension. (Mark Abrams, 1979). In spite of their short spell of post-war affluence their criteria of personal material well-being remained those they had learned as children, adolescents and young adults.

The differences in the sample according to sex, age, social class and the historical experiences of different groups described above are likely – independently and in combination – to influence attitudes, values and beliefs. Before such influence is investigated, however, we need to establish some usable categorisation of values.

A TYPOLOGY OF VALUES

On 123 occasions in the survey the respondent was asked to choose between alternatives and indicate which he/she felt was preferable;

on 98 occasions to express a belief or opinion; and 48 questions were concerned with the respondent's behaviour. An example of each of these is:

Choice: 'During your leisure time do you prefer to be alone, with your family, to be with friends, or to be in a lively place with many people?' (Q.112).

Belief: 'How much trust do you think young people have in older people in Britain today?' (Q.125).

Behaviour: 'Apart from weddings, funerals and baptisms, about how often do you attend religious services these days?' (Q.157)

From the total of 269 questions where the replies provide clues to the respondent's values, 71 have been selected which deal with the six topics of family, religion, patriotism, work, property and sex. On each question whenever the respondent expressed a high regard for family life, religious belief, patriotism, work, property rights and the sexual standards publicly regarded as 'good' before the popularisation of Freud, Kinsey and Spock (R. E. Money-Kyrle, 1932) he or she was allotted 1 point. In each of these areas the number of questions and replies used to construct a global scale was:

	Topic	*No. of items used*
1	Family	10
2	Religion	15
3	Patriotism	7
4	Work	15
5	Property	14
6	Sex	10
		71

On the basis of his or her total score on these 71 questions the respondent was placed in one of three categories, derived in part from the writings of Commager (1962), Geiger (1969) and Chisholm (1946).

1. Those holding *traditional values* scoring 41 points or more (23 per cent of the sample).

2. Those with *ambivalent values* scoring 28 to 40 points (56 per cent of the sample).
3. Those with *anti-traditional values* scoring 0 to 27 points (21 per cent of the sample).

TABLE 2.2   *Per cent of respondents endorsing 'traditional' values*

Value Areas	(a) Traditionals %	(b) Ambivalents %	(c) Anti- traditionals %	(d) (a) as % of (c)
Religion	48	31	21	229
Sex	62	50	37	167
Family	64	53	41	156
Patriotism	65	60	46	141
Work	50	43	37	135
Property Rights	83	78	67	124

The statistically significant differences in the replies of these three groups in each of the six value areas indicate that the scale as a whole and each of its six sub-scales can be accepted as valid measure of the values described here as traditional, ambivalent, and anti-traditional. Table 2.2 shows for each values area the average level of endorsement of the traditional outlook by those designated on the basis of the global scale as 'traditionals', 'ambivalent' and 'anti-traditionals'.

Apparently it is differences in values on religious beliefs, sexual mores, and family life that most sharply divide the traditionalists from the anti-traditionalists. The differences between them are less on issues concerned with property rights, work and patriotism, but on all six sub-scales the differences are substantial.

Responses of the two sexes on the global scale were similar, and as Table 2.3 illustrates, overall class differences were slight.

TABLE 2.3   *Global values by social class*

	ABC1 %	C2 %	DE %	All %
Traditional	25	22	23	23
Ambivalent	55	58	55	56
Anti-traditional	20	20	22	21
Total	100	100	100	100

However, as can be seen from Table 2.4 the three age groups differ substantially in the distribution of value systems. For example:

(i) Among those aged 18 to 34 anti-traditionals outnumber traditionalists by 5 to 1 in all three social classes – though ambivalents predominate numerically in all but class DE.
(ii) Among those aged 35 to 54, approximately two-thirds are in the ambivalent category in their value scores; and of the remaining one-third traditionals consistently slightly outnumber anti-traditionals.
(iii) Among those aged 55 or more, traditionals heavily outnumber anti-traditionals but the excess of the former is not constant. In the middle class the ratio of traditionals to anti-traditionals is almost 5 to 1; in the skilled working class, 4 to 1; and among the DE's, it is slightly less than 3 to 1. Again, ambivalents are in an overall majority.
(iv) Looking at all three age groups, what predominates is the fact that in their values, young middle class people have much more in common with young working class people than with their middle class elders.

TABLE 2.4   *Global values by class and age*

	ABC1 %	C2 %	DE %	All %
(a) Those aged 18–34				
Traditional	8	8	9	8
Ambivalent	51	50	42	48
Anti-traditional	41	42	49	44
	100	100	100	100
(b) Those aged 35–54				
Traditional	22	15	20	19
Ambivalent	63	73	66	67
Anti-traditional	15	12	14	14
	100	100	100	100
(c) Those aged 55 or more				
Traditional	39	37	33	36
Ambivalent	53	54	55	54
Anti-traditional	8	9	12	10
	100	100	100	100

Well over half the traditionals are aged 55 or more, the largest proportion of the ambivalents are aged 35 to 54, and of the anti-traditionalists, two-thirds are in the youngest age group.

The very high degree of similarity in the distribution of values by class and sex may not hold true for all the six value areas that make up the global scale. Each needs to be considered separately. Table 2.5 provides a summary picture and the following sections deal with each value area in detail. As can be seen the major differences are related to age rather than gender or social class.

A. RELIGION

Each respondent's position on this scale was determined by his/her replies to 15 questions or statements about traditional behaviour or beliefs – see Table 2.6.

In this area the average endorsement of traditional values indicated a slightly more positive attitude among women, but with considerable differences between the sexes on particular items. On five of them the level of endorsement by women was much greater than that of men. They were:

1. Regular weekly church attendance (18 per cent women, 10 per cent men).
2. Membership of a religious organisation (28 per cent women, 16 per cent men).
3. Great confidence in the church (24 per cent women, 14 per cent men).
4. Derives great comfort from religion (55 per cent women, 35 per cent men).
5. Parents should encourage religious faith in their children (16 per cent women, 11 per cent men).

In all three social classes, the average level of endorsement for these 15 traditional religious values was approximately 33 per cent; that is to say, class differences were negligible. The relatively low average figure was brought about largely by the fact that in all three social classes an average of almost 80 per cent of those classified as anti-traditionalists on the global scale rejected each of the items on this sub-scale, and by the very low affirmative scores of all three social classes on four items in the religious scale. Very few either

TABLE 2.5 *Percentage endorsement of traditional values by age and social class*

	Total sample	Social class			Age			Gender	
		ABC1	C2	DE	18–34	35–54	55 & over	Male	Female
Religion	32	32	34	33	26	32	40	31	34
Sex	60	59	60	61	52	60	70	60	60
Family	57	53	58	61	51	57	64	58	57
Patriotism	58	58	58	57	51	60	65	60	57
Work	43	46	44	41	42	47	47	45	43
Property	77	77	76	77	72	78	82	76	78

TABLE 2.6 *Percentage endorsement of traditional religious values by social class and age*

Item	Total sample	Social class			Age		
		ABC1	C2	DE	18-34	35-54	55 & over
Q163 Believe in God	76	73	74	81	65	79	85
Q315 Suicide unjustified	72	70	74	74	67	71	80
Q147 Life never meaningless	50	50	54	46	44	51	58
Q315 Killing in S.D. unjustified	46	43	49	48	39	45	56
Q168 Comfort from religion	46	46	40	52	28	46	67
Q359 Disagree future uncertain	37	40	38	32	31	33	25
Q146 Often think about life	34	36	31	33	28	33	36
Q154 Clear guidelines for good/evil	28	27	28	30	21	29	37
Q113 Member religious organisation	22	28	14	23	15	21	32
Q155 One true religion	21	13	25	27	15	19	31
Q349 Great confidence in church	19	15	19	24	8	16	35
Q262 Encourage faith in child	14	14	10	16	7	11	25
Q157 Weekly churchgoer	14	16	11	14	10	13	20
Q113 Member welfare charity	8	5	7	8	5	9	12
Q151 Risk life for religion	4	5	4	3	4	4	4
Average	32	32	32	34	26	32	40

supported the view that parents should take steps to encourage their children to have any religious faith, or themselves attended a religious service once a week; no more than a handful said they were prepared to risk their lives for their religious beliefs, and less than 20 per cent said they had a great deal of confidence in the church. In spite of these very widespread rejections, three-quarters of the respondents in all three classes said they believed in God, and in all three classes at least 40 per cent said they drew comfort and strength from religion.

If the scores of the youngest age group are taken as a proportion of the oldest, the gap between younger and older respondents on religion is greater than on any other values dimension; but even among the latter group, the average level of endorsement was no more than 40 per cent – less than half the support they gave to traditional property values. Of the 15 items, 10 were rejected by more than 70 per cent of the younger adults. Only two received majority endorsements from them: that suicide is never justified, and that there is a God; but even these two were rejected by one-third of younger adults. Indeed, these two items – a belief in God and condemnation of suicide – seem to be the back-bone of religious values in all three age groups and without their widespread endorsement the overall averages would have been even lower than the present very modest levels. Almost the greatest difference between the younger and older age groups is that whereas less than 30 per cent of the former said they derived comfort and strength from religion, over two-thirds of the elderly said that religion gave them these feelings.

B. SEX

The average scores of both men and women on the sub-scale measuring traditional attitudes to sexual behaviour were identical. Women were, however, more certain than men that prostitution was never justified; that adultery was not permissible, and that sex between those under the legal age of consent must be discouraged. To counterbalance these views, men were less opposed to having unmarried mothers as neighbours and more certain that homosexuality was to be condemned.

The average endorsement scores of the three social classes shown in Table 2.7 are also practically identical. In all three, three-fifths of

TABLE 2.7 *Percentage endorsement of traditional sex values*

Item	Total sample	Social class			Age		
		ABC1	C2	DE	18–34	35–54	55 & over
Q315 Under-age sex unjustified	82	82	83	81	75	86	88
Q315 Extra-marital affairs unjustified	74	72	75	77	68	74	83
Q315 Prostitution unjustified	70	66	71	75	61	69	88
Q315 Homosexuality unjustified	65	59	68	71	56	65	79
Q315 Abortion unjustified	60	55	60	66	54	57	70
Q261 Disapprove single parent	47	47	47	45	34	45	65
Q258 Sex needs moral rules	40	46	39	35	34	39	48
Q208 Accept ninth commandment	79	79	78	79	69	82	86
Q208 Accept sixth commandment	78	79	77	77	68	80	87
Q120 Object unmarried mothers as neighbours	3 —	3	4	3	1	2	8
Average	60	59	60	61	52	60	70

the respondents endorse traditional values. On many individual items within the scale, the same class agreement prevails. Occasional divergencies (for example, on homosexuality, prostitution and abortion) indicate more 'laxity' among middle class respondents than among working class respondents. Even so, solid majorities of the former also condemn these practices.

In all three age groups a majority endorsed traditional standards, but among younger adults the majority was slight (52 per cent) while among elderly adults the majority was substantial (70 per cent). Again, this difference was not uniform over all ten items. On five of them – mainly those concerned with the behaviour of married people – there was a much higher degree of agreement between the generations. On the other five – which were largely outside the contractual commitments of marriage – the gap between the younger and older adults was much wider with the former much less condemnatory of prostitution, homosexuality, abortion and so on. What is perhaps surprising is that even among the older adults, over 90 per cent said they had no objection to unmarried mothers as neighbours. Presumably their high regard for motherhood outweighed their distaste for illegitimacy.

C. FAMILY

A little under three-fifths of both men and women endorsed traditional family values (Table 2.5). On three of the ten items comprising the sub-scale, women's ratings were higher than those of men. These were: 'it is important that parents teach their children good manners', 'euthanasia is never justified', and 'it would be good for society if more emphasis was placed on the family'. On the other hand men gave greater endorsement to the statement that 'a woman, for fulfilment, must have children', and to the choice that if they had more leisure they would prefer to spend it with their family.

In this area distinct class differences do emerge (Table 2.8) with the DE's expressing higher approval of traditional values than do the ABC1's. This is almost entirely due to the greater emphasis placed by working class respondents on the reciprocal loyalties that should prevail between parents and children. This was particularly marked when respondents passed judgement on the statement: 'regardless of what the qualities and faults of one's parents are, one must always love and respect them'. At the same time, the DE's were more prone

TABLE 2.8 *Percentage endorsement of traditional family values*

Item	Total sample	Social class			Age		
		ABC1	C2	DE	18–34	35–54	55 & over
Q308 More emphasis on family good	84	82	84	86	79	83	91
Q208 Accept 4th commandment	83	81	84	84	76	85	89
Q260 Parents duty, best for children	71	68	70	76	54	72	84
Q262 Encourage good manners in child	68	60	72	72	63	70	72
Q259 Regardless of faults, respect parents	56	44	58	68	52	53	63
Q315 Euthanasia unjustified	56	56	52	62	51	54	72
Q315 Divorce unjustified	51	46	52	52	44	49	59
Q112 Prefer leisure time with family	48	48	50	45	39	59	48
Q262 Encourage obedience in child	37	30	41	40	36	35	40
Q257 Woman needs child for fulfilment	20	19	19	22	17	21	23
Average	57	53	58	61	51	57	64

than the ABC1's to endorse the statement: 'It is the duty of parents to do their best for their children, even at the expense of their own well-being.'

Among young adults the average level of endorsement of the ten items barely passed the halfway mark (51 per cent), while among their elders it almost approached the two-thirds level (64 per cent). This gap between the two generations is mainly due to the reluctance of the younger age group to agree that parents should sacrifice their own interests when they conflict with those of their children. Their reluctance can possibly be traced to the fact that as parents, younger adults of both sexes had more young children than did their elders. Of all respondents aged 18 to 34, more than half (53 per cent) lived in households that contained four or more persons; among the elderly the comparable proportion was no more than 8 per cent.

D. PATRIOTISM

In the area of patriotism the only significant differences between the sexes were that women were much less willing to fight for their country and had less confidence in Parliament and its workings.

In this domain, too, there is almost complete agreement among the three social classes. This holds true, with two exceptions, for all the individual items in the scale (Table 2.9). Compared with ABC1 people, DE respondents are more prone to say that they are proud to be British and less likely to regard the maintenance of law and order as one of the country's top priorities. All are strongly agreed in their condemnation of violence as a means of bringing about social and political change. In contrast, their confidence in Parliamentary democracy as an alternative is uniformly very slight.

Of the seven items brought together in this scale there is one where the level of endorsement by the younger adults slightly exceeds that of the elderly – willingness to fight for their country if there is a war. On three other items – all concerned with the use of violence to bring about social, political and economic change – there are in all age-bands solid majorities rejecting these means. There are then three other items which could be described as measures of social alienation and on these the younger adults differ markedly from their elders: they are not very proud to be British, they do not consider the maintenance of law and order to be a top priority and certainly they do not have great confidence in Parliament. Clearly this was not a

TABLE 2.9 *Percentage endorsement of patriotic values*

Item		Total sample	Social class			Age		
			ABC1	C2	DE	18–34	35–54	55 & over
Q348b)	Condemn terrorism	84	83	83	86	77	85	81
Q315	Assassination unjustified	82	82	82	82	78	85	85
Q315	Fighting police unjustified	82	83	82	83	75	84	88
Q152	Willing to fight for country	62	61	66	59	59	69	57
Q348a)	Very proud to be British	55	51	55	60	39	54	74
Q277	Maintain order a priority	30	36	31	26	27	32	38
Q249	Great confidence in Parliament	10	10	14	7	5	8	20
Average		58	58	58	57	51	60	65

view that was specific to the then Parliament with a Conservative majority; in the sample as a whole, among those who (on a 1 to 10 scale) described themselves as left of centre, 10 per cent said they had no great confidence in Parliament and of those who said they were politically to the right of the central point of this scale, 15 per cent expressed this view of Parliament.

E. WORK

Fifteen items were included in the work values sub-scale, a number of which, for example alcohol consumption and taking marijuana, are only indirect measures. The overall similarity in the levels of endorsement of work values masks a threefold discrepancy between the values of men and women. On five items women are more positive and this apparently is because men attach less importance to sobriety as a virtue. Only 39 per cent of men, but 49 per cent of women expressed agreement with the statement that alcoholism is now a serious problem. On a further five points, the work views of the two sexes were in broad agreement. For example, 80 per cent of men and 77 per cent of women agreed that it is important to take pride in one's work, and 60 per cent of men and 57 per cent of women said that in one's work it was important to feel that one was achieving something.

The scores for the three classes reveal a steady but small decline from 46 per cent for ABC1's to 41 per cent for DE's (Table 2.10). These averages conceal high levels of assertion, in all three classes (84 per cent ABC1, 70 per cent DE) that respondents take a great pride in the work they do; modest proportions (56 per cent ABC1, 35 per cent DE) who feel that what makes for a satisfying job is the opportunity to use one's abilities, and a handful of respondents in each class (average 16 per cent) who feel that parents should teach children the importance of hard work.

Although the overall averages are very similar for the three classes, there are some aspects of work which have a distinctly higher value for middle class people than they do for DE's; these are:

I take great pride in the work I do.

It is important to have a job
    in which you feel you can achieve something;
    that meets one's abilities;

TABLE 2.10 *Percentage endorsement of traditional work values*

Item	Total sample	Social class			Age		
		ABC1	C2	DE	18–34	35–54	55 & over
Q315 Marijuana unjustified	83	79	85	85	75	85	89
Q135 Take a pride in work*	78	84	78	70	71	83	85
Q132 Achievement important	58	68	60	45	66	56	52
Q308 Decrease importance of work bad thing	58	56	58	54	58	53	54
Q111 Spend leisure doing things	52	52	53	52	57	49	49
Q132 Use of ability important	46	56	45	35	46	48	44
Q338 Drugs very serious problem	46	34	49	60	45	43	61
Q132 Use of initiative important	42	62	42	38	52	51	42
Q338 Alcoholism very serious problem	36	34	34	40	30	37	43
Q132 Chance of promotion important	35	40	35	30	44	28	33
Q134 Look forward to work*	33	33	34	31	31	33	33
Q132 Socially useful job important	30	49	31	25	26	32	35
Q138 Find extra work for extra pay*	18	14	24	21	17	19	22
Q262 Encourage patience in children	16	14	21	14	15	15	21
Q262 Encourage hard work in child	16	14	18	14	13	20	15
Average	43	46	44	41	43	45	45

* Asked only if respondent was in employment.

that gives opportunity to use initiative;
that gives good chances for promotion;
that is useful for society.

These differences may spring from class differences concerning the
purpose of work, or they may simply reflect differences in the sort of
work that the two classes do. A dustman, unlike a professional
worker, is very unlikely to have opportunities to show initiative,
opportunities for promotion, even opportunities to take great pride
in the work he does. Accordingly, he is unlikely to attach much
importance to the unattainable.

On their average scores a majority in all three age groups rejected
traditional values. This majority was very slightly larger among
younger adults (57 per cent) as compared with the rejection score (55
per cent) among older adults. However, the pattern was far from
constant over the whole 15 items. On four of the items, endorsement
of traditional values was higher among younger adults than among
older adults; they were:

In a job good chances for promotion are important.
In a job it is important to feel that you can achieve something.
In a job it is important to have opportunities to use one's initiative.
In my leisure time it is important to me to be doing things.

It is not surprising that to those in the early years of their careers
these traditional values should appear relatively important. What is
perhaps surprising is that to those who are middle aged or elderly
they should seem, possibly in the light of more experience and
greater wisdom, to be relatively less important.

There is a second set of work values where the level of endorsement by the two age groups is practically the same. They were:

It would be bad if there were a decrease in the importance of work in
our lives.
It is important that a job should meet one's abilities.
When the weekend is over I look forward to work.
It is especially important that children learn the value of hard work.

Finally, there were seven items where approval was significantly
lower among younger adults than among older adults. Some of these
related directly to the value of work as such, but others were rather

forms of behaviour which would normally affect adversely the ability to work and were probably seen by younger adults not as work values but rather as parts of a more general youth culture. These seven were:

Taking marijuana is never justified.
I take a great deal of pride in the work I do.
Illegal drug-taking is a serious problem in Britain today.
Alcoholism is a serious problem in Britain today.
It's important that children should learn patience.
Socially useful job important.
Would find extra work for extra pay.

Very broadly, it would seem that the work values of younger adults are more concerned with self-interest than are the work values of older adults; the values of the latter attach more weight to social behaviour that affects the productivity of the work force. This would be a rational view on their part since more than half of all the older adults are aged 65 or more and most of these have a State retirement pension as their main source of income.

F. PROPERTY

In dealing with the fourteen items that measured their standards on matters affecting property (public and private) the respondents in all groups almost invariably endorsed each traditional value with very large majorities. The outstanding exception was the rejection by over 90 per cent of all respondents of the notion that it was important that parents should encourage the quality of thrift in their children. The view that it is desirable and meritorious to 'take the waiting out of wanting' has been adopted by almost everyone; only a handful of adults (15 per cent) remain unconvinced though women express greater support than men. They also endorse more strongly the notion that it is never justified to lie in one's own self-interest.

In the three social classes, the levels of approval for property rights and personal honesty were very high and almost identical. There was a slight falling away in standards where honesty in the public sector was in question (for example, not paying bus fares, or cheating on tax returns). The general picture is similar for age though younger adults exhibit less attachment to personal honesty than older adults. Very few respondents thought it desirable to encourage children to be thrifty – a traditional means, especially among some older working

TABLE 2.11 *Percentage endorsement of traditional property values*

Item	Total sample	Social class			Age		
		ABC1	C2	DE	18–34	35–54	55 & over
Q267 Would never damage property	96	96	95	97	91	99	99
Q267 Would never use violence	95	95	96	95	91	97	99
Q315 Joyriding unjustified	88	88	88	87	86	88	89
Q315 Accepting bribes unjustified	84	85	82	83	81	85	87
Q315 Threatening non-strikers unjustified	83	84	82	82	79	84	87
Q315 Claiming unentitled benefit unjustified	83	83	84	81	79	86	86
Q315 Buying stolen goods unjustified	81	82	80	81	75	83	87
Q315 Avoiding fares unjustified	79	80	80	78	72	82	86
Q262 Encourage honesty in children	78	79	76	80	77	76	79
Q315 Failing to report accidental damage unjustified	76	78	75	76	70	76	85
Q315 Keeping money found unjustified	76	76	75	76	68	82	84
Q315 Cheating on tax returns unjustified	73	74	73	72	67	73	81
Q315 Lying in own interest unjustified	72	72	72	74	68	69	78
Q262 Encourage thrift in children	9	6	10	16	3	11	15
Average	77	77	76	77	72	78	82

class people, of acquiring some property and retaining one's independence.

It is striking that in the domain of property, as with work, the great majority of all adults, irrespective of age, are unwilling to agree that an important parental responsibility is the inculcation of some of the traditional values in their children. There were no items where concern for honesty and property rights was greater among younger adults than among older adults.

CONFORMISTS AND DEVIANTS AND AGE

At the beginning of the chapter it was pointed out (Table 2.4) that whilst 'ambivalents' were the largest category in all age groups, among younger adults anti-traditionalists outnumbered traditionalists by more than 5 to 1. Although comprising a minority of respondents in the 18–24 age group (44 per cent), the young anti-traditionalists can, for the purpose of comparison, be described as conformists and the young traditionalists as deviants. At the same time it was recorded that among the older adults, traditionalists outnumbered anti-traditionalists by over 4 to 1. Among the older adults, traditionalists (36 per cent of the total) might also be characterised as conformists and the anti-traditionalists as deviants. The survey findings are able to throw some light on the distinctive characteristics of the deviants in each of these age groups.

A. Younger adults

In this age group, the average 'deviant', that is those holding *traditional* values, was five years older than the average 'conformist' – that is those holding anti-traditional values – 28 as compared with 23 years of age. In the light of this age difference it is not surprising to find that the proportion of 'deviants' who were married was higher; that few 'deviants' were still students; and that half the 'deviants', but only one-third of the 'conformists' were already parents. Further, those holding traditional values were less likely to be drawn from social class DE and more likely to be materially better off.

The 'conformists' (those holding anti-traditional values) were more prone than the deviant, traditionalist, minority of younger people to question authority; to approve of cheating and lying when these served their own self-interest; to denigrate respect for parents; to disavow any pride in being British; to regard the maintenance of public order as of little consequence; to refuse to accept the idea that there is a clear-out difference between what is good and what is evil, and to have very little contact with organised religion.

The distinctive characteristics of the anti-traditionalist younger adults did not end there. Compared with the traditionalist minority, they more frequently felt lonely, bored and less than happy, and generally felt less satisfied with the life they lead.

B. Older adults

Among the older adults (those aged 55 and over), 'conformists' (those holding *traditional* values) outnumbered the small group of 34 'deviants' (those who rejected traditional values) by more than 4 to 1. In both sub-groups the age of the average member was 66. 'Conformist' elderly persons were, however, more likely than 'deviants' to conform to the average for their age group in respect of owner-occupation, household income, socio-economic grade, marital status and sex distribution. In short, in middle and old age, relatively lower levels of material well-being tend to be associated with above average approval of anti-traditional values among a small, predominantly female, group.

The small elderly 'deviant' minority is more prone to approve of cheating on one's tax returns; to lie if it is to one's interest; to attach less importance to filial respect; to regard Parliament distrustfully; to feel less pride in their British citizenship; to doubt the wisdom of authority; to attach comparatively little importance to the maintenance of social order; to be less censorious of homosexuality; to cut themselves off from organised religion, and to reject the idea of clearly defined boundaries between good and evil. Among older people, those holding 'deviant' values are those most likely to say they feel lonely and bored, not very happy, and much less satisfied with their lives as a whole.

One may conclude that in values and emotions, there is among older people a very small deviant minority which has more in common with the substantial minority of anti-traditionalist young adults. At the same time, there is among younger adults a deviant minority which, in its values, is closer to its elders than to its peers.

This apparent proximity, however, fails to close one important gap. All respondents were asked to say (a) how much trust they thought young people had in older people (Q.125), and (b) how much trust did they think older people had in the young (Q.126). They indicated their opinions by using a 1 to 10 scale in which 1 represented 'none at all' and 10 represented 'a great deal'. The outcome was that the 'deviant' older respondents (those closest to the young anti-traditionalists in their values) registered an average score of no more than 4.8 when assessing the amount of respect that older people received from the young; this was actually less than the 5.1 score recorded by the 'conformist' elderly whose values were furthest removed from the anti-traditionalist younger adults. And in answering the second question 'How much trust do you think older people have in the young?', older 'deviants' gave an average rating of no more than 4.2, while their 'conformist' age-peers recorded the appreciably higher score of 5.1. This suggests that in addition to what might be described as the 'normal' values gap between younger and older adults, there is among the latter, a minority whose alienation from their age-peers is part of a general pessimism about people and social institutions.

SOCIAL CLASS AND CULTURAL INTERESTS

From the data presented it would be reasonable to conclude that broadly all three social classes in this country hold the same value systems; all three contain much the same proportions of traditionalists, anti-traditionalists and ambivalents, and the only distinctive differences between the classes are those of occupation, income, residential tenure and educational background. However, these latter four differences generate class differences in life-styles that are often more important than values in generating and sustaining class divisions. In recent years some of these social/cultural variations have been measured in the Government's General Household Surveys. These are largely in the cultural field, where relative consumption by the middle class substantially exceeds working class consumption, and in the area of physical activity, where the level of middle class activity is similarly higher than that of working class men. The exceptions are playing billiards/snooker, playing darts and doing football pools – three activities where the rate of working class participation runs well ahead of that recorded for middle class men. Similar differences in taste emerge from the National Readership Surveys; well over four-fifths of social classes C2D read the popular tabloids (*Sun*, *Mirror*, *Star*) daily compared to one-fifth of social class AB. Two-fifths of social group E read no newspaper at all.

Apparently there is an acute awareness in this country of this class difference in culture. For example, in February 1983, the press reported that the Labour-controlled South Yorkshire County Council had decided to organise and finance a snooker and pool competition as part of a 'working class culture' programme. According to the *Daily Telegraph* (11 Feb.) 'other planned working class culture activities included whippet and greyhound racing, darts and public house quizzes.' The Chairman was quoted as saying: 'In the past most of our support has gone to opera and ballet which are essentially middle-class activities. There is a wealth of working-class culture in this country ... whippet and greyhound racing, pool and snooker and the games held in pub taprooms are all part of working-class culture.'

PSYCHOLOGICAL WELL-BEING

At various points in the interview questions were asked which sought to measure the respondent's quality of life and state of psychological well-being. Sometimes this was attempted by simple and direct means, for example by asking respondents to rate: their satisfaction with life as a whole (Q.129); their subjective assessment of happiness (Q.129); their loneliness (Q.118); and so on. Responses to such questions revealed similar assessments by both men and women. However, a more refined approach using the Bradburn Affect Balance Scale (see Chapter 9), was also employed (Q.122) and this did reveal a significant difference between the sexes.

In terms of a period specified as 'the past few weeks' the average man appears to enjoy, on balance, more positive psychological experiences and fewer negative experiences than does the average woman. Similarly, despite the fact that the values held by the three social classes are virtually identical, there is not a matching similarity of levels of psychological well-being. Class differences are substantial and consistently show DE class deficits, particularly related to subjective feelings of loneliness, restlessness and lack of control over their lives, compared with middle class levels. These deficits remain, even when the classes are matched on their value systems and although partly related to the greater age of the DE group, this is not the whole explanation. Presumably, common values are not sufficient to neutralise differences between the classes in income, wealth, housing or education. Or, to describe the association between values and class in the reverse direction, differences in income and wealth may lead to differences in subjective assessments of well-being but not to differences in values. Brecht's famous summation of the relationship ('Erst kommt das Fressen, denn kommt die Moral' – 'A full stomach is necessary before one can afford the luxury of morality') lacks support in the findings of the present study of contemporary Britain.

However, the replies to the life satisfaction question (Q.129) in the survey suggest that this is not the last word on the subject of class and values. Respondents were asked to use a 1 to 10 scale to answer the question: 'All things considered, how satisfied are you with life as a whole these days?' (1 = completely dissatisfied, 10 = completely satisfied). This time the mean scores of the DE's and the ABC1's were very similar; the slight gap between the two classes would have been even smaller but for the fact that in the working class the anti-traditionalists, unlike middle class anti-traditionalists, returned markedly low life-satisfaction scores – as Table 2.12 illustrates.

TABLE 2.12   *Average life-satisfaction scores (max. 10.0) in each class*

Values held	ABC1	C2	DE	All
Traditional	7.97	8.73	7.89	8.17
Ambivalent	7.60	8.17	7.41	7.75
Anti-traditional	7.30	6.55	6.87	6.94
Whole class:	7.62	7.90	7.40	7.65

Apparently among middle class people it is possible to hold anti-traditional values and simultaneously to lead a life that one finds highly satisfying. In the working class, however, such a values position is associated with a life that is felt to be much less satisfying. This is not true of the working class respondents with traditional values. Despite their material deficits, their high levels of loneliness and a widespread sense of helplessness, and despite the fact that relatively few of them are very happy, it is still possible for them to express an average life-satisfaction score that is higher than that of the average middle class person. Perhaps this derives from modesty in both their expectations and in their aspirations – traits which themselves have had a long history as distinctive working class values. The age-composition of the anti-traditionalists, however, suggests that this history may be coming to an end.

CONCLUSION

Despite substantial class differences in education, income, housing tenure and leisure interests, the values exhibited by the three main socio-economic groups, in each of the six major value domains analysed, were remarkably similar. Male and female responses also showed little overall variation – though differences were apparent on some individual items within the sub-scales. When the sample is broken down by age groups, however, significant variations are apparent. These are particularly marked in relation to religious values and beliefs, and age-related differences on the sexual morality and family values scales are also substantial. The following three chapters explore these themes in greater detail. Least variation was evident on questions of property rights and work related values – the latter issues are explored in Chapter 7 within a broader European context.

A majority of survey respondents (56 per cent) were classified as ambivalent in their responses on the global scale, a little under one-quarter emerged as traditionalists and about one-fifth as anti-traditionalists. Indeed, ambivalents predominated in all age and class groups with the single exception of those aged 18–34 in social class DE, about half of whom were classified as anti-traditional. Among younger adults anti-traditionalists outnumber traditionalists five to one, whereas among adults over 55 years traditionalists predominate three to one. Anti-traditionalists generally emerge as more lonely, bored, less happy and less satisfied with the life they lead. Among older respondents espousing anti-traditional values, their general pessimism appears to distance them not only from their age-peers but also from those younger people who share their views. Class differences in psychological well-being are apparent, social group DE reporting generally lower levels of well-being, yet these differences – which are explored further in Chapter 9 – do not lead to significant variations in overall satisfaction with life – anti-traditionalists excepted. This may in part be due to the age composition of the DE group and the relatively modest expectations which the older generation appear to maintain.

3 Religious Attitudes and Values

DAVID GERARD

PART I: BACKGROUND

Introduction

Given the limitations of sample size, the material which follows focuses necessarily on Christianity and its contemporary relevance to the neglect of other religious traditions. The impact of the Christian message and the historical processes of conversion, differentiation, secularisation and rejection vary in different cultural and political settings. They involve different degrees of accommodation between Church and State, from persecution and suppression to collusion, establishment and secularised forms of 'civic religion' (Bellah, 1964, 1967; Martin, 1978; Gilbert, 1980; Dobbelaere, 1981; Wilson, 1982).

It has been suggested that the Christian church, as heir to the Jewish and Graeco-Roman cultures, absorbed in its struggle for survival and influence much of the spirit and content of classical culture, internalising old tensions between 'religious' and 'secular' consciousness, between 'sacred' and 'profane' views of the world, and consequently contained within its tradition the seeds of secularisation (Weber, 1977; Gilbert, 1980; Berger, 1967). In contemporary western societies, the legacy of that tradition is manifest in a wide variety of forms of belief and commitment, varying from deep conviction and frequent church attendance to open rejection. In Britain, over 70 per cent of the population seldom or never read the Bible (EVSSG Pilot Study, 1980; Harrison, 1983) and no more than one person in seven attends church weekly. Yet, more than three-quarters of respondents to the Values Study expressed a belief in God and 85 per cent reported membership of one of the main Christian denominations.

Christian values

The message Christ proclaimed was a message of love; the 'good news' of salvation and eternal life offered by a just and compassionate God to all mankind, attained through faith, repentance, baptism and wholehearted commitment to the will of God. In His teaching He emphasised the unity of creation and the universality of God's love, falling like rain on just and unjust alike, and pointed out that the whole of the law and the prophets hung on two commandments; love of God and of one's neighbour. A response to a divine invitation, salvation was not a contractual obligation that God was bound to honour in exchange for fulfilling the external requirements of the law for, as St. Paul argued, no man could be deemed righteous before God, all merited condemnation. God could not perjure himself and declare the guilty innocent. Rather, salvation represented a gift, unmerited and freely bestowed on those who responded in faith to God's call.

The Christian ethic is both an ethic of relationship (person to God; person to person; and persons in relationship, i.e. the Christian community to God) and an ethic of concern – total universal concern for mankind to be expressed in compassionate, dedicated and selfless service undertaken in a spirit of humility (Barclay, 1971).

Central to the Christian ethic are notions of a personal God, family relationship and a community of faith as the concepts of 'Sonship', God as 'Father' and so on imply. The importance, and vulnerability of these notions are recognised by sociologists of religion. Thus, Dobbelaere (1984, p. ii) suggests that the increasingly impersonal nature of relationships and differentiation into specialised roles, characteristic of modern society undermines belief in a personal God and in Christianity itself. Wilson (1982, p. 174), noting the importance of community to all the great religions, argues that 'It is to the passing of natural communities ... that we may look for a significant part of the explanation of secularisation, when the term is used to refer to the transformation of religious consciousness'.

Christianity involves an attitude of irrepressible goodwill and concern for the welfare of others (material, physical, spiritual). It also entails a commitment to objective, universal moral standards. Christians are to live 'in' the world, but not in conformity to the standards 'of' of the world. Rather, they are to provide models for others to emulate, exhibiting truthfulness, compassion, forgiveness and responsibility. They are to refrain from passing judgement, must show forbearance when others exhibit weakness, do nothing which would undermine the community but, rather, seek to build it up. All this is to be accomplished without hint of sexual immorality, drunkenness or greed and in a spirit of charity.

The Christian call to perfection, the very notions of, 'holiness' (i.e. difference) and of 'church' (i.e. those 'called out') which are employed; Christ's own reference to the hostility of the world to His teaching; and the many instances of rejection of its implications in the Gospels suggest that fully committed Christians will be a minority group. Similarly, the notion of Christians as the 'light of the world' and the 'leaven', by definition imply 'darkness' and 'dough'. Yet, the invitation remains for all mankind. As indicated in the introduction, the level of response and intensity of commitment vary within and between cultures, reactions foreshadowed in the parable of the sower (Mark 4:1–20).

Finally, Christianity provides both an integrated belief system and a means of expressing commitment through ritual participation. These two dimensions of Christianity – 'meaning' and 'belonging' – reinforce each other. Whilst it can be argued that some people may join worshipping communities for reasons which are not primarily religious – and yet eventually become fully committed – the direction of causation is primarily from 'meaning' to 'belonging'. Recent studies have suggested that, in a secular society, the compensations obtainable from participation as a member of a religious group are not a 'plausible option' for those seeking comfort, consolation or relief from deprivation (Stark, 1972; Roof, 1978). For the committed Christian, full participation in the life of the community of faith is, on the one hand, a consequence of spiritual transformation and of joyful submission to God. In circumstances in which religious explanation may be defined as 'plausible' by researchers, commitment does provide a source of comfort, refuge and strength. Evidence of prayer and meditation is especially marked among such people in Belgium (Dobbelaere, 1984, p. i). The primacy of 'meaning' over 'belonging' has been the subject of recent comment (Roof, 1979; Dobbelaere 1984, p. ii), and it is to be expected that the higher the level of individual commitment, the greater the degree of institutional involvement.

Secularisation and the decline into emotivism

Secularisation refers to the process of functional differentiation in society (Luhmann, 1977; Martin, 1978) commencing in the Middle Ages and linked to industrialisation, urbanisation and the rise of science. During this process: the church loses its overarching claims (Dobbelaere, 1981), evacuates large areas of social and economic life (Berger, 1967); becomes one among a number of sub-systems of society and its inspirational power and moral authority wane (Sorokin, 1966). The political, economic, social and religious spheres separate out; the world is 'desacralised' and mastered by technology; rationalisation of the institutional sphere occurs. Church and society disengage (Shiner, 1967; Durkheim, 1964). Activities become efficiently organised, bureaucratic, predictable, controllable. Individuals typically adopt 'positions' and perform 'roles'; relationships between persons are reduced to the instrumental/technical level outside of close family and friendship networks (Wilson, 1982; Dobbelaere, 1984, p. i).

The historical process of secularisation and the rejection of theology was paralleled by the philosophical rejection of Aristotelian notions of an essential human nature and of a telos. The coherence of the medieval moral scheme was, MacIntyre (1981) suggests, destroyed; the 'Enlightenment project' of discovering rational secular foundations for morality failed and moral judgements ceased to have clear status. The result, in his view, was to open the way for Nietzche and his successors to mount an apparently successful critique of previous morality leading to a decline into emotivism in the twentieth century and the absence of moral consensus. It is, he suggests, central to the claims of emotivism that there can be '*No* valid rational justification for any claims that objective and impersonal moral standards exist and hence that there are no such standards' (McIntyre, 1981, p. 18). Further, in its social content, emotivism entails the obliteration of any genuine distinction between manipulative and non-manipulative social relations, others are always means, never ends. Where elements of the earlier tradition survive, such as in rural Christian and Jewish communities, they are eroded by the need to participate in public life.

MacIntyre's characterisation of contemporary society is echoed in studies of, for example, the social limits to growth and the problems of developing neighbourhood care. Thus, Hirsch (1977), argued that industrial development, personal mobility and the anonymity implicit in urbanisation make it difficult to see reciprocal obligations in a perspective that has meaning for individuals. The commercial appeal is to individual rather than collective satisfaction. There is a premium placed on making one's time available to others, given pressures to improve personal prosperity and the scramble for 'positional' power, resulting ultimately in an 'economics of bad neighbours'. Similarly, P. Abrams, acknowledged that informal community care was unlikely and uncommon in advanced capitalist societies based on market moralities, possessive individualism and bureaucratic services. He pointed out that neighourhood care involved notions of empathy, duty and collective moral standards and was thus sustained and legitimated by membership of a moral community, especially a religious community (Abrams, 1978; 1981). Wilson commenting on the implications of what he regards as the collapse of community and custom, argues, 'the large scale social system ... seeks not to rely on a moral order, but rather ... on a technical order ... where morality must persist, then it can be politicised, and subject to the direct coercive force of the state' – for example in the case of sexual or racial discrimination (Wilson, 1982, p. 161).

The absence of moral consensus, and of generally accepted criteria of judgement suggests that contemporary morality is more likely to exhibit a negative 'anti-traditional' character, than to take the form of a positive, internally consistent alternative. The result may be manifest in insecurity and confusion at the personal level, with individuals holding values which conflict with each other. Evidence from opinion research provides a degree of confirmation of the latter position (Converse, 1964; Inglehart, 1977). Further, an emphasis on personal autonomy in matters of moral choice is likely to be particularly apparent in areas of private morality, such as sexuality and matters of personal honesty.

The treatment of other persons as means rather than ends in pursuit of personal goals is likely to be reflected in varying degrees of mistrust, an absence of expressed commitment to altruistic ideals and limited involvement in activities demanding the gift of time in the service of others. Finally, the 'collapse of community' and the anonymity of urban life will tend to undermine religious faith and to entail subjective feelings of isolation among vulnerable groups in society.

Religious change and institutional involvement

The form and content of religious beliefs and rituals, the structure and organisation of religious authorities, undergo evolution and change in response to wider social and cultural forces. New religious communities emerge and decline. *Religious change* (Yinger, 1962), therefore, varies over time and from place to place but fundamentally involves either strategies of resistance or strategies of accommodation (Berger, 1967). Such strategies will differ both in the extent to which they emphasise the need for personal values and beliefs to be closely integrated with those of the wider society, and in the definitions they offer of what is 'sacred' – and thus the scope for conflict with other social institutions (Fenn, 1978). Berger suggests that in America the churches have maintained a position of central symbolic importance because they have accommodated themselves to, and support, the American Way of Life, have 'modernised' and marketed their product, adapting it to meet the needs of their constituents. Consequently church involvement has remained much higher than in Europe where 'internal' secularisation and the process of adjusting to the demands of the wider society have proceeded much slower. Both strategies require theoretical legitimation and pose theological problems (Berger, 1961; 1967). The accommodation strategy may reduce conflict and tension between denominations, each being regarded as a different form of expressing a common national identity and common faith (Herberg, 1967).

Apart from hypotheses about adaptations of formal religious groups to the process of social change, other sociologists identify evolutionary developments towards individuation, autonomy and purely subjective 'invisible' religion which undermine institutional forms (Bellah, 1964; Luckmann, 1967). Luckmann argues that society no longer requires religious legitimation and that religion has become transformed into a subjective, private, reality. This reality is, he suggests, characterised by autonomy, choice and personal preference and an emphasis on self-realisation; mobility; self-expression; sexuality and familism. It does not conform to the demands of the specialised institutional form of religion with its defined doctrine, specialised ministry and ecclesiastical organisation. The latter is consequently undermined. Such a private religious reality depends on restricted kin and friendship networks to support it and enables the individual to 'manage' his own relationship to God and to choose with whom he will worship (Parsons, 1967). There is a danger, however, that defining as religious all privately created meaning systems, whether God centred or not, which provide some form of interpretive framework and confer identity, empties the term of content. Such definitions, for example, may encompass – as the Greeley/Geertz formulation (Greeley, 1972) suggests – evolutionism,

Marxism and scientism inhibiting empirical studies of comparative religiosity and rendering the notion of secularisation redundant if every solution to problems of ultimate concern is regarded by definition as 'religious'.

Attempts empirically to validate the existence of some form of privatised religion independent of any institutional framework or doctrinal system of beliefs have been made using student samples. Accepting Geertz's (1968) thesis that man's ultimate values and beliefs are rooted in his reflections about the inevitability of his own death, and the consequent need to determine whether any transcendent reality is benign or malicious, Yinger (1977) developed a religious 'scale' based on experiences of meaninglessness, suffering and injustice. He reported that a religious disposition was as evident among those without any formal religious identity as among adherents to the major religions. Other studies indicate that Yinger's scale lacks internal consistency, being composed of two or three separate dimensions. Further, whilst indicative of some form of non-doctrinal religious commitment, it is clear that the extent of such commitment varies *directly* with traditional forms of religious attachment (Nelson *et al.*, 1976; Roof *et al.*, 1977).

Religious involvement is clearly influenced by the processes of secularisation and change. The evident decline in belief, practice and religious vocations in the post-war period is not uniform throughout all sections of society, but related both to key socio-demographic indicators (age, sex, class, occupation, education) and to moral values.

Some social scientists see religious involvement as primarily a function of social class or as a response to different forms of deprivation (material, social, psychological) – providing consolation, comfort, or substitute rewards in a situation of powerlessness or distorted perception of the cause of disadvantage (Glock, 1965; 1967). Empirical studies, however, indicate that social class differences contribute little by way of explanation of patterns of church involvement (McCready and Greeley, 1976). Similarly, empirical verification of Glock's theory is lacking (Stark, 1972; Roof, 1978).

Luckmann emphasises the degree of involvement in the work process and the spread of functional differentiation and urban culture into rural localities via the media (Luckmann, 1976). Martin (1978) goes so far as to identify specific occupational categories at risk in particular cultural contexts – for example process workers in impersonal, large scale, highly mechanised heavy industrial sectors and employees in large scale farming projects subject to economic uncertainty. Others have stressed the seeming irrelevance, indeed apparent opposition, of the values promoted by the churches to many contemporary concerns (Schmidtchen, 1972).

The importance of value change is often regarded as stimulating a rapid short term deterioration in involvement (Hoge and Roozen, 1979), particularly following the emergence of a 'counterculture' among the younger generation during the 1960s, which emphasised rights, protest, change and the rejection of traditional moral values and constraints on 'permissive' social behaviour (Wuthnow, 1976, p. i). The defence of traditional values was defined in fact by some sociologists as a response of a threatened group to potential loss of social status (Zurcher and Kirkpatrick, 1976).

Wilson focuses on the displacement of symbolism and religious ritual formerly used to celebrate and legitimise social life: to initiate the young; celebrate the harvest; heal the sick; revere the old; and sustain the bereaved. The modern, mobile, large-scale society has little communal life to sustain, legitimise or celebrate. The system relies, he suggests, less on people being good, more on their actions being calculable. The conception of the supernatural as a meaningful reality is remote from everyday life (Berger, 1969). Yet where people's life and work continue to be lived 'in contexts which are familiar and on a human scale, they are more likely to practise Christianity and be sensitive to it' (Martin, 1978, p. 160).

The quality of relationships in the parental home – between mother and father, parent and child – has also been shown to contribute significantly to explanations of religious self-definition and church attendance (McCready and Greeley, 1976). In addition to the family, ethnic-group attachment and local community orientation, as opposed to a wider 'cosmopolitan' perspective, appear to underpin both belief and practice – particularly among 'liberal' protestants and catholics (Roof, 1976; Roof and Hoge, 1980). Dobbelaere, commenting on Roof's research, suggests that 'declining community attachment, more than erosion of traditional beliefs *per se*, is the critical factor in accounting for the decline in church attendance and church support' (Dobbelaere, 1981, p. 141), and that whilst the influence of parental religiosity and social status on church attendance are stronger among 'locals', it is the 'localism' itself which is the 'primary plausibility structure'. Roof further speculates that the increasingly 'cosmopolitan-modernist' sub-culture of the young and better educated and the identification of institutional church membership with

the local-traditional sub-culture is a cause of declining church commitment. The result, he suggests, is likely to be a widening cleavage
between older traditionalists, holding conventional moral values and
involved in the church and the young cosmopolitan embracing the
new morality (Roof and Hoge, 1980). Others see the potential for a
return to the church in middle life – particularly among those whose
parents were religious, or for religious values to re-assert themselves
in later generations not exposed to the counterculture of the sixties
(Wuthnow, 1976, pp. i and ii; McCready, 1981).

PART II: FINDINGS

The population: religious disposition, belief and practice at a glance

It was earlier suggested that Christianity possesses both an integrated
system of beliefs and a means of expressing commitment through
ritual participation; these two dimensions were referred to as 'meaning' and 'belonging'. Whilst they reinforced each other, the former
was held to be prior. In discussing both emotivism and secularisation,
it was also noted that a number of sociologists have argued in favour
of the existence of a fundamental religious disposition, independent
of any explicit attachment to the beliefs and rituals of the major
religious traditions. Rooted in man's capacity for reflection on his
circumstances, and his search for meaning and identity, such a
disposition may find contemporary expression only in subjective,
private realities. Although the EVSSG questionnaire was not designed for the purpose and the indicators available within it are not
necessarily those best suited for the task, the values data do provide
the opportunity to explore all three dimensions and to assess the
degree to which they are related to each other. Table 3.1 provides
selected indicators of religious disposition, orthodox belief and
institutional attachment for Great Britain compared with the overall
European population. Many of these items are later combined to
form a scale to measure the intensity of overall religious commitment.

Three-quarters of the British sample reported a belief in God
(Q.163). As far as evidence of an underlying religious disposition is
concerned, three-fifths identified themselves as 'religious persons'
(Q.158), half regularly felt the need for prayer, meditation or
contemplation (Q.169), half scored above the mid-point on the

'importance of God' scale (Q.167) and a little under half indicated that they drew comfort and strength from religion. Those who identified themselves as convinced atheists (Q.158) comprised only 4 per cent of the population. Indeed, an examination of the responses of the 45 self-confessed atheists reveals that twenty of them claimed some form of denominational attachment, ten believed in the existence of some sort of spirit or life force, ten believed in life after death, one actually believed in a personal God, eight asserted a belief in God (Q.163) and seven were agnostic. The true figure for convinced atheists is therefore nearer 2 per cent.

On the other hand, evidence of a reflective disposition and widespread 'spiritual experience' is limited. Only one-third of the population reported frequent reflection about the meaning and purpose of life; one-in-five reported having a profound spiritual experience; one-in-seven frequently contemplated death. Further, two-fifths of the sample were of the opinion that religion would become less important in future (Q.162) – twice the proportion who believed it would become more important – and the proportion who believed that religious faith was an important value to be encouraged at home among children (Q.262) was low.

The evidence suggests that such general expressions of religious commitment vary both with the degree of orthodox belief and practice and with important socio-demographic characteristics such as age, sex and occupational status. Table 3.2 illustrates the way in which subjective perception of the importance of God (Q.167) – the single most useful summary indicator of religiosity emerging from multi variate analysis of the data – varies with the intensity of church attendance (Q.157), the conception people have of God (Q.166) and the degree of comprehensiveness of the orthodox beliefs held (Q.163). Thus, whilst there is widespread evidence of some form of religious commitment, it remains doubtful whether this is indicative of the existence of a dimension of religiousity which is *independent* of attachment to orthodox Christian teaching. Rather, it appears consistent with previously reported American evidence (Nelson *et al.*, 1976; Roof *et al.*, 1977) which suggests that non-doctrinal commitment varies *directly* with traditional beliefs.

Examination of people's conception of God and attitudes to orthodox belief help to throw some further light on the question. Two-fifths of the population conceive of God as some sort of spirit or life force; a little under one-third believe in a personal God; one-fifth are unsure what to think, and a further ten per cent profess no belief

TABLE 3.1 Indicators of religious commitment, Great Britain compared with the European average/ percentages

Indicators of Religious Disposition:	Great Britain	European average	Indicators of orthodox belief	Great Britain	European average
Often think about meaning and purposes of life	34	30	Believe in personal God	31	32
Never think life meaningless	50	44	(Believe in a spirit or life force)	39	36
Often think about death	15	18	Believe in:		
Often regret doing wrong	8	10	God	76	73
Need moments of prayer, etc.	50	57	Sin	69	57
Define self as a religious person	58	62	Soul	59	57
Draw comfort/strength from Religion	46	48	Heaven	57	40
God is important in my life (6–10)	50	51	Life after death	45	43
Have had a spiritual experience	19	12	The Devil	30	25
			Hell	27	23
			Personally fully accept Commandments demanding:		
			No other Gods	48	48
			Reverence of God's name	43	46
			Holy Sabbath	25	32

Indicators of moral values:	Great Britain	European average
Absolute guidelines exist about good & evil	28	26
Personally fully accept commandments prohibiting:		
Killing	90	87
Adultery	78	63
Stealing	87	82
False Witness	78	73
Agree with unrestricted sex	23	23
Terrorism may be justified	12	14
Following acts never justified:		
Claiming unentitled benefit	78	
Accepting a bribe	79	
Taking marijuana	81	
Homosexuality	47	
Euthanasia	30	
Political assassination	77	
Greater respect for authority: good	73	59
Willing to sacrifice life	34	33

Indicators of Institutional Attachment:	Great Britain	European average
Great confidence in Church	19	21
Church answers moral problems	30	35
Church answers family problems	32	33
Church answers spiritual needs	42	44
Attend church monthly	23	35
Denomination:		
Roman Catholic	11	54
Protestent (Established)	68	29
Free Church/Non-conformist)	6	2
Believe religion will become:		
More important in future	21	19
Less important in future	40	34
Believe in one true religion	21	25
Religious faith an important value to develop in children	14	16

TABLE 3.2 Importance of God to various groups identified by religious disposition, religious practice, conception of God and orthodox belief

| Indicators of orthodox attachment | Indicators of religious disposition | | | | | | | | | | Row total |
| | Belief in God | | | Religious person | | | Comfort & strength | | Thinking about meaning/purpose | | |
	Yes	Unsure	No	Yes	No	Atheist	Yes	No	Often	Rarely*1	Average
Church attendance:											
Weekly	9.02	5.00	4.33	9.02	8.93	1.50	9.11	4.67	9.10	7.71	8.88
Monthly	7.06	5.40	1.50	7.35	4.82	0.00	7.41	4.89	7.37	5.63	6.77
Yearly	6.44	2.69	2.06	7.02	3.53	5.00	7.39	3.91	6.50	4.43	5.62
Seldom/never	6.09	2.76	1.94	6.63	3.25	1.89	7.38	3.41	5.57	4.35	4.78
Conception of God:											
Personal/God	8.03	4.50	3.57	8.34	5.73	0.00	8.56	5.17	8.61	7.17	7.86
Spirit/life force	6.29	3.68	2.29	6.75	4.04	4.00	7.27	4.15	6.54	4.69	5.67
Unsure	5.26	2.46	2.10	5.98	3.02	2.50	6.85	3.16	4.72	3.56	4.03
Neither	6.88	2.63	1.54	5.36	1.70	1.06	8.29	1.60	2.90	2.33	2.25
Believe in:*2											
God/Devil/heaven	7.80	–	–	8.31	5.80	7.50	8.56	5.45	8.51	6.38	7.80
God only	6.36	–	–	7.07	4.77	4.00	7.51	4.80	6.91	5.83	6.36
None of the above	–	2.96	2.00	4.20	2.10	1.28	6.55	2.03	2.98	2.25	2.34
Column average	6.82	2.96	2.00	7.32	3.65	1.97	7.90	3.60	6.79	4.72	5.74

*Q167. "And How Important is God in Your Life" Scale 1 – 10, 1 means 'not at all important'.

NOTES:

1. The category 'rarely think about the meaning and purpose of life' was chosen to illustrate differences, as there is an indication in the data that the 'never' category combines both those who never think about it because they are certain of their ultimate religious purpose and those who are indifferent to such matters.

2. Based on a Guttman scale. The composition of the scale is based on the belief items and affects the distribution of scores under the heading 'Belief in God'.

in either. Given the centrality of the notion of a personal God to the Christian tradition, the data support the view that belief in, and attachment to, a deity persist but that only a minority inhabit the Christian tradition in the full sense. However, as Kerkhofs (1983) has noted, lack of endorsement of the 'personal God' item in the questionnaire may be indicative not so much of outright rejection of the notion itself as rejection of an exclusively anthropomorphic image of God. On the other hand, it is clear that little more than a quarter of the population accept absolute , as opposed to relative, guidelines concerning good and evil (Q.154) and only a quarter accept the full range of Christian beliefs (Q.163) when these are taken to include both Hell and the Devil. These results could be taken to imply widespread rejection of the traditional Christian paradigm which may be manifest in a search for a new paradigm.

The percentage accepting absolute guidelines (28 per cent of the total population) is higher among those who believe in a personal God (45 per cent) than among those who conceive of God as a spirit or life force (37 per cent). More pronounced differences are apparent between these two groups when the full range of Christian beliefs is considered.

More than two-fifths of those who believe in a personal God accept the comprehensive range of beliefs (Q.163). Yet, these results are in themselves indicative of a degree of selectivity in belief among more orthodox Christians. However, the proportion who do so among those who adopt the alternative conception of God is no higher than the population average, less than a quarter accepting the full range of beliefs. These differences are reflected in differing attitudes to personal and sexual morality, and in the need to pray – the former group being stricter.

The most startling contrasts, however, are in the attitudes of the two groups to the importance of developing religious faith in children and in church attendance. Seven out of ten of those who believe religious faith is an important value to develop in children, accept a personal God; only a quarter adopt the alternative immanentist conception. Nine-tenths of those who attend church weekly are drawn from the former group, less than one-in-ten from the latter.

The acceptance of a personal God is correlated with age, the contrast being most marked between the very young (less than one-fifth of those under 25 years adopting such a conception) and the very old (half of those aged over 75 years holding the belief). The notion of God as a spirit or life force is less influenced by age, though it is a belief more prevalent among the middle-aged than among either young or old. Whatever the particular conception of God, however, belief in God is clearly related to age, the proportion increasing from about three-fifths among the 18–24 year olds to about nine-tenths among those aged 75 years or over. Whether this variation is an enduring generational effect or a function of age itself it is not possible to establish on the basis of these data alone.

The widespread rejection of absolute guidelines in favour of a more relativist moral position, tends to bear out one element in MacIntyre's (1981) thesis. Yet, as can be seen from Table 3.1, there remains a very high degree of consensus on moral issues and continuing commitment to the moral commandments of the decalogue. This contradicts another important element in his argument and suggests that his assertion that contemporary moral arguments are interminable and unsettleable is an overstatement. Whether generalised commitment to the existence of God but apparently weak assent to the detail and range of Christian belief will be sufficient to sustain the existing moral consensus is, nevertheless, open to doubt, given MacIntyre's view that in the absence of a teleological framework there is no rational basis for such values. In Chapter 4 Harding and Phillips note the correlation between youth, low levels of religious involvement and moral permissivity. Certainly, the relative lack of confidence exhibited in the church and minority assent to its contemporary teaching authority (see Table 3.1), reflected in low levels of church attendance, and the high degree of indifference to encouraging the development of religious faith among children, require either a revitalisation of the church's pastoral strategies or their displacement by an alternative source of moral leadership.

The following section takes the above analysis a stage further through the development of a number of composite measures of religiousity, religious meaning and institutional attachment, identifying the correlates of commitment, and assessing the degree to which commitment varies throughout important sub-groups in the population.

The approach to analysis and composition of scales

Two recent analyses of the overall European data identified six separate factors underlying religious and moral attitudes, beliefs and values (de Moor, 1983; Harding and Phillips, 1985). The three specifically religious factors are similar to those already described.

1. *Traditional Christian beliefs in*: life after death, heaven, hell, the devil, a soul, sin (Q.163); a personal God (Q.166).

2. *Religiousity* belief in God (Q.163); the importance of God in one's life (Q.167); the perception of oneself as a religious person (Q.158); the need for moments of prayer and contemplation (Q.169); drawing comfort and strength from religion (Q.168).

3. *Confidence in the ministry of the church*: belief that the church is giving adequate answers to the moral problems of the individual, the problems of family life and man's spiritual quest (Q.159).

The moral dimensions included the specifically moral commandments of the decalogue (commandments 4–10), a permissiveness factor and indications of personal honesty. Whilst these separate dimensions were associated with each other, the correlations were typically weak, with the exception of a strong positive relationship between acceptance of traditional beliefs and confidence in the ministry of the church, and a strong negative relationship between placing a high value on personal honesty and adopting permissive attitudes towards sex, marriage and other aspects of social behaviour.

A similar factor analysis was performed on the British data to develop appropriate analytical measures. Interestingly, traditional belief and the religiousity dimension did not emerge as separate factors for Great Britain but rather as one single dimension. The confidence factor remained distinct, however. These two dimensions were, therefore, used as a basis for two separate scales (see Appendix 3.1):

1. *Religious Disposition*: A combination of de Moor's first two factors, together with: the belief that basic truths and meaning are contained in all great religions (Q.155.1); personal acceptance of the first two commandments (Q.208); belief that religious faith is an important value to develop in children (Q.262); an indication of some form of 'spiritual experience' (Q.228.d).

2. *Institutional Attachment*: de Moor's third factor, together with: belief that there is only one true religion (Q.155.2); personal acceptance of the third commandment (Q.208); attendance at religious services (Q.157).

All the items in the religious disposition scale emerge as a single factor with the exception of the belief that basic truths and meaning are to be found in all religions – which was, nevertheless, retained for completeness. The institutional attachment items all form one factor, though again, the reliability of the scale would have been slightly improved if the item, belief in only one true religion, had been dropped. It too was retained.

The absence of a separate religiosity dimension for Great Britain independent of traditional Christian belief, casts doubt on the Luckmann (1967) 'invisible' religion thesis. On the other hand, it raises the possibility that affiliation to the establishment churches of Scotland, England and Wales may function as a kind of 'civil religion' analogous to that attributed by some American writers to the 'American Way of Life' (Bellah, 1964; Herberg, 1967). The possibility will be explored in the section on religious denomination.

For the purpose of analysis the population was split into three broad groupings of similar size (Low; Medium; High) on the basis of the recorded scores on each scale. As Table 3.3 illustrates, there is a high correlation (Gamma: = 0.74) between religious disposition and institutional attachment, with 56 per cent of the sample matching groups on both scales.

TABLE 3.3   *Relationship between religious disposition and institutional attachment*

Religious disposition	Institutional attachment			Row total
	Low %	Medium %	High %	
Low	64	35	3	35
Medium	32	43	33	36
High	5	22	64	29
Column total N = 100%	408	460	365	1233
	33	37	30	100

A further 5-point scale was constructed to measure overall religious commitment combining the above results. The low, medium and high categories were formed from matching groups. Low-Medium, and Medium-High categories were added. The former comprised those who scored low on religious disposition and medium on institutional attachment or *vice versa*. A similar procedure was adopted for the Medium-High category. A total of 32 respondents (2.6 per cent of the sample) scored high on one measure and low on the other. These were dropped from the combined scale. The resulting overall distribution is shown in Table 3.4. A little over one-in-five of the population fell into the lowest category and a little under one-in-five into the highest group.

TABLE 3.4   *Percentage distribution of sample according to overall religious commitment*

1. Low	2. Low-Medium	3. Medium	4. Medium-High	5. High
22	24	17	19	19

An analysis of the 32 respondents omitted from the combined scale suggests that they do not differ significantly from the population at large by sex or social class, though they do appear less likely to be retired people.

It is clear from Table 3.4 that, as suggested in the section on 'Christian values', fully committed Christians are a minority group and the population is evenly spread across a continuum running from high to low.

Finally, it is clear from the analysis of the demographic data in the previous chapter that age is an important discriminating variable. Similarly, as Stoetzel's European review and Dobbelaere's analysis of Religion in Belgium confirm (Stoetzel, 1983; Dobbelaere, 1984, p. i), sex and the working status of women are also important as far as values are concerned. The data on religious attitudes and beliefs have therefore been further analysed using a composite sex and work status variable (males, working females, non-working females) broken down by age group. It will be made clear in the following text whether the combined scale or the two component scales (religious disposition and institutional attachment) are referred to. Generally, however, the combined scale is employed where no substantial differences exist between responses on the component scales.

Socio-demographic profile of religious commitment in Britain

Table 3.5 illustrates the differences in religious commitment (combined scale) among various groups in the population. With the exception of age, these differences are not striking and remain the same whether religious disposition or institutional attachment is considered. In statistical terms the main relationships occur when the population is analysed by age, sex and the working status of women – though their contribution to causal explanation is limited. When the influence of age is accounted for, other differences tend to disappear. Thus, terminal education age influences religious commitment but this is primarily due to the fact that older people had typically left school by the age of 15. When the relationship between religious commitment and education is controlled for the effects of age the correlation falls from 0.15 to 0.017. Importantly neither social class nor physical location significantly affect commitment. The former finding is consistent with contemporary research and with Stoetzel's overall European analysis. The latter finding is indicative of the fact that secularisation has made its impact throughout the country and suggests that the spread of functional differentiation and urban culture into rural localities (Luckmann, 1976) may be complete in Britain.

Table 3.6 illustrates the variation in the intensity of commitment when age, sex and working status are combined into a single variable. The degree of religious conviction is uniformly higher the older the respondent. Similarly, women as a group tend to be more religious than men at any age. However, when the working status of women is taken into account a number of interesting differences emerge. The degree of commitment of working women is relatively stable throughout working life and is higher than that of non-working women well into middle-age. The religious conviction of non-working women varies significantly with age. These findings cast doubt on Luckmann's view (1976) that involvement in the working process is an important factor in secularisation. Rather, it may be that where participation of women in the labour force is uncommon or at a low level, the characteristics of participants are untypical of women in general. When participation is the norm, such differences may disappear.

The least religious group in the sample is the small group of young women at home–typically these had young children. These results are consistent with Harding's analysis of psychological well-being (Chapter 9), in which he refers to the higher levels of 'positive affect' among working women, and the review of research on family life reported by Brown *et al.* (Chapter 5). Harding suggests that substantial differences exist in psychological well-being between women in employment with no children and those at home with young children. The latter group were lonely, remote and exhibited high negative affect. Given his contention that psychological well-being and religiousity are positively associated with each other, the low level of religious commitment of young women at home is not unexpected. The findings point to a major deficiency in the pastoral strategy of the churches. Young women at home are a group which the ordained clergy typically find it difficult to relate to and and yet who are undergoing a major period of adjustment in life (Dominian, 1968, 1980; Thornes and Collard, 1979). The findings also raise further questions about Glock's deprivation thesis (1965; 1967), for in such circumstances religious involvement is not increased. Rather, the results add weight to the contention that participation in religious groups is not a plausible option for those seeking comfort or consolation in contemporary society (Stark, 1972; Roof, 1978) in the absence of fundamental conviction.

The majority of males are found in the 'low commitment' categories. It is only among the *retired* group *without* children that 'highly committed' men predominate over relatively uncommitted males. Among married men with children aged over 15 years, considerable variation is apparent and those in the 'medium to high' range predominate over the uncommitted. Indeed greater variation in commitment is a feature of all the middle-aged groups, though the effects of age and domestic circumstance appear greater for women than men. The presence of, or ages of, children in the family appear to exert little influence on religious commitment; such differences as exist being largely explained by the age of the parents.

Turning to individual components of the religious commitment scale (disposition, belief and institutional attachment – see Table 3.7 for selected items), significant overall differences are found when analysed by the combined age, sex and female work status variable. The sex and occupational status differences alone tend to be statistically significant for most items. Age differences are, however, uncommon among working women; more common among non-working women than among men.

Both age and sex differences are apparent on the three summary measures of religiosity (importance of God, self-definition as religious; comfort and strength), the variations being consistent with the above analysis. On the measures of reflectiveness, however, differences by age for each group tend not to be statistically significant. Similarly, no significant sex differences emerge in relation to reflec-

TABLE 3.5 *Socio-demographic profile*

| | Overall religious commitment: combined scale | | | | | Total sample |
Variable	Low %	Low-Medium %	Medium %	Medium-High %	High %	N = 100%
Age:						
18 –24	39	27	15	11	9	193
25–44	24	31	16	16	14	446
45–64	14	21	19	20	27	335
65 & over	14	11	18	28	28	202
Significance 0.0000						
Gamma 0.29						
Sex/Employment status of women:						
Male	27	25	18	14	15	576
Working female	18	23	17	23	20	311
Non-working F	15	23	14	22	26	314
Significance 0.000						
Gamma 0.21						
Terminal education age:						
14 yrs or under	15	15	18	25	28	361
15–17 yrs	24	29	17	16	14	628
18 yrs or over	26	23	14	15	22	208
Significance 0.0000						
Gamma 0.14						
Locality:						
Village	17	22	19	21	21	322
Small town	24	23	17	19	17	547
Large town	22	27	14	16	21	330
Significance 0.13						
Gamma 0.05						

...socio economic group.

	Low	Low-medium	Medium	Medium-High	High	Total (n)
AB	22	23	17	18	20	192
C1	25	24	16	14	21	263
C2	23	24	19	18	17	387
DE	17	24	15	23	21	353

Significance 0.21
Gamma 0.05

Income level: (327 missing cases)

	Low	Low-medium	Medium	Medium-High	High	Total (n)
Under £3840	15	20	15	25	26	250
£3840 – £7199	19	26	16	17	21	307
£7200 and over	28	27	18	13	15	322

Significance 0.0001
Gamma 0.15

Missing cases 32   Total   22   24   17   19   19 $\overline{1201}$ (max)

TABLE 3.6   *Religious commitment by age, sex and working status of women*

	Males %				Working females %			Non-working females %				Total %
	Under 25	25–44	45–64	65 & over	Under 25	25–44	45–64	Under 25	25–44	45–64	65 & over	
Low	45	29	18	20	23	18	13	54	20	8	9	22
Low-medium	26	35	22	11	28	25	13	29	32	26	10	24
Medium	14	15	22	24	16	17	19	11	16	12	14	17
Medium-High	7	13	16	22	19	25	21	4	11	25	33	19
High	8	9	23	22	14	15	32	0	22	29	35	19
Column total N=100	100	213	160	96	64	142	90	28	92	85	102	1172

(Missing cases 59)

TABLE 3.7 Selected indicators of religious disposition, belief and institutional attachment by age, sex and working status of women

Indicators of religious commitment	Sex/status	Total	Age			Significance levels for age
			30 years & under	Over 30 years not retired	retired	
Often think about meaning and purpose of life	Male	35	29	34	48	N.S.
	W. Female	34	24	37 }	36	N.S.
	Non-W. Female	32	31	31 }		N.S.
(S/S Differences not significant)			Overall difference significance 0.04			
Define self as a religious person:	Male	55	35	60	72	0.0000
	W. Female	64	47	72 }	70	0.001
	Non-W. Female	63	28	73 }		0.0000
(S/S Differences significant)			Overall differences significant 0.0000			
God important in life: (Score 7–10)	Male	36	17	39	57	0.0000
	W. Female	44	28	52 }	70	0.002
	Non-W. Female	57	27	64 }		0.0003
(S/S Differences significant)			Overall differences significant 0.0000			
Belief in God	Male	70	53	75	80	0.0000
	W. Female	77	73	80 }	89	N.S.
	Non-W. Female		67	91 }		0.0000
(S/S Differences significant)			Overall differences significant 0.0000			

	(1212)	(333)	(688)	(191)	S/S Differences significant
Believe in personal God:					
Male	26	23	27	32	N.S.
W. Female	35	33	36 ⎫		N.S.
Non-W. Female	39	28	43 ⎭	41	0.0001
			Overall differences 0.006		
Believe in Hell					
Male	24	25	22	26	N.S.
W. Female	25	26	24 ⎫		N.S.
Non-W. Female	33	21	39 ⎭	34	N.S.
			Overall differences not significant		
Fully accept first commandments					
Male	44	24	49	61	0.0000
W. Female	49	33	57 ⎫		0.001
Non-W. Female	58	29	64 ⎭	70	0.0000
			Overall differences significant 0.0000		
Fully accept third commandment:					
Male	23	9	23	46	0.0000
W. Female	21	16	23 ⎫		N.S.
Non-W. Female	34	12	36 ⎭	47	0.0000
			Overall differences significant 0.0000		
Attend church monthly:					
Male	15	16	14	17	0.005
W. Female	30	25	33 ⎫		N.S.
Non-W. Female	29	6	36 ⎭	40	0.001
			Overall differences significant 0.0005		
Column Total N =	1212	333	688	191	

(S/S Differences significant) appears under each category group.

tion on the meaning and purpose of life. Younger people tend – as Stoetzel's European analysis suggests – to regret doing wrong more frequently than those aged over 30 years but to be less convinced about the existence of sin.

On major items of belief the differences by sex/occupational status are statistically significant in all cases. As far as age is concerned, however, it is only in relation to the first commandment that significant differences *are* apparent between younger and older working women. For non-working women the situation is the reverse; it is only on items relating to the Devil, Hell and sin that differences between younger and older women *are not* significant. Among males substantial age differences are apparent on items relating to belief in the first three commandments, God and the notion that there is one true religion.

A similar picture emerges in relation to institutional attachment, including church attendance. Interestingly, in contrast to other denominations, a higher proportion of young people is affiliated to the Roman Catholic church than among older age groups – one-in-six compared to one-in-twelve.

Regional variation, denominational differences and church attendance

No significant differences were found in levels of overall religious commitment between England, Scotland and Wales even when the regional variations in religious denomination were taken into account. Differences were apparent, however, between those identifying themselves as members of the established churches and both Roman Catholics and Free Church members. More than two-thirds of those who define themselves as not religious, and three-fifths of non-believers, identify with the established churches, as do two-fifths of the small group of atheists. Further, those who identify with the established church are much less likely to attend church frequently than those from other denominations. They also score significantly lower on the scale of overall religious commitment than either non-conformists or Roman Catholics. Table 3.8 illustrates the relationship between denomination (broken down by frequency of practice) and levels of commitment – the correlation $(G = 0.38)$ is moderate and differences highly significant. To avoid contaminating the results, frequency of church attendance (Q.157) has been deleted for the items forming the scale in Table 3.8.

TABLE 3.8 *Religious commitment by denomination and frequency of church attendance*

	Denomination						
Commitment Level	Established Churches		Roman Catholics		Free Church		None	Row Total
	Monthly	Less	Monthly	Less	Monthly	Less		
1. Low	2	22	—	14	1	26	73	22
2. Low-Medium	7	25	1	23	1	22	15	19
3. Medium	11	16	5	15	4	9	7	13
4. Medium-High	34	25	22	29	21	20	2	23
5. High	45	12	73	19	73	24	3	24
Column Total	12	56	6	5	6	7	9	100
N = 100%	135	651	74	54	67	83	102	1166
Significance level 0.0000		Gamma = 0.38						

Those with no denominational attachment are least likely to attend church regularly and exhibit the lowest levels of religious commitment. Among denominational adherents those practising at least once a month exhibit much higher levels of commitment than those attending church less frequently.

Nearly three-fifths of the Roman Catholics and well over two-fifths of the Free Church members attend church monthly. About three-quarters of these regular attenders fall in the highest category of the commitment scale. Less than one-fifth of the established church members, on the other hand, attend monthly and only 45 per cent of these fall in the highest commitment category. Among the infrequent attenders, approaching half of those in the established and free churches and over one-third of the catholics fall in the bottom two categories of overall commitment. These findings are consistent with recent evidence from a local study in North West England of the beliefs and practice of teenage church attenders (Francis, 1984).

The identification of substantial proportions of atheists, and those who do not class themselves as religious, with the established churches and the relatively low levels of practice and commitment exhibited by the general membership raises the question of the degree to which affiliation functions as a form of 'civil religion' analogous to that reported in the USA (Berger, 1961). From an historical point of view it can be argued that mainstream Anglicanism has followed a strategy of accommodation rather than resistance to social forces, accepting enhanced status as a social institution in exchange for declining religious influence during the nineteenth century and demanding minimal commitment in the twentieth 'requiring neither deviation from the generally accepted ethical and social standards of the wider society nor burdensome donations of time, money or energy' (Gilbert, 1980, p. 112). In Scotland the established church has functioned differently, providing an affirmation of regional identity and being concerned more with adaptation of method than accommodation to social forces.

Given the wide variations in church practice an attempt was made using multivariate analysis to assess those factors predictive of frequency of attendance. A total of 36 variables was considered using a stepwise multiple regression procedure; of these 14 account for 46 per cent of the variance in church attendance. In addition to the Beta values shown in Table 3.9, crude estimates of the total number of days respondents would actually attend church each year were computed, depending upon the particular values and beliefs they held

TABLE 3.9   *Values, beliefs and behaviour predictive of church attendance[1] and the estimated number of days attendance attributable to each item*

Values or belief	Beta value	Days attendance attributable per annum
Q.262 Encourage childrens religious faith	0.19	15
Q.113 Voluntary worker	0.20	14
Q.163 Believe in Hell, Devil, Heaven, after-life	0.16	11
Q.208 3 Religious commandments	0.13	9
Q.315 Conduct unjustified[2]	0.08	9
Q.156 Roman Catholic/Free Church	0.10	7
Q.349 Great confidence in church	0.09	6
Q.159 Church answers all needs	0.10	6
Q.150 Regret doing wrong	0.06	6
Q.166 Believe in Personal God	0.10	6
Q.246 Marriage not outdated	0.07	5
Q.228 Had spiritual experience	0.07	5
Q.361 TEA below 16 years	0.08	4
Q.146 Often think about life	0.06	4

NOTES: 1. Code 1 on Q.157 was estimated to equal 120 days for the purpose of the above Regression Analysis.
2. Lying; Extra-marital affairs; Prostitution; Divorce; Euthanasia; Killing in self-defence.

or relevant aspects of behaviour. The belief that it is important to encourage religious faith in children in the home; active participation in voluntary work and a belief in Heaven, Hell and the Devil are the most significant predictors of church attendance accounting for 36 per cent of the variance. Those respondents endorsing these – and *only* these items – would be likely to attend church on 40 occasions annually. Other combinations of the items in Table 3.9 produce different estimates of church practice; those endorsing all 14 items would attend on average twice a week.

The ten commandments

The ten commandments, incorporating as they do both religious and moral dimensions, provide a further useful summary measure of assent to Christian principles. The Values Study (Q.208) asked both for an assessment of the degree to which respondents believed the commandments applied to them personally and the degree to which they applied to most people. Table 3.10 shows the distribution of responses when analysed by the combined scale. In interpreting the results it is important to recall that responses to the first three (religious) commandments in so far as they apply to *oneself*, were included in the scale; the results are therefore contaminated and the very substantial differences between the highly committed and uncommitted are therefore to be expected. The note to Table 3.10 makes this clear. This limitation does not apply to the *moral* commandments of the decalogue or to the perception of others. The distribution of responses falls into three main groups (command-ments 1–3; 4–5; 6–10).

In general, apart from the expected variations in assent to the religious commandments, *personal* acceptance of the moral precepts of the decalogue is generally very high, particularly commandments relating to the prohibition on killing and the demand to honour and respect parents.

The perception of the degree to which *other* people accept the religious commandments is low, but the more religious a person is, the more religious he or she believes other people to be.

Personal assent to the moral commandments though high increases with overall religious commitment, the correlations being moderate, reaching 0.46 on those concerned with marital infidelity (numbers 6 and 9). On the other hand, the perception of the degree to which

TABLE 3.10 Perception of ten commandments as applying to self and others and level of religious commitment

Commandment	Low		Medium-Low		Medium		Medium-High		High		Total	
	Self	Others	Self	Others	Self	Others	Self	Others	Self	Others	Self	Others
1. No other Gods	(6)*	8	(23)*	14	(58)*	24	(70)*	27	(96)*	30	(48)*	18
2. Lords name in vain	(5)*	5	(28)*	13	(48)*	18	(60)*	15	(80)*	22	(43)*	14
3. Sabbath holy	(–)*	3	(9)*	6	(22)*	8	(38)*	14	(61)*	18	(25)*	9
4. Honour patents	71	50	83	60	82	48	88	47	96	47	83	49
5. Do not kill	85	66	93	72	90	60	93	61	96	59	90	62
6. No adultery	61	25	76	31	81	21	87	27	95	29	78	25
7. Do not steal	78	40	89	46	89	35	90	38	97	36	87	38
8. False witness	66	36	78	42	80	35	84	36	94	38	78	35
9. Neighbour's wife	61	29	78	38	83	31	88	37	95	35	79	32
10. Neighbour's goods	62	30	80	40	78	31	87	38	93	35	79	33
N =	259		287		199		223		233			

NOTES: Results indicated as follows: ( )* are contaminated by the inclusion of the item as it applies to 'oneself' in the scale others accept these moral precepts is much lower, particularly so with those relating to honesty, covetousness and adultery.

There is a remarkable degree of consensus about the *degree* to which other people accept the moral commandments which appears to be independent of religious commitment.

A number of observations can be made on the basis of the above results. Perception of the degree to which others are religious is likely to be influenced by the circles in which one moves. In so far as religious people belong to a community of faith they may tend to overestimate the extent to which others share their beliefs and *vice versa*. There is, in fact, an indication in the data that, whilst general levels of tolerance are high, those who score high on the religious disposition scale are somewhat more uneasy in the company of those whose values they do not share (Q.117 and Q.120), a fact which may reinforce their attachment to their religious communities and insulate them a little from other views.

The difference between high personal assent to the moral commandments and the low perception of other people's values may simply reflect attachment to precepts acknowledged as an ideal on the one hand as against the realities of daily life on the other. Yet, it would be erroneous to dismiss the subjective responses out of hand as an unreliable guide to personal values. On the one item for which objective data is available – the commandment to keep the sabbath holy – a little under half of those respondents fully accepting it (25 per cent) attend church monthly.

An alternative explanation is that the responses are a valid indication both of personal belief and of a perception of the world as informed by, for example, media portrayal of reality. Either way, in so far as membership of a community of faith is essential to sustain religious and moral values, then, the belief that others reject values that one cherishes, together with the process of secularisation previously described, will tend to undermine such values and contribute to the confusion and insecurity implied by MacIntyre's analysis. Indeed, from the point of view of the latter thesis, perception of the moral values of others may reflect a realisation of the fragility of the moral consensus when it is deprived of a teleological framework, and that others are unlikely to share one's ideals. What is remarkable is that most people *do* hold such ideals whilst erroneously believing themselves to be untypical in doing so.

Table 3.11 elaborates on the above discussion by again illustrating the variations in beliefs by age, sex and working status of women.

TABLE 3.11 Ten commandments by age, sex and working status of women

Commandment and Sex/status	Total		Age						Significance levels age	
			30 years & under		Over 30 Years Not retired		Retired			
	Self	Others	Self	Others	Self	Others	Self	Others	Self	Others
1. No other gods										
Male	44	19	24	10	49	24	61	17	0.0000	0.002
W. Female	49	20	33	13	57	23 }	70	26	0.001	N.S.
Non W. Female	58	22	29	14	64	24 }			0.0000	N.S.

Self: S/S Differences significant 0.0000 — Self. Significant — Retired 0.000
Most people: Differences not significant — Overall differences: Others — Others. Significant — 0.005

	Self	Others	Self	Others	Self	Others	Self	Others	Self	Others
2. Lords name in vain										
Male	40	14	16	8	45	17	62	17	0.0000	N.S.
W. Female	44	14	33	10	49	16 }	62	20	0.05	N.S.
Non-W. Female	50	16	20	9	55	17 }			0.0000	N.S.

Self: S/S Differences significant 0.01 — Self. Significant — Retired 0.000
Most people: Differences not significant — Overall differences: — Others. Significant — 0.05

	Self	Others	Self	Others	Self	Others	Self	Others	Self	Others
3. Sabbath holy										
Male	23	10	9	7	23	10	46	14	0.0000	N.S.
W. Female	21	6	16	8	23	6 }	47	14	N.S.	N.S.
Non-W. Female	34	13	12	13	36	13 }			0.0000	N.S.

Self: S/S Differences not significant — Self. Significant — Retired 0.000
Most people: Sex differences. Not significant — Overall differences: — Others. Significant — N.S.

80

4. Honour parents

Male	83	54	72	45	86	60	92	54	0.0000	0.01
W. Female	84	51	78	51	86	51 }	89	49	N.S.	N.S.
Non-W. Female	85	46	80	50	86	42			N.S.	N.S.

Self: S/S Differences not significant
Most people: Differences not significant

Overall Differences: Self. Significant 0.000 Others. significant N.S.

5. Do not kill

Male	88	64	82	58	91	67	89	64	0.04	N.S.
W. Female	94	68	94	70	94	65 }	92	61	N.S.	N.S.
Non-W. Female	94	61	91	56	95	64			N.S.	0.02

Self: S/S Differences significant 0.008
Most people: Differences not significant

Overall differences: Self. Significant N.S. Others. Significant 0.01

6. No adultery:

Male	76	29	63	27	79	28	89	37	0.0000	N.S.
W. Female	79	21	72	21	82	22 }	86	28	N.S.	0.04
Non-W. Female	85	27	67	17	91	31			0.001	0.004

Self: S/S Differences significant 0.002
Most people: Differences not significant

Overall differences: Self. Significant 0.000 Others. Significant 0.01

7. Do not steal

Male	84	40	72	40	87	39	94	43	0.0000	N.S.
W. Female	92	39	88	45	94	37 }	92	36	N.S.	N.S.
Non-W. Female	92	39	82	36	95	43			N.S.	N.S.

Self: S/S Differences significant 0.002
Most people: Differences not significant

Overall differences: Self. Significant 0.000 Others. Significant N.S.

TABLE 3.11 Cont'd.

Commandment and Sex/status	Total		30 years & under		Over 30 years Not retired		Retired		Significance levels age	
	Self	Others	Self	Others	Self	Others	Self	Others	Self	Others
8. False witness										
Male	79	42	65	33	83	46	91	42	0.0000	N.S.
W. Female	79	35	69	31	83	36	86	36	0.01	N.S.
Non-W. Female	82	33	67	24	88	37			0.02	N.S.

Self: S/S Differences not significant
Most people: Differences significant 0.05
Overall differences: Self. Significant 0.000
Others. Significant N.S.

9. Neighbour's wife										
Male	79	38	65	36	82	41	92	34	0.0000	N.S.
W. Female	83	32	79	34	84	32	83	36	N.S.	N.S.
Non-W. Female	82	31	67	25	86	31			0.03	N.S.

Self: S/S Differences not significant
Most people: Differences not significant
Overall differences: Self. Significant 0.000
Others. Significant N.S.

10. Neighbour's goods										
Male	78	38	64	36	83	41	88	34	0.0000	N.S.
W. Female	79	31	76	34	80	29	84	33	N.S.	N.S.
Non-W. Female	83	33	64	27	90	35			0.001	N.S.

Self: S/S Differences not significant
Most people: differences not significant
Overall Differences: Self. Significant 0.000
Overall differences:Others. Significant N.S.

The evidence confirms that attachment to the moral components of the decalogue is relatively high regardless of age, sex or the occupational status of women, whereas personal assent to the religious commandments is much lower – with significant differences apparent between major groups.

Age differences are of greater significance than sex differences and this is particularly true of men; though on the basis of these data alone it is not possible to disentangle age and generational effects. Significant variations are apparent between older and younger men on all commandments, whereas among women, age differences are more pronounced on the religious commandments. Once again, all working women exhibit relatively similar attitudes, but older non-working women exhibit greater concern than younger women at home.

Perceptions of other people further illustrate the high degree of consensus which exists throughout all sections of the population; few significant differences being apparent.

PART III: THE CHARACTERISTICS OF RELIGIOUS PEOPLE

The ethic of concern

It was argued in Part I that given the importance of the notion of total universal concern to Christianity, the religiously committed should exhibit significantly higher levels of attachment to values and attitudes indicative of concern. Such values also imply a certain 'openness' and non-judgemental attitude to others. The data indicate that while overall levels of trust (Q.124–126) and belief in the basic goodness of others (Q.149) are not high (a little over two-fifths believe people can be trusted and a little under one-fifth that they are good), religious people are more likely to endorse such attitudes. This is more particularly the case with the degree of trust the old have in the young – religious people tending to be over-represented among older people. Religious people also emerge as significantly more likely to indicate a willingness to sacrifice their lives for a cause beyond their immediate family. One in five would be prepared to do so to save another life, a little over one in ten for their religion. The comparable figures for those who are not religious are one in seven and one in a hundred.

The survey also included one objective measure of concern – the propensity to undertake voluntary work (Q.113b). Religious people emerged as significantly more likely both to be in membership of and to be working for, voluntary organisations. They were also more likely to give higher priority to voluntary work in answer to the question on alternatives to employment (Q.138). This is true whether one considers religious disposition or institutional attachment. The correlation between religious commitment and voluntary work on the combined scale was 0.44. Roughly half of those in the highest category on the combined scale undertook voluntary work; almost nine-tenths of those in the lowest category undertook none at all. The main areas of activity of the religiously committed volunteer – apart from work for church organisations – were in the fields of welfare and youth work (see Chapter 8). Significantly, Harding and Phillips found that those scoring highly on their 'self-interest' dimension (see Chapter 4) were unlikely to be in membership of a voluntary organisation and least likely to be involved in religious groups or welfare charities. In interpreting the results it is important to bear in mind the age differences between the religiously committed and the uncommitted and the tendency for voluntary work to be an activity of the middle years (see Chapter 8).

Despite the above indicators of concern, those who scored highly on the religious disposition scale were, surprisingly, less likely to endorse 'unselfishness' as an important value to develop in children (Q.162); more likely to object to having left-wing extremists, heavy drinkers and people with a criminal record as neighbours. Two possible explanations may be advanced for the latter view. Firstly, religious people tended to be older and to feel significantly more anxious at home (Q.237). Secondly, a certain tension is evident in the teaching of St. Paul between, on the one hand, the need for members of the church to maintain the moral and spiritual integrity of the community of faith and to avoid the company of those who might undermine it, and on the other, to imitate Christ and not shirk the company of sinners in fulfilling the obligation to love one's neighbour. Withdrawal is clearly one strategy of resistance for the elderly in the face of possessive individualism and secularisation.

Family and morality

In addition to concern, a commitment both to the family and to objective moral values were distinguished as characteristic of Christianity. Certainly, the more cohesive and strict the picture of the family emerging from the survey, the more likely it was to be religious. A family cohesiveness scale was developed from items concerned with the closeness of family relationships (Q.248) and the importance of shared beliefs and mutual respect for successful marriage (Q.248). The correlation between family cohesiveness and religious conviction on the combined scale was 0.39. About half of those in the lowest religious category also fell into the lowest of the three cohesiveness categories; conversely, about half of those in the highest religious category also fell in the highest cohesiveness category. Religious respondents tended to value the institution of marriage more highly (Q.246) and to emphasise the importance of shared values more strongly (Q.244/245) than those who were not religious. Similarly, they placed relatively greater emphasis (G = 0.38) on faithfulness in marriage (Q.248), reflected also in their responses to the sixth and ninth commandments and to the lack of justification for extra-marital affairs (Q.315). They believed that greater emphasis on the importance of family life (Q.308) in the future would be a good thing (G = 0.42), disapproved more strongly of single-parenthood (Q.256, Q.261). They were more opposed (G = 0.25) to divorce (Q.315) than those who were less religious and more likely to impose strict conditions for the termination of marriage (Q.255).

Religious people, especially the institutionally attached, were more likely to regard children as important for a successful marriage (Q.248), reflected both in a higher ideal (Q.254) and higher actual (Q.264) family size. They were more likely to have experienced strict parental discipline (Q.236) and less likely to agree that parents should be free to have a life of their own without being asked to sacrifice their personal well-being for the sake of the children (Q.260), less than one-fifth accepting such a point of view compared to two-fifths of those scoring low on the combined scale.

Religious people were significantly more likely to adopt an absolute as opposed to a relative or situationist position with regard to moral rules. A little under half of those in the highest religious category on the combined scale accepted absolute guidelines; more than four-fifths of those in the lowest group adopted a situationist perspective. However, the fact that even among the most highly committed religious people the latter perspective is as common as an absolutist one is an indicator of religious change and may be thought consistent with MacIntyre's contention that the Christian teleological tradition is preserved relatively intact only in closely-knit marginal communities. Whatever their underlying perspective however, the British population emerge (with important exceptions) with a high degree of consensus about morality and a relatively strict perspective (see Chapter 4).

Responses to the ten commandments illustrate the extent of moral consensus. The 'justification scale' (Q.315) further elaborates on the picture seeking opinions about the justifiability of certain forms of social conduct. With limited exceptions (assassination, avoiding taxes or fares on public transport, joy-riding) religious people emerge with significantly different standards, always expressed in terms of strict traditional Christian views. These are most marked in relation to sexuality, personal honesty and other aspects of morality associated with the counterculture of the sixties (abortion, homosexuality, drug taking, euthanasia). Other questions explored some of these issues in greater detail and the results confirm the existence of a positive association between religious commitment (both disposition and institutional attachment) and moral outlook.

Politics

On the basis of Phillips political involvement scale (see Chapter 6) and the various measures of religious commitment developed above, religious people are no more or less likely to be politically active than anybody else – though there is a suggestion of greater passive interest in politics among those who score highly on the religious disposition scale. Nevertheless, religious people do exhibit significant differences in their political outlook which tend to be conservative in character. They express greater pride in their nationality, exhibit relatively greater confidence in Parliament, the Bureaucracy and the security services, favour greater respect for authority; are less likely to participate in protests, demonstrations and boycotts. Although no more or less likely to be close to a political party than other people (Q.343), or to endorse the reactionary response to the question concerned with overall political disposition (Q.276), religious people, more particularly the institutionally attached, place themselves further to the right (Q.275) than those who are not religious, reflected in a greater tendency to be affiliated to the Tory Party among the minority in the latter group who *do* identify with a given party.

Quality of life

Do religious people experience any differences in the *quality* of life compared to others? Is the 'peace of Christ' which was promised to his disciples evident in their lives and does it have an impact on their quality of life? The question is not an easy one to answer because religious people tend to be older and are more likely, therefore, to have experienced bereavement, failing health, social isolation and inadequate income (Kinnard *et al.*, 1981; Rossiter and Wicks, 1982). Such factors affect indicators of the quality of life and psychological well-being; and there is evidence of poorer health, subjective experience of anxieties at home, more frequent loneliness and lower median income among more religious people. On the other hand, the higher the score on the combined scale of religious commitment, the less likely people were to experience life as meaningless. Religious people are certainly as happy as any other group in the population and express themselves as more satisfied with certain aspects of life, principally with the financial situation of their household (consistent with significantly lower emphasis on the importance of money and material possessions (Q.308)) and the quality of their home life. With regard to overall levels of psychological well-being however, it depends upon the measure of religiosity used. Using the Bradburn Affect Balance scale (Q.122) together with various measures of religious commitment described, some variation in levels of psychological well-being according to religious conviction and practice is apparent but the differences are not statistically significant. Harding, however, using specific indicators of religiosity, drawn from the survey data, demonstrates (Chapter 9) that there is a relationship between higher levels of psychological well-being and religious attitudes. This finding is consistent with recent empirical research on the nature of religious experience and its connection with psychological well-being (Hay, 1982).

PART IV: CONCLUSIONS

In Part I it was suggested that two major dimensions of religious conviction could be distinguished: meaning and belonging. It was also contended that whilst fully committed Christians would inevitably be a minority group, the influence of Christian values and beliefs would be more widespread, resulting in a continuum of forms running from open rejection to firm conviction. The evidence confirms the existence of the two dimensions but suggests that they are highly correlated. It supports the view that convinced Christians are a minority (less than one-fifth of the population), and raises the possibility that they will become fewer still, particularly as religious faith was not regarded as a priority so far as imparting values to children was concerned. Yet complete rejection of belief in God is confined to a tiny minority – about 2 per cent of the population – and personal attachment to Christian moral teaching remains high, particularly as expressed in the moral commandments of the decalogue. The impression remains of an enduring but partially absorbed Christianity, to use Martin's phrase (Martin, 1967), varying in intensity according to age and generation, sex, family background and, for women, occupational status.

The attachment to Christian moral precepts prevails despite widespread rejection of the view that absolute moral guidelines exist and, surprisingly, despite the belief that such values are not shared by most other people. The rejection of absolute guidelines is consistent with MacIntyre's thesis concerning emotivism; the continued attachment to moral standards for which (he argues) no rational, as opposed to teleological, basis exists is not. Grounds for the moral confusion which MacIntyre cites are clearly apparent though for somewhat different reasons. Most people maintain that they *personally* accept traditionally high standards of personal morality – standards which, were others to be aware of them, would form the basis for mutual trust. Yet, the majority also believe that others do not abide by such standards with the result that over half the population are of the opinion that 'you cannot be too careful in dealing with people' (Q.124) and young people in particular have the impression that older people do not trust them (Q.126). In so far as membership of a moral community is necessary to sustain shared standards, and membership of a community of faith is necessary to sustain Christian belief, then uncertainty and doubt are increasingly likely to prevail. This is particularly so in the absence of an alternative moral scheme – as opposed to a position based on rejection of prevailing standards – and in the face of relatively high levels of indifference to religious values exhibited by young people. Nearly two-thirds of those aged under 25 years fell into the two lowest categories on the composite religious commitment scale.

It was also suggested that central to the Christian ethic were the notions of community, concern and family relationship, whereas the emotivist thesis entailed the notion of a society of self-absorbed individuals and predominantly manipulative social relationships. The necessity to participate in contemporary social life, tends to undermine the key values of the Christian minority. Evidence of significantly higher levels of social concern, greater attachment to the institution of the family and more cohesive family units were apparent among committed Christians. Given the correlation between involvement in formal voluntary organisations and the propensity to engage in informal helping and caring activities in the neighbourhood (Morgan *et al.*, 1977; Axelrod, 1956) the very low levels of involvement of the uncommitted also provide indirect support for the above view. Further, whilst committed Christians exhibit slightly higher levels of trust and openness, these do appear to be affected by contemporary reservations about other people.

Despite generally high levels of belief in God, it is clearly difficult for many people to articulate their conception of God. Less than one-third accept the traditional Christian notion of a personal God and it is this group which comprises the bulk of regular church attenders. Most people exhibit a relatively vague religiousity and selective beliefs drawn from the Christian portfolio. There is an indication that, for many, the established religions of the two kingdoms may function as a form of 'civil' religion with the established churches adopting strategies of accommodation rather than resistance to secular forces. Roman Catholics and non-conformists exhibit higher overall levels of religious commitment than those in membership of the established churches. The latter group represent more than two-thirds of the population but less than half of those in the highest religious category. Catholics and non-conformists, less than one-fifth of the total population, represent two-fifths of those with the highest level of religious conviction. As far as church attendance is concerned, for some catholics, weekly observance has perhaps as much to do with identity as with deep conviction, whereas for non-conformists it is more a function of the latter. As far as beliefs are concerned, acceptance of the comprehensive range of beliefs appears higher among catholics; the difference may be due to relatively greater attention to dogma in the catholic tradition.

Turning to the question of secularisation, the process of religious change appears to have eroded the moral and teaching authority of the church. Only one-fifth of the population professed to have a great deal of confidence in the church as an institution. Three-fifths of this small group were highly committed Christians, none was drawn from the uncommitted. Similarly, the churches' response to contemporary moral, spiritual and family problems was recognised as authoritative primarily by the committed – between two-thirds and three-quarters of the minority who expressed confidence in the churches' response to these issues were drawn from the two highest commitment categories.

The age profile of the churches is untypical of the population. There is a tendency to emphasise frail and elderly church members as far as ministry and services are concerned as opposed to evangelisation among young people. Low levels of commitment exist among the young – especially young women at home. A radical review of pastoral priorities and resource allocation between different forms of ministry appears to be called for if the apparent moral consensus is to be sustained and – from the churches' point of view – firmly re-rooted in the tradition from which it sprang before it evaporates in the absence of an alternative foundation.

Despite the variation in, and apparently vague religious commitment of, the British population, the data lends no support to the view that a separate, identifiable, more fundamental religious dimension exists to life independent of traditional Christian belief and practice. Indicators both of a tendency to reflect upon life and death and of a general religious disposition were included in the study. Multivariate analysis failed to distinguish such measures as a factor in religion separate from traditional components of belief. Responses to such questions varied directly with those indicative of traditional Christian conviction and church practice. Values associated with Luckmann's invisible religion, for example, moral autonomy and sexuality tended rather to be negatively correlated with indicators of religious conviction as did the moral permissivity of the 'counter-culture'.

From the point of view of the demography of religion, age, sex and the working-status of women are of significance; education, class and income are not when the influence of age is taken into account. As with other recent studies, the data does not support Glock's 'comfort thesis'. No major indicators of deprivation were found to be associated with religious conviction – other than those associated with age itself. Religious people are as happy as any other group in the population and in certain respects more, rather than less, satisfied with life than are the uncommitted.

The process of secularisation appears to have had its effect throughout the country; no major differences emerging between rural, small town and large urban centres. Importantly, insertion in the work process of itself does not appear to lead to the results Luckmann postulated. Rather a complex of factors relating to age, domestic circumstances, levels of social support and psychological well-being appear to be at work. Men are typically less religious than women throughout life. It is true that retired men are more religious than young men, but this is probably a function of generational differences. Working women exhibit relatively stable levels of religious conviction throughout working life – again increasing with retirement – levels which exceed those of non-working women well into middle-age. It is the young woman at home with children who typically emerges with the lowest levels both of religious conviction and psychological well-being.

The narrow contemporary appeal of the teaching authority of the churches, the relative irreligiosity of young adults and the potential fragility of the moral consensus clearly confront the churches with a formidable challenge.

APPENDIX 3.1   RELIGIOSITY SCALES

Religious feeling

Q.155	Code	1		2		6			
	Score	1		0		0			
Q.158	Code	1		2		3			
	Score	1		0		−1			
Q.163	Code Yes	1	2	3	4	5	6	7	8
	Score	1	1	1	1	1	1	1	1
	(Score 1 for each Yes mentioned)								
Q.166	Code	½		3		4			
	Score	1		0		−1			
Q.167	Code	1/2		3/4		5/6		7/8	9/10
	Score	1		2		3		4	5
Q.168	Code	1		2					
	Score	2		0					
Q.169	Code	1		2					
	Score	2		0					
Q.208 (a) self	Code	1		2					
	Score	2		1					

Commandments 1 & 2 only

Q.228 (d)	Code	1	2
	Score	0	1

Religious Faith

Q.262	Code		(all others)
	Score	1	0

Institutional attachment

Q.155	Code 2	Score 1			All others		0
Q.157	Code	1	2	3	(4/5/6)	7	8
	Score	5	4	3	2	1	0
Q.159	Code Yes	(a)	(b)	(c)			
	Score	1	1	1			

(i.e. Score 1 for each Yes mentioned)

Commandment 3 only

Q.208 (a)	Code	1	2
self	Score	2	1

The church

Q.349	Code	1	2	3	4
	Score	3	2	1	0

4 The Structure of Moral Values

DAVID PHILLIPS AND STEPHEN HARDING

INTRODUCTION: THE RESEARCH APPROACH

There is a difficulty in asking people direct questions about the kinds of attitudes or actions which may make them feel personally guilty or feel that they have 'sinned' or transgressed in some way. Ethical standards can be inferred, however, by obtaining respondents' judgements towards behaviours about which there has been some diversity of moral opinion.

The approach adopted in the Values Study (Q.315) was to present respondents with a selection of 'morally debatable' issues; for example, 'suicide' and 'avoiding fares on public transport'. The twenty-two items chosen cover some of the problematical areas of morality which individuals might conceivably have to face in their lives, or at least be expected to have an opinion about. Respondents were asked to rate each of the twenty-two statements on a 10-point 'justification scale' where 1 means that the behaviour is considered 'never justified' and 10 means that the behaviour is 'always justified'. Points in between indicate intermediate levels of justification. To counteract possible order effects which might lead to stereotyped 'response set' answering, half the sample was presented with the items in reverse order. The distributions of responses to the individual statements are shown in Table 4.1, where the items are also ranked by their mean scores from 'least justified' to 'most justified'.

On almost all the items the majority of the British sample are close to the lower 'never justified' end of the scale. Mean scores on many of the items are very low, less than 3.0 for sixteen of the items. On only

TABLE 4.1 *The 22 justification items ranked by mean scores, with percentage response distributions (N = 1231)*

Ranking	Mean score	Item	Never 1	2	3	4	5	6	7	8	9	Always 10
Least justified 1	1.30	Taking and driving away a car belonging to someone else (joyriding)	90	3.5	2	1	1	1	1	0.5	0.5	0.5
2	1.69	Someone accepting a bribe in the course of their duties	77	7	5	4	3	1	1	1	0.5	1
3	1.76	Threatening workers who refuse to join a strike	75	8	5	3	4	1	1	1	0.5	0.5
4	1.81	Claiming State benefits which you are not entitled to	73	8	5.5	4	5	2	1	1	0.5	1
5	1.85	Political assassination	74	9	4	3	4	2	1.5	1	0.5	1
6	1.91	Fighting with the police	68	12	6	3	5	2.5	2	1	0.5	1
7	1.93	Taking the drug Marijuana or hashish	76	4	5	3	5	2	1	1	1	2

8	2.01	Sex under the legal age of consent	71	7	5	3	7	2	2	1	1	1	1
9	2.04	Buying something you knew was stolen	68	7	7	3	5	3	2	2	1	0.5	1
10	2.23	Avoiding a fare on public transport	61	10	9	4.5	8	2.5	2	1	1	0.5	1
11	2.49	Failing to report damage you've done accidentally to a parked vehicle	56	11	9	5	9	3	2	2	2	0.5	2
12	2.66	Keeping money that you have found	51	12	10	5	10	3	3	2	2	1	3
13	2.70	Married men/women having an affair	51	8	9.5	6.5	13	4	3.5	2	2	0.5	1
14	2.82	Cheating on tax if you have the chance	54	9	8	5	8	4	4	3	3	1	4
15	2.88	Suicide	49	9.5	10	6	12	5	3	4	4	0.5	3
16	2.90	Lying in your own interest	43	13.5	12	7.5	11	4	4	3	3	1	2
17	3.14	Prostitution	46	7	9	7	15	4	4	4	4	1	3
18	3.69	Homosexuality	43	4	7	6	17	4	5	5	6	2	7
19	4.14	Abortion	30	7	8	7	21	6	5	5	7	2	6
20	4.45	Euthanasia (terminating the life of the incurably sick)	28	7.5	7	7	17	7	6	6	9	3.5	8
21	5.12	Divorce	14	4	7	8	28	10	8	8	8	3	8
22	5.52	Killing in self-defence	19	5.5	6	5	16	7	8	8	12	5	17

Most justified

one item, 'Killing in self-defence', does the mean value (5.52) exceed the numerical mid-point of the scale (5.5). Evidence from other countries (Harding and Phillips, 1985 forthcoming), however, indicates that low scores such as these are not simply an artefact of the rating scale. Scores for other European samples in the Values Study have tended to be low and skewed towards the 'strict' end of the scale but not always to the same extent as the British sample. French respondents in particular expressed a more 'liberal' attitude on many of the issues – for them at least, the 10-point scale represented a real diversity of moral choice. Viewed in a cross-national context, the British do stand out as being fairly 'strict'.

Greatest strictness is directed towards acts which are illegal. The first eleven items in the ranking all involve breaches of the law; with the possible exception of 'threatening workers who refuse to join a strike', where the illegality is implied rather than actual. Those items with the lowest average justification scores are concerned mainly with violations of private and corporate property and violence against the person. Indeed, it appears that certain offences against property are viewed more seriously than offences against the person. 'Taking and driving away a car belonging to someone else (joy-riding)' (Mean = 1.30) is overwhelmingly regarded as the least justified. Accepting bribes (Mean = 1.69) and 'claiming state benefits which you are not entitled to' (Mean = 1.81) are considered to be more serious than 'political assassination' (Mean = 1.85), which is technically the most serious 'crime' among the items.

By and large, a more 'liberal' stance is taken towards those issues which involve more private concerns, especially aspects of personal and sexual relations, such as divorce, abortion, homosexuality and prostitution. The greatest diversity of opinion is expressed for divorce and for 'killing in self-defence' (Mean = 5.516), which is viewed as the most justified act. This last item encapsulates most clearly a tension that appears to run through the ranking of the items, a tension between the demands of the law and the personal interest of the individual.

The British on the whole appear to be a law-abiding people, and where a formal code of behaviour exists, as embodied in law, it exerts a powerful influence upon the moral view that is taken of particular actions. Where, however, the behaviour is seen to lie in the area of more private, personal concern, there seems to be more scope for a liberal attitude and such acts are more likely to be regarded as morally justified.

ANALYSIS OF THE 'JUSTIFICATION SCALE'

In order to investigate the structure underlying the pattern of responses to the twenty-two justification items, a factor analysis was performed on the data. This statistical procedure detects patterns of inter-correlated items among the data which appear as distinct clusters or 'factors'. The analysis, of which a more detailed report relating it to other research in the area is available from the authors, revealed three such factors which appear to distinguish between three broad areas of moral concern (see Table 4.2).

Factor 1 is composed of a cluster of items with particularly high 'loadings' concerning relational or interpersonal behaviour and sexual conduct. Prostitution, divorce, homosexuality and abortion feature most prominently, followed by suicide, 'married men/women having an affair' and euthanasia. Sexual relations are dominant items in this factor, which we label 'Personal/Sexual Morality', but an additional area of concern is with what might be termed 'matters of life and death' – abortion, suicide, euthanasia – which increasingly nowadays may be seen as legitimate areas of debate for the moral conscience. One characteristic which unites the items in Factor 1 is that they all involve the endorsement or proscription of actions and conduct which have in the past been regarded as 'sinful' by the church.

Factor 2, which we label 'Self-Interest Morality', leads strongly on items which might loosely be described as 'petty fiddling' – 'buying something you know was stolen', 'cheating on tax if you have the chance', 'avoiding a fare on public transport' and 'claiming state benefits to which you are not entitled'. Strictly speaking, these are all activities which contravene the law. They have in common a certain element of minor cheating or dishonesty, evidenced by the prominence of 'lying in your own interest' and 'keeping money that you have found'. They all involve behaviour where there is a certain calculation of interest and where the final decision concerning their rightness or wrongness is largely made by the individual, rather than determined by the state.

Factor 3, which we label 'Legal Morality', appears to involve actions and behaviour which are much more likely to bring the individual into serious conflict with the state. Most prominent among the items

TABLE 4.2 *Factor loadings on individual 'justification scale' items*

F1	Personal/sexual morality	F2	Self-interest morality	F3	Legal morality
0.72	Prostitution	0.65	Buying something you knew was stolen	0.60	Taking and driving away a car belonging to someone else
0.71	Divorce	0.65	Cheating on tax if you have the chance	0.57	Fighting with the police
0.70	Homosexuality	0.59	Lying in your own interest	0.54	Threatening workers who refuse to join a strike
0.67	Abortion	0.57	Keeping money that you have found	0.50	Political assassination
0.54	Suicide	0.53	Avoiding a fare on public transport	0.49	Someone accepting a bribe in the course of their duties
0.47	Married men/women having an affair	0.40	Claiming State benefits to which you are not entitled	0.45	Sex under the legal age of consent
0.47	Euthanasia (terminating the life of the incurably sick)	0.39	Failing to report damage you've done accidentally to a parked vehicle	0.43	Claiming State benefits to which you are not entitled
0.43	Killing in self-defence	0.39	Someone accepting a bribe in the course of their duties	0.40	Avoiding a fare on public transport
0.43	Taking the drug marijuana or hashish				

48% of the variance explained.
The SPSS factor program was used: loadings are orthogonally rotated (Varimax), following principle factoring with iteration (PA2).

loading highly on this factor are 'taking and driving away a car belonging to someone else', 'fighting with the police', 'threatening workers who refuse to join a strike', 'political assassination' and 'someone accepting a bribe in the course of their duties'. All are instances which most people, irrespective of whether or not they might view them as justified, would readily define as law-breaking. Three of these items also involve violence, either actual or implied.

The factor structure that we have identified makes a great deal of sense. The implication is that whether a particular act is regarded as morally justifiable or not is largely influenced by its perceived position in relation to three areas of moral concern: the personal/ sexual area, a self-interest area, and the area of legality. It may be then that these areas provide a context for moral judgement, representing contrasting ethical considerations which influence the taking of a particular decision. After all, this is much in line with the everyday experience of taking a moral decision at the individual level. It makes sense to ask oneself questions along the lines of 'How does it affect me and my relationship with other people? – Is this a private matter for my own conscience?'; 'Is it in my interest? – Can I get away with it?', and 'Are there sanctions if I do this? – Is it against the law?'. These are quite literally key factors which people bear in mind when they come to make moral decisions, and people with differing moral outlooks are likely to vary in the relative importance they attribute to them.

THE SOCIAL LOCATION OF MORAL OUTLOOK

How are these differences in moral outlook related to demographic characteristics of British society, and to what extent do they reflect wider dimensions of personal values? In order to investigate these relationships, individual scores were computed on the three factors. Each respondent obtained three summary scores for:

1. Personal/Sexual morality,
2. Self-interest morality, and
3. Legal morality.

A high score indicates a 'liberal' or 'permissive' outlook, towards the 'always justified' end of the justification scale for items with high loadings on a particular factor, while a low score indicates a more 'strict' outlook.

On all three factors, a respondent's scores are skewed towards the low end of the range, emphasising the general strictness of outlook of the population as a whole. There is, however, greater variation among scores on Personal/Sexual morality than among scores on the other two factors, with least variation on Legal morality. This suggests there is comparatively greater diversity among British people concerning personal and sexual conduct, whereas there is more unanimity of outlook regarding secular issues, especially behaviour which conflicts with the law. To what extent are variations in scores on the three 'justification' factors associated with differentiation in terms of social characteristics?

(i) Age differences

There is, first of all, a strong relationship between the age of respondents and their scores on all three factors. Correlations between the three sets of factor scores and age are negative and fairly high for social survey data of this kind (F1 Personal/Sexual morality, r = −0.32; F2 Self-interest morality, r = −0.31; F3 Legal morality, r = −0.28). Across all three areas, younger people tend to be more liberal in their outlook while older people tend to be more strict.

There are, however, some differences in detail between the individual factors (see Table 4.3). Differentiation of outlook by age appears to take place later in the personal/sexual area than it does in the self-interest and legal areas. On Personal/Sexual morality, a predominantly liberal outlook is found among respondents aged up to 40, while those aged 60 and over tend towards the strictest outlook. On both Self-interest morality and Legal morality, the liberal view predominates only among the under 25's, while those aged 40 and over tend to be more strict. Among the 25 to 39 year-old group, a liberal outlook remains more widespread in the personal/sexual sphere than in the other two areas of moral concern. This suggests that liberality among younger people, at least in the relational and interpersonal area, may be a relatively more extensive and permanent characteristic of moral outlook and not just a transient stage in the maturational process.

(ii) Social class, home ownership and income

There are also systematic relationships between class background and positioning on the three factors. Interestingly, this contrasts with the

TABLE 4.3 *Mean factor scores and one-way analysis of variance results for age, social class, and sex*

	F1 Personal/Sexual	F2 Self-interest	F3 Legal	N of Cases
Age:				
—Under 25	0.22	0.43	0.41	349
—25 to 39	0.20	−0.02	−0.03	327
—40 to 59	−0.04	−0.21	−0.27	284
—60 plus	−0.52	−0.31	−0.23	284
F value	44.20	55.04	51.05	
significance	0.001	0.001	0.001	
Social class:				
—AB Professional/				
Managerial	0.27	−0.26	−0.14	260
—C1 White-collar	0.13	0.05	−0.01	264
—C2 Skilled manual	−0.04	0.10	0.01	337
—DE Unskilled and				
Others	−0.25	0.06	0.09	359
F value	20.06	11.47	3.85	
significance	0.001	0.001	0.01	
Sex:				
—Men	0.05	0.17	0.01	579
—Women	−0.05	−0.15	−0.02	642
F value	3.75	47.75	0.41	
significance	NS	0.001	NS	

analysis of traditional versus anti-traditional values presented in Chapter 2 where class differences in relation to the number of values areas were found to be slight. Within the specific area of moral judgement social class does emerge as a significant predictor of values, particularly in relation to the issues which make up the first factor, Personal/Sexual morality. On this factor, middle class respondents tend to be more liberal in outlook while working class respondents tend to be more strict. The most liberal are those in the AB socio-economic category, from a professional or managerial background; those in the DE category, predominantly semi- or non-skilled manual, are most strict.

While the age trend appears to be general across all three factors, this is not the case with social class where there is clear differentiation between the factors in terms of their content. Although differences are not as pronounced on factors 2 and 3, the general direction of the class relationship is reversed. On Self-Interest morality, AB respondents stand out as being more strict compared with the rest of the population. On Legal morality, the middle class also tends towards a strict view while working class respondents tend to be more liberal.

Similar patterns emerge on other measures of socio-economic status. Home-owners are more liberal than non-owners on Personal/Sexual morality and more strict on both Self-interest morality and Legal morality. Again, respondents with above-average incomes are more liberal on Personal/Sexual morality and more strict on Legal morality compared with below-average income respondents.

(iii) Interactions between socio-demographic variables

The effects of age and class combine together in different ways on the three factors. The age trend on Personal/Sexual morality occurs systematically within each social class grouping, with a steady shift towards a more liberal outlook moving from working class to middle class. Thus, the most liberal group are respondents under 25 years of age from the upper middle class, while the strictest group are those aged 60 and over from the lower working class. The picture that emerges is one of considerable class difference in outlook in this area. Superimposed upon the generally greater liberality among younger people, middle class respondents are more lenient concerning aspects of sexual relationships such as divorce, homosexuality and prostitution; life and death issues like suicide and euthanasia, and abortion which involves both relational and life and death aspects. Working class respondents, by contrast, tend to have a more conservative and restrictive attitude to this area of life.

The direction of the class effect is reversed on the two remaining factors and age and class interact differently. Lower working class respondents under 25 years of age tend to be most liberal on Legal morality while the strictest group are older respondents, aged 40 and above, in the highest (AB) occupational category. Although the differences are less pronounced than for Personal/Sexual morality, we again observe a class differentiation superimposed upon the general age trend, only on legal issues it is the working class, especially younger people, who tend towards a liberal outlook while middle class groups are stricter. It appears that there is slightly greater leniency in attitudes among the working class when it comes to acts which involve breaches of the law, while the middle class are more restrictive.

On self-interest morality, the most liberal group are working class respondents under 25 years of age, the most strict are again AB respondents aged 40 and over. However, there is also a substantial difference in outlook between the sexes on this factor, while no overall sex differentiation emerges on either Personal/Sexual morality or Legal morality. Men tend to be more liberal than women on Self-interest morality, particularly among the younger age groups.

To what extent do these results enable us to locate moral outlook within a social context? Firstly, there is the strong age trend, with younger people tending to display a more liberal outlook in all three factor areas. Two complementary explanations might be advanced to account for these apparent generational differences.

One interpretation would view moral development as part of a socialisation process, a variation on the idea of the 'generation gap'. From this standpoint, the greater leniency found among younger people would be a relatively transitory characteristic, to be modified subsequently as they grow older and pass through successive stages of the life cycle. Certainly, liberal views are most predominant among the youngest, under-25 year-old group, which is some confirmation of such a process.

Another explanation would emphasise age differences as evidence of a more permanent change in moral values with British society becoming progressively more liberal over recent decades, a process accentuated among the post-war generations. It is difficult to establish the existence of such a process of change without the analysis of data over successive time periods. Nevertheless, as the preceding discussion suggested, the evidence that liberality in the personal/ sexual area is carried further into the years approaching middle age is some grounds for concluding that this may be a relatively more enduring change.

Additionally, there is the fact that differences in moral outlook between successive generations are not confined to the younger age groups but are also found between middle-aged and older groups. This too may be the outcome of an underlying shift towards greater permissiveness with each generation (cf. Wright, 1978). It is worth noting that education may be a contributory element in this process. Across all three factors, respondents whose education has been prolonged beyond the current school leaving age tend to be significantly more liberal than those whose formal education was completed by the age of sixteen.

Secondly, there is evidence of some class differentiation in moral outlook, seen most clearly in the contrast between scores on Personal/Sexual morality and Legal morality. Middle class respondents tend to be more liberal than the working class on personal/sexual issues, and more strict on the legal and to a lesser extent the self-interest items in the 'justification scale'. It is difficult to avoid sociological stereotypes when discussing these differences. Among middle class people, with generally higher levels of education and with perhaps greater access to a diversity of moral viewpoints, it may be that a certain 'culture of enlightenment', for want of a more precise description, provides greater opportunity for adopting a 'progressive' moral stance when it comes to sexual conduct and issues like suicide and euthanasia. Working class people appear to be more traditional, more tightly adherent to relational norms and displaying a greater degree of conservatism in their personal lives. Where legality is concerned, the middle class appears to identify more closely with the state and institutionally-defined codes of conduct, while the working class seems slightly more detached. Perhaps there is less certainty among some sections of the working class about the transgression of rules involved in 'fighting with the police' or 'threatening workers who refuse to join a strike'. Similarly, in the area of Self-interest morality, it is much easier to express strong disapproval of the dishonesty involved in buying stolen goods, cheating on tax, keeping money that you have found or avoiding fares, if you come from a professional and managerial background and presumably lack any immediate financial incentive to engage in such acts. It may simply be that people who are less well-off are more likely to recognise that there may be extenuating circumstances in these situations.

Finally, there is a difference between the sexes on Self-interest morality, with men tending to be more lenient than women. The difference is most pronounced among younger people and gradually declines with age; there is little apparent difference in outlook between men and women after 60 years of age. The implication is that women are more conscientious than men. When it comes to actions which may involve some element of duplicity – buying stolen goods, cheating on tax, lying in your own interest, keeping money that you have found, avoiding payment of fares – women are more likely to express approval of the 'correct' behaviour in such matters. Perhaps it is more compatible with the male identity, particularly the competitiveness and bravado of earlier years, to challenge these standards or, at least, to regard their transgression less seriously.

MORAL OUTLOOK IN RELATION TO OTHER VALUES

Those respondents with high scores on each of the three factors (that is, with a more 'liberal' moral outlook) are less likely to describe themselves as religious or to engage in religious practice. The trend is particularly marked on the Personal/Sexual and Self-interest morality factors, and in both cases it is the relatively small group who describe themselves (Q.158) as 'convinced atheists' who display greatest liberality. There would appear to be something in their *'prise de position'* which distinguishes the values of this group from those who describe themselves simply as 'not a religious person'. To some extent it might be expected that differences in religion (and other) values reflect the pervasive variations in moral outlook which occur between different age groups. The greater moral strictness among religious people may partly be accounted for in terms of their greater age, but this is not a totally sufficient explanation. Even when the effects of age are controlled for, a significant relationship still persists between religious adherence and strictness of moral outlook. Irrespective of age, therefore, religious practice and values are predictors of a respondent's moral values.

One explanation for this relationship is that one role of a religion is to carry a certain set of absolute moral values. Thus, it is not surprising that the distinction between high and low scorers also extends to more generalised statements concerning the nature of morality. Asked (Q.154) whether they believe that there are clear guidelines concerning good and evil or whether what is good and evil depends on prevailing circumstances, the liberal, high-scoring respondents (particularly on factor 1, Personal/Sexual morality) tend to align themselves with moral relativity, whereas the more strict, low-scoring respondents tend to show allegiance to a world of moral absolutes, based on clear guidelines. The distinction between moral absolutes and relativism is not merely academic, of interest to philosophers, but clearly separates the population at large, particularly it would appear when the moral issues under consideration are personal-sexual in nature. In other words, we can explain the strictness or liberality of a person's outlook towards, say, homosexuality, or suicide, according to whether they adhere to a clear-cut moral code or see moral situations as depending on prevailing circumstances (cf. Davies, 1975).

Values in relation to the family also show variations according to respondents' positions on the morality factors. Greater strictness on all three factors, for example, is associated with greater reported strictness of upbringing. Despite the difficulty of inferring much from such retrospective reports, the pattern supports a 'socialisation' model of values, whereby an individual's values are seen in part as a product of identification with parental values. In relation to duty and responsibility within the family, and conformity to conventional modes of family life, it is those with high or low scores on the first factor, Personal/Sexual morality, who show the greatest differentiation of views. High scorers on this factor are more likely than low scorers to agree (Q.259) that parents have to earn the respect of their children rather than that children have a duty to respect their parents regardless. They are more likely to disagree (Q.256) that a child needs both a father and a mother, and more likely to approve (Q.261) should a woman want to have a child as a single parent. Freedom of the individual to choose and act in the way that suits them seems to characterise the position of high scorers, whereas low scorers express greater adherence to traditionally accepted standards.

So far we have considered the types of values which cut across all three morality factors, or which highlight those with high or low scores on the first, personal-sexual factor. Are there values which predict respondents' positions on the second and third morality factors? The second factor (Self-interest morality) clusters around items which are concerned with personal gain. Those with high scores on this factor are permissive on issues where they might obtain material advantage: avoiding a bus fare, for example, or keeping money that they had found. Their permissiveness is more 'opportunistic' in nature and has nothing to do with personal or sexual matters. High scorers again tend to report being somewhat less religious than low scorers, but the most marked differentiation occurs on the more secular religious proscriptions, such as the commandments 'Thou shalt not steal' and 'Thou shalt not bear false witness'. Not only do high scorers tend to endorse behaviour likely to be of (pecuniary) advantage to themselves, they also reject more alternative modes of conduct. For example, when asked which organisations they belonged to (Q.113), high scorers were particularly differentiated by their tendency to report 'none'. Least characteristic of them was to belong to a church organisation or 'charities concerned with the welfare of people'. Another characteristic of high scorers, which they share with high scorers on the third factor (Legal morality), is their relative lack of confidence in institutions of public authority (Q.349), such as the police and the legal system. This would seem to accord with their greater tolerance of petty acts, which are nonetheless infringements of societal rules.

Whereas items contributing towards factor two concern offences of a relatively trivial nature, those loading on factor three concern actions whose seriousness casts them unmistakably beyond the law ('fighting with the police', 'political assassination'). It is the items falling in this area which attract greatest censure among the sample, underlining the widespread commitment to legality among the population as a whole. A more 'liberal' endorsement of such actions, then, implies some readiness to reject laws and the institutions which maintain them. The evidence suggests that the moral outlook of those who go this far is linked to a more radical political stance. For example, high scorers are more likely to place themselves towards the left politically (Q.275) and to value social equality over individual freedom (Q.274). The small number of respondents who favour 'radical change through revolutionary action' (Q.276) also score highly on this factor. Taken to extremes, a values system which challenges legal authority may lead to the endorsement of violence for political ends. High scorers on factor three are more likely to agree (Q.348) that 'there may be certain circumstances where terrorism is justified', whereas low scorers condemn terrorism outright.

SUMMARY AND CONCLUSIONS

Questions of morality enter into the arena of public awareness and debate with great regularity. The scrutiny of other people's moral behaviour apparently makes good Sunday morning reading, be it in the form of a Social Security swindle or an MP's illicit love life. At the more personal level, a moral decision to follow a certain course of action may well be among the most heart-searching that we ever have to make.

In this chapter we have considered in some detail attitudes towards twenty-two 'moral' behaviours or situations. Most importantly, the analysis shows that these behaviours are not viewed in isolation, subject to discrete deliberation. Rather, there is a predictability in the way people categorise moral issues for treatment, according to the context of the behaviour in question. The analysis reveals a structure of moral judgement, the basic constituents of a moral code. Of course, the results cannot be viewed as definitive: a house can only be constructed from the materials provided. It is possible that the inclusion of a different, or more extensive, list of items would yield a different pattern from that presented here, though arguably the picture would be enriched rather than altered fundamentally. Analyses performed on data from eight other European countries reveal (with minor variations for Italy and Spain) the same three-factor pattern throughout (see Harding and Phillips, 1985).

On all three factors, two important characteristics are key predictors of respondents' strictness or liberality: age and religious involvement. Though age and religious belief are correlated, it was demonstrated that their effects occur independently. Both greater age and greater religiousness are associated with greater strictness of moral outlook.

Beyond the pervasive effects of age and religion, more specific influences help to explain the variations seen on each individual factor. Class-related differences such as occupational status; income; level of education, and home ownership, interact in differing ways across the three factors. In particular, a more liberal stance on the Personal/Sexual morality factor is associated with a more privileged social position – from a higher status occupational background, being better educated and better-off. Liberality in personal-sexual matters also extends to a more individualistic stance on related issues, such as attitudes towards family structure and responsibility. On the other two factors, Self-interest morality and Legal morality, the reverse pattern tends to prevail, with the more privileged showing greater strictness than those from lower status backgrounds. Analysis of responses to other values questions further corroborates and describes the nature of the morality factors: thus, Self-interest morality is associated with levels of participation in voluntary organisations and charitable activity; Legal morality is related to reported political attitudes.

5 Marriage and the Family

JENNIFER BROWN, MIRIAM COMBER, KAREN GIBSON, SUSAN HOWARD

INTRODUCTION

Our interest in families and marriage today is a reflection of the concern that has been expressed in recent years about the future of these institutions in Britain (See, for example, Home Office, HMSO, 1979). Conflicting moral codes, the well-publicised increase in the divorce rate and experimentation with radical life-styles have all contributed to a climate in which people may feel that fundamental changes have and are taking place at the very roots of society – that is within the family.

The interest of people in the future of marriage and the family rests on a belief that these institutions fulfil certain functions. Butler (1979) noted four possible functions for marriage:

(i) to legitimise sexual union;
(ii) to make a public declaration of a sexual union;
(iii) to make a declaration of the permanence of the relationship;
(iv) to prescribe obligations in the areas of family economy, parenthood and place of residence.

The family is viewed as a fundamental part of the system of controls which regulate our behaviour in the areas of sexuality and the raising of children. Changes in attitudes and behaviour surrounding these institutions are seen as a threat to the overall functioning of society.

This chapter aims to examine both the myths and the facts associated with marriage and the family today and to compare these ı the attitudes and beliefs expressed by the sample of British adults interviewed in the Values Study. It also examines aspects of marital quality from the points of view of the effects of children, of the life cycle of the marriage, and of the differential experience of men and women. Finally, issues of divorce liberality and features of the consequences of divorce are considered.

MARRIAGE AND FAMILY LIFE: MYTHS AND FACTS

Myths about the institutions of marriage and the family are widely held, and to some extent, seem impervious to statistical reality. Current myths include notions such as 'people no longer take marriage seriously'; 'marriage is an outdated institution'; 'feminism has changed attitudes towards women's role in their families'; the so-called 'cereal packet norm' (Leach, 1967) that is 'mother/father/ two children' ideal of family life, is being undermined by widespread single parenthood.

These myths seem to reflect an underlying belief that the institutions of marriage and the family are threatened by individuals' attitudes and behaviour. In this first section recent British research into marriage and family life is highlighted in an attempt to challenge these myths and at the same time provide a context in which the attitudes expressed in the Values Study can be understood.

Statistical background

Examining the statistical evidence for the popularity of marriage, Table 5.1 shows a decline in the overall number of marriages. Yet, in proportion to the population as a whole, marriage was no less popular in the late 1970s than it was in the late 1950s. Despite a recent rise in the number of divorces, the proportion of remarriages has risen. For example, in 1970, only 11.4 per cent of marriages were remarriages but by 1982 that proportion had risen to 29.9 per cent. These figures reflect the popularity of marriage for divorced people despite what may have been unpleasant divorce experiences. The general popularity of marriage is illustrated by the fact that in 1978, 95 per cent of women and 91 per cent of men were married by the age of forty (Rapoport and Sierakowski, 1982).

Taken together these statistics suggest that despite recent large increases in the divorce rate, the proportion of people entering

TABLE 5.1 *Marriage, divorce, previous marital status at marriage and illegitimacy rates England and Wales 1970–1982*

	1970	1980	1982
All marriages (000's)	415.5	370.0	342.2
1st marriage (both parties) %	81.8	65.1	64.1
One party divorced %	8.8	17.5	17.8
Both parties divorced %	3.1	11.4	12.1
One party widow(er) %	6.3	5.9	5.6
Divorces (000's)	58.2	148.3	146.7
Divorces per 100 marriages	14	40	42.9

SOURCE: Office of Population Census and Surveys *Marriage and Divorce Statistics.* Series FM2 HMSO (Annual)

TABLE 5.2 *Number of marriages per 1000 population in United Kingdom*

Year	Number of marriages	
	England and Wales	Scotland
1950	16.3	15.8
1955	16.1	16.9
1960	15.0	15.5
1965	15.6	15.5
1970	17.1	16.8
1975	15.4	15.1
1980	15.0	—

SOURCES (i) Mitchell B.R. (1981) *European Historical Statistics 1750–1975*, Macmillan.
(ii) Offices of Population Census and Surveys. *Marriage and Divorce Statistics* Series FM2 HMSO (Annual).

marriage has declined only very slightly while the increasing proportion of marriages which are remarriages shows that the experience of divorce does little to deter people from marrying again. The propensity of divorcees to remarry was clearly shown by Leete and Anthony (1977) whose survey of one thousand couples divorced in 1973 showed that 56 per cent of men and 48 per cent of women had remarried by 1977, 60 per cent of them within a year of divorcing. Dominion (1982) makes the point that if remarriage rates remain stable, one in five of men and women born around 1950 will have entered a second marriage by the age of 50.

Equality myth

Marriage continues to play a part in the lives of the vast majority of adults in Britain today but it has been argued that the feminist or 'Women's Liberation' movement has attempted to challenge the traditional nature of marriage. It is here suggested that feminist thinking and campaigning on the subject has done little to alter the fundamental position of the majority of women (or more specifically wives). This is because the underlying characteristics of their position – generally lower wages accompanied by the burden of responsibility for domestic and child care tasks – have remained unchanged. The limitations on women's employment potential are reflected in recent figures for average male and female hourly earnings in 1982: male manual workers received an average of 294.7 pence per hour, compared with 202.7 pence per hour for female manual workers. Male non-manual workers averaged 462.3 pence per hour while female non-manual workers averaged 282.2 pence per hour (New Earnings Survey, 1982). What the feminist movement has succeeded in doing is to draw attention to the legal, financial and domestic disadvantages shared by most women.

Researchers have studied many aspects of the position of women. In the domestic sphere it may be concluded that wives' domestic responsibilities are crucial in severely limiting their employment opportunities and earnings potential (Oakley, 1974; 1976; Edgell, 1980; Gibson, 1983). These responsibilities still remain on the shoulders of women. Studies of employment suggest that the position of women is still disadvantaged in the sphere of paid employment due to: high occupational segregation (Hakim, 1978; Adams, 1980); low levels of unionisation (Barron and Norris, 1976); the vulnerability of part-time workers (Hurstfield, 1978); sex-discrimination in the labour market (Chiplin and Sloane, 1976) and employment and redundancy policies (Jenness, 1976; Bruegel, 1979; Armstrong, 1982).

The fact that general inequalities between the sexes are reflected in personal male-female relationships was made clear by Mansfield who concluded from a study of the early years of marriage that contemporary marriage was 'more equal perhaps – but not equal' (Mansfield, 1982, ii). In the light of all the evidence, it is difficult to see how the Women's Liberation Movement has in any real sense influenced the lives of the majority of British women.

Women's attitudes towards their own position is itself at times ambivalent. For example, a recent survey of 'Town's Women' readers showed that 69 per cent thought that going out to work was good for women, but 75 per cent felt that the consequences were bad for the children.

The above literature suggests that the rewards for women in the work place are equivocal. However, data from the Values Study shows that women do not see their fulfilment as necessarily in childbearing. This is a view shared by the majority of men. However, more men (26 per cent) than women (15 per cent) agreed with the proposition 'Do you think that a woman has to have children in order to be fulfilled or is this not necessary?' (Q.257).

'Outdated institution' myth

A second much voiced opinion is that young people today are rejecting marriage. This is thought to be indicated by rising rates of cohabitation. Dunnell (1979) showed that 9 per cent of women marrying between 1970 and 1975 had lived with their husbands before marriage compared with only 1 per cent of those marrying between 1956 and 1960. Brown and Kiernan (1981) found that in 1979, 5 per cent of women were cohabiting; however, Kiernan (1983) points out that cohabitation is not a static state; she suggests that it may simply be a transitional phase allowing for a postponement of marriage rather than a replacement. Consistent with this hypothesis are findings which illustrate young people's hopes and expectations for and about marriage. A survey carried out by the *Sun* newspaper in 1980 found that 70 per cent of 13- to 19-year olds felt that marriage was not out of date. A McCann Erickson survey (Burdus, 1977) showed that 91 per cent of 15- to 19-year old single men and women expected to marry, although 60 per cent acknowledged that divorce was something that might happen to them. Research by the Marriage Guidance Council in 1981 found that 60 per cent of boys and 75 per cent of girls questioned expected their marriage to last until death. The same survey discovered a widespread traditional attitude with 87.5 per cent of boys and 93 per cent of girls expecting faithfulness within marriage.

The indications from the present survey are that, in overall terms

84 per cent of those questioned disagreed with the statement 'marriage is an outdated institution' (Q.246). There is a marginal tendency, however, for those in the 18–24 age group to agree with the statement, although there is not a clear cut linear relationship between age and belief in marriage.

Just eighteen respondents (1.6 per cent) to the Values Study admitted to 'living as married' and of these four thought marriage to be an outdated institution. However, those who were most disillusioned, perhaps not unexpectedly, were the separated or divorced, over a quarter of whom thought marriage to be outdated. Only about an eighth of married couples thought this to be so. Marginally more single people – one in six – indicated their agreement with this statement.

Interestingly, those who do not believe in marriage are more likely to be left wing politically; dissatisfied with their home life; belong to the lower socio-economic classes; unemployed and in either the younger or older age groups. This seems to indicate that disillusionment with marriage may go hand in hand with a broader scepticism about other facets of life in modern Britain.

Till death us do part

Although the Values Study did not deal specifically with attitudes towards permanence in the marital relationship it is worth noting at this juncture that an important myth about the permanence of marriage does exist. Marriage today is sometimes seen as a failing institution because some are relatively short-lived compared with the potential or actual life-span of the couple. However, until changes in public health transformed the notional length of life as 'three-score years and ten' from a potential to a normative span, permanence for many couples involved no more than fifteen or twenty years of marriage before the bond was broken by the death of one partner.

Today, couples marrying in their twenties can expect an undissolved relationship to span forty, fifty or more years; thus the reality of what constitutes permanence has changed considerably. Thornes and Collard (1979) indicated that of the divorced respondents taking part in their research, about a third were divorced during the first five years of marriage, about a quarter during the sixth to the tenth year, one fifth between the eleventh to fifteenth year and a further fifth after sixteen years.

Despite the change in the average potential length of marriage, there is still a tendency to hold to a view that a marriage which ends in divorce after a number of years is a failed marriage. This is partly attributable to the teachings of the Christian Church, exemplified by St Augustine's pronouncement that the three principal characteristics of marriage are permanency; the faithfulness of the couple; and the role of marriage in the procreation and education of children. The ideals of life-long monogamy in the marital relationship are of course fundamental principles of the institution. The Christian tradition underlies English legislation on the subject of marriage and divorce. These ideals are also implicit in most academic work in this area, 'successful marriage' usually denotes a life-long, monogamous relationship.

This Christian tradition is very well established in England. Sexual fidelity has for centuries been at the core of divorce legislation. It was only in 1857 that the need for a divorcing couple to attain an Act of Parliament was abolished. Yet as recently as 1922 a dual standard applied: a wife's adultery was considered to be sufficient grounds for divorce, but a husband's adultery had to be aggravated by some further offence such as cruelty. More recent changes in divorce legislation have extended accepted grounds for divorce to include desertion, cruelty, or insanity (1938) while the 1969 *Divorce Reform Act* changed the grounds for divorce to 'irretrievable breakdown of marriage' as indicated by desertion, separation, unreasonable behaviour or intolerable adultery. Despite the fact that this legislation may allow the couples to judge whether their marriage has broken down and thus makes possible conflict-free divorce, it by no means remains uncontended.

Marriage and parenthood

Another widely held belief is that the nuclear family, or what Leach called the 'cereal packet' norm, is under threat. This norm is described as consisting of two parents and one or more (but not too many) children. Concern has been expressed in religious, governmental and welfare circles about recent increases in the number of illegitimate births which, it is thought, represent a growing rejection of one of the main stays of the orthodox nuclear family – that is the belief that a family made up of a woman and her children must also include a husband/father. That the orthodox nuclear family is not in

TABLE 5.3 *Attitudes to marriage and parenthood*

	Total sample	Marriage is an outdated institution		Approve child outside stable relationship		Child needs both parents		Parents sacrifice well-being for children	
		Agree %	Disagree %	Approve %	Disapprove %	Agree %	Disagree %	Agree %	Disagree %
Sex									
Male	590	16	82	32	46	77	22	73	18
Female	641	12	85	30	48	58	39	70	17
Marital status									
Single	251	17	79	34	42	60	37	66	22
Married	808	12	80	32	47	69	29	73	16
Living as married	18	21	72	39	23	37	59	61	24
Divorce/Separated	46	26	72	33	31	56	41	61	28
Widowed	109	12	87	13	69	76	20	82	11
Age completed education									
16 or under	929	15	83	33	45	66	32	71	20
17/18	165	11	87	37	40	56	41	69	17
19/20	23	16	82	39	45	60	36	64	26
21 or over	112	9	89	30	42	65	32	57	15
Age									
18/24	19	19	76	41	37	55	42	63	25
25/34	251	13	85	48	31	53	43	67	20
35/44	204	15	83	31	41	63	37	63	22
45/54	179	9	90	29	48	70	27	76	11
55/64	189	9	89	22	54	82	18	82	12
64/74	127	18	81	11	72	79	17	76	18
75+	82	15	82	11	75	90	9	86	7

Class

AB	19	67	33	65	51	26	90	9	197
C1	18	70	38	61	44	31	87	11	271
C2	19	70	30	68	47	34	82	16	402
DE	16	77	25	72	47	30	79	17	362
Occupation									
Professional	21	58	38	61	46	28	90	8	108
Non manual	18	69	37	61	40	37	90	8	206
Skilled manual	15	75	28	70	40	37	83	15	219
Unskilled	19	74	39	57	39	38	81	15	148
Student	12	63	29	68	51	26	85	11	29
Unemployed	26	64	12	86	39	33	68	28	70
Retired	16	78	12	86	72	11	74	18	191
Housewife	17	74	35	61	48	31	84	13	221
Political view point									
Left 1/2	18	72	25	70	41	40	55	39	52
3/4	17	66	31	66	45	31	81	17	152
5/6	24	69	33	65	46	34	85	13	506
7/8	18	73	25	73	49	29	88	10	215
Right 9/10	16	80	20	80	66	18	90	9	88
Satisfied with home life									
dissatisfied	17	78	30	70	50	30	61	33	11
	32	60	29	69	46	38	73	24	32
	13	79	38	57	49	31	72	23	118
	21	65	33	63	47	30	85	13	360
satisfied	16	74	25	70	47	31	86	12	706

fact being rejected is evident in much recent research. For example, although Dunnell (1979) demonstrated an increase in the number of couples choosing to cohabit rather than marry, Brown and Kiernan (1981 p. 4) concluded that cohabitation is 'largely a childless period with most childbearing occurring within the framework of legal marriage'. Further evidence was reported by Mansfield (1982 p. 30) who summarized her respondents' attitudes to parenthood as 'inevitable and in most cases a desirable consequence of marriage'. Busfield and Paddon (1977) suggested that the link between marriage and parenthood is self-reinforcing, it makes those who want to have children marry and those who marry feel they should have children. These statements are supported by the fact that between 1979 and 1981 88.1 per cent of families with dependent children were headed by a married couple, while only 2.2 per cent were headed by an unmarried mother as opposed to widows or divorcees (*General Household Survey*, 1981 p. 20).

In addition, figures for 1980 (*Population Trends* 30, p. 10) show the percentage of live births which were illegitimate was 11.8. With respect to this, Wermer (1982 p. 11) noted that 'during the 1960s a higher proportion of the mothers of illegitimate children were separated or divorced than in the previous decade; the proportion who were single was correspondingly lower'. Other evidence suggests that during the 1970s an increasing proportion of women who remarried cohabited with a second partner before marrying him (Brown and Kiernan, 1981). Some of these women may have had a child during this period as the general reduction in age at marital breakdown during the 1970s brought an increase in the proportion of divorces of females of childbearing age (Kiernan, 1983).

Taken together the evidence above suggests that recent rises in the illegitimacy rate do not necessarily represent a widespread rejection of the orthodox nuclear family. In addition, the propensity of divorcees to remarry and the speed with which this is accomplished (Leete and Anthony, 1979) reflects the enthusiasm with which the orthodox nuclear family or 'cereal packet' norm is pursued.

The Values Study confirmed widespread support for this traditional view of family life. For example, 82 per cent of men and 85 per cent of women said they thought marriage was not an outdated institution. Only 31 per cent of respondents approved of the statement 'If a woman wants to have a child as a single parent, but she doesn't want to have a stable relationship with a man do you approve or disapprove' (Question 261): 67 per cent agreed with the statement 'a child needs a home with both a father and a mother to grow up happily' (Question 256). The importance of children's well-being was reflected in the fact that 72 per cent of respondents agreed that 'parents' duty is to do their best for their children even at the expense of their own well-being' (Question 260).

Data on what is believed to constitute an ideal family so far as numbers of children are concerned was gathered in this survey and is shown in Table 5.4 along with similar data gathered in the 1960s and 1970s. This table shows a decrease in the popularity of the ideal of 4 or more children. In 1967, 50 per cent of respondents thought 4 or more children to be an ideal number while by 1982 that proportion was only 9 per cent.

TABLE 5.4   *Ideal family size*

No. of children	1967 %	1972 %	1976 %	Present survey (1982) %
None	0	0	1	0
1	0	1	1	2
2	23	44	65	64
3	22	18	17	19
4	42	28	11	7
5 or more	8	3	2	2

SOURCE: Dunnell K. (1979) *Family formation 1976* (Office of Population Censuses and Surveys) (London HMSO).

Overall therefore, the data collected in this survey tends to suggest a large degree of support for the 'cereal packet' model of family life. A majority of respondents stressed the contemporary relevance of marriage, the necessary presence of both parents for children's well-being and the primary importance of that well-being, all of which is set within a family ideally containing only two or perhaps three children.

MARITAL QUALITY AND DIVORCE LIBERALITY

Having examined some of the myths and facts associated with marriage and the family it is now proposed to look at factors which have been found to be associated with satisfaction within marriage and with the decision to end the relationship. It should be noted at this point that much of the research into both marital satisfaction and divorce liberality is American. It may not therefore be entirely translatable into the British experience, though a recent review by Dominion (1982) highlights certain parallels in British research.

Marital quality

The quality of marital relationships is the most widely studied topic in the field of family and marital research (Spanier and Lewis, 1980). Essentially, marriage researchers are attempting to discover new correlates which may explain the variance in marital quality and marital stability. Marital quality and marital stability are closely but not inevitably linked, and as Lewis and Spanier (1979) note: 'the quality of most ... marriages is the primary determinant of whether a marriage will remain intact.'

Attitudes and values towards marriage are but one of the factors which influence marital quality. However, they are important because they indicate how other factors which affect marital quality will be perceived. Lewis and Spanier (1979) propose a theory which states that marital quality is a function of social and personal resources (premarital homogeneity, premarital resources, exposure to adequate role models, support from significant others); satisfaction with life-style (socio-economic adequacy, satisfaction with wife's working, optimal household composition, community embeddedness) and rewards from spouse interaction (positive regard for spouse, emotional gratification, effectiveness of communication, role-fit and amount and quality of interaction).

Three areas are of particular importance in the study of marital quality: the effects of children; changes in marital quality over the life-cycle of the marriage and differences in the way that men and women experience marriage.

The effects of children on marriage

In the last decade, since Hicks and Platt (1970) there has been considerable research into whether children tend to detract from rather than contribute to the quality of their parents' marriage. Apparently the birth of a child has a negative impact on most marriages, especially for wives (Russell, 1974; Rollins and Galligan, 1978). Houseknecht (1979) compared fifty women who were childless by choice with fifty mothers (matched on education, religion, and participation in the labour force). The women who were voluntarily childless exhibited higher marital adjustment than did the mothers. This research is supported by the findings of the Values Study in that married women who had dependent children (aged ten years or younger) reported lower satisfaction with their home life than did their counterparts who either had no children or older children (see Chapter 9). It may be as Dominion (1982) suggests that the advent of the first child may be accompanied by 'tiredness, irritability and temporal loss of sexual activity... coupled with a diminution of time that spouses have for each other'.

Traditionally, despite the equivocal value of children to their parents' marriage their needs have been paramount within the family. Three-quarters of respondents to the Values Study affirmed their belief that parents have a duty towards their children even at the expense of their own well-being. Only eighteen per cent felt that parents have a life of their own and should not be asked to sacrifice their own well-being for the sake of the children.

Changes in quality over the life cycle

Most studies examining the life-span of marriage have found a U-shaped pattern for marital quality over the marital career, for example Anderson *et al.* (1983), Schram (1979), Spanier *et al.* (1975). Marital satisfaction is found to be at its highest in the early years of marriage, with a decline after the birth of the first child (Belsky *et al.*, 1983), reaching a low point when the eldest child was of school age, and only beginning to increase after the children had left home. More recently, researchers have questioned the uncritical acceptance of the notion of family life-cycle (Rollins and Galligan, 1978), arguing that it was no better a predictor of marital satisfaction than the length of time married or the age of the respective spouses.

However, marital life-cycle research does highlight the fact that individual marriages are not uniformly happy or unhappy over time and that a number of factors can contribute to the relative satisfaction or dissatisfaction the spouses experience at different times in their marriage. Attitudes towards what is required for a successful marriage and what would be sufficient for divorce may also be expected to change during the marriage.

Respondents to the Values Study reported a surprisingly high overall level of satisfaction with their home life (Q.242), but it is not possible to make any estimation of the effects of stage or length of the marriage on marital satisfaction. These particular survey results may be due to contextual effects of the questionnaire in that respondents were being asked to make comparative evaluations across different areas in life rather than concentrating on just marriage and the family. Secondly, satisfaction with home life is perhaps made up of a number of different components, and respondents here are giving a global estimation.

The two marriages

Since Jessie Bernard first indicated in 1972 that husbands and wives experience different marriages, there has been a significant increase in interest in the relationship between gender perceptions of marriage and marital satisfaction. In summary, married men are superior to never-married men on almost all indices of well-being, whether demographic, psychological or social. Furthermore, as Bradburn (1969) found, they report themselves as happier than any other group (divorced, separated, widowed or single). These findings are confirmatory of previous research in which the married consistently reported themselves as happier than the single (Knupfer *et al.*, 1962).

The picture is very different for women. More wives than husbands report marital frustration, dissatisfaction and marital problems or difficulties (Bernard, 1982; Locke, 1951). Also more wives than husbands seek marriage counselling and initiate divorce proceedings (Brannen and Collard, 1982). Wives are more likely to see their marital problems as having started sooner and lasted longer, and are more likely to see a greater density of problems (McMillan, 1969). Additionally, wives are more likely than their husbands to report and experience psychological distress which they tend to blame on their own lack of general adjustment (Gurin, Veroff and Feld, 1960).

Unlike men, single women appear to be psychologically healthier than their married counterparts (Knupfer, 1962) and this has led to the assertion that 'the psychological costs of marriage, in brief, seem to be considerably greater for wives than husbands and the benefits considerably fewer' (Bernard, 1982).

Results of the present survey may be discussed against these findings. Married male respondents by and large expressed the greatest satisfaction with their home life. These findings tend to support previous research, in that the separated and divorced reported the least satisfaction whilst the widowed and single were intermediate between the two. Women reported significantly lower satisfaction with their home life and this finding too is supportive of previous research. However, contrary to earlier findings, married women reported themselves as happier with their home lives than did the single, the divorced or the widowed. Once again, the separated and divorced were the least satisfied.

Features perceived to contribute to successful marriage

There were fewer sex differences than might have been predicted when examining those factors that were felt to contribute to a successful marriage (Q.248). The rank order of factors perceived to be very important is shown in Table 5.5. Men and women were found to hold different views on only four items: faithfulness, sharing the same social background, sharing similar religious beliefs, and sharing household chores. 91 per cent of women think that faithfulness is important compared to 84 per cent of men (Chi-square = 10.62 $p<0.01$); 25 per cent of women think that sharing the same social background is important compared to 18 per cent of men (Chi-square = 7.36 $p<0.01$). Finally 22 per cent of women think that sharing religious beliefs is important compared to 16 per cent of men

TABLE 5.5 *Frequency of attributes considered necessary for a successful marriage (Values Survey)*

	%
Faithfulness	88
Mutual respect	87
Understanding and tolerance	85
Happy sexual relations	73
Living apart from in-laws	61
Having children	58
Sharing tasks and interests	51
Good housing	49
Adequate income	47
Sharing household chores	42
Sharing same social background	24
Sharing religious beliefs	21
Sharing political views	8

(Chi-square = 7.95 $p<0.01$). Conversely, more men than women think it important to share household chores, 44 per cent to 38 per cent (Chi-square = 4.89 $p<0.05$). It is striking that in a sample of this size so few statistical differences were found.

It is possible to build from the Values Study a composite picture of how the attributes believed to be necessary for a successful marriage are related. For each of the 13 attributes, respondents can be scored by whether they thought that an attribute was important or not. Thus, from the patterns of response of each person it can be shown whether there is a discernible underlying pattern to people's views about the ingredients of a successful marriage.

The program used for this analysis was the Guttman-Lingoes Smallest Space Analysis, SSA-I (Lingoes, 1973). This produces a plot of points, each denoting one attribute, so that the stronger the relationship or association between two attributes the closer together are their corresponding points. (See glossary)

From the display of 13 items given in Figure 5.1, three discernible groups are evident. The first group (labelled **personal**) is concerned with the relationship between the couple and includes faithfulness, mutual respect, understanding and tolerance and a good sexual relationship.

The second group of items all refer to the more tangible supporting or **background** features, i.e. adequate housing, money, presence of children, living apart from in-laws, sharing interests and household chores.

Finally, the most fragmentary items occupy the periphery of the display, namely shared social, religious and political views.

These groups of items relate closely to Lewis and Spanier's (1979) components of marital quality; i.e. social and personal resources (cultural), satisfaction with life-style (background) and rewards from spouse interaction (personal).

Having observed these three distinct groups, it is possible to calculate a composite scale of beliefs about successful marriage. Responses were recoded to give the respondent a score of one if he or she mentioned any of the items appearing in a given group. In the subsequent analysis a reliable Guttman Scale (see glossary) was found to account for 1165 or 95 per cent of the sample.

The scale (Table 5.6) may be interpreted in the following way. The personal group of factors is seen as the most important in so far as almost all (99 per cent of respondents) feel that these factors are important for a successful marriage. They are felt to be sufficient on

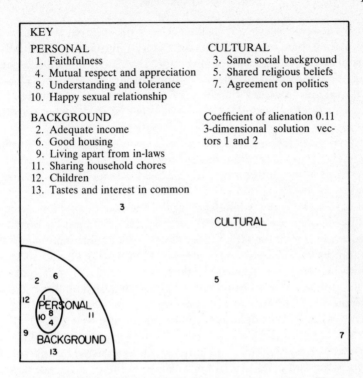

KEY

PERSONAL
1. Faithfulness
4. Mutual respect and appreciation
8. Understanding and tolerance
10. Happy sexual relationship

BACKGROUND
2. Adequate income
6. Good housing
9. Living apart from in-laws
11. Sharing household chores
12. Children
13. Tastes and interest in common

CULTURAL
3. Same social background
5. Shared religious beliefs
7. Agreement on politics

Coefficient of alienation 0.11
3-dimensional solution vectors 1 and 2

FIGURE 5.1 *Aspects contributing to successful marriage SSA-I*

TABLE 5.6 *Guttman scale of factors contributing to a successful marriage*

Cultural	Background	Personal	N	%
1	1	1	433	37
0	1	1	662	57
0	0	1	59	5
0	0	0	11	1
			1165	100

Coefficient of reproducibility = 0.9664
Coefficient of scaleability = 0.8032

their own for a successful marriage by 5 per cent of the sample. Cultural and background aspects only appear in conjunction with the personal items and are not believed to be sufficient in themselves to result in a successful marriage. A small group of 11 people (1 per cent) did not consider that any of these features contributed to success, presumably feeling there were other items not mentioned in the list.

The scale categories are mutually exclusive. Having one profile excludes a respondent from having any other. Thus the scale can be used to examine differences between respondents holding differing views.

If this scale is cross-tabulated against a variety of biographical variables, only age and church attendance are found to produce statistically significant differences. On the one hand, there were no differences between either the sexes or socio-economic status (SES) groups, whilst on the other hand, those who attend church frequently (at least once a month) were more likely to think that all three sets of attributes were important for marriage. Those who attended infrequently placed less emphasis on a shared cultural background.

Interestingly, the older age group (59+) were also more likely to consider success as due to all three groups of items, i.e. personal, background and cultural attributes. Those in the younger age ranges thought that sharing cultural attributes was probably dispensable and the 15–29 year olds were more likely than any other group to think that personal attributes alone were sufficient. This difference suggests that older people believe that a marriage requires a wider range of attributes to be successful than do younger people. This may be a result of their greater experience with marriage. Certainly their attitudes support the theories of marital quality mentioned above.

DIVORCE LIBERALITY

Because of the increasing divorce rate and the number of adults and children involved in this traumatic experience every year, theorists are at pains to arrive at an explanation of why some marriages are stable and others are not. There are two areas of interest: theories of marital instability and correlates of divorce liberality.

TABLE 5.7 Factors from Table 5.6 cross-tabulated against church attendance and age

Factors[1]	Church attendance			Age			
(a)(b)(c)	At least once a month %	Special Holy days %	Never %	15–29 years %	30–44 years %	45–59 years %	Over 59 years %
1 1 1	65	40	27	24	33	48	57
0 1 1	30	51	67	68	61	49	38
0 0 1	3	8	5	7	4	3	4
0 0 0	1	0	1	1	1	0.5	1
N =	255	215	695	454	265	194	256

Chi square = 122
4 degrees of freedom
p < 0.001

Chi square = 92
6 degrees of freedom
p < 0.001

[1](a) = Cultural (b) = background (c) = personal
[2]Cells in the bottom two rows were combined as these had low frequencies

Theories of marital instability

Lewis and Spanier have been influential in recent years in formulating theories of marital instability, arguing that lack of marital quality is an important factor influencing stability (Lewis and Spanier, 1979; Spanier and Lewis, 1980). They see marital stability as a function of the rewards to be obtained from the marital relationship, the personal profit to be derived outside the relationship, and the importance of external influences on the perceived nature of marriage. They propose that:

1. the greater the marital quality, the greater the marital stability;
2. alternative attractions to a marriage negatively influence the strength of the relationship between marital quality and marital stability;
3. external pressures to remain married positively influence the strength of the relationship between marital quality and marital stability.

A large body of research dealing with dissolution indicates that the greater the discrepancy between individual background characteristics, the less the stability of the marital dyad (Falk, 1975). As noted by Edwards and Saunders (1981) these differences, associated with age, religion, socioeconomic status and education, may result in a lower degree of mutal adjustment prior to marriage and a greater instability in the marital relationship itself.

Divorce liberality

In a study of 240 Minneapolis spouses, Jorgensen and Johnson (1980) concluded that 'American spouses are becoming increasingly accepting of divorce as a means of dealing with marital strain and stress'. Their study indicates the importance of spouses' *attitudes* towards divorce, and acknowledges that these to some extent shape the couples' decision to divorce. They found firstly, the presence of dependent children and religious homogeneity acted as relationship barriers which discouraged the dissolution of marriage as a legitimate means of solving marital problems. Secondly the significant correlates of divorce liberality differed for husbands and wives. Wives' attitudes were more influenced by perceived barriers around the relationship such as the presence of dependent children, while the divorce attitudes of husbands appear to be somewhat more sensitive to perceptions of marital quality. Thirdly the most divorce liberal were childless wives.

Booth and White (1980) looked at 1364 married persons, and asked them whether they had given serious consideration to divorce in the past two years. Their results – interesting in the light of the Values Study – indicated that thinking about divorce could occur when couples described themselves as happily married, and occurred in 4 per cent of those who rated their marriages as 'very happy'. However, overall there was a strong correlation between low marital satisfaction and thoughts about divorce.

Booth and White (1980) found that wives were significantly more likely to report considering divorce than were husbands. Other researchers have also noted this increased tendency for women to acknowledge problems in their marriage (Brannen and Collard, 1982). It has been suggested (Hill *et al.*, 1976) that this difference is due to women's increased sensitivity to deterioration in relationships and their ability to make more accurate judgements about the probability of a continued relationship. Dominion in a series of recent articles (*Tablet*, 4 Feb–25 Feb 1984) goes somewhat further. 'Women' he writes, 'have played a crucial role in marital breakdown as they have steadily refused to put up with the lack of love or presence of cruelty'.

In summary these research findings suggest that women are in general more sensitive to deteriorating relationships in marriage and are more prepared to act by either seeking counselling or opting out of the marriage. Evidence from the Values Study (as will be detailed in the next section) shows a correspondence between men and women as to what constitutes unreasonable behaviour as a prelude to divorce. In other words, the differences would seem to be behavioural rather than attitudinal. The Values Study asked what factors are deemed sufficient grounds for divorce. Men and women gave similar answers. It might be hypothesised that the differences in behaviour are the result of varying perceptions of the actual existence of these factors in the person's own relationships. On the one hand, men may recognise these in the abstract, but are less likely to perceive them in their own marriages. On the other hand, women seem to acknowledge problems that may exist in their own marital relationship and are increasingly prepared to act on them.

Thinking about divorce was found by Booth and White to conform in many ways to the actual pattern of divorce. Those married at a younger age, those with pre-school children and those in full-time employment were more likely to think about divorce. Intensity of religious belief however, correlated negatively with thinking about divorce.

When divorce statistics are examined it is possible to generate actual correlates of divorce. These include dissimilarities of culture, social background, religion and age (Thornes and Collard, 1979; Landis, 1962; Dominion 1968); a short or intermittent courtship (Thornes and Collard, 1979); marriage at an early age with premarital pregnancy or the early arrival of children (Thorne and Collard, 1979; Dominion, 1968; Rutter and Madge, 1976; Winch, 1971; Chester 1972); low educational standards (Thornes and Collard, 1979; Komarovsky, 1967; Cutright, 1971); money problems (Thornes and Collard, 1979); and finally child–parent discord possibly indicated by parental disapproval of the marriage (Thornes and Collard, 1979).

Features perceived to contribute to divorce

By using the methods of Smallest Space Analysis and Guttman Scaling, conditions deemed sufficient for divorce may be examined. Ten items were included in the Values Study (Q.255) which sought to elicit from respondents reasons they considered were sufficient for divorce. The percentages for all those responding are shown in Table 5.8.

Any of these attributes alone can be considered grounds for divorce. In examining the groupings of items that respondents

TABLE 5.8 *Percentage of respondents considering items sufficient grounds for divorce*

	%
When either partner is consistently unfaithful	84
When either partner is violent	80
When either partner has ceased to love the other	60
When either partner consistently drinks too much	49
When their personalities don't match	29
Unhappy sexual relationship	24
When they can't have children	6
When they can't get along with each other's relatives	3
When either partner is ill for a long time	2
When they are financially broke	2

considered, their potential for divorce liberality may be revealed. In other words some respondents may feel there is only one basic type of reason for divorce, or alternatively, accept a variety of grounds. The more grounds a person accepts as sufficient, the more 'divorce liberal' he or she is. Alternatively if none or few reasons are considered sufficient, a person might be thought to be divorce resistant.

Three groups of attributes are discernible. Firstly, those associated with **personal** characteristics such as unfaithfulness, drinking, violence, and withdrawing love. The second group are concerned with

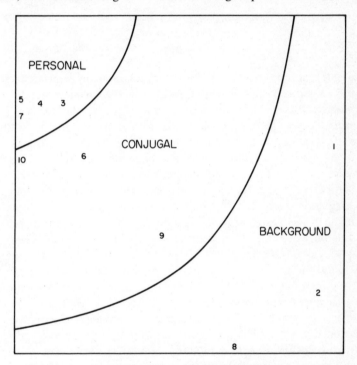

FIGURE 5.2   *Reasons considered sufficient for divorce SSA-I*

KEY

PERSONAL
3. When either partner consistently drinks too much
4. When either partner is violent
5. When either partner is consistently unfaithful
7. When either partner has ceased to love the other

Coefficient of alienation = 0.11
2-dimensional solution

CONJUGAL
6. When the sexual relationship is not satisfactory
9. When they cannot have children
10. When their personalities don't match

BACKGROUND
1. When either partner is ill for a long time
2. When they are impecunious
8. When they cannot get along with each other's relatives

Table 5.9 *Guttman scale of features considered sufficient for divorce*

background	conjugal	personal	N	%
1	1	1	59	5
0	1	1	451	37
0	0	1	571	47
0	0	0	126	10
		Total	1207	100

Coefficient of reproducibility = 0.9886
Coefficient of scaleability   = 0.9420

conjugal relations, e.g. when the sexual relationship is unsatisfactory or the couple cannot have children. Finally, **background** factors such as illness, money difficulties or problems with relatives form an identifiable set. In exactly the same manner as before, these three clusters become the attributes contributing to the divorce scale. Indeed it makes for an even more reliable scale than the previous one and accounts for 1207 of the respondents.

Ten per cent of those questioned indicated they did not consider divorce acceptable for any of these stated reasons; they may be thought of as divorce resistant. Five per cent exhibited the greatest latitude in accepting any of the attributes as a prelude to divorce; they may be called divorce liberal. Forty-seven per cent of respondents restricted the grounds for divorce to personal factors alone.

By unravelling the scale to its separate items, two factors statistically distinguished men's and women's approach to divorce. In this case more men than women thought that an unsatisfactory sexual relationship was sufficient for divorce, 23 per cent men to 17 per cent women (Chi-square = 6.25 $p<0.05$). Similarly, 35 per cent of men to 28 per cent of women thought that personality clashes were sufficient for divorce (Chi-square = 6.72 $p<0.01$).

Socioeconomic status, age, number of children and church attendance all discriminate views about divorce. Lower socioeconomic status respondents were more likely than higher SES groups to be represented at both extreme – the divorce liberal and the divorce resistant – ends of the scale.

Similarly, the older age group (59+) are also represented as being either divorce resistant or divorce liberal. Fewer of the younger respondents (15–29) were prepared to restrict grounds for divorce to personal factors alone.

TABLE 5.10 *SES by divorce index*

Factors	Socio-economic status				Age				Church attendance		
(a)(b)(c)	AB %	C1 %	C2 %	DE %	15–29 %	30–44 %	45–59 %	Over 59 %	At least once a month %	Special Holy days %	Never %
1 1 1	3	4	4	7	5	4	4	6	2	26	6
0 1 1	42	43	38	29	45	38	33	27	30	31	39
0 0 1	42	45	50	51	44	51	48	50	47	38	47
0 0 0	12	8	8	13	7	7	14	17	20	5	6
N =	261	259	330	356	473	274	200	263	272	279	709

Chi-square = 25
9 degrees of freedom
p < 0.05

Chi-square = 44.69
9 degrees of freedom
p < 0.001

Chi-square = 160.8
6 degrees of freedom
p < 0.001

[1] (a) = Background
(b) = cultural
(c) = personal

The number of children the respondent has is also significantly related to the conditions acceptable as sufficient for divorce. As numbers of children in a family increase from none to four the more likely it is that the respondent will be divorce resistant. Curiously, those with families of 5 or more children are potentially more divorce prone. Personal factors alone seem to be more significant for families with 1, 2 or 3 children and less so for childless couples or those with 5 or more children.

Church attendance also significantly differentiates between attributes sufficient for divorce. The most divorce prone are those who only attend church on special holy days such as Easter or Christmas. As might be expected, those rejecting divorce are regular church-goers – 52 per cent of those going more than once a week do not accept any of the attributes as sufficient reasons for divorce, three times as many as any other group.

CONSEQUENCES OF MARITAL BREAKDOWN

The consequences of marital breakdown fall into two related areas: implications for the couple directly involved, and implications for their families and society at large.

In reviewing eleven studies of marital status and incidence of mental disorder, Crago did not find a single exception to the statement that 'for adults, admission rates to psychiatric facilities are lowest among the married, intermediate among the widowed and never-married and highest among the divorced and separated' (Bloom *et al.*, 1978). This trend is replicated in usage patterns of other health facilities, e.g. visits to GP's, and in motor vehicle accidents (McMurray, 1970).

The Values Study (see Tables 5.12 and 5.13) asked respondents to declare whether they often, sometimes, rarely or never felt relaxed, anxious, happy, aggressive, secure, safe and sound (Q.237). A composite score was computed based on the number of positive responses to create an 'adjustment scale'. Results indicated that men who either were married or widowed had the highest scores.

In common with previous research findings (Bernard, 1982) single women reported higher self-adjustment than did single men. It would appear that women tend to find marriage and a family less fulfilling than do men. The separated and divorced scored lowest on adjustment throughout, but, interestingly, single men and divorced men reported approximately equal levels of adjustment.

Changes in divorcees' state of health have been examined. Chester (1971) found that over 90 per cent of his sample of divorced women approached their doctor for help at the time of breakup, while Ambrose *et al.* (1983) reported that 68 per cent of a sample of divorced men sought medical help for newly developed mental health problems and 28 per cent for new physical problems. The same study noted other effects of divorce including men's reactions to loss and change, alteration in their role as father, career and financial implications and relationships with family and friends.

Ambrose's study identifies two groups of men: those least affected, and those most affected by divorce. The first were characterized as non-manual workers with no dependent children. Their relationship with their parents and their feelings about themselves remained largely unchanged by the breakup. The most affected group tended to be manual workers with children of custodial age. They experienced a changed relationship with their parents and changed (usually to the negative) feelings about themselves.

The importance of socioeconomic status and presence or absence of financially dependent children in determining men's reactions to divorce points to a consequence of divorce which was identified by the Finer Committee in their 1974 report. The report commented on the fact that very many one-parent families share a common feature – low socioeconomic status. The vast majority of one-parent families are headed by a woman. Evidence given showed that women's earning potential was severely limited and suggested that many husbands defaulted on or were unable to meet maintenance payments. The consequences for the children of single parent families are potentially serious (Hart, 1976; McGregor, 1970). Some studies have suggested that children from broken homes are prone to a number of problems including alcoholism (Ollerstrom, 1952), poor academic achievement (Douglas *et al.*, 1968) and emotional disorder (Greer *et al.*, 1966). More rigorous studies involving control groups of comparable economic status show that the differences between children from one- and two-parent homes on variables such as school achievement, social adjustment and delinquent behaviour are small or even non-existent (Burchinal, 1964; Thomas, 1968; Murchison, 1974), and when comparisons were made between children from intact but unhappy homes and those from divorced homes the latter showed less evidence of psychosomatic illness or delinquent behaviour, had a better adjustment to parents and did not differ significantly in terms of school adjustment (Nye, 1957; Landis, 1960; Rutter, 1977). Taken together therefore, these studies suggest that problems are not only associated with divorce *per se*, but also the fall in income consequent upon marital breakdown.

FAMILY AND VALUES TYPOLOGY

In order to examine the relationship between family types and value orientation, two classification schemes were adopted. The first is based on biographical indices including marital status, working status of women and presence or absence of dependent children. The second categorisation derives from the Abrams typology of values given in chapter one.

Family types

The family typology distinguishes between those families in which the wives either worked at professional or semi- or unskilled occupations, or were full time housewives. In addition, the family types reflected the presence of dependent children (under secondary school age). Thus the typology takes into account both orthodox and unorthodox types such as single parent families, or dual career families.

Table 5.11　*Family typology*

Marital status /Sex	Presence of children	Working status	N	%
Single:				
Men			200	16
Women	Dependent children		24	2
Women	No dependent children		134	11
Married:				
Men			346	28
Women	Dependent children	Professional	25	2
		Non professional	38	3
		Housewife	88	7
	No dependent children	Professional	56	6
		Non professional	96	8
		Housewife	71	6
Sep/divorced:				
Men			13	1
Women	Dependent children		8	1
	No dependent children		20	2
Widowed:				
Men			8	1
Women	No dependent children		63	5
Women	Dependent children			
			1214	102*

*Percentages are rounded up so total adds up to more than 100 per cent.

Having classified family types in this way, a number of comparisons were made based on questions in the survey. Full details are available as an appendix. Briefly six indices were computed:

1. degree of closeness to parents   Q233 PARCLOS
2. no. of values shared with parents   Q245 PARSHAR
3. no. of values shared with partner   Q244 PARTSHAR
4. family values   Q246, 247, 256, 257, 259, 260,
                                       261 TRAD
5. personal adjustment   Q237 ADJ
6. sexual values   Q247, 258 PERMIS

additionally satisfaction with home life (Q242) was also used.

The statistical procedure (analysis of variance – see glossary) indicated that firstly, the degree of parental closeness (PARCLOS) was not statistically significant. In other words the perceived closeness of father and mother and of self to father and mother were the same for all types of family. However, there were some interesting gender differences which accompany the number of values respondents perceived they shared with their parents (PARSHAR). There was an increment in the number of values which sons shared with their parents if they were single (these shared the least) married, separated or divorced and widowed (these shared the most). These results were statistically significant but there were no significant differences for women.

Values that partners shared (PARTSHAR) were significant for both men and women. Married men shared a greater number of values than did those who were widowed or separated or divorced. Interestingly, divorced or separated women report sharing even fewer values. On the whole, married women who work and have dependent children share more values with their partner than do those women who are at home with young children.

As previously mentioned, married men report the highest levels of satisfaction with their home life. Single women are marginally more satisfied than single men. Of the married women, housewives at home with dependent children report the lowest level of satisfaction with home life whereas women in similar situations, but who have professional occupations are more satisfied.

From these findings it can be concluded that being married is generally better for men than for women in terms of psychological adjustment and satisfaction; single women seem to cope better

138

TABLE 5.12 *Attitudinal indices by men's marital status*

	Married	Single	S/D[1]	Widowed	ANOVA F Value	Level of significance
PARSHAR – Values shared with parents	3.21	2.79	3.64	3.70	5.9	0.001
PARCLOS – Degree of closeness to parents	2.53	2.64	2.15	2.65	2.41	NS
PARTSHAR – Values shared with partner	3.95	–	3.0	3.78	3.68	0.05
TRAD – Number of traditional values held	4.73	3.95	3.62	5.0	11.47	0.001
ADJ – Personal adjustment	2.996	2.73	2.70	3.43	5.19	0.01
CHURCH – Amount of church going	2.00	1.89	1.54	1.86	0.71	NS
PERMS – Degree of moral permissiveness	1.42	1.37	1.33	1.40	0.38	NS
Satis with home life	4.58	4.19	3.46	4.55	16.10	0.001
Total no. of respondents	346	200	13	20		

[1]S/D Separated or Divorced

TABLE 5.13 *Attitudinal indices by women's marital status*

Marital status	Married						Single		Separated Divorced		Widowed			
Dependent children	No			Yes										
Working status	PROF WORK	WORK	HW	PROF WORK	WORK	HW	No	Yes	No	Yes	No	Yes	ANOVA F values	Level of significance
	1	2	3	4	5	6	7	8	9	10	11	12		
Parshar – Values shared with parents	3.51	3.12	3.33	2.92	31.2	3.03	3.15	2.89	3.07	3.17	3.68	2.0		NS
Parclos – Degree of closeness to parents	2.55	2.55	2.43	2.58	2.53	2.53	2.61	2.14	2.47	2.00	2.53	2.0		NS
Partshar – Values shared with partner	3.88	3.58	3.87	3.88	4.06	3.57	–	–	2.20	2.25	4.13	2.67	4.57	0.001
Trad – Number of traditional values held	3.96	4.35	4.97	4.20	4.11	4.08	3.86	3.50	4.00	3.75	5.21	3.33	5.01	0.001
ADJ – Personal adjustment	2.91	2.64	2.90	2.58	2.58	2.71	2.85	2.50	2.31	3.00	2.61	1.50		NS
Church – Amount of church going	3.04	2.31	2.49	3.12	2.29	2.26	2.23	1.71	2.05	3.13	3.14	2.00	3.90	0.001
Permits – Degree of moral permissiveness	1.43	1.32	1.51	1.65	1.22	1.30	1.29	1.43	1.40	1.80	1.39	1.00	2.13	0.05
Satisfaction with home life	4.30	4.34	4.57	4.60	4.55	4.28	4.20	4.0	3.70	3.75	4.21	4.67	2.92	0.001
Total number of respondents	56	96	71	25	38	88	134	24	21	20	71	3		

psychologically than single men; separation and divorce seem to result in more disruption to home life than death of a spouse. Divorced men seem to suffer more in this respect than divorced women, but widows suffer more than widowers.

The stresses and strains on dual-career families did not seem to have an untoward effect with respect to psychological adjustment and satisfactions of home life. Women as single parents however do seem to suffer a significant decrement in self-reported well-being.

Values typology

In an earlier chapter, Mark Abrams describes a typology of value systems. Those holding *traditional* views tend to be older, married or widowed. *Ambivalents* are more likely to be in the 35–54 age group whilst the *anti-traditionalists* more often fall within the 18–34 age group. Being younger the latter are also more frequently represented amongst the single. Class as such did not differentiate people in terms of these global values.

TABLE 5.14 *Values typology by biograpical characteristics[1]*

	Anti-traditionalists %	Ambivalents %	Traditionalists %
Age:			
18–34	67	33	16
35–54	20	39	26
55+	13	28	58
Class:			
ABC1	39	38	37
C2	31	34	30
DE	30	27	33
Marital status:			
married	48	73	68
living as married	2	2	0
divorced	3	2	1
separated	2	2	1
widowed	6	7	16
single	39	15	14

[1] Percentages are calculated on the base figures from Gallop tables of raw data

TABLE 5.15　*Values typology by attitudes towards parents and parenting, marriage and divorce*

Question number from survey	Anti-traditionalists %	Ambivalents %	Traditionalists %
245　Sharing views with parents:			
religion	46	58	71
moral	62	78	85
social	52	61	73
political	43	44	54
sexual	33	33	40
246　Marriage is an outdated institution:			
yes	17	15	9
no	79	84	89
254　Ideal number of children:			
2	64	65	62
3	19	19	19
255　Grounds for divorce:			
drink	52	51	43
violence	84	84	70
unfaithful	81	90	76
260　Duties of parents toward children:			
expense of self	58	71	85
life of own	28	17	9

There are discernible trends in the Values Study that indicate that the traditionalists more often report being happy and experience greater satisfaction with home life. Fewer think marriage is an outdated institution. Anti-traditionalists have the lowest average satisfaction with home life, fewer indicate being happy and more think marriage is outdated. The ambivalents occupy an intermediate position between the other two types.

With respect to the relationship between children and parents, more of the anti-traditionalists believed that parents should have a life of their own (28 per cent to ambivalents 17 per cent and traditionalists 9 per cent). The latter were more likely to be closer to both their parents and to have had a stricter upbringing. They were also more likely to share with them their views on religion, politics, morals, sexual and social issues. Anti-traditionalists were more likely to hold differing views to those of their parents.

Global value orientation also differentiated people in terms of the grounds considered sufficient for divorce. If the main reasons are examined, more of the anti-traditional thought excessive drinking, violence, or unfaithfulness, to be sufficient. The traditionalists were more divorce resistant. Interestingly, the greatest number feeling that unfaithfulness is sufficient reason for divorce were those categorized as ambivalents.

Strictness of upbringing similarly differentiates those with differing global value orientations. The traditionalists had the strictest perceived upbringing, followed by ambivalents and anti-traditionalists. It is also age related. More of the older age groups perceived their upbringing as very strict.

Further examination of the results showed that both reported closeness to parents, and the number of values shared with partner were associated with perceived strictness of parents and these differences were statistically significant. Greater closeness and sharing was related to stricter upbringing.

The traditionalists not only report being closer to both parents but more are happy and satisfied with their home life than either of the other two groups. Global value orientation is also associated with differing values with which parents wish to inculcate their children (Q.262). In overall terms, most parents wish their children to be honest (80 per cent), have good manners (68 per cent) and be tolerant and have respect for others (62 per cent). Traditional parents in addition wanted their children to be obedient, unselfish, have determination and faith. Anti-traditionalists place less emphasis on obedience and faith and greater on having self control and independence. Ambivalents are more likely to give priority to unselfishness than the other two groups. No parents give thrift or leadership as significant values for children to have.

TABLE 5.16 Global values by strictness of upbringing

Number Q236	Parental strictness	Anti-traditionalists				Ambivalents				Traditionalists			
				Age				Age				Age	
		All	18/34	35/54	54+	All	18/34	35/54	54+	All	18/34	35/54	54+
	Very	18	16	16	29	35	25	37	43	38	27	38	41
	Quite	56	58	52	48	44	54	42	36	47	63	41	45
	Not very	23	24	26	15	18	18	20	17	12	7	17	11
	Not at all	2	2	3	5	2	2	2	2	2	1	2	2
	Average	2.9	2.89	2.84	3.05	3.1	3.04	3.13	3.22	3.22	3.18	3.17	3.26

TABLE 5.17 Strictness of upbringing

Q236	those having strict parents	those whose parents were not strict	ANOVA F	Sig
Q233 closeness to parents	2.5	2.4	49	0.02
Q244 no of values shared with partner	3.8	3.5	8.3	0.004

TABLE 5.18   *Global values by attitudes towards parents and present home life*

		Anti traditionalist %	Ambivalents %	Traditionalists %
Q233a	Close to mother:			
	very	55	57	64
	not at all	4	3	1
Q233b	Close to father:			
	very	38	49	53
	not at all	6	6	4
Q236	Strictness of parent			
	very	38	49	53
	not at all	6	6	4
Q237	How happy:			
	often	63	77	78
	average	3.6	3.79	3.77
Q242	Satisfaction with home life:			
	very satisfied	24	34	52
	average	7.91	8.49	8.85

TABLE 5.19   *Global values by child rearing*

Values	All % Rank	Anti-Trad. % Rank	Amb. % Rank	Trads % Rank
honesty	79(1)	72(1)	81(1)	80(1)
good manners	68(2)	56(3)	70(2)	74(2)
tolerance/respect	62(3)	64(2)	61(3)	63(3)
unselfishness	40(4)	39(4)	43(4)	34(6)
obedience	37(5)	28(8)	36(6)	48(4)
loyalty	36(6)	30(7)	39(5)	35(5)
self control	33(7)	37(5)	32(7)	29(8.5)
politeness	27(8)	20(11)	29(8)	29(8.5)
responsibility	24(9)	27(9)	25(9)	20(12)
independence	23(10)	33(6)	22(10)	17(13.5)
determination	17(11)	21(10)	15(11)	17(13.5)
patience	16(12.5)	14(13.5)	14(12)	22(10.5)
hard work	16(12.5)	14(13.5)	13(13)	22(10.5)
faith	14(14)	5(15)	8(16)	33(7)
imagination	11(15)	18(12)	10(14)	7(16)
thrift	9(16)	4(16)	9(15)	15(15)
leadership	4(17)	3(17)	3(17)	5(17)

CONCLUSIONS

This chapter began by looking at some of the prevailing stereotypes of marriage and family life, for example, beliefs that these institutions are being undermined by some of the more strident aspects of feminism or that there is an increase in single parenthood, or that the young are rejecting marriage. The research literature and empirical data from the Values Study however indicate that the institutions themselves are not under threat but rather changes have taken place in the ways that individuals live out their marital and family lives.

Certainly it is the common expectation amongst young people that they will be married. The Values Survey data showed that 84 per cent of those questioned disagreed with the statement that marriage was an outdated institution.

It is not the *fact* of marriage that is being questioned, but rather the *quality* of married life. Despite the increase in the divorce rate there is also an increase in remarriage. Twenty years ago Berger and Kellner (1964) wrote:

Individuals in our society do not divorce because marriage has become unimportant to them, but because it has become *so* important that they have no tolerance for the less than completely successful marital arrangement.

In other words, although increasing numbers of people are rejecting specific marriage partners, the institution of marriage is not threatened and this is underlined by the high rate of remarriage following divorce. It seems too, that women are not only more dissatisfied with the quality of married life, but also increasingly take the initiative in trying to change things or even dissolve the relationship.

There is a high degree of consensus from those taking part in the Values Study of the factors thought to contribute to successful marriage such as faithfulness, mutual respect, and understanding and tolerance. There is a high level of satisfaction with home life, with more of those espousing traditional values reporting being happy and satisfied with home life than those holding either ambivalent or anti-traditional values.

When looking at the relative satisfaction with home life, certainly married women are less satisfied than married men, and housewives with dependent children are the least satisfied of all.

Those holding traditional views are more likely to think that drunkenness, violence or unfaithfulness are not sufficient grounds for divorce. As views move away from the traditional these factors are seen as unacceptable within the marriage.

There is also evidence from the study that those perceiving that they had strict parents report not only being closer to, but also sharing more values with, both their parents and marriage partners. Irrespective of global value orientation, parents wish to impart the values of honesty, tolerance, respect and good manners to their children. The importance of children's well-being is paramount, with a total of 72 per cent of respondents believing that it is the duty of parents to do their best for their children even at the expense of their own well-being.

In both attitudes and behaviour, the respondents to the Values Study showed little evidence of departing radically from traditional views of either family or marriage. Over two-thirds felt that a child needs a home with both a father and a mother, less than 2 per cent said they were living as married, more women with dependent children stayed at home than went out to work, and dual-career families (wives following a professional career) are still in the minority.

It can therefore be concluded that the so-called 'cereal packet' model of family life is still the norm for most families. There is strong support for marriage; the presence of both parents for their children's well-being; and agreement that the setting of that well-being should be within a family of two or possibly three children. Finally, it was evident that similar values are handed on from parents to children. Global value orientation seem to be less of a reaction against, but rather a continuation of, values shared with parents.

6 Participation and Political Values

DAVID PHILLIPS

INTRODUCTION

The Values Study followed a period of considerable change in British politics. Apparent shifts in previously well-established patterns of voting behaviour during the 1970s were attributed by leading commentators to an increasing 'volatility' among voters. The unpredictability of election outcomes was linked to deep-seated changes. These included: a decline of support for the Labour Party among working class people; an expansion of white-collar employment; a shrinking heavy industrial sector; increased affluence and more widespread home ownership. At the same time the British economy was entering a period of structural crisis which coincided with a deepening recession in world trade. Since 1945, both Labour and Conservative governments had shared a commitment to the goal of full employment which they pursued through interventionist fiscal policies. The election of the 1979 Conservative government marked the end of this post-war consensus. The break was followed by polarisation in party politics accompanied by the emergence of a centre alternative in the shape of the Liberal–SDP Alliance.

Against this background, one looks in vain for evidence of sharpening divisions among the sample of respondents surveyed here. Indeed, the large majority of the population appear to share a broadly 'consensual' outlook on political affairs. Attempts, using multivariate statistical techniques like cluster analysis, to identify groupings differing sharply in their political values, under headings such as 'Radical Left', 'Militant Moderate', 'New Right' and so on,

146

were strikingly unsuccessful. Small numbers do exist which can be labelled in this way and there is some limited differentiation between left and right, but most respondents do not fit neatly into such categories. The majority are not highly involved in politics and are not strongly attached to the existing parties. Their outlook is broadly centrist, with widespread agreement on such things as the importance of personal freedom and the desirability of gradual improvement through reform, and they share high levels of national pride and confidence in such institutions as the police and the armed forces.

This chapter reviews the findings emerging from the political items in the questionnaire under three headings. The first section describes the extent of *participation* in politics, identifies certain characteristics which are associated with relatively greater or lesser involvement, and suggests that participation is likely to be greater among more socially advantaged groups. The second section examines *political outlook*, focusing in particular upon orientation on the left–right political dimension, and goes on to describe alignment on a variety of issues: freedom versus equality, patriotism, confidence in institutions, attitudes towards political change and towards political protest. The final section considers whether *political values are changing* and looks to the theory of Inglehart (1977), describing the evidence for a slight age-related shift from conservative 'materialism' to a more radical 'post-materialism' among generations growing up after the Second World War.

POLITICAL PARTICIPATION

The British political system is generally depicted as a highly-developed parliamentary democracy where participation in the political process – in theory at least – is open to all. Apart from General Elections, relatively few individuals participate directly in political decisions. Particular interests are more usually expressed through involvement in pressure groups and voluntary agencies organised around specific aims. Electoral participation involves a relatively advanced notion of political citizenship. It requires a politically-aware electorate, actively concerned in public affairs and committed to the existing framework of political institutions. Without such involvement democracy may provide only a partial expression of political interests and aspirations. To what extent, therefore, do British people participate in the political process? How prominent are political concerns in their lives?

Interest in politics

The broad majority of the population do not appear to take a great deal of interest in politics. While a substantial number of respondents report having some interest, those with an active interest are a decidedly small minority. Well under half the sample (about 2 people in every 5) express interest in politics. Only a small proportion (1 in 20) claimed that their interest was active. The majority (three-fifths in all) reported either that their interest in politics was no greater than their other interests (33 per cent) or that they were not interested at all (28 per cent). The frequency of discussion of political matters with friends shows a similar pattern – the overwhelming majority discuss politics only occasionally (half the sample) or never (two-fifths of respondents).

That active interest is very much a minority phenomenon is supported by figures for membership of political parties or groups: only 4 per cent belong to a political organisation; 1 per cent report that they do some kind of voluntary work for such groups. A much larger proportion of the sample (one-fifth) are members of trade unions, though it is unlikely that nominal membership alone implies involvement in politics. Athough about one in ten take an active interest, more than half of trade union members expressed little or no interest in politics.

Lack of interest is more pronounced among women than men. Just over one-third of all women are not interested in politics at all, compared with one-fifth of all men. More men report an interest in politics (over two-fifths) than women (a little over one-third). The employment status of women appears to make little difference. Among both men and women, interest in politics appears to increase with age. Active interest remains typically low until 55 years of age, after which it tails off – probably as people's physical energy declines. However, non-active interest shows a steady increase across the age groups, rising from about one in five of the 18–24 year-olds to over half among the 65–74 year-olds, declining thereafter, but remaining above average. Complete lack of interest is most pronounced among the youngest 18–24 year-old group, almost two-fifths of whom report no interest at all.

The marked relationship between age and an increasing (non-active) interest in politics is a somewhat unexpected finding. Certainly, it denies one common picture of politics as a passionate interest of the young which declines as they grow older and disillusioned. One possible explanation of this greater interest among older groups is the socialisation process, expressed as a cohort effect. The impact of specific political events in one's formative years may be reflected in later life in the form of a heightened political awareness. Thus, respondents aged 65 to 74, and who display the greatest level of interest in politics, came to political maturity during the turbulent years preceding the Second World War (they would have been aged 23 to 32 in 1939). However, every generation experiences political events in their formative years which are deemed important at the time and it is not immediately clear why certain historical events should have a more persisting influence among particular generational groups. It is more likely that such inter-generational difference stems from a variety of causes, modified by the progressive acquisition of political experience as people grow older.

Differences in class background also appear to have some influence on the levels of interest that respondents have in politics. Both active and non-active interest are somewhat greater among middle class occupational groups than among working class groups. This difference is most pronounced when we compare people from a professional or managerial background with those from a predominantly semi-skilled or non-skilled manual background. Among the middle class, (AB), three-fifths express a specific interest and more than one in ten are active. Among social group DE (one-fifth of whom are retired persons on State pensions only – see Chapter 2), only 2 per cent take an active interest and one-fifth are interested but not active. Thus, middle class respondents appear twice as likely to be interested in politics as working class respondents, indeed less than one in ten of the AB's report a complete lack of interest in politics, compared with two-fifths of the DE group.

While socioeconomic classifications based on occupation are only a crude indicator of social background, the relationship is confirmed by other data. Interest in politics tends to be significantly greater among people with higher incomes, those who own their own homes, and those who have received higher levels of education. Can this apparent class difference be explained? It may be that working class people have less time or energy for political involvement because of the greater physical demands made on them during their working lives, but there is a long and vigorous tradition of working class political activity, especially through trade unions and labour institutions. Again, 'politics' may be experienced as a universe of discourse remote from daily life in which middle class values predominate.

Relatively greater material and educational disadvantage among the working class may constitute an obstacle to involvement which is not experienced to the same extent by the middle class.

Taken together, the background influences of sex, age and social class have an additive effect upon levels of political involvement. Those most likely to take an interest in politics will be older men from an upper middle class background. Lack of interest is greatest among younger women from the lower working class. Between these two extremes, different sub-groups of the population tend to distribute themselves accordingly. Thus younger men from the lower middle class, to take one example, tend to display greater interest than younger women from the same occupational background, and greater interest than fellow young men from the working class. Overall, the pattern of political involvement is patchy. Certainly, it does not appear that interest in politics can be located among specific groups, defined in demographic terms. Rather, such background factors tend to alter slightly the balance of involvement found in the population against a background of low interest levels and widespread distance from politics.

Political involvement and social participation

The low level of political involvement in Britain has been well-documented by political sociologists (Butler and Stokes, 1971; Rose, 1980). Involvement in organised religion is another area, like politics, where people are more or less free to define the extent of their commitment. Politics might be viewed as a secular equivalent of religious belief, with less interest in politics apparent among actively religious people, and less religious involvement among those who are interested in politics. Certainly, among the small group who declare themselves to be 'convinced atheists' (4 per cent of the total sample – but see also Chapter 3), there is relatively more interest in politics. For the large majority, however, this simple 'alternative' relationship between political and religious involvement is not borne out. In fact, interest in politics is more pronounced among people who frequently attend church services (half of whom are interested or involved) and lack of interest is greater among those who hardly ever or never go to church (one-third of whom are interested or involved). Politics does not appear to be a substitute for religion, just as religion is not a substitute for politics. Indeed, political participation appears to be one form of social participation: people with an active interest in one area of life are more likely to take an interest in other areas as well.

This is supported by data from the Study on the interest levels of members of voluntary organisations and people who do unpaid voluntary work (see Chapter 8). Indeed, of the small minority actively interested in politics, two-fifths are also active in some kind of voluntary work. Finally, respondents who take no interest in politics tend to spend more time watching television and also report that they feel lonely more often than those who take an interest in politics.

Attachment to political parties

With only very small numbers actively involved in politics, and where a more detached concern seems typical of less than half the population, it is perhaps surprising that people turn out to vote in the numbers they do. Turnout at General Elections fluctuates between 70 per cent and 80 per cent, although figures drop considerably for local elections. It can be argued that respondents' endorsements of general statements concerning their level of interest in politics provide only a limited indication of their involvement. Such survey questions lack the immediacy of real choices between competing political options. We might expect to learn more by examining people's attachment to actual political parties.

Traditionally, surveys approach this question by 'squeezing' respondents so that they are forced to choose in much the same way as they would at an election. For example, they might be asked who they would vote for if there was a General Election tomorrow, or which party do they think has the best policies. When respondents are uncertain or non-committal, they will be encouraged to state a definite preference. The drawback with such an approach is that it fails to explore the strength of party commitment. More particularly, commitment tends to be over-emphasised and the *absence* of party attachment is minimised. In the Values Study, respondents were first asked whether or not they felt close to *any* political party. Only after an initial commitment had been established were those who did feel close to a political party asked to say which one. The immediately striking observation is that only one person in five reported that they felt close to a political party.

Predictably, those people who identified with a party were more likely to be interested in politics and nearly two-thirds of the politically active minority expressed a definite party attachment. The politically attached are found in slightly greater numbers among male respondents, among the middle class, and among those who received some form of higher education. They are also more numerous among those who do voluntary work, almost one-third of whom express a party attachment – further confirmation of the tendency for activism and commitment in one area to be accompanied by involvement in another.

Among the minority with a definite party attachment, identification reflected well-established patterns of political outlook and social background. Three-quarters of the Conservatives come predominantly from the 'Centre Right' and 'Right', three-fifths of Labour supporters from the 'Centre Left' and 'Left', three-fifths of the Liberals from the 'Centre'. Other political values, such as attitudes towards political change, towards managerial or workers' control in industry, display a similar consistent ideological pattern on the part of the politically attached. Those close to the Conservative Party were likely to come from the middle class, to be female or to be retired. Those attached to the Labour Party are more likely to be working class and male.

The low level of party attachment among the large majority suggests that there is ample room for new political parties to make an appeal. The survey was undertaken in April 1981, one month before the official launching of the Social Democratic Party, so we are not in a position to say very much about the extent of support for the SDP at that time. However, while those with a definite party attachment were more likely to position themselves towards left or right, the unattached appear to be situated much more towards the political centre. For a party like the SDP, which seeks to tap new political loyalties, a strategy directed towards the centre makes a lot of sense.

Predictors of political involvement

An additive score was computed for respondents' overall Political Involvement, ranging from 0 to 6 and based on all relevant items from the questionnaire (see Table 6.1.1). With a mean of 1.43, the distribution of the resulting scores (Table 6.1.2) demonstrates clearly the low degree of involvement among the population as a whole. Close to one-third of the sample are not involved at all in politics and

TABLE 6.1 *Political involvement*

6.1.1 *Components of political involvement score*

Items in scale	Weighting	Percentage of total sample
Active interest in politics	2	6
or Non-active interest in politics	1	33
Member of political party or group	1	4
Discusses politics frequently	2	11
or Discusses politics occasionally	1	52
Close to a political party	1	21

6.1.2 *Distribution of political involvement scores*

	Total Score	Percentage of total sample
No involvement	0	28
	1	31
	2	22
	3	12
	4	4
	5	2
High involvement	6	1

score zero, while three-fifths score no more than 1. Barely one-fifth score more than 2 and only minute proportions achieve high Political Involvement scores. To what extent can we predict these levels of political involvement?

A stepwise multiple regression analysis was performed on the results to examine the relationship between Political Involvement and a number of the measures which the previous analysis indicated might exert some predictive influence. Regrettably, the analysis provides a highly incomplete explanation, the total set of predictor variables accounting for only 15.5 per cent of the total variance in Political Involvement scores. Nevertheless, it gives some support to a tentative model of political involvement. Those predisposed to greater involvement are more likely to be middle class, male, older, members of voluntary organisations and more educated. Whilst not accounting for all possible variations, the model suggests that involvement in politics is greater among relatively advantaged groups, and in particular is indicative of a participatory 'style' more often found in the middle class, where higher levels of material and educational resources provide both physical and cultural means for more effective involvement. Those who are more disadvantaged, or more confined in terms of gender role or lack of (age-related) experience, are likely to be less involved in politics.

POLITICAL OUTLOOK

Although involvement in politics is low and few people identify closely with political parties, it would be wrong to assume that people have no political views. The remainder of this chapter seeks to describe the general political outlook of the British population. How much does it embody values which are generally shared? To what extent is there differentiation between competing political priorities? Are political values linked to other values that people hold and are they associated with differences of social background?

The 'left-right' dimension

Respondents were asked (Q.275) to indicate their general political outlook by positioning themselves on a ten point 'Left-Right' Scale. Almost one-fifth of the sample felt unable, or were unwilling, to position themselves on the scale. The proportion of 'don't knows' is identical to that found by other researchers (Klingemann and Inglehart, 1975; Marsh, 1977) for representative British samples, suggesting that this level of non-response may be a constant feature of the scale. Marsh suggests that conservatives are over-represented among them.

In Figure 6.1 (based on percentage figures excluding the 'don't knows'), respondents' scores have been grouped in '2's and given conventional political labels. The general picture is clear. The British population emerges as slightly to the right of the political centre, the mean score (5.70) being identical to that obtained by Marsh in 1974. Almost half position themselves at the 'Centre', while one-fifth place themselves left of centre and three-tenths right of centre. Among those leaning towards left or right, most occupy the 'Centre Left' and 'Centre Right' positions; very small proportions take up the far 'Left' and far 'Right' positions.

As has been seen, the pattern of orientation among those who felt

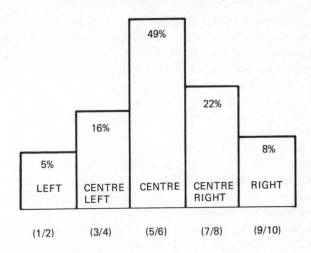

FIGURE 6.1 *Distribution of 'left-right' positions*

close to one of the three main parties is consistent with the scale shown in Fig. 6.1. Only 5 per cent of those identifying with the Conservative Party came from left of centre (1 per cent 'far left') and only 10 per cent of those close to the Labour Party are drawn from right of centre (3 per cent 'far right').

If any single issue can be said to divide left from right it is the approach to property ownership embodied in Clause 4 of the Labour Party constitution, which seeks 'the common ownership of the means of production, distribution and exchange'. One question (Q.143) asked respondents how they thought that business and industry should be managed. Half the sample preferred that full control be vested in the owners; a further two-fifths favoured employee participation in the selection of managers. Less than 10 per cent supported the notion that ownership and control should be vested in the employees, and there was almost complete rejection of nationalisation, with only 2 per cent of the sample in favour.

A highly consistent pattern emerges when these attitudes are tabulated by positions on the 'Left-Right' scale. 'Right' and 'Centre Right' favour control by owners, while joint participation is more popular among the 'Left' and 'Centre Left'. Even among the far 'Left', support for workers' control barely exceeds that for owner-controlled enterprises (22 per cent as against 20 per cent). What support there is for State control is concentrated among the 'Left'.

Alignment on many other political issues in the questionnaire is similarly consistent with differentiation between left and right. For example, those towards the right are more likely to think that 'greater respect for authority' would be a good thing, that 'maintaining order in the nation' is an important priority, and they express greater confidence in the police and armed forces. Greater numbers on the right are very proud to be British and willing to fight for their country in the event of a war. They are also more likely to favour 'valiantly defending present society against all subversive forces', particularly on the far 'Right'. General support for 'personal freedom' over 'equality' is more pronounced on the right, and greater (though still minority) support for 'equality' is only found left of centre. Support for social reform is stronger among the 'Centre Left' and 'Centre', weaker on the 'Right'. Those towards the left are more willing to consider taking part in lawful demonstrations and joining unofficial strikes, and they tend to display more confidence in trade unions.

However, the extent of such left-right differentiation needs to be set against the predominantly centrist outlook of the population as a whole. The large majority (87 per cent) falls within the range 'Centre Left' – 'Centre' – 'Centre Right' and relatively few take up the more extreme positions. It would be quite mistaken, therefore, to view political outlook as sharply polarised between left and right. Differentiation does exist but limited to differences of emphasis among groups which may share substantial areas of agreement on particular issues. Thus, support for social reform is strongest among the 'Centre Left' (four-fifths) but it also receives considerable support among the 'Centre Right' (two-thirds) and the far 'Right' (one-half). Again, greater numbers on the right (over four-fifths) believe that more respect for authority would be a good thing but so do over half of those on the left.

The influence of age and social class on left-right positions

Demographic differences, similarly, are slight but middle class respondents tend to lean a little further towards the right than those from working class backgrounds. Older people also tend to lean more towards the right than younger people (correlation = 0.20). Table 6.2 shows the mean 'Left-Right' scores for groups defined by both age and social class. With one or two exceptions, the general tendency is

TABLE 6.2   *Mean 'left-right' scores by age and social class*

Age group	Social class				
	AB	*C1*	*C2*	*DE*	*All*
Under 25	5.94	5.22	5.35	4.48	5.20
25 to 39	6.09	5.52	5.18	5.45	5.58
40 to 59	5.78	6.00	5.71	5.59	5.77
60 plus	6.92	6.50	6.04	6.04	6.29
All respondents	6.10	5.66	5.51	5.41	

for rightward 'leanings' to increase with age within each social class category. The influences of age and class background act in a complementary fashion. The most leftward-leaning are those aged under 25 from a semi- or non-skilled manual background (DEs); the most rightward-leaning are those aged 60 and over from a professional or managerial background (ABs). The dotted line in the table indicates the divide between those groups which on balance lean left of centre and those which lean to right of centre. Opinion tilts slightly towards the left among respondents under 40 years of age from the working class and also among under 25 year-olds from the lower middle class. There is, incidentally, almost no significant differentiation between men and women across age and class groupings. Among women, however, those with paid employment score slightly below average (mean 5.31).

Left-right positions and other values

The survey provides some evidence that left-right orientation is associated with other values and beliefs which, although not directly political, embody what might be termed an underlying dimension of traditionalism and anti-traditionalism. For example, respondents who agree with sexual freedom (mean score = 5.38) score below average; those who disagree wtih sexual freedom score above average (mean score = 5.89). Respondents who believe there are absolutely clear guidelines about what constitutes good and evil (mean score = 6.18) lean further to the right than those who believe there are no clear guidelines (mean score = 5.49). This suggests that political outlook is not formed in isolation from other human values.

Rather, political values appear to have systematic links with broader value systems which include dimensions of morality and social relations.

Such a connection is seen most clearly in the relation between left-right orientation and certain religious beliefs. The percentage of those who believe in God increases steadily, moving from left to right on the political dimension. Those who are convinced atheists lean more to the left (mean score = 4.78). It should be emphasised that this connection between political and religious orientation exists only at the level of belief and does not extend to religious practice. Indeed, a negative correlation (−0.14) exists between 'Left-Right' score and frequency of church attendance, suggesting that the religiously active are slightly more leftward-leaning in their views.

There is also some evidence of weak association between left-right orientation and particular measures of subjective well-being. Respondents towards the right report slightly higher levels of satisfaction with life as a whole, with home life and with job, but the patterns are not evenly consistent. It makes some sense that the 'Centre Left' are a little less satisfied than those towards the right; to this extent their political outlook may express their greater dissatisfaction. Contrary to expectations, however, those at the far 'Left' report greater overall satisfaction than the 'Centre Left', and the mean level of job satisfaction among the far 'Left' is exceeded only by those on the far 'Right'. Broadly speaking, it is the far 'Right' group which stands out, displaying the highest mean levels of satisfaction. This may simply reflect an underlying age effect: 'quality of life' studies consistently find higher levels of satisfaction among older age groups and three-quarters of those on the far 'Right' are over 40 years of age.

There is a more consistent relationship between left-right orientation and psychological well-being which tends to be higher among those towards the right and lower among those on the left. This is seen most clearly with 'negative affect' (a combination of restlessness, loneliness, boredom, depression and unhappiness, and feeling upset by criticism) which steadily increases from right to left, and is most pronounced among the far 'Left' group. There may be wider social factors involved here. Almost half of the small group on the far 'Left' come from the least privileged occupational background (DEs), where the experience of relatively greater hardship and more restricted opportunities might accentuate both political and personal discontent (see also Chapter 9).

The left-right dimension has assumed its importance in political sociology because it implies a division between political radicalism and conservatism which reflects the formal divide between Labour and Conservative Parties in electoral politics. The preceding discusion, however, suggests that such differentiation is relatively circumscribed. It is associated most strongly with attitudes towards economic issues such as industrial control and confidence in the trade unions, and aspects of authority such as confidence in the armed forces and the police. There is, however, extensive agreement across the political spectrum on these and other issues, and so left-right orientation does not translate directly into alignment around specific political attitudes. More generally, it appears to reflect underlying value differences on a continuum between traditionalism and anti-traditionalism which embraces other areas besides the immediately political. This influence is seen among different age groups, confirming the general pattern of youthful anti-traditionalism and older traditionalism reported in the opening chapters.

Since the 1979 election, commentators have generally concurred in describing recent British politics as a period of increased polarisation, marked by a break with the post-war politics of consensus. The two major parties have become increasingly identified with 'right' and 'left' in the public mind, the Conservative Party through its pursuit of *laissez-faire* and Labour through its preoccupation with internal party democracy. In the 1983 election, both parties obtained their lowest shares of support among the electorate for many years, while support for a 'centre' alternative represented by the Liberal–SDP Alliance increased dramatically. Clearly political parties ignore the broad centrist outlook of the population at their peril. Indeed, Särlvik and Crewe (1983) maintain that neither of the two major parties could count on support from more than one-fifth of the population; both had become factional entities.

Freedom or equality

Respondents were asked to choose (Q.274) between two statements, the first emphasising 'personal freedom' and the second 'social equality'. The two statements imply an underlying distinction between 'individualist' and 'egalitarian' political outlooks, although the choice required is somewhat ambiguous since freedom and equality would not be seen as polar opposites by many people.

Nevertheless, when presented with these two alternatives, three times as many people chose 'freedom' (69 per cent) as chose 'equality' (23 per cent). Relatively few (8 per cent) were unwilling or unable to make a choice. Freedom was the most popular choice across the 'Left-Right' political spectrum although there was relatively greater support for equality (about one in three) among those towards the left and those close to the Labour Party.

Patriotism is more pronounced among those choosing freedom, two-thirds of whom are willing to fight for their country. Of those choosing equality only 50 per cent are willing to fight. Nevertheless, there is not a sharp polarity here and the overwhelming preference for freedom over equality shows that concern for individual liberty is a core political value among British people and suggests that any party programme which adopts 'equality' as a central component will have limited appeal.

The importance placed on freedom is widespread, cutting across class divisions and age group differences. There is almost no relationship between the choice made between freedom and equality and occupational status, although it is worth noting that freedom is more popular among those from a professional or managerial background. Nor is there any systematic relationship with age. Only among the DE group does the preference for freedom increase with age.

Patriotism

The majority of British people appear to be patriotic. If there were to be another war three-fifths of the sample would be willing to fight for their country. Respondents also said they take pride in their national identity; 55 per cent were 'very proud' and 31 per cent were 'quite proud' to be British, while 8 per cent were 'not very proud' and only 3 per cent were 'not at all proud'. National pride is related to age (correlation = 0.29). Greatest pride was expressed by older respondents, four-fifths of those aged over 60 being 'very proud'. Younger people were more likely to express themselves as 'quite proud'. The largest proportions saying they had little or no sense of national pride were also found among the younger age groups, about one-fifth of the under 25 year-olds adopting this position.

While patriotic values vary systematically with left-right orientation, they are, like freedom, very generally held values among all shades of political opinion. Even among the small group on the far 'Left' less than a quarter were 'not very' or 'not at all proud' to be British.

In addition to patriotism, relatively high confidence in the police and the armed forces (Q.349) is expressed by more than four-fifths of the population. There are important exceptions, of course, and sizeable minorities especially, those with more left-wing views, do not endorse these values as fully. Furthermore, the relatively low level of confidence in Parliament (three-fifths lack confidence) suggests that many people feel a certain amount of distance from political institutions. These views are not static and uncritical, as becomes more apparent when we examine attitudes towards change and protest.

Attitudes towards political change

An important question in the survey (Q.276) asked people to choose between three different approaches to social and political change. A very small minority in Britain – less than one in twenty – supports radical change through revolutionary action. Fully two-thirds favour gradual improvement through social reforms, and over one-fifth wish to defend society against subversive forces.

There is consistency between these attitudes to change and political outlook on the left-right dimension, but it is not a simple case of 'revolutionary' left and a 'defensive' right (Table 6.3). Gradual reform is the most favoured option across the entire political spectrum, although it receives relatively greater support among the 'Centre Left' and 'Centre'. Support for 'valiant defence of society' tends to increase from left to right and it is especially pronounced among those on the far 'Right', but even here it is still outweighed by those in favour of reform. Those in favour of 'radical change by revolutionary action' are not confined to the far 'Left', as might have been expected, but are found among all shades of political opinion. The prevailing outlook, then, is one of broadly-based support for

TABLE 6.3   *Attitudes to political change by 'left-right' position*

	Left %	Centre left %	Centre %	Centre right %	Right %	All %
Radical change	6	2	3	5	5	4
Gradual reform	64	82	71	66	49	66
Valiant defence	13	14	21	24	45	22
Don't know	16	1	4	5	2	8
N =	52	152	506	215	88	1231

'moderate' forms of change.

Among the minority of respondents who felt close to a political party, attitudes to change displayed some consistency with party alignment. Four-fifths or more of those identifying with both Labour and Liberal parties, support gradual reform while defence of present society gets little support. Among those close to the Conservative Party, two-thirds also favour gradual reform but three in ten support defence of the *status quo*.

More generally, attitudes to change show consistency with positions taken on other social and political issues (Table 6.4). For example, people in favour of gradual reform or radical change are significantly more tolerant towards homosexuality, abortion and divorce. Those favouring defence of the *status quo* tend to choose freedom over equality in greater numbers. 'Defenders' express greatest pride in being British, are more likely to think that greater respect for authority would be a good thing and that a decrease in the importance of work would be a bad thing. On many other issues, however, this sort of differentiation does not occur and, as with the left-right scale, such differentiation has to be weighed against the

TABLE 6.4   *Outlook on selected issues by attitudes to political change*

			Radical change	Gradual reform	Valiant defence	All
Q.274	Choose freedom over equality	%	57	70	75	69
Q.274	Choose equality over freedom	%	36	24	20	23
Q.348	Very proud to be British	%	55	50	73	55
Q.308	Greater respect for authority (good)	%	74	71	83	73
Q.308	Decrease in importance of work (bad)	%	44	55	59	56
Q.315	Homosexuality (Mean Score)		3.15	3.73	2.73	3.42
Q.315	Abortion (Mean Score)		4.08	4.16	3.69	4.01
Q.315	Divorce (Mean Score)		5.03	50.9	4.76	4.96
N =			54	813	279	1231

NOTE: Tolerance scores for homosexuality, abortion and divorce are scored on range from 1 = never justified to 10 = always justified.

broad levels of agreement found among people with differing views of political change.

There appears to be a connection between these attitudes to change and religiosity. People holding certain religious beliefs appear relatively more change-resistant. Those in favour of defending society are relatively more likely to describe themselves as religious people, to believe in God, and to rate more highly the importance of God in their lives. The tendency for values from comparatively separate life areas to be linked in this way is further confirmation that attitudes to change reflect differences between value systems on a broad dimension of traditionalism and anti-traditionalism. As religious views tend to be more prevalent among older people, this also indicates the existence of some underlying difference in values across generations.

In fact, attitudes towards political change vary systematically between different age groups (See Table 6.5). Majority support for reform is greater among younger age groups and then starts to tail away among older groups: the contrast is most pronounced between those aged under 25 and those aged 60 and over. The youngest group favour gradual reform more than the oldest group, support for defence of society among the over 60's is double that found among the under 25's. Yet, the age trend is confined to 'reform' and 'defence' and there is little variation in support for the 'revolutionary' option. There is no evidence that the radical stance finds greater support among younger people. Differences between social classes are slight although support for reform appears to be slightly greater among respondents from a middle class background. Different age-class combinations show slight variations but the general pattern is one of widespread support for gradual reform, receiving greater emphasis among younger people.

There seems to be little that distinguishes the relatively small numbers who favour radical change by revolutionary action. They are

TABLE 6.5 *Attitudes to political change by age group*

	Radical change	Gradual reform	Valiant defence	(N = 100%)
Under 25 (%)	6	78	16	183
25 to 39 (%)	4	76	20	315
40 to 59 (%)	4	71	25	345
60+ (%)	5	63	32	273

certainly not more left-wing in their views. Of the 54 respondents who chose this option, 6 were left of centre, 17 placed themselves at the 'Centre' and 16 were right of centre (a further 15 were 'don't knows' on the Left-Right scale). Nor is there any simple connection between this 'revolutionary' stance and either social background or other values and beliefs. There is some evidence, however, that this 'radical' group experience lower levels of psychological well-being: they are less happy, less satisfied with life, and more emotionally discontented. The data is discussed in detail in Chapter 9, where it is suggested that the association reflects the outcome of a more general socio-psychological process, linked to the holding of 'deviant' anti-consensual values.

Political protest

Levels of interest and involvement in politics, as we have seen, are generally low and only a small minority are actively involved. Yet, less orthodox forms of political action are available outside the formal political framework by which people might express their views, demands or grievances. There has been a long, if intermittent, tradition of political militancy throughout British history. The numbers involved have often been small but there have been periods when forms of collective action have taken place on a larger scale. Basic democratic rights such as that of every man and woman to vote, and the right of working people to confederate in trade union organisations, resulted from prolonged and sometimes violent political conflicts in the past. More recently, the late 1960s and early 1970s saw an upsurge in radical protest demonstrations and occupations, particularly among students and young people. Today, demonstrations are synonymous in many people's minds with political protest and are employed by a great variety of pressure groups campaigning on many different issues. Over recent years, for example, there have been demonstrations against nuclear weapons, by unemployed workers for jobs, rival groups for and against abortion law reform, for women's rights, for environmental concerns, for animal rights, against the construction of motorways, by elderly, retired people for improved State pensions. In industry, unofficial strikes and factory occupations are common tactics in attempts to protect jobs and to resist closures. It may be objected that these actions usually involve only small and unrepresentative groups among the total population, but such forms of protest seem to be an inescapable fact of British political life. How much support exists for protest action among the general population and to what extent are people prepared to take part?

The Values Study in Q.267 repeated the items, with some slight alteration in the wording, which make up the Political Protest Battery developed by Marsh (1977). Respondents were presented with seven types of political action and asked to say for each one 'whether you have actually *done* any of these things, whether you *might* do it, or would never, under any circumstances, do any of them'. The actions vary in extremity from mild forms of protest like signing petitions to actions which would almost certainly involve breaking the law, such as damaging things or using personal violence (Table 6.6).

TABLE 6.6 *Attitudes to protest actions*

	Have done %	*Might do* %	*Would never do* %
Signing a petition	63	28	9
Attending lawful demonstrations	9	33	58
Joining in boycotts	6	31	63
Joining unofficial strikes	8	16	76
Occupying buildings or factories	2	10	87
Damaging things like breaking windows, removing road signs, etc.	2	1	97
Using personal violence like fighting with other demonstrators or the police	1	3	96

There was clearly a great divide between signing petitions, which more than three-fifths of the sample had actually done at some time, and the other six political actions. The numbers who have taken part in more militant forms of protest are very small and well over half the sample would never do any of them. Only one in ten has attended a lawful demonstration, only one in sixteen has joined in a boycott and only one in twelve has joined an unofficial strike. There is almost universal rejection of the most extreme actions involving violence or damage to property, underlining the strong commitment among the British population to lawful political activity.

Although few have actually participated, there does indeed appear to be greater readiness to contemplate more lawful types of protest.

TABLE 6.7 Mean protest scores¹ by selected characteristics

	Total	Political scale					Interest in politics		Terminal age of education		Trade union membership		Belief in God	
		Left 1/2	3/4	5/6	7/8	Right 9/10	Active	None	-16	16+	Member	Non-member	Yes	No
Signing a petition	1.54	1.49	1.64	1.60	1.64	1.29	1.60	1.43	1.49	1.58	1.65	1.51	1.52	1.57
Attending lawful demonstrations	0.50	0.63	0.75	0.57	0.46	0.23	1.10	0.30	0.34	0.68	0.74	0.44	0.44	0.72
Joining in boycotts	0.43	0.64	0.74	0.44	0.40	0.24	1.08	0.25	0.31	0.57	0.68	0.37	0.37	0.62
Joining unofficial strikes	0.32	0.52	0.50	0.30	0.32	0.14	0.44	0.32	0.32	0.31	0.56	0.25	0.29	0.41
Occupying buildings/factories	0.15	0.37	0.30	0.15	0.10	0.02	0.40	0.11	0.08	0.23	0.26	0.12	0.11	0.30
Damaging things (windows, etc.)	0.05	0.10	0.07	0.05	0.00	0.08	0.15	0.05	0.03	0.07	0.06	0.04	0.04	0.10
Using violence (fighting, etc.)	0.04	0.15	0.06	0.04	0.03	0.03	0.13	0.03	0.02	0.07	0.04	0.04	0.02	0.12
N of cases	1216	50	150	504	211	89	60	336	640	573	250	966	924	189

¹Range of scores: from 0 = 'would never do' to 2 = 'have done' (mid-point = 1.00)

Almost one-third of the sample say they 'might' be prepared to take part in demonstrations and political boycotts. Apart from signing petitions, which are acceptable to most people and which might not be regarded as 'protest' in many instances, the *potential* support for protest action effectively ranges from demonstrations (two-fifths) to occupations (1 in 8), with illegal acts ruled out by almost everyone.

How are attitudes to protest related to other characteristics? Table 6.7 shows the mean protest scores for the seven types of action among various sub-groups. In effect, any score less than 1.0 (the mid-point) indicates that the balance of opinion leans towards no protest rather than active involvement in protest. Apart from signing petitions, almost all the mean scores are less than 1.0, reflecting the generally low level of support for protest activity. Against this background, there are nevertheless predictable variations in protest scores between people with differing characteristics. Those to the left of centre are more likely to have been involved or to become involved in protest compared with those at the centre and towards the right. Noticeably, among the small number on the far 'Left' there is some small-scale support for the most extreme actions. Not surprisingly, there is greater readiness to protest among those with an active interest in politics than among those with no interest. Those who have experienced a longer period of formal education show more support for protest action, except for unofficial strikes where education is likely to be of less importance than work circumstances. Trade union members also display higher protest scores than non-members, predictably for unofficial strikes, less predictably for demonstrations, boycotts and occupations. Again, there is an association between political and religious beliefs, with those who believe in God showing more opposition to protest activity than those who do not believe in God.

Can those who might be prepared to engage in protest be defined in demographic terms? Looking only at demonstrations, in a sense the most typical form of protest action, there are strong associations between protest scores and both age and sex, and a slightly weaker relationship with social class (see Table 6.8). Similar patterns are found for other protest actions but to a lesser degree. In general, younger people are more likely to demonstrate or to take a more favourable view of demonstrations than older people; there is a greater support among men than among women and among middle class respondents than among the working class. Thus the greatest readiness to demonstrate is found among young men from middle

TABLE 6.8 *Attending lawful demonstrations*
(mean scores[1] by age, sex and social class)

Age	Sex	Social class				All classes	Total
		AB	C1	C2	DE		
Under 25	Men	1.17	1.03	0.61	0.67	0.80	
	Women	0.81	0.84	0.54	0.51	0.64	0.72
25 to 39	Men	1.01	0.90	0.63	0.82	0.81	
	Women	0.80	0.51	0.36	0.38	0.49	0.64
40 to 59	Men	0.75	0.64	0.47	0.33	0.52	
	Women	0.52	0.39	0.28	0.32	0.36	0.44
60 plus	Men	0.36	0.28	0.44	0.22	0.34	
	Women	0.38	0.45	0.12	0.14	0.21	0.27
All		0.72	0.62	0.43	0.37		

[1] *Range* of scores: from 0 = 'would never do' to 2 = 'have done', (mid-point = 1.00)

class backgrounds, least readiness and greatest opposition among women aged over 60 from the working class, with other groups distributed accordingly. Younger women, for example, are more likely to be prepared to demonstrate than older men, perhaps reflecting the growth of the Women's Liberation Movement. Indeed, among the over 60's, in the middle class, it is the men rather than the women who display slightly greater opposition towards demonstrations. The difference is barely significant but it is remotely possible that some women in this group have been influenced by feminism.

The general picture accords with expectations. It is not surprising that demonstrators are more likely to be young. Apart from any generational differences in political values, it does after all require some energy to take part in what tend to be fairly vigorous forms of political activity. Again, gender roles enable men to pursue political ends through confrontational forms of action with relatively greater freedom than women. It is perhaps less predictable that younger people from more privileged backgrounds are more ready to consider protest than those from the working class, although this ties in with the notion of 'student revolt'. The strongest influence here is undoubtedly education, particularly the expansion and changes that have taken place in higher education, leading to a greater questioning of accepted political goals among some of the more educationally privileged. Such trends should not be exaggerated, however. Levels of support for political protest are generally low and even among those who view it most favourably, support for protest exists much more at the level of ideas than action.

CHANGING POLITICAL VALUES

Age differences, as we have seen, are associated with variations across many aspects of political outlook. Across all age groups a broad majority favours change through gradual reform but greater numbers of older people support 'valiant defence of society'. How much do apparent generational differences reflect a real change in political values? If such a change is taking place, how widespread is it and does it represent a permanent realignment or is it a more temporary phenomenon?

Ronald Inglehart argues that one of the major developments in Western democracies since the end of the Second World War has been a shift in political priorities from what he terms 'materialist' to 'post-materialist' values, a 'silent revolution' which is transforming social and political life. This shift, resulting from the period of economic expansion, affluence and political stability which the West has largely enjoyed since 1945, marks a change in values from 'an overwhelming emphasis on material well-being and physical security towards greater emphasis on the quality of life' (Inglehart, 1976, p. 3). Older people, maturing in an era of economic hardship and great political insecurity, experienced a process of political socialisation which reinforced political concerns directed towards satisfying needs for security and stability – continuing employment, economic growth, social peace, good housing and work conditions. Younger people, growing up in the relative affluence of the post-war boom years, were freed of these needs and thus able to embrace more outward-looking political goals – participation, equality, social justice, concerns such as world peace and nuclear disarmament and the protection of the environment.

Central to Inglehart's thesis is the divergence between materialist and post-materialist values across different age groups, and more specifically, the shift towards post-materialist values among generations born after the Second World War.

Materialism and post-materialism in Britain

Inglehart's 4-item battery was repeated in the Values Study. Respondents were asked to choose two out of four statements representing alternative national goals (Q.277).

Following Inglehart, those respondents who chose both the first and third statements ('Maintaining order in the nation' and 'Fighting rising prices') are defined as Materialist. Those choosing both the second and fourth statements ('Giving the people more say in important government decisions' and 'Protecting freedom of speech') are defined as Post-materialist. Respondents choosing all other two-statement combinations are assigned to a 'Mixed' category. When responses to the items are combined in this way a pattern emerges replicating that found in other surveys (see Inglehart, 1981).

Materialist	25 per cent
Mixed	62 per cent
Post-materialist	13 per cent

Clearly the Materialist and Post-materialist types together account for only a minority of the total population. Inglehart, however, would not argue that the two 'pure value types' should account for the value priorities of an entire population; they indicate two polar positions at the ends of a continuum. Furthermore, he does not maintain that there is anything inherently post-materialistic about 'freedom of speech' for example, rather it is the *relative superiority* assigned to this goal over 'maintaining order' or 'fighting rising prices' that indicates a post-materialist orientation.

Post-materialists are more predominant among those with left of centre political views, Materialists are more predominant among the 'Centre' and towards the right. Similar differentiation is found on many other political attitudes. For example, Post-materialists are more interested in politics than Materialists; they are more likely to be actively involved; they are more likely to consider taking part in political protest. Thus Post-materialists tend to be more radical, more anti-traditional, Materialists are more conservative, more traditional. Briefly described in demographic terms, Post-materialists tend to be younger, they have received more education and come from more middle class backgrounds.

Age and materialism/post-materialism

Far fewer Materialists are found among the under 25's than in other age groups (see Table 6.9). More strikingly, the proportion of Post-materialists increases steadily moving from older to younger groups, such that Post-materialists (about one-fifth) come to outnumber Materialists (about one-sixth) among the under 25's.

TABLE 6.9   *Materialist and post-materialist value types by age group*

Value Type	Under 25 %	25 to 39 %	40 to 59 %	60 plus %
Materialist	15	25	27	27
Mixed	67	58	62	66
Post-materialist	18	16	11	7

What is the nature of this relationship between age and political values? Inglehart (1981) considers three processes which might account for change in political values:

1. *intergenerational* value change,
2. *life-cyle* effects,
3. *period* effects, arising from historically specific events.

Distinguishing between generational and life-cycle effects is a difficult problem which requires systematically repeated studies of different generational groups over lengthy time periods. The life-cycle argument, put very simply, would explain such political radicalism as exists among the young as a transient phenomenon which would diminish as they grow older and face the pressing materialist demands of work, marriage, children and home ownership (cf. Marsh, 1977). If this were the case we would expect the sharpest difference in post-materialist orientation to occur between the under 25's and the 25 to 39 year-olds but this not the case. The greatest division occurs later on between the under 40's and those aged 40 and over. No doubt life-cycle and period effects exert some influence but the persistence of Post-materialism among the 25–39 age group is much more explicable as a real and permanent generational change in political values. If there is a 'generation gap', it is not a simple division between young maturing adults and older people. Rather, it is a gap marked by a specific change in political values linked to a definite historical turning point. As the present adult population grows older and generational replacement takes place, and in the absence of major changes, we can expect this realignment process to continue, very gradually, as post-materialist concerns achieve greater predominance.

Not all researchers agree that such a lasting shift in political outlook has taken place. Apart from Marsh, other critics have pointed to the minority appeal of Post-materialism and questioned the precise nature of the process of change which has led to generational differences. Nevertheless, Inglehart's theory appears to be standing the test of time. Reviewing the evidence from well over a hundred representative national surveys, he concluded (1981) that inter-generational movement from materialist to post-materialist values in Western societies 'constitutes a distinctive and persisting dimension of political cleavage'.

The unexpected re-emergence of the Campaign for Nuclear Disarmament, the growth of the environmental movement and the more general adoption of conservationist goals may indeed point to an underlying shift in the focus of political values. The change is not dramatic or universal and whether one regards it as a move away from materialist, economic preoccupations towards post-materialist concerns, or as some broader change in values is open to debate. It must also be viewed against the widespread agreement that exists for values such as personal freedom, patriotism, and general improvement through reform. Nevertheless, for significant numbers, particularly among those who have grown up since the Second World War, political concerns are in some sense different and involve new priorities.

7 British Attitudes to Work

MICHAEL FOGARTY

INTRODUCTION

The Values Study addressed three sets of direct questions on work attitudes.

1. How important is work to people, and why? (Q.132, 134, 136, 137)
2. What do people think about the way in which their jobs are designed and managed? (Q.135, 139, 143, 144)
3. What are current attitudes to trade unionism and industrial action? (Q.113, 267)

Answers to these questions are relevant to some of the most heavily debated issues in Britain. This chapter focuses on three: the performance of the British economy relative to others, the impact of unemployment, and the equality of opportunity between men and women. It tests three propositions:

1. *On work organisation and performance*: working people in Britain, by comparison with others in Europe, are strong on the qualities of a reliable subordinate but weak on the critical and dynamic aspects which favour improvement in work, either as a personal experience or in its productivity.

2. *On negative and positive reactions to unemployment*: the unemployed in Britain are for good reason a dissatisfied group, but their

attitudes do not generate effective pressure for improvement in their situation.

3 *On equality of opportunity for women and men*: though the present 'new conventional' division of employment and family responsibilities between women and men remains unsatisfactory for many women, women's own attitudes still support it and limit the effectiveness of pressures for further change.

WORK ORGANISATION AND PERFORMANCE

What has to be explained is why, when relative decline in Britain's economic performance has continued so long, and so much is known about ways in which work performance and organisation might be improved, action to bring about improvements has been delayed so much longer in Britain than in many other industrial countries. What British respondents said of their attitudes to work in the Values Study throws a great deal of light on this.

British people present themselves in the survey (Table 7.1) as committed to their work, though not as strongly or exclusively as some others, and with a distinctive view of what a good job means. They are exceptionally proud of and satisfied with their work, look forward to it, and are even less likely than other Europeans to think that it would be a good thing if work played a smaller part in their lives. In Britain as elsewhere in Europe, the idea of a simpler and more natural life style and of giving less emphasis to money and material possessions is vaguely approved, but not at the price of attaching less importance to work or of abandoning technological development. The British remain more optimistic than most about the usefulness of scientific advances to mankind. If they had more free time without loss of pay they would be more likely than other Europeans to look for additional work for money, to avoid boredom or out of interest in running their own business.

This interest in additional work, however, has to compete with many others, for the British can also think of an exceptionally wide range of other ways in which to use extra spare time. The reality of this competition or mutual interference between work, family, and leisure has been documented elsewhere (Young and Willmott, 1973).

What is most distinctive about British responses is the relatively strong emphasis on work as an interesting and satisfying way of life

TABLE 7.1 *Work and life*

		Britain	West Germany	Ten European countries
		Percentages or score		
Takes a great deal of pride in own work	%	79	15	36
Job satisfaction (average score: scale 1–10)		7.72	7.05	7.29
Looks forward to work/enjoys both work and weekend	%	72	57	60
Good if work played a smaller part in our lives	%	26	30	33
if a simpler and more natural life style	%	76	69	82
if less emphasis on money and material possessions	%	62	56	65
if more emphasis on the development of technology	%	61	55	57
In long run, scientific advances will help mankind	%	48	33	38

(Table 7.2), what might be called work as a consumer good. A good job tends to mean for them above all one which is interesting, with pleasant people to work with – simply 'meeting people', the sociable aspect, is not so important – a chance to achieve something, and one where their time is well used. For the British as for most other Europeans, under-employment in the form of 'not too much press-ure' is not a highly valued characteristic of a job.

When people are asked about the importance of features of a job, the strength of their responses as well as the balance between one feature and another should be noted. There is a particularly striking comparison between responses in Britain and Germany. German respondents attach more importance than British to every one of the fifteen features of a job about which the Values Study enquired, except for 'an interesting job', which they nevertheless name nearly as often as the British and far more often than the European average. They take work more seriously than the British. Possibly for that very

TABLE 7.2 *Important features of a job*
(Average for each group of features of percentages who name the features in that group as important.)

	Britain	West Germany	Ten European countries
Good material conditions (pay, security, hours, holidays)	45	59	47
Work as a consumer good (interesting, can achieve something, pleasant colleagues, meeting people, not too much pressure)	54	59	46
A dynamic job (initiative, responsibility, promotion prospects, full use of abilities)	42	59	41
Socially useful, respected	28	43	32

reason, they are also more critical of their work experience, in spite of their known high achievement both in general economic performance and in areas like training or industrial relations which directly affect the individual worker. They are less satisfied with their work than the British and much less likely to say that they are very proud of it.

The British express relatively high satisfaction not only with their own work but with the general business and industrial framework in which it is set (Table 7.3). Half of them, compared to 35 per cent across Europe, express outright support for capitalist ownership and management. Their confidence in major companies is above the European average, though with a qualification explained below. So is their readiness to carry out orders at work even if not first convinced that they are justified. A large majority take a strong line on economic incentives: pay should be related to personal performance rather than simply to job level.

Though *relatively* satisfied with their work situation, however, British respondents find many points for criticism. Like others in Europe, they tend to be markedly less satisfied with their incomes than with their jobs as such. Two-thirds of British respondents, more than the European average, say that they often or sometimes feel exploited or taken advantage of in their work (Table 7.4). Though most score fairly highly on freedom to make decisions in their job,

TABLE 7.3　*The business and industrial framework*

	Britain %	West Germany %	Ten European countries %
Owners should run or appoint managers	50	47	35
Owners & employees should select managers	37	37	41
Employees should own & appoint managers	7	7	10
State should own & appoint managers	2	2	4
Confidence in major companies:			
a great deal/quite a lot	48	34	39
not very much/none	48	65	56
Orders at work should be followed even when not fully agreeing with them:	49	28	32
only if first convinced/it depends	48	69	64
Two secretaries doing same job – fair to pay better performer higher	65	64	59

TABLE 7.4　*Freedom, exploitation and pay*

	Percentage or score		
	Britain	West Germany	Ten European countries
Freedom to make decisions in work:			
score (scale 1–10)	6.65	6.22	6.47
per cent scoring 0–5	32	37	34
Often/sometimes feels exploited or taken advantage of at work	64	54	53
Satisfaction with financial situation of household (Score – scale 1–10)	6.83	6.92	6.58

one third, including half of all lower-skilled manual workers and nearly half of all under 25, score below the mid-point of that scale. Half of all British respondents, and more than half of those under 25, do *not* think that orders should be carried out without first being convinced (Table 7.3). Nearly half, while not interested in a change in business ownership – the majority against state or even cooperative ownership is overwhelming – would like at least some involvement of employees in the appointment of managers. Though British confidence in major companies is relatively high, half of all respondents nevertheless express not very much confidence in them or none. Other surveys largely confirm these findings (Fogarty, 1982).

One obvious channel for criticism and action is the trade unions. The Values Study confirms (Table 7.5) that Britain has an exceptionally high proportion of union members, but also points to some marked weaknesses in the British trade union movement. Respondents present themselves as *belonging* to unions rather than *active* in them: only a tiny minority claim to work voluntarily for the union. Their level of confidence in unions is very low, but the meaning of this finding about confidence in unions needs to be amplified from other surveys (Fogarty, 1982; 1983). British workers strongly approve of trade unionism in principle, but if asked about actual union performance answers differ according to whether the question refers to their own union, especially at their own place of work, or to 'the unions' in general. When the question is put in the first form, replies are predominantly favourable to the unions. When, as in the Values

TABLE 7.5 *Trade unionism*

	Britain %	West Germany %	Ten European countries %
Trade union member (Q.371):			
Self	29	20	20
Self or spouse	45	30	30
Union member (self) (Q.113):	21	16	13
works voluntarily for union	1	2	2
When holds a strong view, tries to persuade fellow-workers or friends:			
Often/sometimes	42	58	51
Rarely	28	29	25
Never	29	9	21
Confidence in trade unions:			
A great deal/quite a lot	26	36	32
Not very much/none	72	63	64

TABLE 7.6 *Militancy*

	Percentage or score		
	Britain	West Germany	Ten European countries
Has taken/might willingly take part in:			
Unofficial strike	24	13	19
Occupation of factory or buildings	12	11	16
Damaging things (breaking windows etc)	3	2	3
Whether certain forms of violence might ever be justified (score scale 1–10):			
threatening workers who refuse to join strike	1.69	1.71	1.70
fighting the police	1.73	2.07	2.03

Study, it is put in the more general form, it becomes clear that the wider leadership and performance of the trade union movement has in recent years attracted little confidence even from union members themselves. The findings of the Values Study about attitudes to militant action (Table 7.6) are consistent with this. The British are no more enthusiastic than other Europeans about plant occupation, violence against blacklegs, or fighting the police, but the minority who have joined or would willingly join in an unofficial strike, irrespective of the views of higher union leadership, is exceptionally large.

These findings suggest, on the one hand, important strengths on which good leadership can build: commitment to and satisfaction in work: and readiness to accept the existing pattern of ownership and management and to respond to strong management, provided that its style is right in matters like fairness to individuals – freedom from exploitation and a fair relation of pay to performance – and the design and interest of jobs. There is an interest in involvement ('more say') within, rather than as a challenge to, the existing industrial order, and a growing interest in information and explanation as a basis for authority. White and Trevor's study (1983) of British workers under Japanese management illustrates the remarkable response which can be obtained where conditions like these are met by managements which are also strong in the sense of forcefulness and insistence on high standards of performance.

The other side of the coin, however, is the relatively uncritical climate of attitudes to work in Britain, and the low level of confidence in possible agents of change. People in Britain criticise many aspects of their work, but against the background of exceptionally high satisfaction with their jobs, the overall system of work organisation, and life in general, a wide range of interests alternative to work, and a not very strong emphasis, compared in particular to the Germans, on the importance of the various features of a job. They are ambivalent in their views on the actual usefulness of unions and reluctant to work actively for them, and have less confidence in the competence of management as they actually encounter it (Fogarty, 1982) than in answering the generalised question about 'major companies' in the Study. The data suggest a 'grumbling appendix' in British attitudes to work, and not a dynamic drive for change.

Findings on other questions not immediately related to work point in the same direction. For example, British people are less likely than the European average, and much less likely than the Germans, often or from time to time to set out to persuade others on matters on which they hold a strong view. One could predict from this that the British would be exceptionally likely to back off from changes which might involve strong and prolonged controversy. Several recent studies show that an important reason why British managers back off from change, or approach it abruptly and clumsily is in fact the fear, rather than the reality, of obstruction to change by unions or the work force. This 'apprehension factor' is much more marked in Britain than in Germany (Jacobs, 1978; Marsh, 1981; Wilson, 1982; Northcott, 1982; Bessant, 1982).

On these findings, the proposition that British attitudes to work reflect the reliability of a good subordinate rather than capacity for criticism and change is justified.

The Values Study took a snapshot of work attitudes in Britain at a particular time. Will there be a change? The responses tell us little about willingness to accept the price of change, but they do show how, if the process of change in the British economy were accelerated, this acceleration would tend to be self-reinforcing. The changes in the occupational and industrial structure likely to be required in a more dynamic economy would themselves shift the balance of attitudes in Britain towards greater dynamism.

Let us suppose that, as a result of accelerated economic development, the occupational structure in Britain came to resemble more closely that now existing in Germany, and that attitudes in educational and occupational groups in Britain remained as they were at the time of the Values Study. There would then be an increase in the proportion of the population interested in:

1. Dynamic features of a job such as initiative, responsibility, promotion, and full use of abilities, in a close relation of pay to individual performance, and in the chance to run their own business: though not simply in working longer to earn more money or because of lack of other interests.
2. Readiness to argue and persuade, and to work voluntarily for a union or professional association.
3. A stronger relative emphasis, as a result particularly of the rise in educational standards, on the dynamic aspects of children's education (Table 7.7). At present, British people put less emphasis than

TABLE 7.7 *Qualities important for children to learn (For each group of qualities, average or percentages who named qualities in that group as important.)*

	Britain	West Germany	Ten European countries
'Passive' qualities: (good manners, politeness, neatness, honesty, patience, tolerance/respect for others, self-control, unselfishness, obedience, loyalty)	44	30	36
'Dynamic' qualities: (independence, hard work, responsibility, imagination, leadership, thrift determination/perseverance)	15	39	23
Net dynamism score (dynamic minus passive)	−29	+9	−13

the European average, and much less than Germans, on developing dynamic qualities in their own children.

4. The quality of life, in the sense of less emphasis on money and material possessions: but with no implication that work should play a smaller part in our lives.

Can attitudes in the various educational and occupational groups, however, be expected to remain the same as at the time of the Values Study? The findings on work attitudes in different age groups show no clear sign to the contrary.

Younger workers have in some respects different attitudes from those older and more experienced. They are, for example, less satisfied with their jobs, and have less pride in their work. These, however, could be life cycle rather than generation differences, and a longitudinal study would be needed to decide this. There is no clear age trend in 'the importance of work in our lives' or in preference for a simpler and more natural life style or less emphasis on money and material possessions. By the age of marriage and starting a family young people in Britain express as much conviction of the value of money and material possessions as their elders. People under 35 do give more weight to the dynamic features of work: but they are also the more educated and occupationally qualified, and the tendency for emphasis on these dynamic features to increase with education and occupational level is particularly strong. When it comes to bringing up their own children, younger people do not have significantly different views from their elders on the balance between passive and dynamic qualities.

A shift in the political balance, on the other hand, could be expected to have implications for work attitudes. Left-right attitudes at the time of the Values Study were spread more evenly across occupational groups than might have been expected (Table 7.8), though with some differences at the extremes. There were relatively high proportions of lower-skilled manual workers among the far left and of employers and managers in small businesses among the far right. On the findings a political swing to the left might be expected (Table 7.9) to carry with it:

1. A much stronger emphasis on employee involvement, and rejection of traditionalist capitalist ownership and systems of authority. Preference for State ownership is noticeable only on the far left,

TABLE 7.8 *Left-right orientation by occupation*

	Column percentages Position on left-right scale				
	1/2 *(left)*	*3/4*	*5/6*	*7/8*	*9/10* *(right)*
Professional/managerial	11	14	14	19	17
Other non-manual	17	26	27	27	25
Skilled/supervisory manual	19	23	23	17	23
Other manual	41	29	28	25	25

and then only as a small minority view. Preference for employee involvement in the control of business and industry, however, is strong on the left, and significantly stronger than in the centre or on the right. The soft left emphasise employee involvement in the appointment of managers, and the hard left prefer co-operative to State ownership. Trade union activism, such as it is, is characteristic of the left rather than the centre or right: but the centre share with the left a preference for a participative style of management in which orders must be explained and justified before being carried out.

2. A stronger, though minority, view that work should play a smaller part in our lives.

3. Less emphasis on the dynamic features of work, opportunity to run one's own business, or a strict relation of pay to personal performance, and somewhat less conviction about the need to emphasise the further development of technology.

Examination of differences in work attitudes by religion, or lack of it, yields less clear-cut results. Catholics, for example, express less interest than Protestants in relating pay strictly to performance, but more in initiative on the job and exactly equal interest in promotion and responsibility. Protestants are less ready to accept orders without question, but also less interested than Catholics in employee involvement in the appointment of managers. If there is a distinctive Protestant work ethic, it does not appear in these findings. Two clear findings do stand out. One is the very strong support of active church

184

TABLE 7.9 *Work attitudes by left-right orientation*

	Percentages Position on left-right scale				
	1/2 (left)	3/4	5/6	7/8	9/10 (right)
Dynamic features of a job – average of percentages thinking each of these features important	37	42	45	45	41
If 3-day week without loss of pay, would use extra time to run own business	7	12	16	17	12
Fair to pay according to individual performance	41	55	71	69	73
Works voluntarily for a union	7	2	0	0	0
Often/sometimes seeks to persuade where holds a strong view	33	55	45	40	32
Ownership and management of business and industry:– owners should run and appoint managers	26	30	52	60	57
owners and employees should select managers	42	55	37	33	36
employees should own and select managers	17	9	7	3	3
state should own and appoint managers	9	3	2	2	0
Orders at work should be followed only if first convinced, or 'it depends'	45	57	54	36	37
Good if:– less emphasis on money and material possessions	60	69	62	68	66
work played a smaller part in our lives	35	36	24	26	22
more emphasis on the development of technology	26	30	52	60	57

members (weekly or monthly attenders) for the idea that it would be good if there were less emphasis on money and material possessions. The other is that on several indicators people of no religion or convinced atheists express more dynamic and radical attitudes than believers. They put more weight on the dynamic features of work, are more interested in running their own business, and are less inclined to endorse capitalist ownership without qualification. The Values Study cannot, however, show how far this distinction would persist if unbelief or non-attachment to a religion became the view of the majority instead of a small and marginal minority.

TABLE 7.10 *The unemployed sample in the Values Study*

	Unemployed N = 70 %	Total Population N = 1231 %
Age:		
18–24	48	16
25–34	14	20
35–44	9	17
45–54	6	13
55–64	23	15
65+	–	17
Men	72	48
Women	28	52
Single	49	20
Living with parents	38	13
Chief earner	36	53
Family in lower income economic group	53	27
Managerial/professional or middle non-manual	0	26
Junior non-manual	11	12
Skilled manual	24	22
Other manual	51	31
Occupation N/A	14	10
Trade union member	19	29

NEGATIVE AND POSITIVE REACTIONS TO
UNEMPLOYMENT

The unemployed in the sample (Table 7.10) were predominantly
either young – two out of five still living with their parents, half not
yet married – or near retirement. They were mainly from manual
occupations, half being semi- or unskilled, and from low income
families. Nearly three-quarters were men. Overall, their attitudes to
work resembled those of the general population of similar age and
occupation (Table 7.11).

It is hardly surprising that the unemployed were dissatisfied (Table
7.12), particularly with the financial situation of their household,
though more expected that it would improve in the next year than

TABLE 7.11　*Attitudes of the unemployed to work*

	Unemployed	Percentages or score whole population	
	Age 18–24	Manual (semi- and unskilled)	All
Good if:			
Decrease of importance of work in our lives	18	22	28	26
Less emphasis on money and material possessions	47	46	57	62
More emphasis on the development of technology	59	52	65	61
Average of percentages (see Table 7.2 on features important in a job:			
Good material conditions	49	45	47	45
Work as a consumer good	54	58	52	54
A dynamic job	39	46	30	42
Socially useful, respected	20	24	23	28
Average of percentages (see Table 7.8) on qualities important to develop in children:			
passive	45	44	43	44
dynamic	15	15	15	15
net score	−30	−29	−28	−29
Pay should be related to individual performance, not job specification	53	58	57	65

TABLE 7.12 *Levels of satisfaction of the unemployed*

	Unemployed	Percentages or score whole population	
	Age 18–24	Manual (semi- and unskilled)	All
Financial situation of your household:			
satisfaction now (scale 1–10)	5.10	6.43	6.81	6.83
in next 12 months likely to get better	42	43	31	31
Psychological well-being: average score (0–5) on:			
Positive items (excited/interested, proud/pleased with compliment/accomplishment, on top of world, things going your way)	1.83	2.57	2.43	2.31
Negative items (restless, lonely/remote, bored, depressed/very unhappy, upset with criticism	1.58	1.47	1.39	1.22
Net positive score	+0.25	+1.10	+1.04	+ 1.09
Often/sometimes feels:			
very lonely	41	39	42	33
life is meaningless	40	32	30	26
Health very good	30	44	44	39
Satisfaction with home life (scale 1–10)	7.71	7.89	8.35	8.44
At home often feels:			
happy	62	70	67	74
secure	68	74	68	77
All things together, very happy	27	34	42	38
Satisfaction with life:			
5 years ago	7.08	6.59	7.40	7.34
now	6.78	7.25	7.60	7.67
5 years hence (expected)	7.47	8.21	8.14	8.15

that it would get worse. On the psychological well-being scale they scored high on negative items such as restlessness, loneliness, boredom and depression, and low on positive items. They were more likely than the general population to think life meaningless, and less likely to report very good health. They expressed relatively low satisfaction with their home life, and were less likely than others to say that at home they felt happy and secure. They were also less likely than others to say that they were happy or satisfied with their life in general, and recorded a fall in their satisfaction compared to the past, though they looked forward to a large improvement in it in the years ahead.

Yet the unemployed were not particularly radical in their views either on society in general or on the organisation and management of work. Table 7.13 sets their views on some general issues about society and religious or moral beliefs alongside those of the whole population of younger people and of lower-skilled manual workers. Seen in this context, only two of their views were clearly distinctive: unusually strong support for equality, and relatively low confidence in some political institutions including the armed forces and police, the legal system, and Parliament. The unemployed, like the rest of the population, overwhelmingly supported the gradual reform of society, and those who took a different view were, as in the population as a whole, more likely to be 'valiant defenders' of the existing order than radical revolutionaries.

Table 7.14 similarly sets in context the views of the unemployed on some issues about management of work. Major companies, like some political institutions, attracted little confidence from the unemployed. Their confidence in trade unions was no higher than that of the rest of the population. It is probably a reflection of both these factors that the unemployed scored marginally high on readiness for direct action such as unofficial strikes and plant occupations.

They showed a particular interest in co-operative ownership of business and industry, but rejected State ownership as emphatically as anyone else. Overall, however, their views cannot be said to have had a sharply distinctive pattern.

The proposition to be tested is not simply about radicalism among the unemployed. It is that, however dissatisfied the unemployed may have been, the attitudes which they expressed in the Values Study were not such as to make them an effective force for improvement. The fact that they had not developed a radically different view of

TABLE 7.13 *The unemployed: orthodoxy, reform, and radicalism – general*

| | Unemployed | Percentages or scores whole population | | |
		Age 18–24	Manual (semi- and unskilled)	All
Prefers freedom to equality	55	67	65	69
Confidence in political institutions (a great deal/quite a lot):				
armed forces	70	75	82	81
police	72	79	85	86
legal system	51	60	57	66
parliament	28	31	35	40
civil service	44	40	51	48
Political views (scale 1 = left, 10 = right)	5.18	5.15	5.26	5.70
Very proud to be British	41	35	58	55
Most important of four possible aims for the country in the next years:				
more say for the people in government decisions	41	36	28	26
maintaining order in the nation	26	27	25	32
Our society needs to be:				
radically changed by revolution	4	4	6	4
gradually reformed	69	72	58	66
valiantly defended against subversive forces	19	15	21	22
Don't know	7	8	15	8
Confidence (a great deal/quite a lot) in:				
educational system	57	53	55	60
the Press	34	23	33	29
the Church	40	34	51	48
Your church's answers are adequate on:				
moral problems/needs of individuals	29	21	25	30
problems of family life	31	23	30	32
man's spiritual needs	36	36	39	42

TABLE 7.14 *The unemployed: reform and radicalism–work-related issues*

	Unemployed Age 18–24	Percentages or scores General population Manual (semi- or unskilled)	All
Confidence (a great deal/ quite a lot)	35	51	49	48
in major companies in trade unions	27	26	26	26
Who should run business and in-dustry?				
owners should run and appoint managers	38	38	46	50
owners and employees should select managers	35	44	41	37
employees should own and select managers	20	11	6	7
State should own and appoint managers	1	3	3	2
Orders at work should be followed:				
even if not fully agreeing with them	42	44	50	49
must be convinced first/it depends	57	54	47	48
Pay should be related to individual performance rather than to job level	53	58	57	65
Have/might join in:				
unofficial strikes	42	36	28	24
plant etc occupation	27	23	13	12
damage like breaking windows	8	8	3	3
violence, fighting other demonstrators	14	10	4	4
May ever by justified (scale 1–10):				
threatening workers who refuse to join in a strike	1.95	2.35	1.80	1.69
fighting the police	2.52	2.75	1.60	1.73

society is relevant to this, but the most relevant findings in Tables 7.13 and 7.14 are about their attitude to institutions which could be used to improve the working of society with or without major changes in its structure. Low confidence in unions, management, and political institutions is not an encouraging beginning to a drive for change. The unemployed were low on union membership, not particularly active in politics, and low on organisation membership and activity generally. The more detailed findings of the Study show that the organisations in which they were members or activists were chiefly in the areas of religion, youth, or charitable work.

Nor was the low confidence of the unemployed in political and economic institutions offset by any high level of confidence in their fellow-citizens generally. The unemployed were exceptionally likely to say that most people cannot be trusted and that people are less willing to help each other than in the past, and doubted as strongly as anyone else whether other people's moral standards were as high as their own. The Values Study cannot answer the question whether there *will* at some time or in some conditions be a rise in radicalism and organised militancy among the unemployed. What it shows very clearly is that at the time of the study the typical attitude among the unemployed was that of the discouraged worker, distrustful of other people and alienated from many of the institutions which might help towards improvement, rather than of the militant for change.

EQUALITY OF OPPORTUNITY BETWEEN MEN AND WOMEN

Women's employment as shown in the Study follows what came in the 1960s to be called the 'new conventional' pattern (Fogarty, 1971; 1972): full engagement in the labour market or as students before acquiring 'housewife' status, generally a break during the years of starting a family, then resumption, but mainly part-time. As with the New Penny, time has made 'new' obsolete: this may now be called simply the conventional pattern.

A 'housewife' is defined in the Study as: 'The person who is in charge of the household arrangements such as shopping, cooking and cleaning. She need not necessarily do the household chores herself, and she may also be going out to work.' This classification of course overlaps the usual distinction by marital status, since the great majority of housewives are or have been married and have had children, whereas the great majority of non-housewives are young, single and still living with their parents. It puts a useful emphasis, however, on the difference between women who do or do not under present social conventions have the principal responsibility for managing a household.

The proposition to be tested is that the present conventional pattern of women's employment remains in a number of ways unsatisfactory to women, and yet that women's own attitudes give it substantial support. The Values Study has one important limitation: it did not ask housewives *not* in employment about their attitudes to employment or their intention to return to work. Subject to this, three different patterns of satisfaction emerge (Table 7.15).

The young and mainly single non-housewives have a profile of both work and other satisfactions very similar to the average for all men and women aged 18–24.

Housewives in full-time employment are a relatively favoured category. They exceed men as well as other women in job satisfaction, pride in their work, and satisfaction with their family finances; feel freer than other women to make decisions at work, and are less likely than men to feel that they are exploited in their jobs. These work satisfactions are not at the expense of satisfactions in other directions. The general life satisfaction of these housewives is above the average for both men and women, and so is their score on the positive items of the psychological well-being scale and on the net balance between its positive and negative items. Compared to other housewives, in or out of employment, they are as satisfied with their home life and more likely to say that at home they often feel relaxed, and less likely to say that they often or sometimes feel anxious.

Housewives employed part-time score favourably on several indicators in Table 7.15 by comparison with non-housewives. One exception is the positive items of the psychological well-being scale: as the columns for all respondents aged 18–24 and 35–44 show, this difference is strongly associated with age. Compared to housewives employed full-time, however, or to all men or all respondents in their own median age group, most of their scores are unfavourable. Like housewives employed full-time, they are less conscious than men of being exploited at work, and on the psychological well-being scale they score about the average for their median age group. On the other indicators in the table they score at least marginally on the unfavourable side and sometimes, as on freedom to make decisions in their work, strongly so. They are less dissatisfied with their family finances than housewives not in employment, most of whom are either in the age bracket where they are likely to be out of the labour market and relying on a single earned income or at or above retirement age: but they are dissatisfied on this by comparison with all but the youngest group of women or men in employment.

TABLE 7.15 *Work and other satisfaction – men and women*

	All men	All women	Non-housewives	All respondents aged 18–24	H'wives in employment F/T	H'wives in employment P/T	All respondents 35–44	H'wives not in employment
Percentage or scores								
Job satisfaction (score 1–10)	7.88	7.49	6.95	7.16	7.95	7.42	7.73	–
Takes a great deal of pride in work	80	77	65	61	85	75	79	–
Freedom to make decisions in work (score 1–10)	7.17	5.91	5.83	5.79	6.27	5.67	6.59	–
Often/occasionally feels exploited in work	67	61	73	69	59	57	69	–
Satisfaction with (score 1–10):								
life in general	7.77	7.57	7.10	7.25	7.94	7.55	7.72	7.59
home life	8.59	8.31	7.87	7.89	8.38	8.32	8.46	8.41
family finances	7.08	6.60	6.76	6.43	7.48	6.73	6.90	6.20
At home:								
often feels relaxed	79	69	78	74	79	65	69	64
often/sometimes feels anxious	51	70	59	53	65	75	66	73
Psychological well-being scale – Score on:								
Positive items	2.40	2.22	2.65	2.57	2.70	2.24	2.13	1.96
Negative items	1.08	1.36	1.29	1.47	1.11	1.15	1.08	1.55
Net Score	+1.42	+0.86	+1.36	+1.10	+1.59	+1.09	+1.05	+0.45

At one level, these differences in satisfaction can be explained by differences in the three groups' work situation (Table 7.16). Non-housewives, like young men of similar age, are beginners at work, and work satisfactions tend to rise with age. Housewives employed full-time are predominantly in higher skilled jobs – half in middle non-manual or professional work, only one in five in a lower-skilled manual job – whereas two-thirds of those employed part-time are in lower-skilled manual work.

It has also to be asked, however, why it is that, after young men and women start with similar levels of satisfaction, the spread of satisfactions among women opens out so sharply. Why do some women achieve the relatively satisfying mix of home and working life experienced by housewives employed full-time, whereas so many others do not? One reason is again the objective conditions of the labour market: sex discrimination is a reality, but one which the Values Study did not explore. There are also, however, reasons in women's attitudes, and on this the study has four findings.

First, men's and women's attitudes to the importance of the various features of a job diverge after marriage in a way unfavourable to women's careers. Young men and women still living with their parents express similar views on these features. The one notable difference is that the women give less weight to a job making full use of their abilities. After marriage, men tend to outscore women in interest in:–
—the dynamic features of a job
—running their own business
—pay
—taking on extra work to earn money
—job security
—holidays
—the social respect (status) and usefulness of a job.
Whereas women tend to express a stronger interest than men in pleasant people to work with, meeting people, and (at ages 25–54) good hours.

There are variations within this pattern. Women aged 18–24 and those with relatively short education and in low-skilled manual work score close to or above men on taking extra work to escape from boredom, rather than simply to earn more money. Married women in skilled manual work, on the other hand, express as much interest as married men of the same grade in pay, promotion, and status. Married women graduates have as much interest as graduate men in a

Table 7.16 *Occupational and other characteristics of housewives and non-housewives*

Occupation (previous if none current)	Non-housewives %	Housewives Employed F/T %	P/T %	Not in employment	All women %	All men %
Professional/managerial	16	24	9	7	10	16
middle non-manual	16	26	12	14	16	13
other non-manual	42	24	12	16	21	5
skilled/supervisory manual	5	5	2	15	8	37
other manual	21	21	64	47	44	26
(N/A omitted) Forces	0	0	0	1	0	2
Chief earner of household	20	28	14	31	25	82
Dynamic features of a job: average of percentages for "think important"	46	38	31	33	35	48
Member of:						
Trade Union (Q.371)	33	38	27	2	18	41
Professional Association (Q.113)	12	14	5	4	7	11
10 types of voluntary organisations						
Member of at least 1	50	59	51	39	46	58
Voluntary work for at least 1	13	28	24	20	21	16
Often/sometimes argues & persuades when holds a strong view	44	43	35	26	33	51
Frequently/occasionally discusses politics	53	67	58	47	54	74
When growing up was close to:						
Mother	59	55	68	62	62	55
Father	49	56	57	52	53	40
Educated to age 17+	46	38	21	15	24	25
Children:						
has had children	14	61	93	82	72	63
ideal number	2.45	2.22	2.46	2.44	2.41	2.40
Children are *not* very important for the success of a marriage	23	33	24	12	20	16
Parents should:						
Do their best for their children even at the expense of their own well-being	63	68	68	75	70	73
Earn their children's love and respect	44	52	37	33	38	40
Elements in children's upbringing:						
dynamism score	16	19	16	14	15	15
net score (dynamic-passive)	−31	−21	−28	−32	−29	−29

job with opportunities for initiative, and more in a job which meets their abilities. Even in the case of women with skills and higher education, however, many of the standard divergencies between married men's and married women's attitudes appear. Women graduates express less interest than men in promotion, running their own business, or taking on extra work for money, and married women in skilled manual work express less interest than similarly qualified men in responsibility, initiative, or full use of abilities.

Secondly, if marriage today were symmetrical in the sense defined by Young and Willmott (1973), with an equal division of employment and domestic commitments, one would expect the partners and especially the wives to see the equal division of household work as important for the success of their marriage. In fact, however, in the Values Study women gave this a consistently low rating (Table 7.17), and the only group of women who rated it higher than men were those still living in their parents' home.

Thirdly, at a number of points the Study suggests that hard-edged attitudes on work or work-related issues develop later among women than among men, so that women are at a disadvantage in an economy

TABLE 7.17 *Sharing household chores is very important for a successful marriage*

	Men %	Women %
Still living with parents	29	34
Married/living as married: Age		
18–24	50	34
25–34	44	31
35–44	40	36
45–54	52	28
55–64	53	43
Terminal education age		
15/16	45	35
17/18	32	17
21+	46	36
Professional/managerial	37	25
Non-manual	49	31
Skilled manual	45	26
Other manual	54	40

where career opportunities and patterns tend to be determined early in life. At age 18–24 women express much less interest than men in a job with opportunity for initiative and one which fully uses their abilities, but at age 25–34 their interest in these features of a job rises sharply and catches up with men's. Older rather than younger women take a strong line on relating pay to individual performance, and insist more strongly than men that orders at work should be explained and justified, while also upholding more strongly either than men or than younger women the existing systems of ownership and managerial authority. Married women's scores on the emphasis to be laid on dynamic qualities in bringing up their own children are in a number of cases higher in middle or older age groups, compared especially to age 18–24, and in those age groups compare better with men's on: independence, responsibility, hard work, and, so far as these are stressed at all, thrift and leadership (Table 7.18). In the case of imagination women's scores tend to drop with age, but men's scores drop even faster, so that older women outscore older men.

Last but not least, housewives employed full-time appear by comparison with those employed part-time as a select group, with special characteristics in other respects besides their higher occupational status. Current occupation may in fact be a misleading indicator of differences between the two groups, since the range of part-time jobs available is limited, and the Values Study did not ask what occupations part-time workers previously held.

Housewives employed full-time have a unique family background. They are the only group of either women or men who say that while growing up they were as close to their fathers as to their mothers. They are more highly educated than part-timers. They are more active and outgoing, in or out of their profession: more likely to be union or professional association members, to be active in these or in special interest groups, to argue and persuade where they hold a strong view, and to discuss politics. They attach more importance to the dynamic features of a job, and give greater relative weight to dynamic qualities in their own children's upbringing. They have also a different attitude to children. They are not less caring, in the sense of readiness to do their best for the children even at the expense of their own well-being. They are more likely, however, to say that they must earn their children's love and respect rather than expect it unconditionally, and less likely to say that children are very important for a successful marriage. Their ideal number of children is 2.22, compared to 2.44 to 2.46 for other groups of women. Though nine

TABLE 7.18 *Dynamic factors in children's upbringing: men and women still living with their parents or married/living as married, by age*

	Still living with parents	Percentage seeing each factor as specially important married/living as married				
		18–24	25–34	35–44	45–54	55–64
Independence:						
Men	24	28	25	19	19	8
Women	27	22	32	26	29	29
Responsibility:						
Men	19	17	25	27	27	21
Women	22	12	34	32	33	27
Determination/perseverance:						
Men	17	16	19	19	19	18
Women	15	19	16	21	17	11
Hard work:						
Men	16	20	15	16	26	19
Women	14	8	8	13	23	10
Imagination:						
Men	16	22	24	16	7	3
Women	13	17	15	10	13	7
Thrift:						
Men	4	6	2	8	7	14
Women	3	5	3	9	17	14
Leadership:						
Men	5	8	5	0	1	4
Women	2	0	0	1	15	7
Average:						
Men	14	17	16	15	15	13
Women	14	12	15	16	21	15

out of ten have been married, and the same proportion are over 25, two out of five have had no children at all. Compared to part-timers, they started higher on the road to a career, show more drive and activity, and travel lighter.

How far do the special characteristics of housewives employed full-time account for their occupational success and the satisfactions which go with it, and how far does occupational success reinforce them – for example, their outgoing and dynamic attitudes or their attitudes to children? *Prima facie* the answer is a mixture of the two, but neither in this case nor in the three others just mentioned are the Values Study findings enough for a full analysis of how present attitudes to the division of responsibilities between men and women are generated or how they might be changed.

The Values data are, however, enough to justify the proposition from which this section started. Women's own attitudes do in many ways support the 'new conventional' division of responsibilities in family and work, even though for many of them it is unsatisfactory: with the rider that there is at least one alternative pattern which, for those women who can and do attain it, proves relatively and absolutely more satisfying.

PRESENT AND FUTURE ATTITUDES TO WORK – HOW FAR WILL THE VALUES STUDY TAKE US?

The thread running through the three sections of this chapter is that, on the evidence of the Values Study, people in Britain might indeed prefer several important aspects of their working life to be otherwise than they are, but many of their attitudes are unhelpful for bringing the relevant changes about. Others have reached such conclusions by other routes. Alan Fox argues that Britain is pre-eminent as a society in which, through a long course of historical development, the points have been set for the free and independent pursuit of individual and group interest without too much regard for overall consequences. When this conflicts with, for example, the need in a highly organised modern economy for common and consistent rules for industrial relations or co-ordination of local and national bargaining procedures, the result is confusion and stalemate (Fox, 1979). Beesley and Evans similarly argue that Britain is a country with widely dispersed power in industrial matters, but low agreement, not so much on desirable objectives in policy for work – few actually want unemployment, inflation, or an industrial relations system prone to unnecessary disputes – as on the relevance of these to group and individual conduct (Beesley and Evans 1978).

To judge propositions like these, however, it is necessary to take a longer perspective than the Values Study provides. It is important once again to remember that the survey is a snapshot taken at a particular moment. There is another thesis that the low pressure, unhurried, and apparently disorganised process by which major social and economic changes are brought about in Britain is better described as polycentric and 'organic', and so in line with what is known about effective decision-making in new and complex situations. As the early studies of small groups by authors like Bales (1951) and Bavelas (1956) showed, this process is slower than that of centralised decision and at some stages seems more confused, but in solving new and complex problems is more effective in the end. There is historical evidence that, as it operates in Britain, it does in fact lead over periods of a generation or more to the identification of new issues, the unlocking of old assumptions, and the emergence of effective consensus on how the new issues are to be handled. One such period of new consensus (not the first) was the time of the foundation of the welfare state from the middle of the 1930s to the end of the 1940s. If past experience is a guide, it can be argued that the issues about economic development, or unemployment, or equal opportunity which emerged through the 1960s and 1970s needed time for a new agenda to be defined and its practical consequences worked out: but the polycentric process of debate and experiment goes on, and new and widely agreed solutions can be expected to emerge towards the end of the century.

Is past experience, however, still a useful guide, and what will be the parameters of the new solutions? Do the findings about British attitudes to work reflect constant characteristics of the British, or an intermediate stage of unfinished business when obsolescent attitudes survive but new ones are on the way, or perhaps a mixture of the two? The Values Study raises questions like these, but cannot provide answers.

8 Values and Voluntary Work

DAVID GERARD

INTRODUCTION

When the Values Study commenced, previous research into the British voluntary sector had been limited, much of it impressionistic. This general nescience was the subject of informed comment at the time (Newton, 1976; Wolfenden, 1978). Recent studies continue to remark on the lack of empirical research and coherent theory (Kramer, 1981; GHS No. 11, 1983). Although its interest in the voluntary sector was indirect – assessing correlates of altruism and service to the community – the Values Study does yield evidence about public perceptions of charity; factors influencing participation in voluntary work and the characteristics of both volunteers and beneficiaries.

PUBLIC PERCEPTIONS OF CHARITY

The Values Study reveals both a high regard for charities and a favourable view of voluntary workers. More than three-fifths of the population believe that whatever governments may do, charities will be necessary. Two-thirds believe that voluntary work should be free from governmental control and about seven out of ten regard those who undertake it as unselfish and dedicated people. Nevertheless, a significant minority (two-fifths of the population) have reservations. Half of them believe that the existence of charities enables government to avoid its social responsibilities, the other half regard volunteers as either well-meaning but misguided, or primarily solving their own problems. The dominant view of charitable work, however, is favourable, and similar attitudes prevail in the USA (Humble, 1982).

These attitudes are remarkably consistent throughout the main groups in the population, with little or no variation by age, sex or marital status. Observable differences relate to political and religious disposition and to education or occupation. Thus, those who place themselves left of centre, those who are in manual employment and those who left school at 15, are slightly less well disposed (but not hostile) towards voluntary agencies, whereas the better educated, non-manual and religious respondents (groups from which voluntary workers are typically drawn) are rather more supportive. These differences are in the main not substantial, though they are statistically significant.

As far as the desirability of government control of voluntary agencies is concerned, neither politics nor religion appear to influence opinion, though there is a suggestion of a greater preference for government supervision of activities among older people.

PARTICIPATION IN VOLUNTARY WORK

Contemporary survey evidence (Morgan *et al.*, 1977; Hatch and Mocroft, 1977; Humble, 1982; GHS No. 11, 1983) suggests that participation in voluntary work, though increasing, remains a minority activity and is correlated both with important socio-demographic indicators (middle-age, upper income and social groups, extended education) and with family composition (dependent children of school age). The participation rates of men and women appear to vary, not so much as a consequence of any differences in willingness to volunteer, but rather according to the definitions of activity used by researchers and the coverage of the enquiry – for example, whether union involvement and church affiliated groups are included or excluded (Nelson *et al.*, 1978; General Household Survey, Office of Population Censuses and Surveys [OPCS] No. 11, 1983).

Responses to the Values Study suggest that over half the adult population is in *membership* of, and about one-fifth undertakes *unpaid work* for, some form of voluntary organisation, including charities, political parties, trade-unions and professional associations but excluding sports and recreational groups. As far as charities are concerned, the proportion in membership is a little under two-fifths of the population with one-sixth donating time. With the exception of trade-union activity the commitment of time to one form of voluntary activity is associated with active involvement in other fields also, a finding confirmed by volunteers' preferences for alternatives to paid employment (compared to non-volunteers) in answer to Q.138. The EVSSG estimates are broadly consistent with the 1981 General Household Survey results though the definitions and coverage of the two enquiries differed in important respects (OPCS, 1983).

Roughly three-quarters of those in *membership* of, and five out of six of the volunteers *working for*, charities were involved in youth, welfare, and religious groups – here defined as 'old-style' charities (Gerard, 1983). The minority actively engaged in 'new-style' charities such as informal education, arts, human rights, conservation and animal welfare comprised no more than 3 per cent of the adult population.

When all forms of voluntary activity are studied, men appear more likely to be *members* than women. When charitable activity alone is examined, no significant differences emerge in membership. The distinction is, clearly, complicated by trade union membership which is no longer a voluntary act for many employees. When voluntary *work* is considered, a higher proportion of women than men is involved, and the differences are statistically significant for involvement in *charitable* activity – only one in eight men compared to one in five women acting as volunteers. Overall, women are more involved in welfare and religious organisations; men in union affairs. Similar variations are apparent from the General Household Survey which points not merely to different preferences between fields of activity but to differences in the actual nature of the work undertaken also (OPCS, 1983). Recent American studies reveal a similar pattern (Nelson *et al.*, 1978; Morgan *et al.*, 1977).

The values data confirms that volunteers tend to be busy middle-aged people with children. About 60 per cent of the voluntary workers were aged between 35–64 years, over 70 per cent were married and half of them had children aged 5–15 years. Young adults appear unlikely to be involved in voluntary activity of any kind. In fact, only 10 per cent of all volunteers in the sample fell into the 18–25 age group. It also emerged that three-fifths of young married people under 30 years of age are *not* in membership of any voluntary body, the proportion rising to seven-tenths for those in the age group with children. This appears largely explained by the lack of involvement of young housewives. The participation of males and working women is little affected by age, whereas the involvement of housewives increases after the age of 30 years, as does participation when children reach school age – events which may coincide.

The Values data point to certain interesting age differences among those taking part in charitable activity. With increasing age there is a tendency towards greater involvement in religious organisations. Only 12 per cent of the under 25 age group report membership of a religious charity compared to 46 per cent of the over 75 year olds, with steadily increasing participation in the intervening years. It is not possible to say whether these differences are due to age alone or to a secular trend resulting from generally reduced religious commitment over time, but a similar pattern is evident from the GHS and from US data (Nelson *et al.*, 1977). Although new-style charitable activity has only minority appeal, and young people are predominantly inactive, the former is nevertheless, relatively more attractive to younger age groups and to the more highly educated. In fact the sample breaks at 45 years as far as age preferences for newer and older style activities are concerned and 30 per cent of those in new-style activities had benefited from education to the age of 21 years.

The Values Study confirms the relationship between education and voluntary work reported in other studies (Morgan *et al.*, 1977; Humble, 1982; OPCS, 1983). One-fifth of all volunteers in the EVSSG sample had been educated to age 21 years compared to only 7 per cent of those not involved as volunteers. In fact, moderate correlations (Q = 0.4) exist between education and both association membership and voluntary work. Nonetheless, three-fifths of all volunteers had completed their education by the age of 16, due to the small overall proportion of the population which had benefited from further or higher studies.

Moderate correlations are similarly apparent between involvement in voluntary activity and occupation (Q = 0.35), and social class (Q = 0.46). A majority of both volunteers and members of voluntary organisations are drawn from non-manual occupations and from the upper social groups. The evidence is consistent with the conclusion of the 1983 GHS that 'those in the professional group were more than three times as likely to do voluntary work as those in the unskilled manual group' (OPCS, 1983, p. 162). In the Values Study, however, four-fifths of all volunteers fell outside the upper of the three income bands used.

THE MOTIVES OF VOLUNTARY WORKERS

Although education, income, age and social class have been found to correlate with volunteering, they account for only a small proportion of the variation in people's willingness to undertake such work – between 4 and 10 per cent, (Morgan *et al.*, 1977; Nelson *et al.*, 1978). Morgan *et al.* concluded that altruistic syndrome differences remain which we can't explain – nor indeed could their respondents, most of whom, it seemed, had never really examined their motives. The Values Study provides the opportunity to explore some of the underlying attitudes.

In so far as there is a prevailing explanatory framework for interpreting individual participation in voluntary associations it is in terms of social exchange and reciprocal benefit. To the extent that such explanations are based on crude exchange theory, such as Homans (1962), they appear an inadequate account of the variety of human motives. A reliance on the reciprocity/social exchange perspective also suffers from other disadvantages. First, it tends to be rooted in a 'subjective' rather than 'objective' view of morality and appears to embody the emotivist perspective and its accompanying 'modes of practice ... which involve us in manipulative relationships with others', that MacIntyre argues have come to characterise the contemporary moral view (MacIntyre, 1981, p.66). It will be argued that a majority of volunteers are more likely to hold an *objective* moral view, deriving either from Kantian notions of duty and acts of will (Nagel, 1970; Collard, 1978) or from a teleological moral tradition within a framework of theistic beliefs.

Second, as Blau and Gouldner have recognised, the application of notions of exchange to all social conduct becomes tautological. The concept, therefore, needs to be restricted to those actions which are *contingent* upon some reciprocal benefit (Blau, 1964; Gouldner, 1973). Clearly, much helping behaviour falls outside this definition.

Third, where empirical studies have employed notions of reciprocity and exchange in the voluntary sector, researchers have found it necessary to retain the concept of altruism also (Abrams, 1979; Qureshi *et al.*, 1983; Mostyn, 1983). Finally, as noted in Chapter 3, the possessive individualism, mobility and anonymity characteristic of urban societies raise the opportunity cost of time devoted to others and make it difficult to place notions of reciprocal obligation within a context that has meaning for individuals (Abrams, 1978; Hirsch,

1977) with consequent implications for participation in voluntary work.

This is not to deny that reciprocal benefits are relevant in volunteer motivation. The reciprocal element may imply no more than an openness to another's giving, the value of expressions of gratitude, or the accordance of respect, in helping to sustain voluntary activity in the face of high personal costs. For some it may extend to include certain instrumental benefits such as access to training opportunities and for a minority may serve as a vehicle for more serious material, social or political ends. Nonetheless, for the above reasons it seems unwise to accord to reciprocity paramount status in explaining motives for voluntary action. Other, more specifically altruistic, norms are of equal relevance and should be incorporated into the analytical framework. For present purposes, therefore, three norms underpinning voluntary action will be distinguished. These are reciprocity, beneficence and solidarity.

Reciprocity demands that people should help and should not injure those who have helped them. Beneficence calls upon people voluntarily to give something for nothing in response to the need and condition of others. It stems from a moral view which stresses notions of duty and compassion, frequently associated, Gouldner suggests, with religious values, supernatural sanctions or some form of moral absolutism (Gouldner, 1973). Solidarity, in contrast, entails notions of fraternity and identity with the deprived, and attends to the assumed causes of inequality (Gerard, 1983). Whereas beneficence accepts inequality as in some sense 'given', and sustains the social order, solidarity is typically concerned with political and social change.

Essentially, therefore, reciprocity is an *exchange* relationship based upon what the recipient *does* or *offers*, not upon what he *is*; beneficence is a hierarchical relationship of *dependency* based upon what the recipient *is* and not what he *does*; solidarity is a relationship involving *identification* with someone seen as of equal worth and based ultimately upon a view of other persons as an *extension of oneself*.

The three norms are interwoven with each other and share elements in common. Yet, they entail different levels of cost to the donor and appeal to increasingly smaller minorities as the focus moves from reciprocity, to beneficence, to solidarity. Further, each norm is associated with a particular form of institutional expression: reciprocity to mutual aid agencies; beneficence to social-order based charities; solidarity to agencies devoted to social change. These distinctions are likely to be reflected both in the activity preferences of volunteers and in the 'philosophy-of-operation' of the organisations for which they choose to work (Gerard, 1983).

THE CHARACTERISTICS OF VOLUNTEERS

The collapse of community, its replacement by a large-scale, insensitive, instrumental/rational social system (Wilson, 1982), the related isolation, self-absorption and manipulative social relations characteristic of the 'decline into emotivism' (MacIntyre, 1981), the market morality and 'possessive individualism' evident in economic life (Abrams, 1978; Hirsch, 1977) all suggest that a willingness formally to engage in institutionalised voluntary work will be characteristic of a minority. This minority, it is suggested, will tend to be unrepresentative in its values and beliefs: more trusting, more altruistic. Further, volunteers are, it is suggested, more likely than the population at large to emphasise and exhibit objective moral standards in their behaviour (Nagel, 1970; MacIntyre, 1981); to stress notions of duty and empathy (Gouldner, 1973; MacIntyre, 1981; Abrams, 1978); to be members of a moral community (Abrams, 1979) which in view of its 'ethic of concern' (Barclay, 1971) will, typically, be Christian (Abrams, 1981; Gouldner, 1973). In view of their objective moral perspective volunteers will tend to find greater meaning in life (Gouldner, 1973).

Turning to the survey findings it is clear that only a minority of the population believes that people are as, or more, willing to help each other (Q.119) than a decade age. Three-quarters of non-volunteers believe them to be less willing, as do three-fifths of volunteers; Americans are even more pessimistic (Roper Center, 1982). Similarly, four-fifths reject the notion that people are 'basically good' (Q.149) perceiving both good and evil in everyone, and those who believe most people can be trusted (Q.124) are in a minority (43 per cent). No more than one-third would be willing to sacrifice their lives for any person or cause beyond their immediate family.

Taking the latter issue as an indicator of altruism, then, as Table 8.1 illustrates, voluntary workers emerge as having a significantly more favourable view of other people, are more trusting, and more willing in principle to consider the ultimate personal sacrifice.

As far as Christian conviction is concerned, the enduring import-

TABLE 8.1   *Characteristics of volunteers, compared to non-volunteers*

Attitudes towards other people	Percentage reporting attitude/value or belief		
	Voluntary workers	All others	Correlation
Everyone basically good	25	17	0.24
Most people trustworthy	52	40	0.24
People as/more helpful than 10 years ago	40	25	0.33
Willing to sacrifice life itself	52	30	0.43
Religious commitment			
Perceive self as religious person	71	54	0.35
Believe in life after death	65	41	0.46
Attend church at least monthly	51	16	0.60
Gain comfort and strength from religion	69	40	0.54
Have had profound religious experience	30	17	0.35
Indicators of reflectiveness:			
Often think about the meaning of life	45	31	0.29
Often/sometimes think about death	67	56	0.23
Pray, meditate, contemplate	70	45	0.48
Attitude to material factors Importance to successful marriage of:			
good housing	38	52	−0.28
adequate income	38	49	−0.22
Desirable future changes:			
less emphasis on money and possessions	76	59	0.38
Important aspect of job:			
good pay	49	62	−0.26
N=	230	1001	−

ance of religious motivation in all forms of voluntary activity is among the most striking results of this study. Over 70 per cent of all volunteers describe themselves as 'a religious person' and over 50 per cent attend church at least monthly. About a third report having had a profound religious experience, compared to less than one-fifth of the remaining population. Table 8.1 provides indicators of the extent of religious commitment among volunteers. These findings are consistent both with Abrams' results concerning the importance of religious motivation in UK neighbourhood care and with recent American survey data (Abrams, 1981; Research & Forecasts, 1982). In the latter case only 6 per cent of those with minimal levels of religious commitment reported frequent volunteer work compared to 38 per cent of those with the highest levels.

Those who undertake voluntary *work* (of all kinds) emerge as more active churchgoers than *members* of the voluntary bodies they serve (37 per cent of whom attend church monthly). Significantly, those who are neither volunteers nor in membership of any type of voluntary association appear least active, only 7 per cent attending church once a month or more.

When the 230 volunteers in the total sample are split between the ten Voluntary Activity categories used in the study, the numbers are such that firm conclusions cannot be drawn. Nonetheless, in only two categories, trade unions and conservation/animals, were regular churchgoers a minority among volunteers. Given the above findings, religious conviction emerges as potentially an important general explanatory variable affecting motivation towards voluntary work.

The religious orientation of volunteers is reflected in their social attitudes and values. Voluntary workers are firmly committed to marriage and the institution of the family. They adopt similar views to others about factors leading to success or breakdown in marriage, though with slightly greater emphasis on the need for respect and tolerance between husband and wife and rather less on material factors – such differences being however on the borderline of statistical significance. They appear more likely to share the social attitudes of their partners than of other people, as did their parents before them. They are more likely to insist upon the importance of a stable family unit for children to grow up in, to favour tolerance, respect and religious faith as values to develop in children and to disagree (Q.247) more strongly (72 per cent) with the notion that people should have the chance to enjoy unrestricted sexual freedom (compared to 55 per cent of other respondents).

Voluntary workers also tend to adopt, as hypothesised, a stricter interpretation than others on a range of social and moral issues. Respondents were asked to indicate (Q.315) whether certain forms of conduct were justified, using a 10-point scale. On a wide range of issues concerned with social morality and with offences against persons, property and the state, volunteers emerged with consistently

TABLE 8.2 *Justifiable social conduct: voluntary workers and others compared*

Form of conduct	Average score for group on 10-point scale		
	Voluntary workers Mean score	All others Mean score	Significance level
Claiming State benefits unentitled	0.46	0.72	0.01
Avoding fare on public transport	0.78	1.12	0.01
Cheating on tax	1.13	1.81	0.001
Buying stolen goods	0.41	0.97	0.001
Lying in own interest	1.29	1.82	0.001
Married men/women having an affair	1.27	1.57	0.05
Sex under age of consent	0.53	0.82	0.01
Accepting a bribe	0.45	0.65	0.05
Divorce	3.55	4.05	0.05
Fighting with the police	0.56	0.77	0.05
Euthanasia	2.83	3.48	0.01
Suicide	1.46	1.79	0.05
Failing to report accidental damage to parked vehicle	0.94	1.42	0.001
Killing in self-defence	3.94	4.42	0.05

NOTE: The EVSSG scale runs from 1 to 10, the above scores have been adjusted to run from 0–9 for ease of comparison.

lower scores than others. Table 8.2 summarises the main results. On thirteen out of the twenty-two issues considered (three-fifths of the total), volunteers differed significantly in their scores from other respondents. This is especially true of matters relating to personal honesty – a correlate, it has been suggested, of maturity (Maslow, 1973).

Voluntary workers in all fields – charitable and non-charitable – appear to be more reflective in disposition and less concerned with material aspects of life than others not so involved (see Table 8.1).

Volunteers express a greater need for moments of contemplation, meditation or prayer in their lives, think more often about the meaning and purpose of life, are, as Gouldner suggested, more likely to find meaning in life and also to reflect more frequently on death.

There is a suggestion in the data that voluntary workers may be less concerned with the material aspects of life than other people. This suggestion arises from responses to three different sets of questions in the Values Study concerning family, work and social issues.

First, in considering the elements necessary for a successful marriage (Q.248), volunteers give a lower ranking to good housing and relatively less emphasis to adequate income, than other respondents. Second, among the social issues respondents were asked to consider, was a question (Q.308) concerning their attitudes to a number of possible changes in the near future, among which was the possibility that less emphasis might come to be placed on money and material possessions. Volunteers were more likely to endorse such a development. Finally, volunteers tend to give lower priority to 'good pay' as an important aspect of a job, ranking it seventh in importance compared to third among non-volunteers.

In interpreting these findings it is important to take account of the relatively more comfortable position of voluntary workers compared to others. The majority are in the upper half of the social scale, over two-thirds own their own homes (compared to a little over half of other respondents), and they are relatively satisfied with the financial position of their household. Controlling for the influence of social class suggests that while socioeconomic status has some effect on attitudes to housing and income as important elements in a successful marriage, it does not explain attitudes to pay or the desire to see society place less emphasis on money and material possessions in future.

IMPLICATIONS FOR PSYCHOLOGICAL WELL-BEING

Aside from the dictates of prudence and common sense as determinants of co-operative behaviour (Downie, 1971; Hart, 1961) and related evidence from biological and cultural evolution (Thorpe, 1974; Montague, 1976; Crook, 1980), the need for human beings to 'belong', to 'relate' and to 'love' each other as essential conditions of maturity and fulfilment, forms a key part of the various needs theories developed by psychiatrists and clinical psychologists, particularly of the humanist school (Fromm, 1955; Maslow, 1970). Such theories have been criticised, both as empty and confused on philosophical grounds (Peters, 1959), and as formulated in ways which are difficult to test and evaluate by social scientists (Hall and

Nougaim, 1968). Significantly however, both philosophers and social scientists tend to accept the importance of the need for warm, affectionate and co-operative relationships with other people (Wahba and Bridwell, 1976; Alderfer, 1969; Benn and Peters, 1959). Indeed, the clinical psychologist Maslow concluded that 'the best helpers are the most fully human persons' (Maslow, 1973, p. 364).

Whilst the empirical evidence is limited, both the comprehensive review of the literature of altruism by Krebs (Krebs, 1970) and Bradburn's studies of psychological well-being in the USA (Bradburn, 1969), indicate a positive association between social participation, altruism and psychological well-being. The Values Study included the Bradburn Affect Balance Scale. It is possible, therefore, to assess a level of psychological well-being exhibited by volunteers and to test two propositions, derived from the clinical insights of the psychologists referred to and from Bradburn's own studies in the USA. These are that volunteers should score more highly on measures of psychological well-being than others in the population not involved in voluntary work, and that volunteers' scores on the Bradburn Affect Balance Scale will be principally the result of reportedly higher levels of 'positive' experience rather than lower levels of 'negative' occurrences.

The voluntary workers surveyed reported better health and a greater preference for active pursuits; were less likely to spend long periods watching T.V. than other respondents. On the basis of the interviewers' own assessment, they emerged as more self-assured. Voluntary workers similarly felt a greater degree of domestic financial security and reported less anxiety about the future than those not involved in voluntary activity. They were less likely to view life as 'often meaningless', more likely to be 'often happy' at home.

In all the above instances the reported differences between voluntary workers and other respondents were statistically significant. On a range of other quality-of-life indicators related to subjective feelings of happiness, loneliness and satisfaction, voluntary workers consistently scored higher than others, though the differences were not statistically significant.

Overall, the findings do suggest the possibility of a higher level of psychological well-being among volunteers. Responses on the Bradburn Scale confirm this (Table 8.3) and, as expected, suggest that it is principally due to higher levels of positive experience. However, 'positive affect' is a correlate of both socioeconomic status and extended education, as is participation in voluntary work. It is necessary, therefore, to control for the influence of education and

TABLE 8.3 *Psychological well-being: voluntary workers and others compared, using the Bradburn Affect scale*

Dimension	Average score for group		
	Voluntary workers	Others	Significance level
	Score	Score	
Positive affect	3.00	2.55	0.001
Negative affect	1.06	1.26	0.05
Affect balance	1.94	1.29	0.001

social class on volunteers' psychological well-being. The results (Table 8.4) both confirm the significantly higher overall scores of volunteers and provide a number of other interesting comparisons.

Summarising, in the wider population, excluding volunteers, the expected correlation between extended education and higher levels of psychological well-being is confirmed. Among volunteers, however, no such difference is apparent. The volunteer with a low terminal education age exhibits a significantly higher level of psychological well-being than the non-volunteer of similar educational background, and an equally high level of psychological well-being to those with benefit of an extended education.

The picture emerging from the analysis of social class is similar to the findings for education. Highly significant social class differences in psychological well-being are apparent in the wider population but not among volunteers. Voluntary workers differ significantly from non-volunteers in both the upper and lower social groups; volunteers in the lower social group exhibit levels of psychological well-being equivalent to non-volunteers in the upper social group.

The conclusions from the above analysis involving the use of education and social class as control variables support the propositions put forward and suggest that the issue is worthy of further investigation.

POLITICAL ACTIVISM

Data from the Values Study throws light on the question of political activism and pressure group activity by charitable organisations. The demand for a higher degree of freedom for charities to engage in

TABLE 8.4 *Psychological well-being, controlling for education and social class: voluntary workers and others compared*

Bradburn Scale	Terminal education age				Social class			
	Under 18 yrs		18 yrs and over		ABC1		C2DE	
	Volunteers	Others	Volunteers	Others	Volunteers	Others	Volunteers	Others
Positive score	2.99	2.47	3.01	3.02	3.14	2.76	2.81	2.45
Standard error	0.128	0.051	0.186	0.127	0.132	0.084	0.170	0.058
Significance level		0.001		NS		0.05		0.05
Negative score	1.06	1.26	1.07	1.27	0.96	0.10	1.19	1.34
Standard error	0.093	0.045	0.137	0.103	0.091	0.068	0.129	0.052
Significance level		0.5		NS		NS		NS
Affect balance	1.93	1.21	1.94	1.75	2.18	1.66	1.62	1.11
Standard error	0.159	0.071	0.223	0.153	0.156	0.110	0.215	0.080
Significance level		0.001		NS		0.000		0.05
N =	161	855	69	146	129	339	101	663

political activity appears to have been over-estimated. Charity Law, based on a norm of beneficence and developed on the basis of the trust form, explicitly recognises and sustains the religious and moral values associated with the old-style, social-order, model of organisation; a conservative, hierarchical view of society and service-based activity. Judges, furthermore, are reluctant to distort the original intentions of donors in changing economic and social circumstances (Gerard, 1983). A social-change model of voluntary organisation is difficult to accommodate to the norm of beneficence. In reality it is based on a rejection of 'charity' in favour of an 'identity with' the deprived; social equality and individual rights. Secular and participative; critical of the conservative value base of the established law and anxious to effect structural change; its values, priorities and 'new-style' methods cannot really be handled within the framework of law developed to operationalise the norm of beneficence. Hence the difficulties relating to attempts to qualify for the privileges of charity whilst rejecting the operational restrictions and perspective which accompany the definition of charity in law. Given the concentration of volunteer effort in 'old-style' beneficence-based service activities, it is to be expected that a majority of volunteers will not be seeking an active political role; political activism will be a minority activity largely confined to those involved with new-style solidarity-based organisations.

As Phillips makes clear in Chapter 6, the politically active proportion of the population is very low – only 5 per cent of the total. The Values data reveals, however, that of this small minority, more than three-fifths are members of voluntary organisations and over two-fifths are also active as volunteers. The fact that political activists are a small minority of members and little more than one-tenth of all volunteers, yet over-represented in the voluntary sector as a whole, may help to account for the demand for greater freedom for charities to engage in politics (which an active minority can voice) and also the very low degree of organisational involvement in politics reported in charities – due to relative lack of interest among the majority of workers and supporters (Gerard, 1983).

The interest of voluntary workers in political issues is manifested both in a tendency to engage in political discussion more frequently than others and in a higher overall affiliation to political parties (Table 8.5). With the single modest exception of signing petitions they are, however, no more likely than others to take part in protests, demonstrations or boycotts, and an overwhelming majority (95 per cent or more) reject violent protest, including damage to property.

TABLE 8.5 *Political participation and voluntary work*

Political involvement	Percentage reporting involvement		
	Voluntary workers	*All others*	*Correlation*
Active interest	11	3	0.60
Never discuss politics	28	38	−0.22
Identify with particular party: any party			
of which:	31	18	0.34
Conservative	15	7	0.40
Labour	8	8	N.S.
N =	230	1001	1231

Almost one-third of voluntary workers consider themselves close to a political party, compared to about one-fifth of the remaining population. Of those that do identify with a given party, 50 per cent are Conservative and about 30 per cent are Labour. The over-representation of Conservatives is not manifested, however, in any statistically significant differences between the volunteer sample and non-volunteers on the left-right scale included in the study, nor in a right wing response to the question concerning people's view of society (Q.276).

Volunteers do endorse law and order – a general priority in the English sample – more strongly than others (Q.277) yet, at the same time, exhibit a more compassionate attitude to imprisonment (Q.279) emphasising education rather than punishment. They are more willing than others to tolerate as neigbours individuals with a criminal record (Q.120). They also appear to have greater confidence in the church as an institution and less in trade unions than other people (Q.349).

Members of voluntary organisations share a similar perspective to voluntary workers. As anticipated, the data suggests a degree of politically related preference for involvement in particular activities. Those who place themselves right of centre appear more likely to favour 'old' style charitable organisations, with those on the left favouring 'newer' style activity and trade unions. Involvement in political, conservation and professional associations, however, appears largely independent of political perspective. Indeed participation in conservation and animal charities is not correlated with the political and religious variables associated with other forms of charitable work and may tap different values – a view consistent with other studies (Cotgrove and Duff, 1981). The general conclusion, therefore, is of a moderate-reformist political disposition among volunteers, with a very slight tendency towards conservatism.

RESOURCE ALLOCATION: WHO BENEFITS?

The question of resource allocation, both to and by charities, has been the subject of informed comment in recent years (Wolfenden, 1978; Austin and Posnett, 1979; Charities Aid Foundation, 1983). The Values Study helps to throw light on one aspect of the problem, that is the nature of the beneficiaries of charity.

The importance of the Tudor period in establishing the framework of charity law is generally acknowledged. Significant distortions introduced into the operation of charity law by the courts since Tudor times (Chesterman, 1979; Keeton and Sheridan, 1971) have, however, so broadened the concept of 'charity' that the original unifying purpose – to relieve poverty and ease the financial burden on the State – has been lost. Indeed, since Lord MacNaughten's judgement in the 1891 Pemsel case it can be argued that charitable resources are unlikely to be directed primarily at meeting the needs of the deprived, but, rather, benefit rich and poor alike; indeed, given the general relevance of the norm of reciprocity as a subsidiary factor in volunteer motivation, it is likely that volunteers themselves will emerge as an important class of beneficiaries.

The Study enquired (Q.D.) whether respondents had ever personally sought, or been offered, financial assistance, practical help, advice, information or counselling from a charitabe organisation. The results indicate that about one-fifth of the population has benefited in some way from the activities of charitable organisations. One in ten reports financial help, and similar proportions report either practical help or advice and counselling support; some individuals clearly benefiting from more than one service.

Detailed examination (Table 8.6) of the results suggests that charities do not positively discriminate in favour of those groups which – on the basis of demographic and other indicators in the survey – are most likely to be in need, such as the poor, the unemployed, the elderly, the widowed and families with young children (Fiegehen *et al.*, 1977). Conversely, those who received no benefit at all, mirror in their distribution the main economic, social and demographic groupings in society.

TABLE 8.6 *Beneficiaries of charitable organisations, analysed by income, occupation, marital status, age and age of children*

Analysis group	Form of assistance			N
	Financial	Practical	Advice/ counselling	
	%	%	%	
Income group:				
Upper	11	11	11	166
Middle	10	11	12	407
Lower	10	13	11	332
Occupation group:				
Manual	8	6	8	367
Non-manual	11	12	11	314
Unemployed	6	5	6	70
All others	11	14	11	479
Education to:				
17 years & over	13	14	17	302
16 years & over	9	9	8	929
Age group:				
18–34 years	10	10	12	450
35–64 years	9	9	9	572
65 & over	10	12	8	209
Marital status:				
Single	7	10	10	251
Married	10	9	9	806
Widowed	8	12	7	109
Divorced/separated/ cohabiting	22	22	28	64
Childrens' age:				
Under 5 years	8	6	10	178
5 years & over	10	10	12	322
Happiness:				
Unhappy	22	12	13	57
Others	9	10	10	1174
Loneliness:				
Frequently lonely	10	19	16	92
Others	9	9	10	1139
All charity volunteers	13	20	14	210
All not involved in charity	9	8	9	1021
Total sample	10	10	10	1231

Others in need of help, for example those who may be suffering emotional problems (indicated by such things as unhappiness, loneliness, dissatisfaction and lack of meaning in life) do not emerge as significantly more likely to benefit from the activities of charities. Exceptions to the general picture exist with regard to financial help for the unhappy, practical help for the lonely and significantly greater amounts of all forms of assistance for those divorced, separated and cohabiting. All three groups are small and the results need to be treated with caution. The results suggest, however, that charities may be better at directing help to those emotionally at a low ebb than to the materially disadvantaged. One relatively privileged group does appear to benefit. Those educated to 21 years or over report relatively high levels of counselling or advice – over one-fifth obtaining such assistance.

Finally, the results indicate that volunteers do benefit from charities (though not necessarily those they work for). A moderate correlation (Q = 0.48) exists between working as a volunteer for charity and receiving practical benefits. Examining the breakdown between the various categories of activity, it would appear that those engaged in old-style charitable work benefit more than the minority in new-style agencies though this may be due to the overwhelming predominance of the former group.

Given the characteristics associated with the disposition to give time, that is to say trust, altruism and religious commitment; given also volunteers' relatively higher levels of mental health and lower concern for material well-being, it seems unlikely that the benefits accruing to volunteers are the result of deliberate self-seeking. Clearly, those working in the voluntary sector may be better informed of the possibility of help if and when they need it, and in view of their occupational and social class backgrounds may be better able to obtain it. Again, some enter the field precisely because they have *been* helped or have experienced problems within their own network of family and friends. One example would be self-help groups for single parents. Another example would be the experience of, or close contact with, physical or mental handicap, leading to participation in the organisation and development of support services. It is worth noting in this connection that an assessment of assistance to the handicapped is not possible from the Values Study data and that practical help would be an important component of such assistance. The evidence, as it stands, is capable of more than one interpretation. It may be the case that the personal qualities associated with a disposition to give are similarly associated with a disposition to receive. Such a disposition, together with the type of reciprocal exchanges implied by the other examples above, may account for the association between volunteering and practical benefit from charity services. What is clear is that tangible benefits do flow to volunteers, in addition to psychological rewards.

FACTORS AFFECTING PARTICIPATION IN VOLUNTARY WORK

In the preceding sections, a range of factors has been shown to be particularly associated with participation in voluntary work. It is possible, using multiple regression techniques, to assess the relative importance of these factors and their contribution to the explanation of variations in voluntary work. Standardised regression co efficients are listed in order of significance in Table 8.7 and indicate the likely percentage increase or decrease in volunteers given a 1 per cent change in each predictor variable.

A number of conclusions emerge from the analysis. First, education, age and income – which have emerged as predictors in other studies (Morgan *et al.*, 1977) are absent, though the variable 'dependent school-age children', indicative of age, is present. Second, the importance of religious factors in the motivation to voluntary work is confirmed – in fact, attendance at religious services accounts for 12 per cent of the variance in volunteering. Third, trust does not feature as a key predictor, but indicators of psychological well-being, altruism and attitudes to material well-being are relevant factors in this respect. Finally, an active interest in politics is confirmed as positively

TABLE 8.7 *Factors affecting participation in voluntary work*

	Predictor variables (in order of significance)	Beta coefficients
1.	Attendance at religious services at least once a month	0.22
2.	Social class ABC1	0.09
3.	Believe religious faith an important value to develop in children	0.10
4.	Felt bored in past few weeks	−0.10
5.	Take an active interest in politics	0.10
6.	Gain comfort and strength from religion	0.10
7.	Have confidence in trade unions	−0.08
8.	Willing to consider sacrificing life for cause apart from family)	0.07
9.	Believe good housing important to a successful marriage	−0.07
10.	Less emphasis on money and material possessions would be a good thing	0.07
11.	Felt proud because complimented about something done in past few weeks	0.06
12.	Have children aged 11–15 years	0.07

influencing volunteering, whereas confidence in trade unions is negatively associated with participation in voluntary work.

The above variables interact with each other. These interactions tend to underline the importance of religious motivation which, to a degree, can act as a compensating factor influencing participation among those with a negative score on certain indicators of psychological well-being. The results explain about 20 per cent of the variance in volunteering overall, compared to between 4 per cent and 10 per cent reported in other studies (Morgan *et al.*, 1977; Nelson *et al.*, 1978).

Volunteers differ among themselves to the degree that they are attached to new or old-style activities, though remaining closer to each other than to the general population. The characteristics exhibited by the *majority* of volunteers are more particularly correlates of the norm of beneficence associated with a preference for old-style charitable activity. A *minority* of volunteers, typically educated and/or young (Levitt, 1973) will, it is suggested, reject charity; be more influenced by the contemporary relativist moral perspective; stress political and social values, the importance of rights, protest and moral autonomy (MacIntyre, 1981); and the necessity for structural change. They will emphasise solidarity and adopt more permissive attitudes to social behaviour.

Given the hypothesis that different factors are relevant in the motivation to work for old and new-style agencies, an attempt can be made, using both multiple regression and discriminant analysis to assess those factors which appear particularly significant in each case and to test how accurately they can be used to predict whether individuals will volunteer or not. Three types of charitable organisation are distinguished for the purpose:

—old-style excluding religion (i.e. welfare and youthwork);
—religious groups;
—new-style (education/arts; human rights; conservation/animals).

In addition, a separate analysis is undertaken for all charities except religious groups.

Despite limitations in the range of charitable activities covered in the survey, the results are revealing. Table 8.8 sets out, for each of the sub-groups, those factors identified from among all significant correlates of volunteering as the best predictors of old and new-style activities.

TABLE 8.8 *Predictor variables & Beta coefficients for main sub-groups of voluntary activity*

	All vols (except religion)	Old-style	New-style	Religious groups
Gain comfort and strength from religion	0.15	0.10	0.09	
Religious faith important for children	0.08	0.07		0.23
Believe in life after death		0.06		
Attend church monthly				0.17
Politically active	0.09		0.11	
Social class AB	0.08	0.09	0.06	
Have felt bored in last few weeks	−0.11	−0.09	−0.07	
Excited			0.08	
Upset			0.07	
Have felt 'on top of the world' in past weeks				0.07
Willing to sacrifice life for others	0.10	0.08		
Believe people basically good			0.07	
Most people trustworthy		0.06		
Good housing important in marriage	−0.07	−0.07		−0.09
Less emphasis on money etc. desirable	0.07			
Good pay important in job		−0.07		
Have had a 'peak experience'				−0.08
Often think about meaning of life				0.08
Abortion favoured	0.08		0.06	
Suicide justified			0.07	
Lying in own interest justified				−0.07
Children aged 5–15 yrs.	0.07			0.05
Percentage of variance explained	11	8	8	20

The results confirm the general importance of both religious motivation and indicators of psychological well-being for participation in all forms of voluntary work. As expected, they confirm the significance of political activism for new-style (solidarity based) activity and also its absence as an important predictor of old-style charity (and the associated norm of beneficence). Finally, the findings are indicative of the relatively stricter interpretation of moral standards associated with beneficence, not so much through their emergence as predictors of old-style activity, but rather through the confirmation of permissive social attitudes as predictive of new-style activity.

Of the three main sub-groups, the largest, *old-style* activity, exhibits a majority of the hypothesised correlates of volunteering as key predictors, such as religious conviction; high social class; an emphasis on altruism and trust in others, and a lack of stress on material factors. Psychological well-being is also relevant, the key factor being the absence of negative affect (specifically boredom), indicative perhaps of an active disposition.

For the *new-style* group, political activism and permissive social attitudes are important predictive factors, but religious conviction is not unimportant. In view of the link between material standards and social justice, the fact that new-style volunteers do not exhibit the less materialistic perspective of other charity workers is not unexpected. Also relevant for the new-style group is a belief in the basic goodness of other people; an attitude which may be associated with the notion of identity which, it has been suggested, is central to the norm of solidarity.

Important interactions occur between a number of the above factors affecting participation in new-style voluntary activity. Thus, among social group AB, religious conviction, political activism and positive psychological well-being (excitement) reinforce each other (beta coefficient 0.26). When one of these is absent the coefficient is reduced, psychological well-being apparently being of greater relative importance than religious conviction. For other social groups such an interaction is not apparent, political activism alone emerging as the dominant factor. The relationship between indicators of psychological well-being and participation in new-style activity is interesting. A negative relationship between 'boredom' and participation in voluntary work, and a positive relationship between 'excitement' and such involvement is not surprising. What *is* surprising is the emergence of an indicator of negative affect (having been 'upset' recently) as predictive of participation in new-style activity.

The picture which emerges of those involved in new-style agencies is of an activist, emotionally sensitive minority, holding progressive social values and a belief in the goodness of others. However, the new-style group may not be homogeneous for, as has been seen, those involved in conservation and animal groups may differ in important ways from other volunteers.

Positive psychological well-being, a lack of emphasis on material standards and a reflective disposition emerge as important predictors of involvement in *religious* groups. What is surprising, however, is the negative influence of 'peak experience' (a profound spiritual or psychological experience) on work for religious groups. As with new-style activity, there are interactions among the factors affecting participation in religious groups. Lack of emphasis on material standards and indicators of religious conviction reinforce each other in the absence of a 'peak experience' (beta coefficient 0.43), but in all cases in which indicators of participation are present, together with evidence of peak experience the beta coefficient is reduced.

Having identified the factors influencing participation in the various forms of voluntary work, discriminant analysis was then applied to test the success with which the selected variables effectively discriminated between volunteers and non-volunteers. The technique combines the discriminating variables into a linear function which will maximise the separation of two (or more) groups – in this case volunteers and non-volunteers – along a continuum, with volunteers clustered at one end of the spectrum and non-volunteers at the other. Each case is assigned to its group on the basis of probability and the analysis illustrates the accuracy of the discriminant function by indicating the percentage of grouped cases correctly classified. As can be seen from Table 8.9, the factors identified do discriminate quite effectively between volunteers and non-volunteers in each of the main sub-groups.

Inspection of the data reveals that what the predictive factors are able to do quite accurately is to discriminate between non-volunteers and *potential* volunteers. Only a minority of the latter group will, for various reasons, be active at any given time as Table 8.10 illustrates.

Table 8.9 *Percentage of volunteers grouped by activity correctly classified*

Old-style (excluding religion)	New style	Religious groups	All volunteers (excluding religion)
73	89	90	72

TABLE 8.10 *Percentage of volunteers and non-volunteers, grouped by activity*

	Activity category			
Predicted group	Old style	New style	Religious	All volunteers (except religious)
Non-volunteers	95	99	98	94
Volunteers	25	17	33	28

Clearly, whereas the ability to predict non-volunteers is very accurate, the proportion of those who *possess* the characteristics associated with voluntary work within the various sub-groups, and *are actually undertaking* it is low. A number of reasons might be responsible for this, including age; opportunity; or participation in informal rather than formal care arrangements.

As has been seen, the peak period for *formal* voluntary work (the data relates only to work for formal organisations) is during the middle years. Young people aged 18–25 years are relatively uninvolved. The participation of housewives increases after the age of 30 years and when children are of school age.

Family and work commitments and the attitude of spouses may well diminish opportunities for those who might wish to be involved. Further, there is evidence both from the UK and the USA that the entry into voluntary work is primarily in response to personal approaches from family, friends, and neighbours, or through experiences and activities related to the needs of family and children. Direct initiatives to seek out voluntary work uninvited are much rarer.

Thirdly, given the association between informal care and work for formal organisations (Axelrod, 1956; SCPR, 1982; Morgan *et al.*, 1977) it may be that a proportion of the potential volunteer labour force is, in fact, active in the informal sector rather than currently involved in established charities. It is suggested that the potential significance of the above findings would warrant further investigation.

Finally, the distinction between *non*-volunteers and *potential* volunteers in the sample does provide the opportunity to indicate the likely limits to the recruitment of volunteers to broad categories of activity, an issue of some current interest. The figures shown in Table 8.11 provide only a crude approximation, based on a comparison of potential volunteers with the relevant sample total, and there is a degree of overlap between categories. Nevertheless, the data suggest

TABLE 8.11 *Percentage of total adult population comprising the potential volunteer work force, by category of activity*

Old style (excluding religion)	New style	Religious	All volunteers (excluding religion)
31	11	12	33

that only about one-third of the adult population is likely to be attracted to voluntary work for formal organisations (excluding religious groups). Within this group, new-style activity will, as expected, have minority appeal and the prevailing interest will be in old-style activity. As has been seen, however, various constraints will reduce the proportion of active volunteers well below the theoretical ceiling.

9 Values and the Nature of Psychological Well-being

STEPHEN HARDING

INTRODUCTION

This chapter examines the role of individual psychological factors, with particular reference to life circumstances and emotional experiences contributing towards positive mental health, happiness or well-being. (Happiness and well-being are frequently used synonymously in the research literature). How much are they valued by people? Are people frequently upset, pleased, excited, lonely? How much do these emotions affect the overall level of satisfaction with life? How much do different life experiences, a satisfying job, a happy home life, or loss of a spouse, affect a person's psychological state? These are some of the questions which data from the European Values Survey lead us to address.

Psychologists with an interest in emotional experiences have devoted more attention to negative states, depression, anxiety, and more severe emotional and personality disorders, than they have to 'positive mental health' (cf. Jahoda, 1958). This is understandable, given the need to find suitable treatments for these often incapacitating conditions; but should we conclude that a state of psychological well-being is nothing more than the absence of psychopathology? It is surely significant that we may be able to recall times of great happiness in our lives, which we would be loath to describe simply in terms of the absence of negative emotions.

The 'humanistic' approach in psychology, pioneered by Carl Rogers, Fritz Perls and Abraham Maslow, focused attention on the development of the self, and on the enhancement of well-being through positive emotional experiences and life events. This largely qualitative approach can take a quantified form, especially for social scientists involved in national surveys aimed at assessing subjective correlates of 'quality of life' (e.g. Abrams, 1973; Andrews and Withey, 1976; Szalai and Andrews, 1983). These researchers have pointed to the need for a more global conceptualisation of well-being encapsulating negative and positive emotional states, and a detailed subjective evaluation of the circumstances in which an individual is living.

This chapter reports on several of their measures which were incorporated into the European Values questionnaire. The first section will attempt to cast light on an area largely untouched by Quality of Life researchers: the relationship between well-being and values. This will be followed by a consideration of some of the most important differences in measures of well-being, illustrated with examples from various sub-groups of the British population. The chapter will conclude with an attempt to integrate these different measures in a model of well-being, the implications of which will then be discussed.

MEASURES OF PSYCHOLOGICAL WELL-BEING

The assessment of psychological well-being was attempted in the European Values questionnaire by means of three different measures, chosen because of their proven capacity to highlight different components. The measures have been used separately in previous surveys, but never together on such a scale.

The first consisted of a short, summary evaluation which simply asked respondents: 'Taking all things together, would you say you are: very happy; quite happy; not very happy; not at all happy?'. This measure has the virtue of providing a general snapshot of respondents' psychological state, highlighting important variations between sub-groups in the population, and providing a valuable contrast with the two other measures – satisfaction ratings, and the Bradburn Affect Balance Scale.

Quality of Life researchers, interested in evaluating the relationship between the objective circumstances in which people live their lives (for example their income, local facilities, type of employment), and their subjective appreciation of those circumstances, have developed a measurement technique based on 'satisfaction ratings'.

Respondents rate their level of satisfaction with various areas of their life, on a numerical scale (typically a ten-point scale, where 1 equals 'dissatisfied' and 10 equals 'satisfied'). This approach was adopted in the current enquiry, using the following ratings: satisfaction with life as a whole; life five years ago; life in five years' time; job; home life; and financial situation.

The third measure of psychological well-being included in the European Values questionnaire is explicitly designed to tap the transient, emotional or 'affective' component of well-being: the Affect Balance Scale (Bradburn, 1969). The scale contains five items concerned with positive emotional experiences ('positive affect'), and five items concerned with negative emotional experiences ('negative affect') (Table 9.1). It yields three scores: one (ranging from zero to five) for positive and negative affect respectively; and one 'affect balance score' derived by subtracting negative affect from positive affect scores. The positive and negative affect scores have been shown to be mutually independent, each relating to other measures of well-being. However, it is the balance score which is found to be the best predictor of reported well-being, thus leading Bradburn to postulate that this psychological state requires conceptualising as a *balance* between positive and negative emotional experiences.

(i) Overall distribution

When asked to evaluate their state of happiness, just over one-third of respondents declared themselves to be 'very happy' (38 per cent), and a little under two-thirds described themselves as 'quite happy' (58 per cent). This leaves only a small minority (4 per cent) who said that they were 'not very happy', and virtually no-one said that they were 'not happy at all' (Table 9.2).

On the second measure of well-being, most people tended towards the 'satisfied' end of the scales. For example, an average score of 7.7 was found on 'satisfaction with life as a whole', with only 15 per cent of respondents using the bottom five points of the ten-point scale.

Scores on the third measure, the Affect Balance Scale, also revealed a trend towards positive self-rating. Respondents were more likely to endorse the items comprising the 'positive affect' scale than they were to endorse those dealing with 'negative affect'. Hence, the average score (out of five) was higher for 'positive affect' (2.6), than

Table 9.1 *Percentage responses to the items comprising the Affect Balance Scale*

			(Percentages down)[1]			
		Total	Men	Women	Professional/ managerial	Unemployed
During the past few weeks, did you ever feel:						
1. Particularly excited or interested in something?	(+)[2]	47	50	45	66	42
2. So restless that you couldn't sit long in a chair?	(−)	36	32	40	33	39
3. Proud because someone complimented you on something you had done?	(+)	49	45	52	61	35
4. Very lonely or remote from other people?	(−)	14	10	17	12	19
5. Pleased to have accomplished something?	(+)	65	66	63	83	49
6. Bored?	(−)	31	29	33	19	45
7. On top of the world?	(+)	43	46	40	49	37
8. Depressed or very unhappy?	(−)	25	22	28	18	37
9. That things were going you way?	(+)	60	62	58	70	50
10. Upset because someone criticised you?	(−)	16	15	18	23	17
	N=	1231	590	641	108	70

[1] Percentages are those responding 'yes' to each item.
[2] Items followed by (+) comprise the positive affect scale; items followed by (−) comprise the negative affect scale.

it was for 'negative affect' (1.2). The composite 'affect balance score' (ranging from −5 to +5), was 1.4.

(ii) Psychological well-being and values

Is psychological well-being as assessed by these three measures related to the kinds of values a person holds? The question can be approached in more than one way, depending upon the definition of values which one endorses. A starting point is the commonly-accepted definition by Rokeach (1973), for whom a value: 'is an enduring belief that a specific mode of conduct or end-state of existence is personally or socially preferable to an opposite or converse mode of conduct or end-state of existence'.

This gives us two types of values – 'modes of conduct' on the one hand, and 'end-states' on the other; (elsewhere he refers to these as 'instrumental' and 'terminal' values respectively). Starting with the second, might psychological well-being be regarded as a personally/socially preferable end-state? The answer is an unequivocal 'yes', as research conducted during the preliminary stages of the European Values project demonstrated (Harding, 1979; Heald, James and Harding, 1981). In an attempt to elicit an unprompted list of terminal values, a nationally representative British sample was asked the following open-ended question, during a Gallup omnibus survey conducted in June 1979: 'What values or goals in life do you think are most worth striving for, either for yourself or for society as a whole? Please mention up to three.' The results obtained by coding the open-ended responses demonstrated that 'happiness' or 'being generally happy' was the most frequently cited terminal value.

There is little doubt, therefore, that happiness or well-being is a state which people value, and will strive for. However, it should be noted that not everyone puts a predominant emphasis on this value. Rokeach (1973), found in an American survey, that happiness was ranked fourth, following 'a world at peace', 'family security' and 'freedom'. In addition, an empirical evaluation of terminal values, whether open-ended or using a structured format such as Rokeach's, does not give any insight into the *nature* of people's happiness or well-being, other than telling us that it is regarded as important by most. An investigation of the nature, or correlates of well-being, appears to be more fruitfully achieved by examining the extent to which respondents' happiness can be predicted from their satisfaction with various specific life domains, and from the quality of their emotional experience. This will be attempted later in this chapter.

What is the relationship between well-being and Rokeach's second type of values: 'modes of conduct' which a person chooses as personally/socially preferable? As has been seen, the European Values questionnaire contains a large number of items in which respondents were given the opportunity to state a preferred 'mode of conduct', be it in relation to their job, politics, religion, personal or social ethical issues, and so on.

The data demonstrate that reported well-being is related both to political and religious values. In each case a more anti-traditional or radical values stance was associated with lower well-being, when compared with those respondents who expressed more traditional or conservative values. The level of well-being of a substantial body of individuals who expressed non-committal or middle-of-the-road political or religious views was approximately average. The trend occurs across all three measures of well-being, and is most marked on issues where extreme preferences may be given. I shall highlight the result by considering two such items: one from the religious domain, the other political. Respondents were asked 'Independently of whether you go to church or not, would you say you are: a religious person, not a religious person, or a convinced atheist?'. Table 9.2 shows how those who consider themselves to be religious have slightly higher average scores on the measure of well-being than those who consider themselves non-religious, although neither group differs significantly from the norm. A more marked difference is apparent, however, between the religious group and those who described themselves as convinced atheists: on each measure this latter group emerged with consistently lower well-being scores. In this instance, then, it is those who *reject* a religious interpretation of life who apparently experience a lower level of well-being, as opposed to those who accept such an interpretation, and those who neither actively accept nor reject such a view.

Turning to politics, respondents were asked (Q.276) to endorse one of three opinions, indicative of a radical, reformist or conservative political perspective. A similar trend occurs: those expressing the conservative stance emerged with the highest average levels of well-being across all three measures; although, once more, their scores were not significantly higher than those of respondents who expressed the second, middle-of-the-road opinion (two-thirds of the sample). It is the radical minority, however, those who would choose

TABLE 9.2 *Psychological well-being in relation to religious and political values*

	Religious person	Not religious	Convinced atheist	Belief in God		Society needs			Terrorism justified		Fight for Country	
				Yes	No	Change	Reform	Defence	Sometimes	Never	Yes	No
N =	708	437	45	931	192	54	813	270	144	1036	762	336
Happiness question (% down)												
Very happy	39	38	33	39	37	31	38	42	33	39	40	36
Quite happy	57	56	60	57	55	64	57	54	61	56	56	58
Not very/not at all happy	3	6	7	4	7	5	4	4	4	6	6	4
Satisfaction with life												
(average on 1–10 scale)	7.8	7.5	7.1	7.8	7.2	7.2	7.7	7.9	7.4	7.7	7.7	7.6
Affect balance score	1.6	1.3	1.0	1.5	1.3	0.5	1.5	1.7	1.2	1.4	1.6	1.1

revolutionary action, whose scores showed the marked discrepancy, being considerably lower than the two other groups on all three measures of well-being.

What are we to conclude from these results? Why should those who express strong disaffection with orthodox religious or political views experience less happiness, lower satisfaction from life, less enjoyable emotional experience? To some extent, particularly on the two items we have considered in detail, it might be expected that we are dealing with the same set of respondents: it would, perhaps, not be surprising for a convinced atheist also to endorse revolutionary social change, and *vice versa*. However, further analysis reveals the overlap to be quite small, of the order of ten per cent. The average age of the two groups turns out to be quite different: more than two-thirds of the convinced atheists were under 34, whereas those in the radical group were fairly evenly distributed across the age spectrum. Hence, the reasons for the lower well-being in the two groups may be different in each case.

If there is a common cause for the lower reported well-being of these two groups, it may be connected with the fact that the values they hold are divorced from, and antithetical to, the consensus values of society at large. Society may not be very demanding in relation to non-adherence to religious beliefs and political indifference. However, declared rejection of consensus values may be a different matter: one is alienating oneself from the accepted views of the conforming majority, and it is well known from both sociological and psychological studies, that society finds it hard to tolerate those who might be labelled 'non-conformist' or 'deviant' (cf. Parkin, 1968; Aronson, 1980). The effects of social pressure and isolation resulting from holding 'deviant' values, might well explain the lower levels of well-being seen in these groups. The suggestion has some empirical support; at least for one of the social groups we have been considering. Both convinced atheists and radicals when asked how often they felt aggressive feelings at home, emerged with a significantly higher frequency of aggressive feelings than the norm. Whilst the result may be attributed to the relatively young age of the atheist group (reported frequency of aggressive feelings is negatively correlated with age), this cannot be the cause with the radical group; hence, their aggressive feelings may be the result of defensiveness in the face of social hostility. Secondly, when asked if they ever felt lonely, the radical group admitted to being more lonely than those who did not share their revolutionary views. Some 41 per cent of the radical group reported feeling lonely 'often' or 'sometimes', as opposed to 33 per cent of the 'reformers' and 30 per cent of the 'defenders' of the *status quo*. It seems possible, then, that the non-conformist political views of some respondents have led to social estrangement and isolation. The atheist group did not show a similar pattern – indeed, if anything, the evidence pointed towards the religious group being more lonely. However, once more, the result should be interpreted in the light of the different ages of the atheist and religious groups.

To sum up then, the low levels of well-being seen in certain groups may be a function of holding deviant social values. Both convinced atheists and those respondents who would prefer social change to be achieved by revolutionary means, reported considerably lower levels of well-being than those who chose more orthodox options. The greater incidence of aggressive feelings and loneliness among individuals in the radical group may offer some support for the 'deviant values' hypothesis. However, it has to be said that the results may be amenable to alternative explanations. In particular, it should be noted that our hypothesis proposes a specific causal path between the variables; namely, that one's state of well-being is affected by the values one holds. Yet a reverse ordering of the variables also offers a not implausible explanation of the findings; that is, that a low level of well-being, dissatisfaction with life, is more likely to lead to a rejection of *status quo* values, and, for some, a desire for a fundamental change in the structure of society.

(iii) Demographic variations in well-being

Turning to specific demographic variations within Britain provides an illustration of the contrasting approaches to the measurement of well-being, and the need to evaluate it by means of different measures. A summary of results is provided in Tables 9.2–9.4.

MARITAL STATUS

Little evidence was found that the three measures of well-being are sensitive to sex differences, although there was a slight tendency for women to generate higher negative affect scores and lower positive affect scores than men (refer to Table 9.1). Marital status on the other hand, showed marked differences (Table 9.3). It should be noted in this respect that the eighteen respondents describing them-

TABLE 9.3   *Psychological well-being in relation to marital status*

	Single	Mar-ried	Divorced/separated	Widowed
N=	251	808	46	109
Happiness question (% down):				
Very happy	28	45	16	15
Quite happy	68	52	69	69
Not very/not at all happy	3	3	14	15
Satisfaction with life as a whole	7.4	7.8	6.8	7.4
–home life	8.0	8.7	6.7	8.3
–financial situation of your				
household	6.9	6.9	5.9	6.2
Affect Balance Scale:				
–Positive affect	2.8	2.7	2.5	1.9
–Negative affect	1.3	1.6	1.3	1.7
–Affect balance score	1.5	1.1	1.2	0.2

selves as 'living as married' are not included in this analysis. Married respondents were much more likely to declare themselves 'very happy' than the single. They were also more likely to consider themselves 'satisfied with life' than single people, although the two groups did not differ significantly on the third measure, affect balance. In the remaining two groups, the divorced and separated and the widowed, happiness would appear to be the exception rather than the rule. In both groups, only one in six respondents said that they were 'very happy' and almost a similar proportion described itself as 'not very happy' or 'not at all happy'. In both cases the loss of a spouse, either through the break-up of a marriage or through death is associated with a very marked drop in reported happiness.

Does this imply that the experiences of being separated or divorced, and of widowhood are psychologically equivalent? Some researchers have taken such a view, arguing that the central psychological characteristic in each case is the same: a state of *loss*, frequently accompanied by an adjustment reaction, a prolonged and frequently painful period of transition (cf. Parkes, 1972). This might explain the low level of happiness observed. However, inspection of the other measures of well-being reveals that the similarity between states goes no further; indeed the dissimilar pattern which can be seen suggests rather diverse psychological experiences for the divorced/separated on the one hand, and the widowed on the other.

In the first instance, on the satisfaction scale the divorced/separated group had a much lower level of reported satisfaction with life (average = 6.8) than all other groups. The widowed had similar average satisfaction scores to single people (average = 7.4), being somewhat lower than those who are married (average = 7.8). Therefore, on this measure, requiring an overall evaluation of satisfaction with life, the divorced/separated group stood out as being particularly badly off. Indeed, such low levels of satisfaction were seen only in one other demographic group: the unemployed (average = 6.8).

On the Affect Balance Scale, however, a different pattern emerges. In this case the widowed had the lowest levels of well-being, particularly as a result of their relative lack of positive emotional experience (low positive affect), and also their somewhat high levels of negative emotional experience (high negative affect) (see Table 9.3). Hence, in comparison with other marital status groups, their overall affect balance score is particularly low (i.e. positive affect is all but cancelled out by negative affect). The divorced/separated group on the other hand, showed levels of affect not significantly different from other groups.

Thus, it would appear that the relatively low levels of happiness reported by the divorced and separated, and by the widowed, may well reflect different sorts of deficit in their psychological well-being. For the divorced/separated group, the low level of happiness seems to be related to a low evaluation of satisfaction with life, whereas for the widowed group, it seems to be more a question of lack of positive emotional experience.

The lack of positive affect in the widowed group is not hard to understand. Positive affect depends upon the occurrence of pleasurable experiences, and it seems reasonable to assume that, for many married couples, these experiences are derived from shared activities and interactions with their spouse. This seems particularly likely in older people (who are also more likely to experience widowhood), for whom other potentially reinforcing roles, such as having a job or bringing up children will have been relinquished. Thus, the loss of a spouse is also the loss of a major source of positive psychological input; a loss which, in older age, is hard to redeem.

The loss of a spouse through separation or divorce on the other hand, does not appear to have such an adverse impact on the potential for positive emotional experience. As a group, the divorced and separated are younger than the widowed and therefore probably have more opportunity for social interaction at a variety of levels. In this respect, the divorced and separated seem closer to single people than to the widowed.

But how are we to account for the very low satisfaction of the divorced and separated as compared with other groups, including the widowed? This requires some understanding of the way in which the word 'satisfaction' is interpreted by respondents. Researchers who have used satisfaction ratings have suggested that these measures involve a cognitive or intellectual evaluation by respondents of their life circumstances according to their wants, needs, expectations, comparisons with their own situation in the past, and the situation of other people (cf. Campbell, Converse and Rodgers, 1976). Furthermore, satisfaction with life as a whole is thought to depend (to varying degrees) on the satisfaction which individuals experience with various specific circumstances in their lives; for example, their job, leisure time, financial situation, etc.

TABLE 9.4   *Satisfaction with home life and household financial situation by marital status*

Satisfaction	Single	Married	Divorced/ separated	Widowed
Home life: average (1–10 scale)	8.0	8.7	6.7	8.3
Household finance: average (1–10 scale)	6.9	6.9	5.9	6.2

One circumstance which has been found to be particularly likely to impinge on individuals' overall satisfaction with life, is the degree to which they feel satisfied (or dissatisfied) with their home life. In this respect, the divorced/separated show a very marked deficit in comparison with other marital status groups (see Table 9.4). The widowed group show levels of satisfaction which are not significantly lower than the married. It would appear then, that in terms of home life the widowed have adjusted to their loss; perhaps because at an older age widowhood is part of the nature of things to be expected. The divorced and separated, on the other hand, have failed to achieve a comparable level of satisfaction, possibly because they have wants and needs which their current home life does not fulfil, or possibly because they experience social stigma from a society in which divorce and separation are negatively regarded. More than 40 per cent of the divorced and separated sample have children and this, too, is likely to impose a burden on home life for some respondents. Finally, financial obligations may weigh heavily on some of this group, although this is also true of the widowed, as Table 9.4 demonstrates.

AGE AND LEVEL OF EDUCATION

Previous studies suggest that older people are less happy, but more satisfied with life (for example, Campbell, 1976). One explanation is that older age is seen as a time for accommodation and acceptance (or possibly resignation), whereas younger people are thought to be more aspiring. Some slight evidence for this trend was found in the current study. Similarly, it has previously been reported that both positive and negative affect decrease with age. Younger people are thought to be more emotionally labile, more likely to experience both 'highs' and 'lows' from life, whereas for older people, life is thought to be more bland. Again, a slight trend in this direction was observed, but it was less marked than in previous studies (for example, Harding, 1982).

More striking differences in reported well-being were related to the amount of education, and again there is a discrepant pattern among the well-being measures. Those who had left school at a younger age were likely to be somewhat more satisfied with their lives than those who had experienced more (particularly post-school) education (see Table 9.5). However, the group with less education had lower affect balance than those with more education, due mainly to differences in levels of positive affect. Put another way, the more highly educated appear on the one hand more dissatisfied, yet on the other, their affective well-being is higher than that of other groups.

One possible consequence of a longer education may be that it generates higher expectations of what life might be like, hence the possibility of greater dissatisfaction with one's current situation (cf. Campbell *et al.*, 1976, pp. 138–40). At the same time, it would appear to open the door to greater frequency of positive emotional experience. To some extent these results replicate the age trend discussed above, as those with lower levels of education are also likely (though not invariably so) to be older. However, as we saw, age differences generated only rather weak trends, and controlling for this effect reveals that education levels had an impact on the data over and above any differential effects of age.

TABLE 9.5 *Psychological well-being in relation to age and level of education*

	Age groups			Terminal education age				
	18–34	35–54	55+	–15	15	16	17–18	19+
N=	450	383	398	378	276	275	167	135
Happiness question (% down)								
Very happy	40	39	35	35	40	40	40	36
Quite happy	57	56	59	59	55	55	56	59
Not very/not at all happy	3	5	6	6	4	4	3	5
Satisfaction with life								
(average on 1–10 scale)	7.5	–7.6	7.9	8.0	7.6	7.6	7.6	7.4
Affect Balance Scale:								
Positive affect	2.9	2.7	2.5	2.4	2.5	2.7	3.0	3.0
Negative affect	1.2	0.9	1.1	1.3	1.2	1.3	1.2	1.1
Affect balance	1.7	1.8	1.4	1.1	1.3	1.4	1.8	1.9

INCOME

Does money bring happiness? For once we have a chance to evaluate that cliché empirically. Relating reported levels of income to self-perceived well-being reveals a consistent trend across all three psychological measures: those in the highest income group apparently experience greater happiness, more satisfaction with life, and also higher affect balance scores than those in middle and lower income groups. However, the difference between upper and middle income groups is less marked than the difference between these two and the lower income group (see Table 9.6). Thus it would seem wiser to state that more money does not necessarily bring greater happiness, but a relative lack of money is more likely to be associated with unhappiness and a lower level of psychological well-being.

Those in the low income group who were working tended also to be less satisfied with their job; felt less free to make decisions in their job, and were more likely to say that they are exploited at work, than those in the middle and upper income groups. However, the experience of low income does not cloud all of life: those in this group were as satisfied with their home life as those in the upper income group.

OCCUPATION

A trend towards greater reported happiness and positive affect was evident among professional and managerial workers when compared with unskilled manual workers. Differences between those currently in employment, and those not working (either due to unemployment or retirement), were more marked (see Table 9.6). The retired group showed relatively high levels of satisfaction with life, but somewhat attenuated levels of happiness and affect balance. The unemployed, on the other hand, showed marked deficits on all three measures of well-being, highlighting the apparently deleterious psychological effects of unemployment (cf. Warr, 1978; 1983). A comparison of the professional and managerial group with the unemployed on the individual items of the affect balance scale underlines the very marked differences in psychological experience between the two groups (Table 9.1, columns 4 and 5).

TABLE 9.6 *Psychological well-being in relation to income and occupation*

	Income groups			Profession-al/ managerial	Non-manual	Skilled manual	Unskilled manual	Unemployed	Retired
	High	Middle	Low						
N =	166	407	332	108	206	157	213	70	191
Happiness question (% down):									
Very happy	44	42	30	43	34	40	42	27	28
Quite happy	55	54	59	54	62	58	52	61	67
Not very/not at all happy	1	3	9	3	4	2	5	10	4
Satisfaction with life (average on 1–10 scale)	7.8	7.7	7.4	7.7	7.6	7.9	7.6	6.8	7.8
Affect Balance Scale:									
Positive affect	3.2	2.7	2.3	3.3	2.8	2.8	2.7	2.1	2.2
Negative affect	1.2	1.1	1.5	1.1	1.0	0.9	1.3	1.6	1.2
Affect balance	2.0	1.6	0.8	2.2	1.8	1.9	1.4	0.5	1.0

WORKING WOMEN

What effect, if any, does employment have on the well-being of women? An examination of the three psychological measures revealed no significant difference in happiness or satisfaction with life between working and non-working women. However, on the affective measure, working women emerged with distinctly higher levels of well-being than women not in employment, with full-time workers apparently being best off (see Table 9.7).

TABLE 9.7 *The psychological well-being of women with and without a job: scores on the Affect Balance Scale*

	Women working full-time	Women working part-time	Women without a job
N =	163	144	335
(Average scores)			
Positive affect	3.0	2.6	2.4
Negative affect	1.1	1.2	1.6
Affect balance	1.9	1.4	0.8

On the face of it, it would seem that employment has a highly beneficial effect on the well-being of women. However, the comparison is a gross one, based on all the women in the sample, young and old, married or not, with or without children. Hence, the differences in well-being may be related to any one of a number of factors, rather than to working *per se*.

Further analysis shows the greatest contrast to be between women with no job and with children under 16 on the one hand, and women in employment with no children or grown-up children (16+) on the other. The well-being score of the first group is lowered by a relatively high negative affect component, suggesting that their psychological state is adversely affected by unpleasant, possibly stressful emotional experience. Reported feelings of loneliness and remoteness are twice as common in this group (21 per cent versus 11 per cent). Almost half of the non-working 'young mums' report feeling bored, in comparison with a quarter of the working women with no (young) children. The contrast is also seen on an item concerned with feeling aggressive at home: 63 per cent of the first group report feeling aggressive often or sometimes versus 42 per cent of the second.

TOWARDS A MODEL OF PSYCHOLOGICAL WELL-BEING

This section attempts to sum up the results presented in the chapter and to demonstrate their place in a model aimed at clarifying the nature of the experience of psychological well-being.

The demographic results show that the experience of well-being is not a simple state which can be ascertained merely by asking people how happy they are; for different patterns of well-being emerged at times across the three measures used in the questionnaire. For example, we saw in the case of the divorced/separated and the widowed, that a low level of reported happiness may be associated with different kinds of shortfall in well-being – a lack of satisfaction with life in the former group's case, and a low level of positive affective experience in the latter group. Furthermore, in addition to the three measures of well-being, we also saw some evidence for a further 'stress' factor, which appears to affect the quality of life of certain sub-groups in the population such as women, not in paid employment, at home with young children (cf. Campbell, 1976).

Thus, we are drawn to the conclusion that happiness or well-being is not a one-dimensional experience. Rather, it seems more appropriate to refer to 'components' of well-being, (cf. Beiser, 1974), which will, in different measure and to varying degree, constitute an individual's sense of well-being.

Analysis of the different measures of well-being threw light on two of these components: one cognitive, the other affective. The cognitive component, it has been suggested, is more adequately revealed by asking people how satisfied or dissatisfied they are with certain personal or environmental circumstances; the affective component is more adequately elicited by asking people about their recent emotional experiences. If in comparison to others, certain people live in poverty, or in slum housing, or in conflict with their family, the dissatisfactions that result are bound to colour their perception of life, making it hard for them to claim to be 'very happy'. On the other hand, even with long-standing circumstances leading to an evaluation that life is more, or less satisfying, we are also subject to transient positive and negative feelings that result from the way in which we respond to current environmental events. The feeling of pleasure aroused by an enjoyable evening out, the 'low' which accompanies being criticised by someone we respect, these everyday ups and downs are also part of the flux of life events which contribute to an assessment of whether at a particular time, we feel happy or not.

Thus we arrive at a simple model, based upon cognitive evaluations of our life situation, and upon our transient affective state, which are jointly seen as providing a composite framework out of which our sense of psychological well-being or happiness is structured (see Figure 9.1).

Can we go further and test how well the model stands up in practice, using data from the Values project? This can be done, using a 'multiple regression' to establish the relative importance of our different components as predictors of happiness.

We start with an estimation of satisfaction with life and affect balance as predictors of happiness. Independent of affect balance, the correlation between satisfaction and happiness is $r = +0.42$. Independent of satisfaction, the correlation between affect balance and happiness is $r = +0.23$. Thus, relative to each other, satisfaction with its implied cognitive component is a more powerful predictor of happiness than is affect, although both are clearly important.

We can extend this simple model by including the other satisfaction ratings, and certain other psychological variables. The analysis reveals that after overall life satisfaction (Beta = 0.32) and affect balance (Beta = 0.18), the other measures were also able to make an independent contribution to the model of happiness. Satisfaction with home life (Beta = 0.17) is the next most important predictor, followed by state of health (Beta = 0.11). Satisfaction with household finances, left-right political perspective, feelings of aggression and anxiety at home, and the importance of God, all make modest additional contributions (Beta = 0.05) in each case. Satisfaction with one's job was a less powerful predictor.

Obviously any model is limited by the number and nature of the items included in the original research instrument. Other research has made use of a more extensive list of satisfaction ratings including satisfaction with one's house, neigbourhood, town, etc. This adds to the predictive power of the model, although the pattern is little changed from that seen here. (For alternative models, see Campbell *et al.*, 1976; Andrews and Withey, 1976; Hall and Ring, 1974; McKennell and Andrews, 1980.)

As well as satisfaction ratings, stress factors appear to play a role, strongly affecting the psychological experience of some groups in the population. Items concerned with feeling anxious and aggressive appeared to highlight a stress component: including these two items in the multiple regression model added to the predictive power of the model, but only marginally.

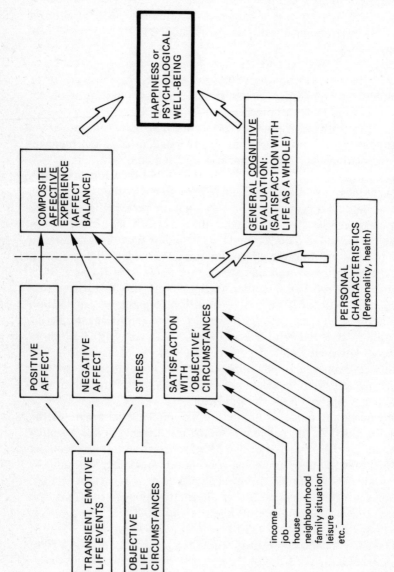

FIGURE 9.1   A model of happiness or psychological well-being

In addition to stress, long-standing personal characteristics have also been considered to predict levels of well-being. One such characteristic is personality. Owing to the time demands of the questionnaire, personality characteristics of respondents were not systematically evaluated though certain stable, enduring personality traits, namely extraversion and neuroticism, have been found to correlate positively with positive and negative affect respectively. More extravert people are likely to have higher positive affect scores, whereas more neurotic people are more likely to have higher negative affect scores (Costa and McCrae, 1980).

A second personal characteristic which clearly and drastically affects individuals' well-being is their state of health. A self-evaluation of health was included in the questionnaire: respondents were asked whether their state of health was very good, good, fair, poor or very poor. A very close correspondence occurs between responses to this health question and the measure of well-being, particularly affect balance (see Figure 9.2). Thus, one's self-reported state of health plays a critical role in mediating one's experience of well-being: those claiming less than good health being far more likely to have lower levels of well-being than average. Furthermore, the impact of health as a predictor of happiness is clearly indicated in the regression model, where it emerges as the fourth most important of the variables included.

Finally, what about the values items? It was seen earlier that certain political and religious values positions were associated with lower affective well-being. Including the values items in the regression model, however, showed them to have very low predictive power. Outside of specific sub-groups, then, they were unable to explain variations in well-being. Two more generalised values items relating to politics (the left-right scale), and religious conviction (the importance of God in the respondent's life) similarly had a relatively minor impact, particularly the latter item.

However, if we regard the model as an expression of terminal rather than instrumental values, an interesting observation can be made. For the list of predictor variables in descending order of importance, approximates very closely to the ranking of terminal values obtained from the open-ended question used in the pilot stage of the project. For whilst 'happiness' features as the most important value, the next most frequently cited values were precisely those emerging as most significant from the regression analysis: namely having a happy home life, good health, enough money. However,

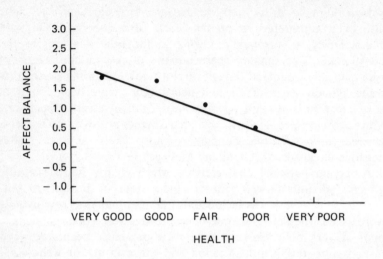

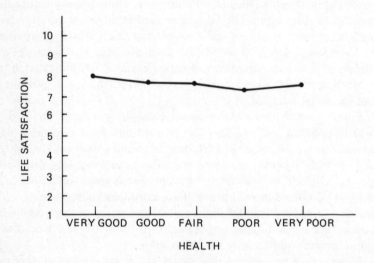

FIGURE 9.2 *The relationship between psychological well-being and self-reported health*

rather than construing these values as independent of one another, and sought after in their own right, the analysis reveals that they are mutually related, combining to constitute that most important terminal value – a person's sense of happiness or well-being.

ENHANCING WELL-BEING: THE ROLE OF ACTIVITY AND SOCIAL PARTICIPATION

What, if anything, can be done to enhance a person's well-being? We shall not concern ourselves with individuals exhibiting psychopathological conditions, but, rather, with the general population.

The model of well-being has established that satisfaction with various circumstances in one's life plays an important part in determining well-being: some circumstances being more important than others. The policy implication is that by identifying those dissatisfying circumstances which take the greatest toll on a person's well-being, one has the opportunity of affecting the most beneficial social change, by channelling the available resources into the area of greatest subjectively felt need. However, the objective is clearly one which depends upon the co-operation of policy makers and their paymasters. Even so, within certain areas some success has been achieved using the approach: architects and planners, for example, are increasingly drawing on research data which provides them with feedback on the needs, wishes and satisfactions of those who use the facilities they create (cf. Lee, 1975; Willcocks, Peace and Kellaher, 1982).

With reference to the affective part of the model, however, a further, more immediate possibility for directly enhancing well-being suggests itself. Psychological well-being rests in part on the experience of emotionally rewarding positive events. The simple corollary to this statement is that those who expose themselves to such positive events are more likely to enjoy a higher level of (affective) well-being. Some hints of such a process at work have been seen during the course of our discussion: those in professional and managerial jobs, the more highly educated, working women without children, all experience relatively high positive affect; the widowed show the reverse (cf. Phillips, 1976). It is suggested that, in each case, the effect reflects the presence (or absence) of social participation and rewarding activity, which in turn affects the way in which those respondents answer the positive affect items.

A more direct test of the proposal is available, however, by considering those items in the questionnaire which concern themselves with social participation, and with the active, rather than passive use of leisure time. The following items indicate whether the respondent belongs to any social organisation, for example youth work, professional associations (Q.113a); whether the respondent does any voluntary work (Q.113b); whether he ever goes to church (Q.157); whether he watches a lot or a little television (Q.116); and whether he prefers to relax or be active during his leisure time (Q.111). When these items were considered in relation to scores on the affect balance scale a consistent trend emerged: those engaging in or preferring greater social participation and activity had quite markedly higher affect balance scores than those involved in less social participation and activity: the effect being largely due to an elevated average positive affect score (see Table 9.8).

Whilst positive emotional experience appears to be considerably enhanced by these activities, certain negative emotions also appear to be less in evidence: respondents engaged in greater activity reported feeling less bored, less depressed, and were less likely to find life meaningless than those involved in less activity.

As mentioned earlier, psychologists have spent little time studying the nature of pleasurable psychological experience, and what has been done tends to relate to rather circumscribed contexts and social groups.

However, two pieces of research from differing areas are worth mentioning, as they apply directly to the results under discussion. The first is an investigation by Csikszentmihalyi (1975) which considered why people find sport and games (among other things) enjoyable. The author demonstrated that these activities are fulfilling in themselves; that the reward is intrinsic to the activity and directly enhances well-being. The second line of research comes from studies on ageing, which have led to an 'activity theory', in relation to the well-being and psychological adjustment of the elderly (cf. Neugarten, 1968; Bromley, 1978). The theory forms a counterbalance to another: 'disengagement theory' which contends that the process of ageing is one of withdrawal from the mainstreams of social activity and interaction. According to activity theory there is a natural inclination in many to continue to participate and associate with others. Moreover, providing suitable facilities and encouragement to motivate the elderly to participate in activities has been shown to be linked to an increase in life satisfaction and happiness.

The evidence from these rather contrasting researches points to the role of social interaction and voluntary activity as a means of enhancing personal well-being. The data presented here suggests that their relevance extends far beyond the subject groups to which they have been thought to apply. Engaging in rewarding social activity is not simply a process to enhance the well-being of sportsmen and the

FIGURE 9.8 *The effects of activity and social participation on psychological well-being (Affect Balance scores)*

	Belong to an organisation	Do not belong	Voluntary worker	Not a voluntary worker
N=	646	585	230	1001
Positive affect	2.9	2.5	3.0	2.6
Negative affect	1.2	1.4	1.1	1.3
Affect balance	1.7	1.1	1.9	1.3

	Hours per day watching TV		Sometimes go to church	Never go to church	In leisure time prefer to:		
	−3	+3			relax	be active	both
N=	722	509	659	571	308	658	263
Positive affect	2.8	2.5	2.8	2.5	2.3	2.9	2.8
Negative effect	1.2	1.3	1.1	1.3	1.3	1.3	1.1
Affect balance	1.6	1.2	1.7	1.2	1.0	1.6	1.7

	Percentage who feel:		
	Bored	Depressed	Life meaningless (often or sometimes)
Belong to an organisation	29	22	21
Do not belong	39	28	32
Voluntary worker	19	22	18
Not a voluntary worker	34	26	28
−3 hours TV per day	31	23	25
+3 hours TV per day	40	27	29
Sometimes go to church	26	25	22
Never go to church	37	25	31
Prefer to relax	37	31	31
Prefer to be active	33	23	26
Both equally	30	21	24

elderly. Rather, the findings from the Values survey suggest it to be an ubiquitous phenomenon of general relevance to the population at large. The nature and implications of the result clearly require further investigation. We cannot say at this stage, for example, that greater well-being is the direct consequence of greater social activity, although they are strongly related. Moreover, the nature of the effects needs further study: to what extent is the sense of enhanced well-being the result of fulfilling activity *per se*, or the result of rewarding interaction with other people? Are there certain activities which are most likely to enhance well-being? All these questions need to be considered in future research. However, the result remains important and also encouraging. For whilst the eradication of dissatisfying social conditions may not be achieved overnight, and may be to an extent beyond the individual's direct ability to control, the finding that affective experience is related to voluntary social activity suggests that, at least as far as this component of the model is concerned, an individual's well-being may well be in his own hands.

10 Theological and Pastoral Reflections

JOHN MAHONEY

In their preface to Stoetzel's *Europe at the Crossroads* (1983, p. viii), de Moor and Kerkhofs express the hope that the findings of the European Values Systems Study Group (EVSSG) will prove of use, among others, to Church leaders. The purpose of this contribution to an examination of the British findings is to offer some reflections of a theological and pastoral nature on how they may be received by the churches and individual Christians. The conclusions which will be advanced are:

1. that, as a matter of theological principle, the individual churches, and the Church as a whole, should be disposed to receive positively the results of the Values Study findings as 'signs of the times', in order to learn from them;
2. that the very disappointing results on religious values and on how religion is understood in Britain constitute a serious challenge to the Church, both to review its presentation of the Gospel and to accept the implications of diminishing membership for its own self-understanding; and
3. that, in the context of the consistently high support among individuals in Britain for moral values, Christians may learn that these are not essentially dependent upon religion and cannot be simplistically applied in a changing society; but that the Church's moral role within British society is primarily to exemplify those human and Christian values which express both the Church's own nature and man's calling as one of *koinonia*, or active fellowship.

253

1.   POSITIVE RECEPTION BY THE CHURCH

How might the churches respond to these findings? One line of approach would be to use the findings as a check-list indicating to what extent people accept the church's teaching on faith and morals today. What is lacking in such a school-report approach, however, is any consideration of whether the curriculum *itself* is in need of revision, whether the genuine needs of the 'students' are being sufficiently considered rather than taken for granted, and whether the entire 'educational system' of the churches is ripe for re-assessment in terms of its goals, and not just of its pedagogical methods.

Another line of reaction could adopt the metaphor of the production and advertising industries. The results of the enquiry might be considered in terms of consumer-wishes and how the product and its packaging might be designed more appealingly and attractively to entice or satisfy the customer. The main questions which arise here, however, are whether the great British public wants the product at all; whether consumer-resistance should be met with an intensified selling campaign, or whether the church should settle for satisfying a minority interest of committed consumers and occasional patrons, after the manner of Radio 3 or the health-food industry. Underlying these two contrasting images of teaching and of the market lie fundamental questions which face the Church in every age, and in particular that of whether its message is to be imparted or to be discovered.

Among the most sustained explorations of this Christian tension in modern times must be classed the work of the Second Vatican Council (1962–64), and particularly its concluding *Pastoral Constitution on the Church in the Modern World*, in which the world-wide body of Roman Catholic bishops set for their church the programme of 'a new humanism', a work of identifying and furthering what was most human in contemporary living. In this *volte face* for the RC church would be seen no watering down or fashionable accommodation of the Christian message, but a genuine attempt to establish an ever present continuity between God's work as Creator and the flowering and culmination of that work in the person, activity and Church of Jesus Christ.

The implications of such an approach were two-fold. First, it embraced a method of theologising 'from below', starting from contemporary man and human experience, in the belief (*sic*) that this reflective journey would terminate in God as ultimate meaning and fulfilment. It was a form of what Henri de Lubac had years earlier termed, not a 'closed' humanism, but an 'open' humanism. It would walk side by side with purely secular and other forms of humanism, as setting out from a shared starting point. But it would also be forever encouraging other humanisms to lengthen their stride, and to take those extra steps towards the full perfection of which man is capable, and the form of human society which alone could do full justice to man who is also the image of God.

The other implication of this 'new humanism' led the Council to refer to the need to 'study the signs of the times', thus adopting as a methodological principle the reproach of Jesus to his own contemporaries as they demanded of Him 'a sign from heaven' as warrant for his programme: 'You know how to interpret the appearance of the sky, but you cannot interpret the signs of the times' (Mt 16:1–3). In other words, God is to be found continually at work in human history, whether collective or individual; and the Spirit of Jesus Christ is to be detected and acknowledged not as some remote oracle but in events as, in the phrase of Macquarrie, 'God in his nearness to us' (1978, p. 61).

Allied to this methodological approach was the acknowledgement, always present in the RC church but more thoroughly espoused in other Christian bodies, that the ability to recognise God at work in contemporary experience is, in principle, an activity shared by all who have been baptized into Christ. The two standard difficulties of such an understanding of 'the (Christian) sense of the faithful', of course, are that it appears to endorse a majority-vote approach towards the discovery of truth and goodness, and that it is unduly trusting in the religious and moral integrity of the individual believer. Nevertheless, if the doctrine of a 'Christian sense', to which most churches, even – with some reluctance – the RC church, appear to subscribe, is to have any meaning in practice, then the views of 'ordinary' Christians, whether as individuals or collectively, must be accorded some theological significance, and cannot be simply discounted.

The theologian, then, will peruse with interest the findings of the Values Study which deploy the various values which appear operative in the lives and decisions of Christians among the general population. But he will not necessarily stop there, particularly so far as the recording of moral values is concerned. The prolonged contemporary search for the 'specificity', or unique quality, of Christian ethics serves most of all to show the resilience in Christian thinking, despite the pessimism of Augustinian, Calvinist and Jansenist currents, of a positive attitude in principle towards strictly human resources for moral reflection, quite apart from any specifically Christian moral revelation. Biblical warrant for such a recognition is found primarily in Paul's contention (Rom 2) that the Gentiles, who had not been vouchsafed the divine revelation of God's law in the Jewish Decalogue, were nevertheless 'a law to themselves', not in the quite contrary modern sense of disregarding all law, but showing by their behaviour 'that what the (Jewish moral) law required is written on their hearts', in contrast with the law written for the people of Israel on tablets of stone (cf. Exod 34:27–28). And it has continued to be characteristic of a Catholic current in Christian thinking to regard human moral exploration with a measured optimism about its powers of perception, if not necessarily about its powers of performance. From within such a view of every individual's genuine, if fallible, capacity for natural moral insight, a positive, if guarded, attitude can be expected towards the Values Study recording of non-Christian as well as Christian expressions of values.

What is more, the traditional distinctions between reason and revelation, and more generically between nature and grace, have for many theologians become increasingly regarded more as conceptual tools designed to safeguard the freedom of divine initiatives, and less as reflecting identifiably distinct factors in human history and personal experience. Rather than viewing reality in some double-decker fashion as (sinful) nature topped in some (Christian) cases by a stratum of grace, the prevailing tendency today is not to view the Christian as the man seated upstairs in the Clapham omnibus, but to consider all men as susceptible to, and continually (even if unknowingly) solicited by, the fullness of divine undifferentiated attraction.

It is considerations such as these which identify the role of the Church in human culture as one of dialogue. Of listening just as much as of uttering; and not just of listening in order to be able to provide the appropriate response, but in order also to sift and scrutinise its own instinctive responses. To do otherwise would be to lapse into the assumption, as John Robinson pointed out (1960, p. 20), 'that what God is doing in the world he must be doing through the Church, that the space to watch, as it were, if one really wants to see what God is up to, is the Church papers.' And the disjunction between the Church and society can also be a more subtle one. In *A Strategy for the Church's Ministry*, Tiller quotes Jurgen Moltmann (1983, p. 11) to the effect that 'the church always belongs *within the context of the world* ... but the context is not *the text*, and we must never allow it to become so. The church's context is society. But its text is the Gospel of Jesus Christ'. Here, in a delicate form, we appear to be in the presence of the first metaphor with which we opened this chapter, in which the Church can be compared to an educational system. The reality is more complex. An incarnational religion will tend more to consider society, the continuing work of God's hand, as both text and context; will acknowledge that 'in these last days he has spoken to us by a Son', but that this divine utterance is the climax and centre of all God's other utterances 'in many and various ways' (Heb 1:1). Similarly, the Gospel is, to be sure, God's definitive and normative utterance in Christ, but it is expressed through the medium, and in the context, of one stage and culture in human society. The text and context are interdependent. The early theologian, Justin Martyr, saw authentically human values in his culture as 'seeds' of the Word. And similarly, in considering contemporary human values in general, and as recorded in the Study findings, in examining these 'signs of the times' in our culture, the churches may do well to be on the lookout for divine glosses on the Word of God and its content for today.

2. A CHALLENGE TO THE CHURCH

It will be to the findings on religious values (Chapter 3) that many Christians will first direct their attention, and with those we may begin; raising first some considerations of a theological nature about the questions posed in the survey on religious beliefs and attitudes. It is a feature of all religious language, referring as it does to a unique and transcendent being and activity, that it must nevertheless adopt, and strain almost to breaking point, the ordinary concepts and terms of mundane experience. And when one adds to this intrinsic poverty of human descriptive resources the propensity of the human imagination to fill in, not so much for 'the God of the gaps' as for the gaps in God, then even such apparently unexceptionable terms as 'heaven', 'hell' and 'sin' can take on such a variety of personal interpretations, as individual variations on traditionally picturesque themes, that it is exceedingly difficult to assess what to make of a simple 'yes' or 'no' accorded to beliefs in the reality to which they refer.

It was the awareness of this irrepressibly pictorial approach to religious realities, of course, which led John Robinson to write his best-selling *Honest to God*, to be met with the expostulations of many theologians and churchmen that he was only stating in over-dramatised, if not mischievous, terms what professional theology had always taken for granted. But the reception of Robinson's popular-isation of the theologians' dissatisfaction with traditional descriptions of religious themes and realities should still challenge the Christian bodies on the adequacy of their presentation of the Christian message for twentieth-century adults. The Values Study, with its findings on religious values, raises for the Church in an acute form the frighten-ing questions as to what degree the apparently widespread lack of belief in the fundamental tenets of Christianity is to be viewed as a justified dismissal of a badly conceived and wrongly presented portrayal of Christian beliefs, and to what extent it would be an evasion for the Church to write off such disbelief as reluctance to accept the personal implications of the Gospel, rather than an indictment of its own educational apostolate.

How to map out what Francis Thompson termed the 'world intangible' in separate religious statements or features also introduces the question of how they are interrelated between themselves and as a whole, and where they figure in what has come to be called the 'hierarchy of religious truths', not in the sense that some are more true than others, but in the sense that some are more fundamental, and closer to the centre of religious reality and the Christian world-view. Evidence that ambiguities, or even incoherence, can abound in people's religious scheme of things can be noted in the fact that, while 57 per cent profess a belief in heaven (markedly more than the European average), only 45 per cent believe in life after death. And most noticeably, what at first sight appears a highly impressive 76 per cent of British respondents professing a belief in God – which must be the basis of all other religious beliefs – evaporates under further enquiry into only 31 per cent conceiving of a personal God. Taking into account such other findings as the importance of God in individuals' lives, the comfort derived from religion, and the importance of passing on one's religion to the next generation, it is difficult to avoid the conclusion that Britain is at present largely a society possessed of a vague religiosity which should not be probed too far and which makes little conscious impact on people's lives. It might even appear that the characteristically British attitude to the deity is to encompass it within the generally tolerant benevolence of 'live and let live'.

At any rate, it does not appear, whether in questions or answers, that attention is addressed with full awareness to the point of religion, or to the fact that it relates to a transcendent, intelligent and benevolent being whose primary aim in our regard is to give rather than to receive, and whose purpose is to sustain his creation in a joint enterprise of ultimate love. Thus it is possible, and not uncommon, to depict the Judaeo-Christian scheme of things in terms of moral obligations of belief and behaviour, at the expense of centring them upon the divine purpose of election, and with little reference to divine grace or forgiveness. It is only such omission or neglect of an over all purpose and context of divine concern which can give credibility to systematic distinctions between the 'sacred' and the 'profane' in society, and to descriptions of 'secularisation' as the gradual displacement of God from His creation. The Christian realisation of God's saving will as universal was to push out the frontiers of the 'sacred' from particular places, times and interventions to embrace the whole of created reality, and to make 'secularisation' not a question of whether God is active in His world, but one of how He shares His purpose for society with mankind, according to it a certain autonomy and an active sharing in his own providence. Rather than the world being in God's hands as some deterministic form of 'automatic pilot', man is seen as co-pilot in the directing of human affairs.

The emergent awareness on man's part of his own historical and cultural responsibility, as described in Bonhoeffer's famous 'man come of age', can have the effect of religion's becoming marginalised in society, as the history of Europe has evidenced. But the reaction of the churches to this human bid for complete autonomy should not be one of repression or of attempting to cow man back into a primitive 'sacral' mentality with anathemas or charges of Adamite hubris. It must be a more discerning and patient response which positively encourages man to recognise and accept his world-wide responsibility for his own and future generations, and which seeks to discover and to foster what is characteristically human not just in man's self-questioning or loss of nerve, but in all human activity and enterprise. The Christian religion, as then seen, becomes not an ever-shrinking distinct sector of mental and social activity and behaviour in a shifting border-dispute between the 'sacred' and the 'secular', but an interpretative dimension of all living; not just a series of itemised tenets and rites, but the 'spiritual worship' of a 'transformed' attitude to the whole of life (Rom 12:2).

From the Values Study findings there is little evidence of such an approach to religion in Britain, unless it exists among those who 'belong' to the churches in more or less regular attendance at their services. The survey confirms what has long been acknowledged by the churches, a steady absolute and comparative decline in such participation, to a present small minority of committed Christians in British society. Factors contributing to such a decline in the established Church of England are identified by Tiller (1983, pp. 12–16) in Britain's becoming a post-industrial, permissive and pluralistic society. The Church, he observes (pp. 59–68), is moving from having been historically a 'communal' institution roughly co-terminous with society to an 'associational' type of religious body characterised by voluntary, rather than automatic, membership, and by active pursuit of its aims as a 'local Christian family' within wider social groupings. The social inevitability of this, as also the only positive way forward for all the churches, appears borne out by the data identifying the pattern of consistently active involvement on the part of only a minority of the population in Britain in the various social institutions, including the political parties, the trade unions, voluntary organisations and the churches, as is noted elsewhere in this volume. But it is not unique, of course, either to the Church of England or to this part of the globe. The phenomenon is to be observed elsewhere, including Latin America and the United States, in the emergence of 'basic Christian communities', of which the most theologically and socially coherent account has been proposed by Rahner in his various writings on the Church as a *diaspora* community.

Taking up the Old Testament theme of the people of Israel's being 'dispersed' and scattered like seed, Rahner sees the situation of Christians in today's increasingly pluralistic society as scattered similarly throughout the world, to be found everywhere but increasingly in an, at least comparative, minority. Sharing in a cultural situation where politics, economics, science, the arts and social well-being and welfare are formally non-Christian, and living within a sovereign non-Christian population which is at best religiously indifferent, betokens for many believers a new kind of Christianity, relying now not on a natural growth in numbers but on individual choice, not on social supports but on personal decisions and on options which were scarcely possible for the majority in previous generations. If the Church is to remain alive at all, Rahner concludes, it will be in permanent dependence on the active goodwill of its ordinary members, who will have to be encouraged to view themselves, not just as objects of the Church's pastoral attentions, but as the Church itself in all its self-awareness. Unable now to compete with public institutions and agencies, such a Church will become more immediately religious, concentrating on 'what is her own most vital sphere' (1963, p. 37).

Such an analysis could, of course, lead to a spirit of defeatism for the churches. Rahner's positive and realistic point for the Church, however, is that, being freed now by history from the temptation and the burden (or the illusion) of omnicompetence in society, the Church is in a position to take its own initiatives, choosing objectives suited to its limited resources rather than wasting energy in fighting the inevitable or in trying to perpetuate a vanished culture. No longer able to dominate, or even compete with, society, or to enforce its values, it must eschew any 'fanatically intolerant attack' (p. 40), but seek common ground on which to build, realising that the Church is by no means the only channel of God's grace into the minds, hearts and institutions of men. Such a patiently consensus approach, of course, will cover much more than explicitly religious values, and in fact, from the Values Study findings, it seems clear that it may well find much broader and sounder foundations in other value areas shared with non-believers and perfunctory believers, as we shall explore later in this chapter. For committed believers in a *diaspora*-type Church, however, the recruiting figures will always remain comparatively small, and be drawn from the numbers of those typically identified in the chapter of this study devoted to voluntary organisations. Nevertheless, a serious attempt by the Church to articulate and explain its beliefs along the lines previously mentioned, and especially within a re-vitalised view of its nature and role in modern society, may well do something to increase the ranks of committed Christians.

The permanent temptation for the churches, of course, faced with such an analysis of their present situation in society to confirm their gloomiest experiences, is to take refuge in becoming a sect. The choice is summed up by Hessert (1968, p. 109) in his observation that the *diaspora* Church is not aimed to save individuals from the world, but to proclaim Christ's lordship in the world. Such minority 'exclusive' bodies have ever recurred in the Christian spectrum in every age, and are readily identifiable in Britain today. What is of more concern, however, is the possibility of such defeatist tendencies growing in numbers and influence within the major Christian bodies. Tiller (1983, p. 61) refers to a view within the Church of England which would presage its becoming more explicitly a 'Eucharistic sect', and other observers have noted tendencies within the Roman Catholic community which may lead to similar results (Hornsby-Smith, 1984). Nor would this be particularly surprising in the aftermath of the Second Vatican Council. Excitement, defensiveness, enthusiasm, disillusionment and bitter resistance are all to be noted in the RC Church, in Britain as elsewhere, in the twenty years since the Council ended, stemming fundamentally from contrasting visions of a Church open to society and a Church on the defensive against society.

To the weakness of Christian fragmentation and the attractions of self-sufficient sectarianism, many today would oppose the positive force of ecumenism; and the enhanced value of joint evangelical witness in society is a commonplace of the ecumenical movement. It is interesting, however, that Tiller urges upon the Church of England the need for regular ecumenical collaboration with other churches at local levels, but that on the more fundamental question of mutual recognition by the churches of their Christian ministries – an issue central to the quest for Christian unity – he found it 'impossible in writing this report to presuppose anything about the progress of Church unity over the next forty years' (1983, p. 51; cf. p. 83). The failure of recent attempts at reunion no doubt provides sober grounds for such realism. Notwithstanding the impressive measure of doctrinal agreement achieved by the members of the Anglican-Roman Catholic International Commission (ARCIC) in its *Final Report* (1982), it is doubtful whether such eventual unity as appears currently envisaged will really make a major contribution in terms of numbers to Christian unity between these two major religious bodies and their adherents in Britain, or whether it will result in a more united presentation of the Christian gospel.

If the goal in view is a 'merger' of the two bodies, the result is likely to be not one new church but three, taking into account those Roman Catholics and Anglicans who would resist or decline to accept such unification. Such a type of union, however, is not that entertained by many Anglicans and some Roman Catholics, subscribing as they do to the ecumenical principle of 'united, not absorbed' dating from the Malines Conversations (Halifax, 1930), apparently alluded to by Pope Paul VI (*AAS* 62 (1970) p. 753) and recently explored by the Archbishop of Canterbury (*CIO*, 1981). And yet, should such corporate reunion eventually come about, the likelihood is that the Church of England in Britain will effectively absorb many of the Roman Catholic community as the consequence of not being itself absorbed by Rome, and that, again, whatever may be forecast for the Church of England, a Roman Catholic remnant will remain, embittered at both Canterbury and Rome, and the more disposed to retreat into the characteristics of a defensive sect.

Whether the new English Church would then take on a fresh lease of religious living and apostolic activity would remain to be seen. But more important is the underlying consideration of whether such possible consequences should be permitted to dictate the Church's activity in this field, or in any other area of its life and development. In an age characterised for 'committed' Christians (the modern and revealing substitute for 'devout' Christians) by what Hessert (1968, p. 102) terms 'the rediscovery of the Church', the Christian body of Christ in the world is acquiring a fresh awareness of its mission within human society, not as constituting the only means of grace and salvation in God's world but as called to be an outstanding expression, embodiment and agent (in other words, a sacrament) of God's love for the world and of mankind's response to God. This is very different from the traditional view of the Church as the ark of salvation designed to save as many passengers as possible from a sinful and perditious world and to carry them safely to their heavenly destination. Nor is it compatible with the view of the Church entertained by those who look to it 'only for the satisfaction of their wholly private "religious needs"' (Rahner, 1974, p. 116), or who subscribe to what Tiller (1983, p. 161) describes as 'that privatised religion which is the peculiarly English heresy and which fits so neatly and so dangerously into the wider privatisation of life today.' But it is a view which Rahner considered calls for a comparative 'neglect' of whose 'who will not want to fulfil the very serious demands which the new community makes on them' (1974, p. 115).

Such a 'thinning-out' policy, however, raises for the Church, with regard to many of its adherents, what traditional moral theology termed the problem of 'scandal', or the degree to which one's decisions and actions may constitute a 'stumbling block' to others by undermining their beliefs and behaviour. In the light of Paul's concern about the effects which the actions of knowledgeable, 'strong' Christians could have upon the consciences of their 'weaker brethren' (Rom 14–15; 1 Cor 8), the avoidance of such 'scandal of the weak' has subsequently become in many Christian bodies almost a pastoral principle regulating official attitudes to any innovation, and concerned with protecting the faith and peace of soul of those who are often also termed, or tacitly considered, the 'simple faithful'. Paul's ultimate answer to this problem was to educate the 'weak' out of their mistaken views, however, and the difficulties of canonising as a principle what was only the first step in his solution are several. Apart from its being a possible cloak for paternalism or for other motives for inaction, it does not take into account that the faithful are not all that 'simple' or weak, particularly today. And those most vociferously conservationist on their own or others' behalf are more accurately to be described in terms of what traditional moral theology distinguished as 'Pharisaical scandal', a determination to take offence at anything undermining their most cherished religious – or cultural – views, more akin to 'hardness of heart' than to the Pauline vulnerability of the uncertain.

The major pastoral objection, however, to accepting the avoidance of 'scandal of the weak' as a principle regulating all religious or moral innovation arises from its being in effect a policy that 'the convoy shall proceed at the speed of the slowest vessel.' The context is one of protection from hostile forces, where stragglers may be picked off one by one, and casualties must be kept to a minimum. It is the ark of salvation adapted to modern wartime conditions as the convoy of salvation. But what it completely fails to take into account is the fate of the 'strong', and the possibility of other types of casualties, both within the Church and among those to whom its message is addressed. For there can also be, and increasingly so today, a paradoxical 'scandal of the strong' in the churches and in society: those to whom theological and pastoral indecisiveness and procrastination constitute a 'stumbling block', for their faith in the Church particularly, and whose impatience and frustrated zeal can reveal a vulnerability and a 'weakness' of a different, but equally real, nature, when compared with traditionalism and conservationism.

In choosing its identity and therefore its adherents for the future, the Church in Britain appears to be faced with the hard, even ruthless, choice of deciding whether it would rather risk losing the 'weak', or the 'strong' who are weak in their own way. It might appear, however, that such a view of the churches' policy for the future is coming perilously close to the second metaphor with which we began this chapter, that of a Church adapting itself to market forces and packaging its product according to consumer wishes. In point of fact, what is really at issue is not simply a consequentialist calculus of which Church policies will retain or secure the greater number of adherents, if only because, as every anti-utilitarian knows, quality is at least as important a factor as quantity. It is more ultimately theological for the churches, whether individually or in union, to decline to play the 'numbers game' and to recognise that absolutely every decision by the Church will please some adherents and spectators and offend others. The best policy is to dismiss this incalculable factor from consideration, and to pursue saving truth as it emerges in the awareness of the Church from its contemplation of the Gospel and the signs of the times, trusting to the Spirit of truth to be also a strengthener or a consoler as appropriate.

Just as the gospel and its context may not be too simply distinguished, however, so also truth and its expression should not be too facilely separated; and here another consideration may be added in the light of our viewing the Church in each locality as *diaspora*. The Greek root verb *speiro* can mean either to scatter like seed or to sow seed. And the *diaspora* Church of today and tomorrow, while to all appearances socially negligible and vulnerable, is at the same time possessed of divine as well as human vitality. 'The seed is the Word of God' (cf. Lk 8:11). But there is no inherent necessity for its growth throughout the world to be identical. Indeed, to be an intelligible and flourishing Word in time and place it must accept the characteristics of each time and place. This is the ultimate rationale in theological terms for religious diversity and pluralism, whether successively throughout history or simultaneously in differing societies, to ignore which is to ignore both the incarnational propensity and adaptability of the Word and the inherently transitory nature of his Church. Herein lies the challenge to the British churches to discover a Church for Britain today, not nostalgic for dwindling heritages but building upon the present particular strengths and aspirations of a society which is also impoverished and challenged socially, racially, economically and culturally.

To do this at all effectively, attention will then have to be directed to the possible sources and resources from which such a Church can emerge, and here the Values Study findings for Britain appear to present both a promise and a problem. Given the 'associational' (Tiller) and '*diaspora*' (Rahner) nature of the Church here envisaged, the chapter in this work devoted to 'Values and Voluntary Work' is of particular relevance. Participation in various types of voluntary work is there distinguished in terms of *reciprocity* as mutual aid and exchange, *beneficence* as an 'old-style' service to dependents within a conservative attitude towards the current social order, and *solidarity* as a 'new-style' identification with equals in a joint programme of social change. The comment is made that these three norms 'appeal to increasingly smaller minorities as the focus moves from reciprocity, to beneficence, to solidarity'. It may be suggested that an illuminating parallel can be drawn between these three types of attitude to voluntary work, and the varying attitudes which exist towards the churches. It appears that most of the minority of church-adherents subscribe to a reciprocal and stable *individualistic* attitude to church membership of an almost contractual nature (*do ut des*), while fewer adopt an active but traditional view of the Church as a *service* provided for the needy, and fewest of all *identify* with it in solidarity as a witness to God's love and an agent for change, both in itself and in society.

In analysing the findings on the one-fifth of the population undertaking 'unpaid voluntary work', and on the one-sixth of these who are involved in the 'solidarity' type of activity, Gerard identifies the characteristics of a group, both actual and potential, within British society upon whom the churches, seeking recruits for a more active and participatory involvement in church life and activities, might do well to focus their efforts. Such appears to be the promise contained in the Values Study findings.

The allied problem contributed by the findings is the propensity towards conservatism to be found in so many unpaid volunteer workers in Britain. Such a propensity, which indicates a leaning more to what Abrams describes as 'traditionalism' than 'anti-traditionalism', while providing one direction for the expression of personal altruism and religious motivation in society which Gerard identifies as the 'old-style' service of beneficence, might also imply a certain resistance to such altruism being focused through a more participatory model of the Church and a programme for social change, whether within the churches or elsewhere. On the other hand, not all voluntary workers in Britain, whether actual or potential, are so conservatively minded or 'traditionalist'. And if the churches could look more to, and appeal more to, even so small a dynamic sector of British society, the result would be a transformation not only in the life of the Church but in its influence in society.

One final reflection may be offered on religious values as evidenced by the Values Study. If the true reading of the data is that of a 'snapshot' of individuals at a particular stage of their progress through the seven ages of man (and woman), then the clear evidence that younger people are less religiously inclined and committed than older people could be met with the rather standard response, sometimes despairing and sometimes worldly-wise and comforting, that the young will 'come back' in time, once they have 'settled down' in life, especially if they have had a 'good religious education'. And rather like a patient father, the Church need, or perhaps can, only await the return of the prodigal son to its forgiving embrace. On the other hand, various commentators place the Values Study findings within a general context, provided by other sources, of a progressive decrease in adherence to traditional, especially religious, values from generation to generation. This is supported by Tiller, and most recently by the survey, sponsored by the British Council of Churches, of *Teenagers and the Church* (Francis, 1984). The findings themselves also tend to confirm that religion will become even less important in Britain in the future, both as a general conclusion agreed to by a majority of respondents, and almost as guaranteed by the low proportion who considered it important to encourage religious faith at home among children.

If, then, a steady, or accelerating, decrease in commitment to religious values is seen as evidence of a qualitative change in British society, as elsewhere, rather than a transitory stage in the lives of many individuals, the attitude of the Church cannot be a patient one of waiting for the wandering sheep to return to the fold, but must be a more active policy of revolutionary response to what is being slowly identified as a revolution in society. Such a policy cannot be simply one of slight adjustments, tinkering with translations or redrawing diocesan boundaries. It must entail a fundamental re-thinking of the churches' membership, ministry and message in the light of these 'signs of the times'.

3. THE CHURCH'S MORAL ROLE

Attitudes to moral values were tapped in the Values Study through explicit questioning about the Decalogue and also through more circumstantial questions eliciting moral reactions to various, sometimes controversial, situations (Qq.208, 315, etc.). The analysis of 'the structure of moral values' (Chapter 4) points to the clear conclusion that, over all, a tendency to moral strictness appears a characteristically British feature. Of particular interest within this context of consistently high support for moral values is what commentators describe as the degree of relativism or absoluteness which respondents accord to them. In questions about 'wrong' behaviour where the choice afforded was not just between 'never justified' and 'always justified', but gave considerable scope for increasing degrees of qualification or justification, the results show that 'on almost all the items the majority of the British sample are *close to* the lower "never justified" end of the scale'. The most frontal, but also the bluntest, approach to the matter in general was the choice forced upon respondents (Q.154) either of accepting that 'there are absolutely clear guidelines about what is good and evil..., whatever the circumstances' or of acknowledging that 'there can never be clear and absolute guidelines... [It] depends entirely upon the circumstances at the time'. On this, Phillips and Harding comment that liberal respondents to specific situations tend to align themselves with moral relativity, while the more strict 'tend to show allegiance to a world of moral absolutes, based on clear guidelines'. And Gerard also refers to 'the widespread rejection of absolute guidelines in favour of a relativist moral position'.

The churches in Britain will doubtless be gratified at the evidence of a consistently high level of commitment to moral values in British society, if only to counter the impression frequently given by selective and sensational media coverage, and notwithstanding what appears to be a marked decline in adherence to religious values. One question, however, might particularly occupy their attention: why is it that the religiously committed are more strict and 'absolutist' in their application of moral precepts, and less inclined to take circumstances into account? No doubt, part of an answer to this question is to be found in their respect for the authority of the Bible and/or of church teaching based on the Bible, which is taken to be clear, comprehensive and uncompromising. And such reliance upon authority is in harmony with Abrams' conclusion that both religious commitment and respect for authority are of a piece in being strong elements of a consistently 'traditionalist' approach to values in society, most notably in 'values on religious beliefs, sexual mores and family life', but also marked 'on issues concerned with property rights, work and patriotism'. What appears to emerge, then, as characteristic of the religiously committed as a group is a generally traditionalist attitude (no doubt expressing itself in, and in turn reinforced by, traditional religion) which is, on the whole, resistant to change, and in this case to moral flexibility. It is an attitude which is not disposed to leave much room for manoeuvre in face of the circumstantial variety, and today's increasing complexity, of moral situations.

It is worth remarking, however, that the forced choice between, on the one hand, absolute moral guidelines regardless of any circumstances, and, on the other hand, morality *entirely* dependent on circumstances, can be misleading. The absolute is by definition uncompromising and exceptionless, but the relative admits of degrees. And this is much more in evidence in the findings related to the ten-point scale of justifying or mitigating circumstances introduced for the replies to the variety of moral situations with which respondents were confronted. There, as noted, the majority of British respondents in almost every case give a slightly qualified subscription to the moral value in question.

Is there something here which the British churches and their members, at least in some cases, have to learn from the Study findings, namely, a greater moral sensitivity to specific situations and a corresponding humility in their moral attitudes and teaching? Various Christian traditions and their theologians have found themselves constrained to discover some device to take account of circumstances without exposing themselves thereby to complete moral improvisation. The Aristotelian tradition of Aquinas distinguishes between 'primary' and unchangeable moral precepts and 'secondary' conclusions deduced from them which, although still precepts, do not invariably apply in all circumstances. More modern analyses distinguish between first-order principles and second-order rules, or develop 'middle axioms', to account for the contingent nature of reality. Others seek to refine moral terms, such as 'lying' or 'murder', with increasing qualifications. A more biblical approach invokes 'hardness of heart' to justify at least moral tolerance of certain types of behaviour. And, at a more systematic level, recognition is accorded by others that at times such is the nature of things that the morally best one can do is adopt 'the lesser of two evils'. What may be noted of all such approaches is that they are not designed so much to discover whether exceptions to moral norms may be morally acceptable, as to justify what may already be perceived, at least potentially, as exceptions to the received moral norms, without jettisoning such norms or subscribing to a view which would make of morality merely a matter of the circumstances prevailing at the time. It might also be argued that such moral flexibility in the light of circumstances, far from betokening a decline of morality into chaotic, incoherent or 'subjective' relativism, indicates, at least in principle, a more refined degree of moral sensitivity which is respectful of the complexity and of what Macquarrie calls the 'facticity' of reality, and is not wishful to straitjacket it into unreflected moral categories or stereotypes.

An allied question raised by the Values Study findings concerns the relationship between the impressive moral consensus which appears to exist in Britain and the very poor and apparently declining value placed upon religion. It might be presumed from this that, as religion declines further in Britain, so the adherence to moral values will disintegrate. But this is to over-identify morality with religion. As we have observed, Christian morality does not, any more than 'human' morality, necessarily call for moral absolutes 'irrespective of cir-cumstances'. Rather, despite the findings that committed Christians find it particularly difficult to allow for circumstances, it requires attention to circumstances. Moreover, in the light of what was said at the beginning of this chapter, reference to morality as 'Christian' requires careful handling. If it denotes the moral precepts as taught for centuries within the Judaeo-Christian tradition, then as a matter of simple description it is unexceptionable. But if it implies that such precepts are the exclusive prerogative of Christian moral teaching, to stand or fall with Christian religious values, then it is making access to such moral precepts too restricted altogether. For the broadly Catholic approach to morality has always maintained that the human mind, unaided by a special revelation, is at least in principle capable of attaining to the basic principles of a human morality such as are (also) to be found in the Judaeo-Christian Decalogue.

It may be answered that, as a matter of historical fact, it has been at least primarily through the Christian Church that these moral rules have entered into the consciousness of men and of Western society. It may also be shown, as from the Values Study findings, that the more religiously committed have a rather deeper attachment to them than do others. But it could be that this deeper attachment is to be explained, in part at least, by religious motives of devotion and loyalty to God as the originator of such precepts, and not necessarily in terms of a heightened moral sensitivity; particularly when, as has been noted, it is the more committed Christians who tend to be more unwilling to qualify them according to circumstances. Whatever may be the explanation for stricter adherence, it can certainly be argued that those who are not committed Christians are slightly less attached as a group to the moral precepts in question, though still impressively espousing them. From this it could not however be concluded that if and as they depart increasingly from Christian religious beliefs, so they will correspondingly cease to give adherence to the human moral principles preached by the Church. There could well be a level of moral awareness beneath which they would not, on the whole, be disposed to sink regardless of their religious attitudes. Consequently, one cannot simply conclude that the impressive moral awareness evinced by the great majority of the population of Britain is to be explained solely in terms of its living on a rapidly dwindling historical Christian capital, to vanish progressively as that capital itself ceases to exist.

If not solely on religion, then on what, or partly on what, might such continuing adherence to moral values be based? It is over-ambitious to treat the British public in general as if it were composed of moral philosophers preoccupied with consistency and with ethical systems. On the one hand, a true account of the moral agent might be that of C. P. Snow, at the end of his *Last Things*, when he has his central character reflect on his son, 'He might know already, what had taken me so much longer to learn, that we made ends and shapes and patterns in our minds but that we didn't live our lives like that. We couldn't do so, because the force inherent in our lives was stronger and more untidy than anything we could tell ourselves about it.' And on the other hand, such moral inconsistency and fluctuation as may be detected may be ascribed less to the agent and more to the increasing intractability of objective situations, as Abrams' large class of moral ambivalents would tend to confirm.

It may be surmised from the British Values Study findings that we are today in presence of an avowal of certain moral values, influenced to some extent by the Christian religious past, but in principle capable of standing on their own moral feet, despite certain defects to which we shall refer later. Perhaps largely inarticulate, it appears to have the characteristics of a blend of popular intuitionism and a basic sense of justice. The difficulties of identifying justice, and the dangers of competing intuitions, are well known. But what the data seem to witness to are what Hampshire refers to (1978, p. 15) as 'elementary decencies', and attitudes exemplifying his view that 'in decisions of substantial moral concern, inferences of the intuitive kind have a proper place alongside inferences of the explicit and fully articulated kind' (p. 36). In the case of British respondents to the Values Study these may be identified, and in varying degrees articulated, in rather popular terms of fairness, tolerance and a general attitude of 'live and let live' which may be considered not to fall very far short of the Golden Rule to be found in the Gospels (cf. Mt 7:12) and other ethical sources.

It is such inherent characteristics and dispositions that the churches could well confirm and encourage, and upon which they could build. But with care to respect the changing realities and relationships of modern living, and above all concerned to propose, as Rahner expresses it, 'morality without moralising'. 'We are moralising if we expound norms of behaviour peevishly or pedantically, full of moral indignation at a world without morals, without really tracing them back to that innermost experience of man's nature, which is the source of the so-called principles of natural law and which alone gives them binding force' (1974, p. 66). And the rejection by the churches of such moralising is not just a self-denying ordinance. It also has positive implications:

> It is a fact that man and his environment ... have become much more complex and unfathomable than formerly. Because they were formerly more simple, ... because they were also much more stable and unchangeable, it was possible to assert relatively simple and stable norms of behaviour, by which man could come to terms with himself and his environment. The consequences of what a person might do had already been often tested and could be sufficiently clearly foreseen; it was therefore possible to provide very clear moral norms of behaviour, which were relatively simple to manage ... . Today these human realities are both much more complex and at the same time left to man's control to a greater extent; they include elements which formerly simply did not exist as objects on which man could exercise his freedom and thus did not demand any moral norms. This very much more complex world, however, is for that reason much more difficult to understand and therefore no longer so easily provides simple and manageable norms for man and for the Church (pp. 67–8).

The role, then, for the churches is not intensified moral instruction which provides pre-packaged answers, but sustained moral education, in which there is 'a very important change of emphasis in Christian proclamation: consciences must be formed, not primarily by way of a casuistical instruction, going into more and more concrete details, but by being roused and trained for autonomous and responsible decisions in the concrete, complex situations of human life which are no longer completely soluble down to the last detail, in fields never considered by the older morality, precisely because they were then unknown and even now cannot be adequately mastered by a rational casuistry' (p. 68).

THE MISSION OF THE CHURCH

Of course, the Church's primary mission so far as it concerns morality is not to propound it, but to exemplify it; and this not in calculated terms of setting a good example or trying to make its moral message more credible to others, but by working to be itself what it is called to be. The Church *is* its message; its being *is* its witness. Barth, for instance, concluded (1958, p. 721) that 'the decisive contribution which the Christian community can make to the upbuilding and work and maintenance of the civil consists in the witness which it has to give to it and to all human societies in the form of the order of its own upbuilding and constitution', which he saw pre-eminently expressed in (p. 726) internal 'righteousness, peace and freedom'. Rahner, as we have seen, concluded that the refinement of its self-awareness which history is forcing upon the Church is leading it to concentrate on what is its own 'most vital sphere'. And in his study on '*Rethinking the Mission of the Church*' (1978, ch. 1), Dulles compares events in the RC Church in the United States after the Vatican Council with what had happened among the Protestant churches there in the 1930s, in the disillusionment of the 'social gospel' movement leading to a growing appeal to 'let the Church be the Church'.

Such views of apparently concentrating on asking the Church to rediscover itself are not, however, to be seen as expressions of isolationism or as aspirations for a cloistered existence, or as acquiescing in exasperated injunctions for the churches to 'keep out of politics'. They are no more than a continual reassertion of what should be the Church's priorities in mission, a reminder of the teaching to seek first God's kingship around which all else will fall into place, a recalling of perspective for the Church. 'A Church centred on God and on God's gift in Jesus Christ should not obstruct the praiseworthy endeavours of building human communities and of transforming social structures. It should powerfully assist its members to do both' (Dulles, p. 25). Or they are perhaps to be seen as the ever necessary reminders of Chaucer's sardonic comment on the humble parson, in contrast with others, that

'Christ's lore, and his Apostles' twelve
He taught – and first he followed it himself.'

If the 'law', in classical Reformation theology, is conceived as primarily a 'mirror to sin', confronting man with the depths to which he is capable of sinking and may have sunk, then by contrast, it may be suggested, the Church is called to be a 'mirror to grace', holding out to man the heights to which he may aspire and rise, and already has in some measure. 'Come and see' (Jn 1:39) should therefore be the primary command and invitation of all the churches, with the corresponding obligation incumbent on them to be such a mirror, and to draw their own and then others' attention to features which today require especial consideration, so that those human qualities which appear lacking or dim in society at large may be shown in the Church as being accorded careful highlighting. And one such general quality, to which the Church is particularly called by its own nature and constitution, and which the Study findings appear on the whole to show as lacking in Britain, is what the New Testament describes as *koinonia*, weakly translated as 'fellowship', or something of what Gerard refers to as the active 'solidarity' with others regularly subscribed to by only a tiny percentage of the population.

In the previous section we advanced the suggestion that the impressive adherence in Britain to moral values could be seen as so many expressions of a general attitude of 'live and let live'. But the maxim is capable of a minimalising or individualistic interpretation which expresses general benevolence coupled with an emotional and psychological, almost guarded, distancing from other individuals. And in the Values Study data for Britain this latter feature also appears to be a characteristic underlying many responses. Trust in others is not a conspicuously British trait. We have already seen how small is the percentage actively involved in voluntary work, even of the 'dispensing charity' type. In analysing British attitudes to work, Fogarty notes no great appreciation of the 'sociable aspect' of work, a widespread reluctance to work actively for trade unions and what may be a general endorsement of the free and independent pursuit of individual and group interest without too much regard for overall consequences. Evidence of a general inclination towards uninvolvement appears also from Phillips's analysis of *Participation and Political Values* (Chapter 6). And on the forced choice between 'personal freedom' and 'social equality' he notes a three-to-one preference for the former, which 'shows that concern for individual liberty is a core political value among British people and suggests that any party programme which adopts "equality" as a central component will have limited appeal'. It is not difficult to see how such attitudes can coalesce and harden into the 1980s version of Disraeli's 'two Nations' analysed recently by the Bishop of Liverpool in his contrast between 'Comfortable Britain' and 'the Other Britain' (Sheppard, 1984).

It is perhaps in marriage and the family as social institutions that one would traditionally look for the greatest solvents of individualism and disinclination to go out of one's way for others, especially since, as the chapter on 'Marriage and the Family' notes, various current myths about marriage and the family seem to centre on a belief that they 'are threatened by individuals' attitudes and behaviour'. The facts show that marriage (including re-marriage) remains highly popular and still tends to be regarded as permanent, even although 'the reality of what constitutes permanence has changed considerably' in terms of greatly increased life expectancy. Overall, it is concluded, the institutions themselves are not under threat but rather changes have taken place in the ways that individuals live out their marital and family lives. The quality of personal relationships (faithfulness, mutual respect, understanding, tolerance) is seen as the most important ingredient of a successful marriage, and women in general are 'more sensitive to deteriorating relationships in marriage'. Finally, there is a high recognition of parents' duties towards their children 'even at the expense of their own well-being'.

The churches, concerned about increasing marital breakdown, will certainly peruse with interest the pre-marital and marital factors which enter into divorce and, in our present context and in the light of rising expectations, those of a personal character. They might well also consider that it appears to be within the marital and family relationship, particularly as conceived by committed Christians, that recognition is more likely to be accorded to values expressive of active commitment for others which, if more prevalent throughout British society, could do much to give greater other-directedness and enrichment to those 'elementary decencies' already to be found there in large measure. And a 'mirror' manifesting such 'marital' (or, for the Christian, 'covenant') values as faithfulness, mutual respect, understanding and tolerance as particularly esteemed and practised in the life of the churches could well be the most appropriate expression of the Church's witness within Britain today.

For these all appear also to be particular expressions of that *koinonia* ethics to which the Church is called, and of which man, made in God's image, may be thought to possess intimations. The term *koinonia*, meaning fellowship, or 'communion', occurs frequently throughout the New Testament. At its most practical it refers to the collection contributed to by many of the early Christian communities coming to the aid of the Jerusalem Church. But it also denotes a 'sharing' of other resources, including the spiritual, based on a prior, or simultaneous, shared reception of God's own gifts, notably in the fellowship of Christians; in the Eucharistic meal; in the Lord, and even in God's own being as 'partakers of the divine nature' (2 Pet 1:4). As a sharing which is at the same time receptive and outgoing, *koinonia* is 'the term that most aptly expresses the mystery underlying the various New Testament images of the Church' (*ARCIC*, 1982, p. 6).

It may also be suggested, on the other hand, that such *koinonia* is not something extraneous to man which is superimposed by grace as a Christian collectivism suppressing man's 'natural' individualism.

> An influential model of man which has developed in Europe over the last few centuries, in reaction to despotism and absolutism, whether political or economic, has been that of the individual possessed of a full panoply of human rights which he is prepared to defend stoutly against all comers, and some of which he will grudgingly cede or delimit for the compensating benefits of living and working at peace in the company of others. It is not entirely easy to see how this philosophical isolationist view of man, which is a pure abstraction, accords either with the Aristotelian and Thomist view that man is by nature a social being, or with the Christian ideal and command of living for others (Mahoney, 1981, p. 251).

To the contrary, man as a being made for community, not just a 'company', or Tönnies-like *Gesellschaft*, and man as created in the image of God are to be interpreted, it is suggested, as pointing to one and the same constitutional feature of man. Where earlier centuries saw the 'image' of God in man, or that in which he resembles his Creator, as the human endowment of reason, or the human capacity for control or craftsmanship in nature, a modern view, strongly influenced by an increasing awareness of human sexuality, inclines to a more dynamic understanding of the divine image in man as his calling to reflect in his own being the interpersonal life which is at the centre of divine Being as Father, Son and Holy Spirit. Man's calling from creation is to live in relationship, whether with God, or in the 'covenant' of marriage and family, or in the 'communion' of the

Church, or in the wider nexus of the whole human family. So much so, that, it may be suggested, it is not each individual, but the totality of interrelated mankind, which will come fully to image forth the interpersonal fullness of God.

This progressive purpose of divine love not only finds its fullest expression for the Church as an ethics directed towards expressing and building up *koinonia* with God and within humanity. It also imparts to the Church the mission of reflecting within human society that the 'image' of God in man which founds human ethical values makes of these at root an ethics of community, of generous concern, which will find its flowering and fruit in the *koinonia* ethics to which Christianity is committed. The mission of the Church, then, is to *show* (not just to teach) man what he is called to be and what he is already capable of becoming as made after the image of God. In this is rooted the task of the Church, as Dulles (1978, p. 25) describes it, 'of building human community and of transforming social structures', commencing always with itself and ever aiming, in Barth's expression (1958, p. 636), 'to offer the witness which is the meaning of its existence in world-history'.

In the British responses to the European Values Study there is to be found little, if anything, of this view or vision of the Christian Church, and such absence constitutes major challenges for the churches in Britain to share their appreciation of the Gospel (and of 'religion') and their aspirations for the Church in ways communicable to modern man in a changing society. In the Study, perhaps in the nature of the case, there is also little to be found on the global problems confronting society, the issues of nuclear war and energy, and the running sores of hunger and injustice which project onto a giant world screen the Gospel parable (Lk 16: 19–20) of Lazarus outside the gate of Dives, compared with which some of the items in the questionnaire may at first sight appear parochial, or even trivial. Nor does it appear possible from the findings to explore to any great extent what differences may obtain between values as individually espoused and the collective values generated in human groups, of which Niebuhr's *Moral Man and Immoral Society* was so pessimistic. Nevertheless, life begins with individuals and, in the Christian scheme, ends with individuals in community and their attitudes and values. And within the limitations of enquiry into the overt and implicit moral values and attitudes of individuals in Britain there appears much for which the churches may give the glory to God, if not to themselves. For the God of creation is also the God who saves. In welcoming such intimations of 'Christian morality', the Church's task might well be to receive them as signs of God's times, to be itself challenged by them, and to encourage and foster them, and thus share in furthering the work of His hands.

11 Subjectivism and Social Planning

DAVID WATSON

INTRODUCTION

A study of moral value systems must have a plausible account of how *moral* values are to be identified. This, the Values Study lacks. According to Stoetzel, 'morality represents the collection of rules which govern our behaviour' (1983, p. 2), but this will not do. To begin with, he neglects the question of the *source* of those rules: perhaps we govern our own behaviour through moral rules; perhaps others govern us by this means. Further, talk of moral *rules* is problematic (see Melden, 1959; Phillips and Mounce, 1969; Warnock, 1971). According to de Moor and Kerkhofs, 'Man defines his own identity by ordering his thoughts and deeds according to a fundamental set of principles which are drawn from a logical system of values' (Stoetzel, 1983, p. vi). This too is problematic. As Warnock has pointed out, 'there is absolutely no reason to assume that the needs, wants, and interests of any one individual will just naturally form what might be called a consistent set, or coherent programme' (1971, p. 19). If this is true for the individual, there is even more reason to doubt that such consistency occurs across a whole society.

De Moor is conscious of the lack of a clear conception of moral values, but what he offers by way of assistance is too brief, and serves only to highlight the imprudence of the omitted research (de Moor, 1983). He comments that 'the concept of value is not well-defined in the scientific literature'. This is unsurprising, for the questions 'what is a value? and 'what is a moral value?' are not scientific questions;

the philosophical literature is richer (see Wallace and Walker, 1970). I have chosen to offer a discussion presenting a reasoned, and, I hope, constructive scepticism in relation to the account of moral values dominant in the Values Study and the policy implications of its findings. I shall argue that the dominant account of moral values assumed in the Values Study, and the reports of its results to which I shall refer, make it impossible that the results will be useful to anyone. This conclusion must be approached one step at a time, and the first step is clarification of what I regard as the dominant conception. Evidence of its *actual* dominance in the Values Study is presented as the second step. I shall then draw the awkward conclusion.

It is perhaps worth adding that the dominant account of moral values in the Values Study is a feature of a particular sociological perspective not unique to this Study, and that authors contributing to this volume were often engaged to analyse data gathered within a research design to be taken as given.

STEP ONE

Subjectivism

The conception of moral values dominant in the Values Study is based in what moral philosophers call 'subjectivism'. Like any view with a lengthy history, subjectivism comes in various guises, and that of contributors to discussion of the Values Study is not consistently in just one form. Two forms recur most frequently, and may be embodied in the following statement:

> A person's moral judgements merely state, or express, his or her own attitudes: moral judgements cannot be proved true, or shown to be sound; they are merely matters of individual opinion.

My purpose here is not to try to *prove* the view ill-founded. I aim simply to show that, in the absence of argument, those who accept subjectivism[1] beg a number of important conceptual questions with the following results, among others: they adopt a conception of moral values which is itself highly problematic, and which entails equally problematic accounts of the genesis of moral values, and the policy implications of citizens' moral values. The philosophical criticisms of subjectivism which I shall report and develop, all flow from the fact that subjectivism severs the connection between moral values, attitudes and judgements, and reasoning.

Moral judgements as statements or mere expression of attitudes

Let us begin with the assertion that a person's moral judgements *state* his or her own attitudes. In what way is this problematic?

If moral judgements *describe* the speaker's own attitude, conversation on moral issues becomes significantly flat: 'So', you say to me, 'this is your house, this is your dog, and these are your moral attitudes; mine are all quite different – how fascinating'. And there is nothing more to be said. Subjectivism severs the connection between moral judgement and reasoning: moral judgements are not conclusions reached by reasoning, so when attitudes are stated, there is no scope for discussion of the adequacy of that reasoning. Subjectivism removes any suggestion that a difference of moral value, attitude or judgement, can amount to a clash to be resolved by reconsideration of the grounds leading us to our different views. No attitude taken by one person challenges the logic of any attitude taken by another: there can be no interpersonal moral disagreements in which 'something's got to give' as a matter of logic; we may differ in the attitude we do take to certain circumstances, but we cannot disagree over, and debate, the right attitude to take (see Williams, 1972, pp. 29–30). This corollary of subjectivism, in the form in question, should at least make us sceptical of its capacity to illuminate human social life, if only because in eliminating the possibility of interpersonal moral disagreement, it offers a more spartan conception. Alternatives which accommodate the phenomenon excluded by subjectivism in this form may be more valuable in discriminating importantly different types of human behaviour and corresponding types of explanation.

Let us next concentrate on the idea that a person's moral judgements *merely express* his or her attitude. Again, the force of the words emphasised is that moral judgements cannot be proved true, or shown to be soundly reasoned. As Williams has pointed out, to assert that moral judgements merely express attitudes is *not* to deny that such attitudes are to be taken seriously; in some cases it may be 'that they are attitudes which we get disturbed about; that it matters to us to secure similarity of attitude within society' (1972, p. 31). However, because subjectivism in this second form also severs the connection between moral judgement and reasoning, though there is scope for moral attitudes to be 'taken seriously' in the sense outlined, there is *no* scope for them to be taken seriously in the sense which requires examination of the reasoning by which the moral judgement is reached, to determine whether or not the speaker's judgement, or one's own if different, is well-grounded. Again, subjectivism's spartan conception of moral values entails a simpler picture of human social life, but one which may be too crude to illuminate our experience. Further, and what is also problematic, subjectivism in this form leaves no possibility for us to include in our social planning attempts to secure similarity of attitude, even in part, by demonstrating by argument that a particular attitude is well-grounded, and all others at least less well-grounded. Goodbye democracy.[2]

The genesis of moral judgements

Non-subjectivists who conceive of moral judgement as the conclusion of reasoning, face the difficult task of discriminating sound from unsound moral reasoning; subjectivists avoid this task, but must offer *some* account of the *genesis* of such utterances. If moral judgements are not the conclusions of a process of thought, are they plausibly the result of an act of *will*, a matter of *choice* and *decision*? As with use of the word 'judgement', we may be reluctant to regard utterances not based on reasoning as the results of 'choice' or 'decision', since each usually carries the implication of preceding consideration of grounds for one choice or decision as opposed to another. However, though the utterances in question are not supported by reasons, they may have a 'background' of a different kind. The soundness of reasoning from grounds to judgement is a public matter: your logic must survive scrutiny by others; on the other hand, the adequacy of this 'background' to which you refer, as a means of explaining your judgement, may be a private matter: no objections to it which I might raise can require you to change your mind. Consider how we might treat your judgement that 'you ought to spend more time beside the sea because you find it bracing'. Thus moral judgements are assimilated to mere expressions of taste or preference.

Reduction

Such assimilation is often part of *reduction*; that is, 'of regarding all interests, ideals, aspirations and desires as on the same level, and all respresentable as preferences, of different degrees of intensity, perhaps, but otherwise to be treated alike' (Sen and Williams, 1982, p. 8). Reduction simplifies theories, but has costs 'in the context of justification, criticism and practical deliberation' (see Sen and Williams, 1982, p. 8). Reduction makes all 'preferences' equal, so that a preference grounded in desires would be as weighty as a preference grounded in a person's interests or ideals. To accept this is to abandon the notion of *rights* as a component of our moral outlook. Rights presuppose a *ranking* among 'preferences', so that rights may be sustained, defended, by reference, say, to a person's interests over opposition grounded in mere desires. In severing moral values, attitudes and judgement from reasoning, subjectivists deny the existence of a context of justification, criticism and deliberation in which judgements figure as conclusions, and in which rights may be recognised.

Suppose you come across someone who is drowning. On the present account it is an adequate 'defence' of letting him drown, that you don't like getting wet. Even if you hold the 'view' that human life ought to be saved when the person in question wishes to be saved, when this 'view' is reduced to the level of a mere preference, and matched against a conflicting preference for staying dry, then priority may be determined only by the relative intensity of your preferences; no criticism could properly attach to your decision.

A causal account of the genesis of moral judgements

At this point subjectivism is revealed as having its roots in a *causal* theory of moral values. That causal theory may be more or less elaborated. It may simply gesture towards 'the evident extent to which attitudes are modified by factors such as the desire to conform with one group or nonconform with another – the groups themselves not being chosen in the light of moral reasons, but rather determined by the individual's situation and needs' (Williams, 1972, p. 32). Or it may more robustly assert that, because of their lengthy past use in emotional situations by which we have been conditioned, moral judgements have the causal power to express and evoke attitudes: the occurrence of an emotion, it may be said, causes us to utter the associated moral judgement, and in turn evokes an attitude in the hearer.

Firstly, as Urmson has argued, 'since one cannot evoke in a hearer an attitude that he already fully shares' (1968, p. 39), causal theories of the type in question cannot satisfactorily explain our making moral judgements in the presence of hearers known to share fully our attitude. The causal theory leads us to the view that in conversation on moral matters with anyone who shares our attitudes, and is known to do so, to utter moral judgements is to say things we know to be redundant, and which our audience, and we ourselves somehow, do not find tedious.

I suppose it may be suggested that our continuing to utter moral judgements in the presence of hearers known to share fully our attitude to a certain *type* of behaviour, say, may alert them to the occurrence of the evocative behaviour on this *particular* occasion, rather as the cry of one bird, in response to a predator, alerts others fully sharing its attitude.

Or, perhaps, the awkward class of utterances in question might be explained by pointing out that we are often less sure that our attitude is *fully* shared than the criticism allows, so that such utterances are unlikely to be thought, and may often not be, *wholly* redundant. Their point would be to evoke a more corresponding attitude in others with attitudes already partly corresponding.

However, each of these explanations presupposes a degree of self-consciousness and a capacity for control in relation to our utterances where there is good *reason* to exercise control, something inconsistent with a purely causal theory which makes such utterances mere responses.

Further, at least consistently, it might be suggested that however redundant from the point of view of evocation it may be to make a moral judgement in this context, one simply cannot help oneself, the utterance being caused by the presence in us of the emotion it expresses; rather like involuntary wind, it is something to be tolerated by fellow-travellers.

Secondly, among those who fully share our attitude, we may reasonably expect to number ourselves. Since, on the type of causal theory in question, to make a moral judgement is merely to respond to an attitude or emotion one *already* has, what are sometimes called 'self-directive' moral judgements are particularly puzzling. It can hardly be suggested that self-directive moral judgements are caused by our not fully sharing our own attitudes. Of course, we may not always or often be wholly committed in a particular attitude, but then that condition should evoke a correspondingly ambivalent utterance.

'Moral attitudes', within a non-causal account of moral judgements

Within causal theories an attitude is manifested in our making moral judgements which are caused by our emotions. Non-causal theories connect emotions and attitudes much more loosely, and in the case of some attitudes, not at all. As Urmson puts it:

My attitude to something is not more or less the same thing as my emotional relation to it; one's emotions and attitude can indeed be in conflict ... emotion is only one among the relevant factors in the case of any attitude, and always a factor which can be outweighed by others .... Thoughts, beliefs, words and deeds are all also relevant, and will be expected, as a matter of logic and not merely of psychological appropriateness, to vary in character according as the attitude is one of interest, indifference, disdain, aloofness, friendliness, benevolence, hostility, or, let us add, approval .... .

Now our emotions are relatively beyond our control ... we may try to suppress them, to discipline ourselves in ways which we expect to modify them, or to have them modified for us by psychotherapists; but we cannot simply choose which emotions to feel. We can, however, choose our words and deeds, or most of us can most of the time. Because of this we can to a great extent choose our attitudes and thus be immediately responsible for them, particularly those attitudes to which word and deed are of paramount importance. This, in its turn, explains why we can and do speak quite naturally of people adopting attitudes and maintaining them, of people being argued out of them, of logically consistent and inconsistent sets of attitudes, of well-based and ill-considered attitudes, and so on. But we do not adopt or maintain our feelings and emotions; we are not argued out of them; though they may be appropriate, they can hardly be well-based (1969, pp. 31–43).[3]

The intelligibility of 'preaching to the converted' and 'self-directive judgements' within a non-causal account

Moral judgements in the presence of hearers known to share fully our attitude may be understood by making rather different use of the fact that attitudes are to types of behaviour as well as to tokens of that type. That a particular episode is an example of behaviour of a type to which we have a common attitude is something to be established by *argument*. What I say must be grounded in features of the behaviour in its context, which warrant my classification of it, and extension to it, of our attitude towards 'that sort of thing'. So, for example, I may make the moral judgement that our employer ought to be strongly and publicly reprimanded because his behaviour is sexist. I know that you share my hostile attitude to sexism. But in any particular case my judgement may be well-grounded or ill-grounded, and one obvious advantage in making that judgement in the presence of hearers known to share one's attitude fully is that it provides an opportunity for the soundness of one's judgement to be examined. Causal theories imply that 'in face of a mere matter of fact we could always *without logical fault* maintain any attitude whatsoever' (Urmson, 1968, p. 19, emphasis added). Non-causal theories, on the other hand, recognising an essential connection between moral judgement and reasoning, leave room for an audience fully sharing our attitude to persuade us of the unsoundness of the reasoning by which we justify extending the attitude in question to the particular behaviour in question, so that we *must* change our attitude, faced by the facts (see also Williams, 1972, p. 50).

How are self-directive moral judgements to be understood? Given the connection between moral judgement and reasoning, we may explain such judgements as the conclusions of your own reasoning about the situation in which you find yourself; revised self-directive moral judgements reflect re-appraisal of your former reasoning. Further, given the connection between moral judgement and reasoning, such judgements may themselves be reasons for reaching further conclusions on which you ought to act, and figure in your thinking about the implications of your judgement.

We have considered the costs of more robust causal theories of the genesis of moral judgement. What of the costs of less robust causal theories? I want to confine myself simply to the point that the much less robust form briefly indicated earlier may be compatible with non-causal explanations, because neither claims to tell the whole story. One may recognise an essential connection between moral judgement and reasoning and still believe it possible to 'overestimate the extent to which people are led by rational considerations to modify their moral views' (Williams, 1972, p. 32). Moral attitudes and judgements are not always well-reasoned, of course, and sometimes reasons advanced are rationalisations, but the *undue* influence of motives (interests and desires) is measured by appraisal of the soundness of the moral reasoning.

STEP TWO

I have argued that in severing moral values from reasoning, a subjectivist conception makes a highly problematic contribution to our understanding of human social life. I turn now to textual evidence of the actual dominance of such a conception in the Values Study.

Subjectivism has its roots in the *causal* explanation of human social behaviour, and I should like to begin by reviewing textual evidence within the Values Study of such an account of the genesis of moral values.

A causal account of moral judgements

The direction of the search to be conducted is fixed in the published preliminary descriptions of the Values Study: 'The study will explore values ... in a variety of *settings* ... The study will attempt to validate or refute a number of hypotheses', including the hypothesis that 'variables previously thought to provide *causal explanations of values* such as social class, income and education are less important than the age, spiritual and political disposition of the *respondent* and his or her stage in the life cycle' (EVSSG, 1980, p. 3, emphases added). Grounds for holding a particular moral view might, with strain, be described as its 'setting', but the other emphasised phrases suggest that a person's moral values, attitude or judgement, is to be explained not by reference to reasoning he has found convincing, but by reference to what Stoetzel places under the broad heading of 'sociological factors': 'The significance of moral judgements is clarified by the sociological factors to which they are linked, and which produce significant differences ... In the moral arena ... the most important are a person's age, his level of education, as well as his political and religious outlook' (1983, p. 16). 'Sociological factors' are investigated with a view to the discovery of statistically significant *correlations* (see de Moor, 1983).

At various points Stoetzel talks of a 'system of moral values' (p. 17) or of morality as a 'collection of rules' (p. 2); others, such as de Moor and Kerkhofs talk of 'principles ... drawn from a logical system of values' (preface to Stoetzel, 1983, p. vi), and de Moor (1983) of 'value patterns' and 'value orientations'. Such phrases may seem to distance the authors from a causal account of the genesis of moral judgements, if only because of their ambiguity. However, in every case it turns out that the search is for 'objective factors' such as social class, work, sex, age and education (de Moor, 1983) on which 'value orientations' are dependent. Only to someone committed to a causal account of the genesis of moral judgements could it be a striking finding that, generally speaking, it makes no difference to value orientations held whether one is male or female, living in urban or rural areas, belonging to higher or lower professional groups or to higher or lower income categories (de Moor, 1983); only someone committed to a causal account could regard it as worthy of note that 'politics does not appear to be a substitute for religion, just as religion is not a substitute for politics' (Phillips, Chapter 6 in this volume). In each case, someone recognising an essential connection between moral values and reasoning would expect such a result. In the first case, because the soundness of our reasoning is independent of our sex, where we live, or whatever, and people in *any* of the categories might reason soundly, or unsoundly. In the second case, because though religious conclusions may have implications for politics, and vice versa, in general the subject-matter of reasoning in religion and politics is quite distinct.

The passage just quoted from Stoetzel is interesting in classifying features such as age and political outlook under one heading. This parallels the preliminary Values Study document's classification of age and 'political disposition' as both possible 'causal explanations of values'. Each thus begs the question I wish to raise, and which subjectivism precludes: is there not a non-causal form of explanation of a person's moral values, attitudes and judgements, in which features such as 'age' cannot figure, whereas features such as 'political disposition' can play a part? The former, even if positively correlated with a judgement, is never in itself a reason which may be seriously given for reaching that judgement. To answer the question 'On what grounds do you come to the conclusion that "video-nasties" ought to be illegal?' by saying 'I'm 64' would be deeply puzzling. On the other hand, a political disposition, considered as a system of beliefs, may itself have moral implications and so provide a reason for the assertion of a particular moral judgement.

If all this is correct, then direction of our search for understanding of moral values away from non-causal explanation stands in need of justification for it seems that we will have no understanding without it. Dissatisfaction with causal explanation is encouraged by strikingly unilluminating descriptions of the relation between the 'sociological factors' and moral judgement: they are 'linked' (Stoetzel, 1983, p. 16) as an 'effect' (Stoetzel, 1983, p. 19) all of which indeed leaves obscure 'what *processes* take place' (Stoetzel, 1983, p. 19, emphasis added).

Features which can, and features which cannot figure as a reason may both be significantly positively correlated with a particular moral value and yet only non-causal explanation provide understanding. This may occur in a number of ways. First, because some reasoning is unsound and widespread. Think of the many occasions on which 'because you're a man (woman)' is offered as a reason in a context in which it is irrelevant. Second, some features irrelevant in themselves as grounds for a moral judgement, are nevertheless correlated with experiences which, in general, provide opportunities for a person to better appreciate certain reasons for a moral judgement: being older, better-educated, richer and better housed may all be features of this kind (see Abrams, Chapter 2 in this volume).

Of course, the correlated experiences may be taken to provide reasons for activity which there are other, perhaps better, reasons to undertake. Thus Gerard notes 'the enduring importance of religious motivation in all forms of voluntary activity' (Chapter 8 in this volume): there may be other sufficient reasons for participation, though not widely recognised by volunteers.

Further, not only causes, but also effects may be positively correlated with a particular moral value, and yet only non-causal explanations provide understanding. Thus, according to Gerard (Chapter 8 in this volume), 'on a range of ... quality-of-life indicators related to subjective feelings of happiness, loneliness and satisfaction, voluntary workers consistently scored higher than others'. However congenial, the effects of moral practice are not necessarily its objective, and so not necessarily a reason for its being undertaken; doing what you think is right may have the effect of making you feel happy without it being true that you did what you did *so that* you might feel happy.

Finally, if only non-causal explanation is illuminating, then any features which do not point towards a person's reasons, but are correlated with particular moral values, are likely to prove unreliable predictors of moral values over time, for their irrelevance may be identified in moral reasoning and the person led, whatever his or her age, for example, to a revised moral judgement.

Moral education: moral development

The causal account of the genesis of moral values implies a particular conception of *moral education* which also surfaces in the texts. Education is reduced to 'a socialisation process' in which moral values are 'inculcated in the individual' (de Moor and Kerkhofs, Preface to Stoetzel, 1983, p. vi). In many passages moral education is not so explicitly cut off from reasoning as 'inculcation' requires. Thus 'the means of mass communication, the Press, radio and television, when discussing these subjects (divorce, abortion and euthanasia) treat them in a generally favourable light and, without doubt, this is a contributory reason for the fact that these actions are more often condoned than some ... others' (Stoetzel, 1983, p. 13). Though provision of sound argument for a moral judgement might be called 'treating it in a favourable light', it seems likely that what Stoetzel has in mind, rather, is mere assertion of 'the undoubted wisdom' of the judgements in question, their description as 'what anyone who has given the matter a little thought' would believe, and so on. Such passages favour the conception of moral education as severed from reasoning, and in the form of 'inculcation'. Other passages are more explicit.

Phillips and Harding (Chapter 4 in this volume) suggest that we might understand the Values Study results by thinking of 'moral development as part of a socialisation process', in which changes in our moral values, attitudes and judgements are to be explained *not* as the result of growing consciousness of morally significant distinctions, for example, between power and authority, law and morality, acts and omissions, attitudes and emotions, or of the rashness of our generalisations exposed in experience and debate, but rather as a feature of growing older and passing 'through successive stages of the life-cycle'. In the past, when we were young, we said 'Abortion should be free on demand', but now that we are older we say, perhaps, 'Abortion should not be tolerated in law'; we move from one utterance to the other, over time, just as our hair turns from brown to grey; a moral value is neither more nor less than 'a relatively transitory characteristic', and one which changes, like others of a person's characteristics, independently of reasoning.

Reduction to preferences

We have seen evidence of commitment to causal explanation of moral values, and of its implied conception of moral education and development. What kind of thing is to be inculcated? Consistent with subjectivism, the answer, of course, is preferences. According to Stoetzel (1983, p. 17), the Values Study identified 'contrasting preferences for, on the one hand, imagination and independence and religious faith on the other'. Leaving aside the implausibility of such context-free characteristics, it is worth noting that Stoetzel explains preferences by reference to a range of 'sociological factors' which are their causes: 'these contrasting preferences are linked to the contrasting socio-ideological beliefs of the respondents, according to their age, level of education and political and religious outlooks'. In this case the explanation is obscurely phrased, but we have earlier seen Stoetzel's commitment to causal explanation and non-discrimination among items called 'sociological factors' (1983, p. 16).

On a causal account of moral values it is impossible to discriminate for separate empirical investigation the question, 'What personal goals or ideas are *preferred*?' from the question 'What personal goals or ideas are thought *preferable*, and "form the basis of moral judgement"?' On a non-causal account of moral values, what is preferred *may* be distinguished from what is thought preferable: the former is what we desire to do, the latter what we are prepared to argue there are good grounds to do. On a causal account of moral values, moral judgements do not have grounds; what we think preferable, like what we say we prefer, is just what we desire to do. The distinction is important if a non-causal theory is adopted, but it cannot be accommodated by a causal theory. Within a causal account of the genesis of moral values, with moral judgement severed from reasoning, there can be no grounds to bear in mind, or to use in debate, in justification, for there is no place for the phenomenon of justification. Gerard (Chapter 8 in this volume), recognises the importance of 'reflection', but has in mind the exercise of a disposition to think about such obscure questions as 'the meaning of life'. Consequent voluntary work is seen as an effect, and so 'reflection' turns out not to be reasoning.

Subjectivism and social planning

Let us now turn to the policy implications of the Values Study.
Doubts are encouraged by the method of inquiry. Answers to
questions about a person's attitude towards joining in unofficial
strikes (Phillips, Chapter 6 in this volume), or towards 'questionable
moral behaviour' like euthanasia (Stoetzel, 1983, p. 14), which rely in
the main upon the subject's self-knowledge and imaginative extra-
polation from it, may be a poor predictor of behaviour when an issue
must be faced in the context of their own lives and the lives of those
who deserve their loyalty. However, a more fundamental criticism
may be levelled: the dominant account of moral values presupposed
excludes the possibility that the results could be useful to anyone.
This is a precise point, and should not be confused with the claim that
the results are necessarily without use. Contributors to the Study
adopt a causal account of the genesis of moral values *and* believe the
results useful to policy-makers; my contention is that a causal account
makes results useful in policy-making logically impossible.

My conclusion follows from the fact that a causal account severs
moral values, attitudes and judgements from reasoning, *and* a
conception of policy-making as presupposing *reasoned* comparative
and normative judgement. The kernel of the causal account is well
expressed in the statement quoted earlier from Urmson (1968, p. 19):
in face of a mere matter of fact we could always without logical fault
maintain any attitude whatsoever. It follows that in face of the mere
matter of fact that one, two, ten, or however many people have a
particular moral value or attitude, or make a particular moral
judgement, we may without logical fault maintain any attitude
towards that fact whatsoever, and pursue any policy whatsoever
consistent with the attitude. If moral values are severed from
reasoning, then normative policy-making is severed from logic, and
any policy may be pursued whatever the facts: the facts have no
implications constraining judgement, because judgement is non-
rational.

Those who are determined to explain human social life by reference to 'sociological factors', offering only causal explanations, may
quite consistently escape this conclusion by further embracing a
conception of policy-making as itself severed from reasoning, so that
a policy is an effect of facts, *contingently* related to them, such
relations being strictly a matter for empirical discovery. Others,

uncommitted to subjectivism, may now need even more convincing.

We may be distracted from taking note of the necessary absence of policy implications by any one of the following lines of thought. First, the line of thought that though a policy-maker might without logical fault pursue any policy whatsoever in the face of the fact, say, that a substantial percentage of citizens have a particular moral value or attitude, he or she would be *imprudent* not to pursue a policy consistent with their attitude, if they are a majority (or to pursue a policy compromising with their attitude, if a substantial minority). In each case the policy-maker recognises difficulties of enforcement likely to arise. Results of the kind reported in the Values Study therefore do have policy implications for prudent rulers. Short shrift for this argument is as follows: it presupposes that prudent policy-making is reasoned policy-making, something ruled out by a causal account of the genesis of moral values. Results of the kind reported in the Values Study therefore cannot have policy implications for prudent rulers, for within a framework of causal explanation prudence cannot exist.

Further, the argument presupposes that a person will be disposed to *act* in a way consistent with the attitude expressed in response to questioning. Within a causal framework our words cannot be a reason to act in a certain way, we are not committed by them, and in any case we may be caused to act inconsistently with our words by changed circumstances (even assuming that what causes us to say our attitude is so-and-so also causes us to act in a way consistent with our words, which phenomena such as hypocrisy and weakness of will discourage us from believing). I said earlier that, within this conceptual framework, in face of the mere matter of fact that however many people share an attitude, we might without logical fault maintain any attitude whatsoever, and pursue any policy whatsoever consistent with it. We now see that we may in fact pursue any policy, consistent or not.

A second line of thought that may distract us begins with our identifying a certain set of moral values as 'traditional'. If we take the view that 'a role of a religion is to be the carrier of a certain set of absolute moral values' (Phillips and Harding, Chapter 4), then the set in question may well be those moral values promulgated by the institutions of a particular religion; in Europe, our set will be made up of the fourth until the tenth of 'the ten commandments' promulgated by the Christian Churches (de Moor, 1983). For each commandment we might then investigate which and how many people believe it still applies for themselves. So far, our results clearly have no policy implications. We are not even in a position to say that *change* has occurred, for we can hardly presume total past adherence.

However, we might be tempted to think that our results had policy implications if we described them by means of a distinction between 'moral strictness and permissiveness'. This is harmless enough so long as it is simply a contrast between what is sometimes called 'absolutism' and 'non-absolutism' in morals; that is, a contrast between the view that moral rules or principles are unconditional and apply whatever the circumstances (strictness), and the view that such rules or principles are conditional, their applicability being a matter settled by reference to the particular circumstances in which they are to be followed (Phillips and Harding, quoted above; Stoetzel, 1983, p. 12). But talk of 'strictness' and 'permissiveness' is of course ambiguous. If we believe that 'the time has come to take stock of the moral strictness of Europe today' (Stoetzel, 1983, p. 12), and also take the view that 'many people believe that our lifetimes have witnessed a change of values, and more particularly, a general lowering of moral standards' (Stoetzel, 1983, p. 2), then we may mistake results classified 'permissive', evidence of the extent of conditional acceptance of particular moral rules or principles, to be evidence of declining adherence to standards worthy of support. In this context our results seem to have policy implications: the decline must be halted.

So one may gently note that 'abortion laws are more liberal than the large majority of citizens', leaving unstated the implication that a change in law is thus warranted (de Moor, 1983), or one may openly presume (Stoetzel, 1983, p. 8) that in the groups where between 7 and 8 out of 10 respondents were non-absolutist about moral rules or principles, the results 'hardly' indicate 'a presence of moral scruples or show a great maturity and the habit of reflecting upon the consequences of each act'. Why not? Well, they are 'those on the left politically ... people who believe in complete sexual freedom, the young, people who do not believe in God, those who believe that terrorism can sometimes be justified, those who are permissive, and students'. The answer is hopelessly unsatisfactory. All that is clear is that such people are different in age, occupation or belief from Professor Stoetzel; it's not clear that they therefore lack moral scruples.

Idealisation

In introducing the category of 'traditional' moral values, and a measure of 'strictness and permissiveness' relative to it, the Values Study opens the way to *idealisation* (Sen and Williams, 1982, pp. 9–11). This is a common ploy for those social theorists who reduce all interests, ideals, aspirations and desires to preferences, differing only in intensity, when they face the policy implications of their reduction. In order to justify not doing some of the unreasonable things some, perhaps many, people would prefer, they inconsistently introduce a distinction between actual wants and preferences, on the one hand, and 'ideal', 'true', or 'perfectly prudent' preferences, on the other. As we have seen, the subjectivism of the Values Study includes reduction; it also includes a tendency towards idealisation: actual preferences may be distinguished from 'traditional' preferences; traditional preferences are to be implemented in policy, actual but permissive preferences are to be approached with caution: perhaps they can be changed. For those arguing an essential connection between moral values and reasoning, permissive and traditional preferences can have policy implications only if soundly reasoned, and classification as 'traditional' or 'permissive' or 'more adjusted' is no indicator of that.[4]

NOTES

1. It may be helpful if I distance my account from Gerard's remarks about 'a "subjective" rather than "objective" view of morality' (Chapter 8 in this volume). The 'subjectivism' I shall outline, like his, may be contrasted with what is sometimes called an 'objective' view of morality: of moral judgements as capable of appraisal as soundly or unsoundly argued. However, Kantian notions, said by Gerard to be the source of the views he calls 'objective', are not an essential ingredient in the non-subjectivist alternative I shall describe; nor would I accept that explanation of voluntary work in terms of reciprocity or exchange *must* be rooted in a subjectivist view of the kind I shall describe; on the contrary, there are sound arguments for reciprocity and exchange in certain contexts (Titmuss, 1970; Arrow, 1972; Singer, 1973). The 'subjectivism' I shall describe, like that mentioned by Gerard, may be derived from a philosophical theory called 'emotivism', and I shall show how. It might be worth saying that Gerard mistakes emotivism to be a view the implementation of which involves us in 'manipulative relationships with others', and mistakes Alasdair MacIntyre to share his conception. What MacIn-

tyre correctly says of the emotivism behind subjectivism is that it 'entails the obliteration of any genuine distinction between manipulative and non-manipulative social relations' (MacIntyre, 1982, p. 22).

2. In his critical discussion of subjectivism, Williams relies upon 'appealing ... to the ways in which moral judgements are actually made and treated' (1972, p. 31), which he takes to establish what kind of judgements they are most plausibly thought to be. A further question always arises: what use and treatment of 'moral judgement' best informs our understanding of human social life? A question which cannot be settled by the kind of appeal Williams employs.

It is unsatisfactory, therefore, to reject the subjectivist reduction of moral judgements to autobiographical statements simply on the grounds of its inconsistency with the fact of our use of such judgements to make 'a sort of claim which is being rejected by someone who utters a contrary moral judgement' (p. 30); it is therefore also unsatisfactory to reject the subjectivist reduction of moral judgements to 'mere' expressions of attitude not derived from reasoning, simply on the grounds of its inconsistency with 'the undoubted facts that a man may be in a state of moral doubt, which he may resolve – that a man can nonarbitrarily change his mind about a moral matter, not merely in the individual case, but on a general issue, and for reasons' (p. 32).

Comparison of rival conceptions of the use and treatment of moral judgements may usefully include evidence of inconsistency with other conceptions, so that the full extent of commitment to a particular conception is exposed. What Williams has to say about subjectivism is useful *not* because he shows it to be inconsistent with 'ordinary use', but because he shows it to be inconsistent with a use and treatment of moral judgements which is *arguably* more enlightening.

3. Urmson presents his account of an attitude as a description of how 'we can and do speak quite naturally' (1968, p. 43). He may be right, but it does not follow that we ought to go on speaking thus. An alternative way of speaking might render reality more intelligible (see Watson, 1983). It seems to me that Urmson's account of an attitude is valuable, not in accurately recording 'ordinary use', but in detailing an account of moral attitudes as essentially connected to reasoning. In so far as our attitudes are manifested in what we say or do, they may be appraised as well- or ill-grounded, and *reasons* given to maintain or change our attitudes. The conception of moral values, attitudes and judgements of which it is a component is to be preferred to the conception implied by the causal theories in that it renders intelligible the two common classes of utterance discussed earlier.

4. I should like to thank David Barker, Michael Banton, Gwynn Davis and Noel Timms for letting me know what they thought of an earlier draft of this paper.

General Appendix: Research Approach and Questionnaire Details

Conceived as a multi-disciplinary enquiry in 1978 the design of the main Study was preceded by: a survey of the research literature undertaken by the Allensbach Institute; a series of exploratory discussion groups held in England by Gallup UK; a limited number of depth interviews conducted in Germany by the Allensbach Institute; a review of material from the archives of the fieldwork agencies represented on the Technical Group including studies conducted for the EEC by IFOP/Fait et Opinions, Paris. Pilot studies were conducted in 1980 in four European countries and the final questionnaire was approved by the Steering Committee following an intensive two-day workshop held at the Oxford Centre for Management Studies, involving all the fieldwork agencies participating in the European Study together with representatives from the affiliated study groups in the USA and Japan.

The main fieldwork took place in the period April–June 1981. A target of 1200 interviews (including a booster sample of 200 young adults aged 18–24 years) was set for each country, and sampling was to continue until the target number of interviews had been achieved. A total of 12 463 personal interviews of approximately one hour's duration was completed in nine European countries. The Study was subsequently replicated in a further eighteen countries.

The fieldwork for the British study was undertaken by Social Surveys (Gallup Poll) Ltd. A nationally representative two-stage probability sample was used with polling districts as the primary sampling units. The sample was stratified by region and town size. Individuals in households were selected using a Kish grid (a technique permitting the random selection of respondents from an alphabetical listing compiled by the interviewer of the eligible persons within each household). The booster sample was based on quotas set for age and terminal education. The resultant total sample was weighted to reflect the proportions by age, sex and socio-economic group in the total population. The over-sampled group of 18–24 year olds were similarly weighted back to reflect their proportion in the population as a whole for general analysis purposes. Gallup reported a response rate of 60 per cent on the active sample (largely due to the need to make prior appointments and to indicate both the length and detail of the interview), a high degree of interest, few fieldwork problems and little interview fatigue. Non-response was primarily due to interview length.

The Pilot Study had included the Marlowe-Crowne scale to test for socially desirable responses. The main survey included trend items from previous studies, and repeat items. The number of interviews per interviewer was restricted (to three each in the UK) to reduce bias and each interview was back checked. On the basis of such tests, the Steering Committee was confident that the results were reliable and consistent across the main European countries. The problem of validity is more difficult. Converse (1964) concluded from a study of belief systems in the fifties, that mass surveys tended to show surprisingly little coherent structure in such systems, though this was disputed at the time. Inglehart (1977) reviewing the evidence concluded that while opinion surveys are not ideal instruments for studying values, they possess inherent advantages, which outweigh the fluctuations in response at the individual level and, skilfully used, are one of the most powerful research tools available. The assessment of responses to the EVSSG study confirmed some socially desirable response (e.g. to questions relating to marital satisfaction), but the conclusion reached was that the survey suffered no more from this difficulty than is generally reported (Campbell *et al.*, 1976) with instruments of this type.

LEISURE

111. Thinking of the way you spend your leisure time, what is more important to you – relaxing as much as possible or doing things, being active?

1 Sitting and relaxing as much as possible
2 Doing things, being active
3 Both equally
V Don't know

112. And during your leisure time do you prefer to be alone, to be with your family, to be with friends or to be in a lively place with many people?

1 Alone
2 With family
3 With friends
4 In a lively place
5 All equally
V Don't know

SHOW CARD A

113a. Which, if any, of the following do you belong to? (Mark in col. (A) below)

b. And do you currently do any unpaid voluntary work for any of them? (Mark in Col. (B) below).

	A	B
Charities concerned with the welfare of people	1	1
Churches or religious organisations	2	2

118. Do you ever feel very lonely? (Read out reversing order)

1 Yes, frequently
2 Yes, sometimes
3 Seldom
4 Never
V Don't know

119. Do you think that people today are more willing or less willing to help each other than they used to be, say ten years ago?

1 More willing
2 Less willing
3 Equally willing
V Don't know

SHOW CARD B

120. On this list are various groups of people. Could you please sort out any that you would not like to have as neighbours. (Mark all mentioned)

1 People with a criminal record
2 People of a different race
3 Students
4 Left wing extremists
5 Unmarried mothers

Trade unions ... 4
Political parties or groups ... 5
Organisations concerned with human rights at home and abroad ... 6
Conservation, environmentalist or animal welfare groups ... 7
Youth work (e.g. scouts, guides, youth clubs. etc.) ... 8
Consumer groups ... 9
Professional associations ... X
None of these ... V

115. Do you regularly read a daily newspaper? That is, at least four out of every six issues?

1 Yes
2 No

116. Could you estimate how many hours you spend on an average weekday, that is from Monday to Friday, watching the TV? Is it: (Read out)

1 Less than one hour
2 Between 1 – 2 hours
3 Between 2 – 3 hours
4 Between 3 – 4 hours
5 More than 4 hours
6 Never watch TV

117. Do you dislike being with people whose ideas, beliefs or values are different from you own? Is that: (Read out reversing order)

1 Very much
2 Quite a lot
3 Not very much
4 Not at all
V Don't know

---

7 Right wing extremists
8 People with large families
9 Emotionally unstable people
X Members of minority religious sects or cults
V Immigrant/foreign workers
R None marked

121. All in all, how would you describe your state of health these days? Would you say it was: (Read out, reversing order for alternate contacts)

1 Very good
2 Good
3 Fair
4 Poor
5 Very poor
V Don't know

122. We are interested in the way people are feeling these days. During the past few weeks, did you ever feel: (Read out, reversing order for alternate contacts. Mark one code for each statement).

	Yes	No
Particularly excited or interested in something	1	1
So restless you couldn't sit long in a chair	2	2
Proud because someone had complimented you on something you had done	3	3
Very lonely or remote from other people	4	4
Pleased about having accomplished something	5	5
Bored	6	6
On top of the world/feeling that life is wonderful	7	7
Depressed or very unhappy	8	8
That things were going your way	9	9

124. Generally speaking, would you say that most people can be trusted or that you can't be too careful in dealing with people?

   1   Most can be trusted
   2   Can't be too careful
   V   Don't know

125. How much trust do you think young people have in older people in Britain today? *SHOW CARD C*

1	2	3	4	5	6	7	8	9	10
None at all   A great deal

   V   Don't know

126. How much trust do you think older people have in the young in Britain today? *SHOW CARD C*

1	2	3	4	5	6	7	8	9	10
None at all   A great deal

   V   Don't know

127. Some people feel they have completely free choice and control over the way their lives turn out, and other people feel that what they themselves do has no real effect on what happens to them. Please use the scale to indicate how much freedom of choice and control you feel you have over the way your life turns out. *SHOW CARD C*

1	2	3	4	5	6	7	8	9	10
None at all   A great deal

   V   Don't know

128. Taking all things together, would you say you are:
(Read out, reversing order for alternate contacts)

   1   Very happy
   2   Quite happy
   3   Not very happy
   4   Not at all happy
   V   Don't know

129. *SHOW CARD D*: All things considered, how satisfied are you with your life as a whole these day?
Please use this card to help you with your answer.

1	2	3	4	5	6	7	8	9	10
Dissatisfied   Satisfied

   V   Don't know

130. *SHOW CARD D*: And where would you rate yourself as you were five years ago?

1	2	3	4	5	6	7	8	9	10
Dissatisfied   Satisfied

   V   Don't know

131. *SHOW CARD D*: And where do you expect you will be in five years time?

1	2	3	4	5	6	7	8	9	10
Dissatisfied   Satisfied

   V   Don't know

SUB-SECTION; VOLUNTARY WORK OR CHARITIES
(ASK AFTER Q. 131)

A. People have different ideas about the role of charities and voluntary groups in our society. Which of the following statements comes closest to your own view? *(read out, reversing order for alternate contacts. Mark one only)*

  1 No matter what the government does, charities will always be necessary

  2 The work of charities goes hand-in-hand with government action

  3 The presence of charities means that the government does not have to fulfill its social responsibilities

  V Don't know

B. It is sometimes suggested that charities and voluntary groups should be closely controlled by the government, to supervise their activities. Other people believe that charities and voluntary organisations should be free from government control. Which do you think?

  1 Should be closely controlled by government

  2 Should be free from government control

  V Don't know

C. People undertake voluntary or charitable work for many different reasons. Which of the following statements comes closest to your own views about why people do voluntary work? *(read out, reversing order for alternate contacts. Mark one only)*

  1 Generally speaking, those who do voluntary or charitable work are unselfish and dedicated people

  2 Those who undertake voluntary or charitable work are usually well-meaning but misguided do-gooders who create more problems than they solve

  3 Those who undertake voluntary or charitable work usually do so with their own problems more in mind than the problems of the people they are trying to help

  V Don't know

D. Have you personally ever asked for or been offered any of the following, by a charitable organisation? *(read out, mark an answer for each)*

	Yes	No
Financial assistance	1	1
Practical help	2	2
Advice, information, counselling	3	3

WORK SECTION

ASK ALL:

132. Here are some aspects of a job that some people have said are important. Please look at them and tell me which ones you personally think are important in a job.
(SHOW CARD E – Mark all mentioned)

1 Good pay
2 Pleasant people to work with
3 Not too much pressure
4 Good job security
5 Good chances for promotion
6 A job respected by people in general
7 Good hours
8 An opportunity to use initiative
9 A useful job for society
1 Generous holidays
2 Meeting people
3 A job you feel you can achieve something
4 A responsible job
5 A job that is interesting
6 A job that meets one's abilities
7 None of these

Ask if working full, or part-time: if not, skip to Q140.

134. Do you really look forward to your work when the weekend is over or do you regret that it is over?

---

138. I should like you to imagine for a moment that the government and employers agree to shorten the working week to 3 days – each of 8 hours – but continue to offer the same pay as for a full week. Which of these, if any, would you do?
(SHOW CARD G – Mark all mentioned)

1 Work 3 days for your employer and then attempt to find extra work for the rest of the week to earn more money
2 Use the spare time to study or improve yourself
3 Spend the time with family and friends
4 To avoid getting bored, find some additional work even if this doesn't bring in much extra cash
5 Use the spare time to do something for your local community, eg voluntary work, local politics, the church, etc.
6 Spend your time following your hobbies
7 Run your own little business in your spare time
8 Spend the time relaxing, not doing anything special
X None of these
V Don't know

SHOW CARD H

139. Overall, how satisfied or dissatisfied are you with your job?

1   2   3   4   5   6   7   8   9   10

Dissatisfied   Satisfied
V Don't know

1 Look forward to work
2 Regret the weekend is over
3 Enjoy both the weekend and work
V Don't know

135. How much pride, if any, do you take in the work that you do? (*Read out*)

1 A great deal
2 Some
3 Little
4 None
V Don't know

136. Thinking of your job, do you often or occasionally feel that you are being taken advantage of or exploited, or do you never have this feeling?

1 Often taken advantage of
2 Sometimes
3 Never
V Don't know

SHOW CARD F

137. How free are you to make decisions in your job? Please use this card to indicate how much decision-making freedom you feel you have.

1   2   3   4   5   6   7   8   9   10

None at all   A great deal
V Don't know

ASK ALL:

SHOW CARD H

140. How satisfied are you with the financial situation of your household?

1   2   3   4   5   6   7   8   9   10

Disatisfied   Satisfied
V Don't know

141. How do you think the financial position of your household will change over the next 12 months? (*Read out.*)

1 Get a lot better
2 Get a little better
3 Stay the same
4 Get a little worse
5 Get a lot worse
V Don't know

142. I'd like to relate an incident to you and ask your opinion of it. There are two secretaries, of the same age, doing practically the same job.

One of the secretaries finds out that the other one earns £10 a week more than she does. She complains to her boss. He says, quite rightly, that the other secretary is quicker, more efficient and more reliable at her job. In your opinion, is it fair or not fair that one secretary is paid more than the other?

1 Fair
2 Unfair
V Don't know

143. There is a lot of discussion about how business and industry should be managed. Which of these four statements comes closest to your opinion?
(SHOW CARD I – Mark ONE only)

1   The owners should run their business or appoint the managers
2   The owners and the employees should participate in the selection of managers
3   The State should be the owner and appoint the managers
4   The employeers should own the business and should elect the managers
V   Don't know

GO TO MEANING AND PURPOSE OF LIFE

SHOW CARD J

144. People have different ideas about following instructions at work.
Some say that people should, in principle, follow the instructions of their superiors related to their job, even when they do not fully agree with them.

Others say no-one should be expected to follow their superior's instructions in a job without being convinced that the instructions are right, rather than as a matter of principle.

Which of these two opinions do you agree with?

1   Should follow instructions
2   Must be convinced first
3   Depends
V   Don't know

169. Do you take some moments of prayer, meditation or contemplation or something like that?

1 Yes   V Don't know
2 No

208. *SHOW CARD P*: Here is a card on which are the Ten Commandments. Please look at them and tell me, for each one, whether it still applies fully today, whether it applies today to a limited extent, or no longer really applies today (a) for yourself, and (b) to most people? *(Write in code number 1, 2, 3 or V under column for 'Self' and 'Most people'.)*

1 Applies fully
2 Applies to a limited extent
3 Doesn't apply
V Don't know

	Self	Most People
1 I am the Lord thy God, thou shalt have no other gods before me	--	--
2 Thou shalt not take the name of the Lord thy God in vain	--	--
3 Thou shalt keep the Sabbath holy	--	--
4 Thou shalt honour thy mother and thy father	--	--
5 Thou shalt not kill	--	--
6 Thou shalt not commit adultery	--	--
7 Thou shalt not steal	--	--
8 Thou shalt not bear false witness against thy neighbour	--	--
9 Thou shalt not covet thy neighbour's wife	--	--
10 Thou shalt not covet thy neighbour's goods	--	--

158. Independently of whether you go to church or not, would you say you are: *(Read out reversing order)*

1 A religious person
2 Not a religious person
3 A convinced atheist
V Don't know

169. Generally speaking, do you think that your church is giving, in your country, adequate answers to:
(Read out and mark an answer for each)

	Yes	No	Don't Know
a) The moral problems and needs of the individual	1	1	1
b) The problems of family life	2	2	2
c) Man's spiritual needs	3	3	3
V not applicable			

162. Do you think that religion in the future will be more important, less important, or equally important for people in this country?

1 More important
2 Less important
3 Equally important
V Don't know

163. Which, if any, of the following do you believe in? *(Read out and mark an answer for each)*

Yes | No | Don't know

	Yes	No	Don't know
God	1	1	1
Life after death	2	2	2
A soul	3	3	3
The Devil	4	4	4
Hell	5	5	5
Heaven	6	6	6
Sin	7	7	7
Re-incarnation	8	8	8

166. *SHOW CARD N*: Which of these statements comes closest to your beliefs?
1 There is a personal God
2 There is some sort of spirit or life force
3 I don't really know what to think
4 I don't really think there is any sort of spirit, God or life force
V Don't know

167. *SHOW CARD O*: And how important is God in your life? Please use this card to indicate – 10 means very important, and 1 means not at all important.

1 2 3 4 5 6 7 8 9 10
Not at all   Very
V Don't know

168. Do you find that you get comfort and strength from religion or not?
1 Yes
2 No
V Don't know

228. Did you ever have any of the following experiences?
(Read out each item and mark an answer for each)

	No Never	Yes	Don't know
a) Felt as though you were in touch with someone when they were far away from you	1	2	3
b) Seen events that happened at a great distance as they were happening	1	2	3
c) Felt as though you were really in touch with someone who had died	1	2	3
d) Felt as though you were close to a powerful, spiritual life force that seemed to lift you out of yourself	1	2	3

ASK ALL SAY 'Yes' at d). Others go to Q.233

232. Has the experience altered your outlook on life in any way? Would you say: *(Read out reversing order for alternate contacts)*
1 Not at all
2 Slightly
3 A fair amount
4 Quite a lot
5 A great deal
V Don't know

MEANING AND PURPOSE OF LIFE

Now for some questions about life in general.

145. In the long run, do you think that scientific advances we are making will help or harm mankind?

1 Will help
2 Will harm
3 Some of each
V Don't know

146. How often, if at all, do you think about the meaning and purpose of life? (Read out, codes 1–4, reversing order for alternate contacts)

1 Often
2 Sometimes
3 Rarely
4 Never
V Don't know

147. How often, if at all, do you have the feeling that life is meaningless?

1 Often
2 Sometimes
3 Rarely
4 Never
V Don't know

148. Do you ever think about death? Would you say:
(Read out)

1 Often
2 Sometimes
3 Rarely

152. Of course, we all hope that there will not be another war, but if it were to come to that would you be willing to fight for your country?

1 Yes
2 No
V Don't know

153. SHOW CARD K: How likely do you think it is that there will be another major war in which your country will be involved in the next five years?

1　2　3　4　5　6　7　8　9　10
Not at all　　　　　　　　　　　　Very
V　Don't know

154. SHOW CARD L: Here are two statements which people sometimes make when discussing good and evil. Which one comes closest to your own point of view?

A: There are absolutely clear guidelines about what is good and evil. These always apply to everyone, whatever the circumstances.

B: There can never be clear and absolute guidelines about what is good and evil. What is good and evil depends entirely upon the circumstances at the time.

1 Agree with Statement A
2 Agree with Statement B
3 Disagree with both
V Don't know

4 Never
V Don't know

149. Some say that there is good and evil in everyone. Others say that everyone is basically good. Which point of view do you agree with?

1 Good and evil in everyone
2 Everyone is basically good
V Don't know

150. Does it ever happen that you regret having done something you felt was wrong? Is that:
(Read out)

1 Often
2 Sometimes
3 Rarely
4 Never
V Don't know

151. Apart from your family, in your opinion, is there anything that you would consider worth sacrificing everything for, even risking your life if necessary?

1 No, nothing
   Yes *(Write in AND code)*
   ----
2 My country, nation
3 To save another's life
4 Justice
5 Freedom
6 Peace
7 Religious beliefs, God
X Other

155. *SHOW CARD M: These are statements one sometimes hears. With which would you tend to agree?*

1 There is no one true religion but there are basic truths and meanings to be found in all the great religions of the world
2 There is only one true religion
3 None of the great religions has any truths to offer
V Don't know

156. What is your religious denomination?

1 Roman Catholic
2 Church of England, Scotland or Wales (Protestant)
3 Free church/non-conformist
4 Jew
5 Muslim
6 Hindu
7 Buddhist
8 Other
   (Write in): ----------------------
X *None*

157. *Apart from weddings, funerals and baptisms, about how often do you attend religious services these days? (Mark one only)*

1 More than once a week
2 Once a week
3 Once a month
4 Christimas/Easter day
5 Other specific holy days
6 Once a year
7 Less often
V Never; practically never

FAMILY LIFE

I'd now like to ask a few questions about your childhood.

233. a) During the time you were growing up, would you say that your father and mother were very close to each other, quite close to each other, not very close or not at all close? (Mark answer in 1st column below)

b) How about you and you mother? During the time that you were growing up, were you very close to each other, quite close, not very close or not at all close? (Mark answer in 2nd column below)

c) And you and your father? During the time that you were growing up, were you very close to each other, quite close, not very close or not at all close? (Mark answer in 3rd column below)

	(a)	(b)	(c)
Very close	1	1	1
Quite close	2	2	2
Not very close	3	3	3
Not at all close	4	4	4
Don't know	V	V	V

235. Some parents are quite strict with their children telling them clearly what they should do or should not do, what is right and wrong, while others do not think they can or should do so (are less strict). How strict were your parents?

1 Very strict
2 Quite strict

244. Do (did) you and your partner share any of the following? (Read out and mark all mentioned)

1 Attitudes towards religion
2 Moral standards
3 Social attitudes
4 Political views
5 Sexual attitudes
6 None of these
V Don't know

ASK ALL:

245. And how about your parents? Do (did) you and your parents share any of the following? (Read out and mark all mentioned)

1 Attitudes towards religion
2 Moral standards
3 Social attitudes
4 Political views
5 Sexual attitudes
6 None of these
V Don't know

246. Do you tend to agree or disagree with this statement? (Read out)

"Marriage is an outdated institution."

1 Tend to agree
2 Tend to disagree
V Don't know

3 Not very strict
4 Not at all strict
V Don't know

237. Please look at this card and tell me for each word, how often you feel this way at home?
SHOW CARD Q (Mark answer for each)

	Often	Some-times	Rarely	Never
Relaxed	1	2	3	4
Anxious	1	2	3	4
Happy	1	2	3	4
Aggressive	1	2	3	4
Secure, safe and sound	1	2	3	4

242. *SHOW CARD R*: Overall, how satisfied or dissatisfied are you with your home life?

1	2	3	4	5	6	7	8	9	10
Dissatisfied									Satisfied

V   Don't know

243. Are you currently: *(Read out and mark ONE only)*
1 Married
2 Living as married
3 Divorced
4 Separated
5 Widowed
6 Single – *skip to Q245*

247. If someone said that individuals should have the chance to enjoy complete sexual freedom without being restricted, would you tend to agree or disagree?
1 Tend to agree
2 Tend to disagree
3 Neither/it depends
V Don't know
R Not answered

248. *SHOW CARD S*: Here is a list of things which some people think make for a successful marriage. Please tell me, for each one, whether you think it is very important, rather important or not very important.

	Very	Rather	Not Very
Faithfulness	1	1	1
An adequate income	2	2	2
Being of the same social background	3	3	3
Mutual respect and appreciation	4	4	4
Shared religious belief	5	5	5
Good housing	6	6	6
Agreement on politics	7	7	7
Understanding and tolerance	8	8	8
Living apart from your in-laws	9	9	9
Happy sexual relationship	X	X	X
Sharing household chores	V	V	V
Children	1	1	1
Tastes and interests in common	2	2	2

254. What do you think is the ideal size of family – husband, wife and how many children?

_____ children

255. Which of the following would you consider sufficient reasons for divorce?
(Read out, reversing order for alternate contacts, mark all mentioned.)

1 When either partner is ill for a long time
2 When they are financially broke
3 When either partner consistently drinks too much
4 When either partner is violent
5 When either partner is consistently unfaithful
6 When the sexual relationship is not satisfactory
7 When either partner has ceased to love the other
8 When they can't get along with each other's relatives
9 When they can't have children
X When their personalities don't match
V None of these

256. If someone says a child needs a home with both a father and a mother to grow up happily, would you tend to agree or disagree?

1 Tend to agree
2 Tend to disagree
V Don't know

257. Do you think that a woman has to have children in order to be fulfilled or is this not necessary?

1 Needs children
2 Not necessary
V Don't know

259. Which of these two statements do you tend to agree with?
SHOW CARD T

A: Regardless of what the qualities and faults of ones parents are, one must always love and respect them
B: One does not have the duty to respect and love parents who have not earned it by their behaviour and attitudes

1 Tend to agree with Statement A
2 Tend to agree with Statement B
V Don't know

260. Which of the following statements best describes your views about parents' responsibilities to their children?
SHOW CARD U

1 Parents duty is to do their best for their children even at the expense of their own well-being
2 Parents have a life of their own and should not be asked to sacrifice their own well-being for the sake of their children
3 Neither
V Don't know

261. If a woman wants to have a child as a single parent but she doesn't want to have a stable relationship with a man, do you approve or disapprove?

1 Approve
2 Disapprove
3 Depends
V Don't know

258. If someone says that sex cannot entirely be left to individual choice, there have to be moral rules to which everyone adheres. Would you tend to agree or disagree?

1 Tend to agree
2 Tend to disagree
3 Neither
V Don't know
R Not answered

262. SHOW CARD V: Here is a list of qualities which children can be encouraged to learn at home. Which, if any, do you consider to be especially important? Please choose up to five.
(Mark FIVE only)

	Important
Good manners	1
Politeness and neatness	2
Independence	3
Hardwork	4
Honesty	5
Feeling of responsibility	6
Patience	7
Imagination	8
Tolerance and respect for other people	9
Leadership	X
Self-control	V
Thrift, sparing money and things	1
Determination, perseverance	2
Religious faith	3
Unselfishness	4
Obedience	5
Loyalty	6

264. Have you had any children?
1 Yes
2 No

How many (write in): _____

CONTEMPORARY SOCIAL ISSUES

I'd now like to talk about something else.

266. *SHOW CARD Y:* Which of these statements comes nearest to describing your interest in politics?

1   I take an active interest in politics
2   I am interested in politics but don't take any active part
3   My interest in politics is not greater than other interests
4   I'm not interested in politics at all

267. Now I'd like to you to look at this card. I'm going to read out some different forms of political action that people can take, and I'd like you to tell me, for each one, whether you have actually *done* any of these things, whether you would do it, might do it, or would never, under any circumstances, do any of them. *SHOW CARD Z (Mark an answer for each)*

	Have done	Might do	Would never do	Don't know
Signing a petition	1	2	3	V
Joining in boycotts	1	2	3	V
Attending lawful demonstrations	1	2	3	V
Joining unofficial strikes	1	2	3	V
Occupying buildings or factories	1	2	3	V
Damaging things like breaking windows, removing roads signs, etc.	1	2	3	V

276. On this card are three basic kinds of attitudes vis-a-vis the society we live in. Please choose the one which best describes your own opinion. *SHOW CARD CC*

1   The entire way our society is organised must be radically changed by revolutionary action
2   Our society must be gradually improved by reforms
3   Our present society must be valiantly defended against all subversive forces
V   Don't know

277. There is a lot of talk these days about what the aims of this country should be for the next ten years. *(SHOW CARD DD)* On this card are listed some of the goals which different people would give top priority. Would you please say which of these you, yourself, consider the most important? And which would be the *next* most important?

	1st	Next
Maintaining order in the nation	1	1
Giving the people more say in important government decisions	2	2
Fighting rising prices	3	3
Protecting freedom of speech	4	4
Don't know	V	V

279. When a person is sentenced by a court of law, what should be the main aim of imprisonment? *SHOW CARD EE (Mark one only)*

A: To re-educate the prisoner

B: To make those who have done wrong pay for it

C: To protect other citizens

D: To act as a deterrent to others

1 Agree with A
2 Agree with B
3 Agree with C
4 Agree with D
V None/don't know

308. *SHOW CARD FF*: Here is a list of various changes in our way of life that might take place in the near future. Please tell me for each one, if it were to happen whether you think it would be a good thing, a bad thing or don't you mind?

	Good	Bad	Don't mind
Less emphasis on money and material possessions	1	2	3
Decrease in the importance of work in our lives	1	2	3
More emphasis on the development of technology	1	2	3
Greater emphasis on the development of the individual	1	2	3
Greater respect for authority	1	2	3
More emphasis on family life	1	2	3
A simple and more natural lifestyle	1	2	3

Using personal violence like fighting with other demonstrators or the police   1   2   3   V

274. *SHOW CARD AA*: Which of these two statements comes closest to your own opinion?

A: I find that both freedom and equality are important. But if I were to make up my mind for one or the other, I would consider personal freedom more important, that is, everyone can live in freedom and develop without hindrance

B: Certainly both freedom and equality are important. But if I were to make up my mind for one of the two, I would consider equality more important, that is that nobody is underprivileged and that social class differences are not so strong

1 Agree with A
2 Agree with B
3 Neither
V Don't know

275. In political matters, people talk of 'the left' and 'the right'. How would you place your views on this scale generally speaking? *SHOW CARD BB*

1 2 3 4 5 6 7 8 9 10

Left   Right

V Don't know
R Not anwsered

315. Please tell me for each of the following statements whether you think it can always be justified, never be justified or something in between, using this card.
(SHOW CARD GG with justification scale. Read out statements, reversing order for alternate contact. Mark an answer for each statement.)

1	2	3	4	5	6	7	8	9	10
Never									Always

V   Don't know

	Write in no.
Claiming state benefits which you are not entitled to	_____
Avoiding a fare on public transport	_____
Cheating on tax if you have the chance	_____
Buying something you knew was stolen	_____
Taking and driving away a car belonging to someone else (Joyriding)	_____
Taking the drug marijuana or hashish	_____
Keeping money that you have found	_____
Lying in your own interest	_____
Married men/women having an affair	_____
Sex under the legal age of consent	_____
Someone accepting a bribe in the course of their duties	_____
Homosexuality	_____

338. In Britain today, how serious a problem do you think is a) illegal drug-taking and b) alcoholism?

(a) Drugs

1   Very serious
2   Quite serious
3   Not very serious
4   Not at all serious
5   Don't know

(b) Alcoholism

6   Very serious
7   Quite serious
8   Not very serious
9   Not at all serious
V   Don't know

339. Do you approve or disapprove of abortion under the following circumstances? *SHOW CARD HH*

	Approve	Dis-approve
Where the mother's health is at risk by the pregnancy	1	1
Where it is likely that the child would be born physically handicapped	2	2
Where the woman is not married	3	3
Where a married couple do not want to have any more children	4	4
Don't know	V	V
Not answered	R	R

...when you, yourself, hold a strong opinion, do you ever find yourself persuading your friends, relatives or fellow-workers to share your views or not? If so, does this happen often, from time to time or rarely?

1 Often
2 From time to time
3 Rarely .
4 Never
V Don't know

342. When you get together with your friends, would you say you discuss political matters frequently occasionally or never?

1 Frequently
2 Occasionally
3 Never
V Don't know

343. Do you consider yourself to be close or not to any particular party?

1 Yes
2 No – *skip to Q.346*

344. To which party?

1 None
2 Conservative
3 Labour
4 Liberal
5 Nationalist
6 Other *(write in)* ------------
V Don't know
R Not answered

345. Do you feel yourself to be very close to this party, fairly close or merely a sympathiser?

1 Very close
2 Fairly close
3 Merely a sympathiser
4 Close to no particular party
V Don't know

Prostitution

Abortion

Divorce

Fighting with the police

Euthanasia (terminating the life of the incurably sick)

Suicide

Failing to report damage you've done accidentally to a parked vehicle

Theatening workers who refuse to join a strike

Killing in self-defence

Political assassination

337a) Do you consider yourself as a total abstainer, occasional drinker, do you drink rather often or do you consider yourself as a regular drinker?

1 Regular drinker
2 Drink rather often
3 Occasional drinker
4 Total abstainer
5 Not answered

b) Generally speaking do you, yourself, drink less alcholic drinks than most people, the same or more alcoholic drinks than most people?

6 Less than most
7 Same as others

GO TO DEMOGRAPHIC INFORMATION

346a) *SHOW CARD II:* To which of these geographical groups would you say you belong to first of all?

b) And the next?

	a	b	
1	1	Locality of town where you live
2	2	Region or country where you live*
3	3	Your country as a whole
4	4	Europe
5	5	The world as a whole
V	V	Don't know

* *Respondents saying Scotland, Wales, Ulster, England to be coded as 2*

348a) How proud are you to be British?

1 Very proud
2 Quite proud
3 Not very proud
4 Not at all proud
5 Don't know

b) Terrorism is everyday news. In principle, most people are against it, but there is still room for differences of opinion. Which of these two statements do you tend to agree with? (*Read out*)

A: There may be certain circumstances where terrorism is justified

B: Terrorism for whatever motive must always be condemned

6 Tend to agree with A
7 Tend to agree with B
8 Neither
V Don't know

349. *SHOW CARD JJ:* Please look at this card and tell me, for each item listed, how much confidence you have in them, is it a great deal, quite a lot, not very much or none at all? (*Mark an answer for each item*)

	A great deal	Quite a lot	Not very much	None at all
The church	1	2	3	4
The armed forces	1	2	3	4
The education system	1	2	3	4
The legal system	1	2	3	4
The press	1	2	3	4
Trade unions	1	2	3	4
The police	1	2	3	4
Parliament	1	2	3	4
Civil service	1	2	3	4
Major companies	1	2	3	4

359. Do you tend to agree to tend to disagree with the following statement? (*Read out*)

"The future is so uncertain that it is best to live from day to day."

1 Tend to agree
2 Tend to disagree
V Don't know

DEMOGRAPHIC INFORMATION

Chief Wage earner:

Industry: ....

Job: ....

	Contact	CWE	
	Contact	*CWE*	
	1	1	Employers and managers of large establishments (over 500 employees)
	2	2	Employers and managers of small establishments (under 500 employees)
	3	3	Professional workers – lawyers, accountants, teachers etc.
	4	4	Middle level non-manual – office worker etc
	5	5	Junior level non-manual – office worker etc
	6	6	Foreman and supervisor – manual
	7	7	Skilled manual workers
	8	8	Semi-skilled manual workers
	9	9	Unskilled manual workers
	0	0	Farmers – employers, managers and own account
	X	X	Agricultural workers
	V	V	Member of armed forces

369. Are you the Chief Wage Earner?

1 Yes

2 No – *go back and ask Q365/367 for chief wage earner and ring codes in 2nd col.*

370. *ASK ALL EMPLOYED:* How many people work in your department or part of your organisation?

1   1

2   2

6   26–99

7   100–249

360. a)

Do you live in a house or an apartment?

1 House

2 Apartment

3 Other *(Write in)* ——————————

b)

And do you or your family own your own home or do you rent it?

4 Own – paid for, buying with mortage

5 Rent from municipality/council

6 Rent privately

7 Hostel, lodging, squatters, etc.

361. And what age did you (will you) complete your full-time education?

1 12 or under

2 13

3 14

4 15

5 16

6 17

7 18

8 19

9 20

X 21 or over

362. How many people are there in your household, including yourself and children?

.... Total

How many 18 or over?   7 .... 18+

IF ANY UNDER 18:

That means ... under 18

8 16–17

9 11–15

0 5–10

X 1–4

V .... Under 1

364. IF RESPONDENT UNMARRIED, ASK:

Do you live with your parents?

1 Yes
2 No

ASK ALL:

365. Are you, yourself, employed now?
If Yes: About how many hours a week?
(Mark an answer in 1st column below)

Contact	CWE	Has paid job:
	1	Full-time (30 hours a week or more)
	2	Part-time (less than 30 hours a week)
	3	Self-employed
		No paid job:
	4	Unemployed
	5	Retired; pensioned
	6	Housewife not otherwise employed
	7	Student

367. a)

In which profession/industry do you/did you work? (write in below)

b)
What is/was your job there? (write in below and code in first column)

Contact: ....

Industry: ....

	3	3–5	8	250–1000
	4	6–9	9	More than 1000
	5	10–25	V	Don't know

ASK ALL:

371. a)
Do you (or your spouse) belong to a trade union?

1 Yes, self
2 Yes, spouse
3 No

371. b)
Sex of respondent:

4 Male
5 Female, housewife
6 Female, not housewife

372. Can you tell me your date of birth please?
(Write in)

....

374. Would you say you live in a:

1 Rural area or village
2 Small or middle sized town
3 Big town

375. Region: (write in first box of your interviewer number)

376. SHOW INCOME CARD:

Here is a scale of incomes and we would like to know in what group your family is, counting all wages, salaries, pensions and other income that comes in. Just give me the number of the group your household falls into before tax and other deductions.

Name and address of respondent: *PLEASE PRINT*

Mr/Mrs/Miss ....

Address ....

....

.... Tel. No. ....

INTERVIEWERS: CODE BY OBSERVATION ONLY.

377 a)
Ethnic group:

1   Caucasian (white)
2   Negro (black)
3   Asian (brown)
4   Oriental (yellow)
5   Arab
6   Other non-white
    (specify)

....

b)
Socio-economic status: *(Code from occupation)*

7   AB   (professional/managerial, above average life style)
8   C1   (sales, clerical and other non-manual)
9   C2   (manual workers–skilled i.e. served an apprenticeship
X   DE   (semi-skilled, unskilled or unemployed or pensioner)

378 a)
During the interview the respondent was

1   Very self-assured
2   Fairly self-assured
3   A bit unsure of him/herself
4   Fairly unsure

378 b)
On the whole the respondent looked:

5   Quite cheerful
6   Not so cheerful
7   Impossible to say

I hereby attest that this is a true record of an interview made strictly in accordance with your requirements, with a person who is a stranger to me. This form was completed entirely at the time of interview.

Signed: ....   Date: ....

This form is the property of:

© *SOCIAL SURVEYS (GALLUP POLL) LTD*
   202 Finchley Road
   London NW3 6BL

How was this contact selected?

1 Contact interviewed according to grid
2 Contact 18–24, interviewed at given address, but not selected according to grid
3 Contact 18–24, found on quota basis, not within address list

Technical Appendix and Glossary of Terms

The aim of this brief appendix is to summarise the statistical techniques adopted in the Values Study and to outline what they involve for those unfamiliar with survey analysis. The procedures used are largely elementary. Apart from limited use of multi-variate techniques (e.g. multiple regression, discriminant analysis, factor analysis and smallest space analysis) the main approach has been to **cross-tabulate** the data, plotting the changing scores or **values** of one variable (a characteristic or attribute such as 'sex' or 'age') against another variable (such as 'political preference' or 'religious commitment'). Relatively simple **statistical tests** and **measures of association** have then been employed to evaluate the results. The cross-tabulations have been **elaborated** in some cases to **control** for the influence of other variables. These procedures are explained below.

In any observed relationship between two variables there exists the possibility that the apparent association (or **correlation**) may be due entirely to chance (that is to the random behaviour of variables that are not, in fact, correlated at all). **Significance tests** are a means of evaluating the evidence for or against the existence of a real relationship (**the null hypothesis**) and assessing the probability that the apparent association is therefore due to chance. If the outcome suggests that the observed relationship will occur by chance less than once in twenty times (less than 5 per cent of the time) then in the social sciences the convention (a purely arbitrary rule of thumb) is to reject the hypothesis that there is no relationship and accept that the association is a genuine one. Similarly, we may wish to show that two groups being analysed exhibit very **different characteristics**; so different, in fact, that they cannot be assumed to be drawn from the same 'parent' group or population. For example, we may wish to demonstrate that 'anti-traditionalists' exhibit certain characteristics which clearly distinguish them from the rest of the population. The negative assumption is made that there is no difference, that they are drawn from the same parent group, and the probability that the observed differences are due to chance is assessed. Again, if the likelihood is that such differences will occur by chance less than once in twenty times (0.05) it is normal practice to conclude that the **difference is statistically significant**. If the probability is even lower, say one in a hundred (0.01) or one in a thousand (0.001), then the difference may be termed very significant or highly significant.

It is important to emphasise that, in a given case, there either is, or is not, a statistical association. There is, or is not, a genuine difference. The use of significance tests does not **prove** the point one way or another, it simply indicates the degree of risk attached to drawing the wrong conclusion from the evidence. **Confidence** is placed as much in the procedure as in the result. Even if the test suggests that the possibility of an observed relationship occurring by chance is only one in a thousand, we have no way of knowing whether the particular result we have observed is that (1 in 1000) chance result. We merely acknowledge that the risk is very low and proceed on the assumption that a genuine relationship exists, that is to say that the variables are **correlated**. From the above discussion it is clear that the judgement we make on the basis of the probabilities we have calculated may involve one of two possible errors. We may accept that a relationship (or significant difference) exists in a particular case when, in fact, no relationship does exist. Conversely, we may reject the possibility of a relationship (or difference) when, in fact, a relationship is present. The lower the probability level, the lower the risk we run.

When a relationship between two variables is observed and the correlation is a significant one, we may endeavour to **predict** the value of one variable from our knowledge of the value of the other. Yet, the possibility remains that the relationship is apparent rather than real. It may be due to **both** variables being associated with, or dependent upon, a third variable. In such cases the third variable may be responsible for the observed relationship between the first two. If this third variable can be isolated, and its influence on the other variables **controlled for**, then we may observe important changes in the relationship between the original pair of variables. The original relationship may disappear or alter in unexpected ways. The technique of **elaboration** can be used for this purpose. Simply stated, the process of elaboration involves the introduction of a third variable (and perhaps additional variables) into an existing analysis of a relationship between two other variables. The additional variable(s) are usually termed **'test factors'** or **'control variables'** and are used to test the validity of the original relationship, or to specify the conditions under which it can be said to hold true. When the control variable is introduced, the apparently observed relationships between the original variables may continue to hold or even increase in size. On the other hand, the observed relationship may disappear. It may hold in certain cases but not in others, or it may occasionally suggest that the opposite of the original interpretation is in fact the true position. When a given relationship increases, following the introduction of a test variable, then the latter is said to have **'suppressed'** the true relationship. When the relationship disappears, or is reduced to negligible proportions, the test variable is said to **'explain'** or **'account for'** the apparent association between the original variables, which is then often rejected as **'spurious'**. When the relationship holds under some circumstances but not others (perhaps for men but not for women), then the control variables act to

'specify' the nature of the relationship. Finally, on the rare occasions when the observed relationship is reversed, the test factor is termed a **'distorter'** variable. One of the main advantages of the introduction of test factors is that they may point to a causal sequence or chain connecting various related variables (Rosenberg, 1968).

Elaboration involves an expansion of the tables used in the analysis, each table being broken down into two or more sub-tables depending upon the number of test variables employed. Thus, in Chapter 9 the relationship between psychological well-being and voluntary work is controlled for both social class and level of education. The relationship between psychological well-being and voluntary activity for each main education and class group is assessed separately. The correlations calculated from the sub-tables are termed **conditional** and **partial – correlations.** They are helpful in 'unpacking' or decomposing the overall relationship into its component parts, illustrating the way two variables change, or fail to change, in association with each other when other variables are held constant.

It must be stressed that a high correlation is not necessarily statistically significant and, conversely, a low correlation may be significant. Each value must therefore be subjected to a test of significance. In general the larger the sample size the greater the likelihood that relatively small differences will turn out to be significant. Judgement is then necessary to determine whether small but significant differences are substantively important. In reporting correlations for survey data, it is common practice to summarise the strength of association using the terms negligible (±0.01 to 0.09), low (±0.10 to 0.29), moderate (±0.30 to 0.49), substantial (±0.50 to 0.69) and very substantial or high (±0.70 to 0.99).

Two main measures of association are used in the Values Study. The **Pearson product-moment correlation coefficient** and **Gamma** or, in the case of **dichotomised** variables (variables split into just two categories, for example males and females), **Yules Q,** a special case of gamma. The Pearson correlation coefficient, 'r', summarises the relationship between two variables (or between two pairs of variables), indicating both the strength of the association and whether the correlation is **positive** (an increase in the value of one variable being associated with an increase in the other) or **negative** (an increase in the value of one variable being associated with a decrease in the other). The Pearson coefficient can, however, only be used in cases in which variables can, at least, be ranked or ordered according to some acceptable criterion, e.g. social class groups AB, C1C2, DE (**ordinal** level measurement), or better still when the differences between variables can be measured either in terms of fixed units such as degrees (**interval** level measurement) or proportionate magnitudes (**ratio** level measurement). The Pearson measure is not appropriate for assessing relationships between **nominal** variables, such as sex, religious denomination or region, in which the categories cannot be ordered on a numerical scale. Dichotomised nominal variables can, however, be treated as if they were ordered on an interval scale and in such cases, Yules Q provides a reliable guide to the strength and direction of the association between them. The data are set out in a four **cell** table (two columns and two rows) and the cross-products (formed by multiplying the diagonally opposite cells) are used to obtain a coefficient Q, which is simply the difference between the cross-products divided by the sum of the cross products. 'Q' will vary from zero to ±1. A coefficient of zero indicates that the variables are **independent** from one another – that the reported cell frequencies are exactly what would be expected if there were no association between the two variables. A coefficient of ±1 indicates that is is possible to **predict** the value of one variable perfectly given the value of the other. A Q value of 0.5 indicates that one would do 50 per cent better than chance by predicting the value of one variable on the basis of knowledge about the value of the other. One advantage of Q is that it is insensitive to multiplication or division of row or column frequencies by a positive constant and can therefore be calculated direct from percentages in a table without reference to the raw data (Davis, 1971). Gamma ('G') is a similar measure of association between ordinal level variables and involves the comparison of every possible pair of cases in a table to ascertain whether or not the ranking on one variable is the same as the ranking on the other, and what the probability is of correctly predicting the order on the former variable from the order on the latter.

As far as tests of significance are concerned, the **Chi-square** (x^2) test is simple and widely used. Two, three or more independent groups or samples are compared to ascertain whether significant differences exist between them (or whether some systematic relationship is present). It involves a comparison of the **expected** cell frequencies which would occur if no relationship was present (or no differences existed) with those which have actually been observed. The result is compared with the values in a Chi-square table to ascertain the relevant probability level. Before using the table, however, it is necessary to calculate the number of **degrees of freedom** in the data being tested. Simply stated, the number of degrees of freedom refers to the number of items in a group which is free to vary given some overall limitation on the size of the group (for example, if there are three numbers which must add up to 10 and two of those numbers are known then the third number is fixed and there are two degrees of freedom involved).

In Chapter 9, the psychological well-being of volunteers is compared with a sample representative of non-volunteers in the population using the **Bradburn Affect Balance Scale**. The scores of the two groups are averaged and their **arithmetic means** (the total **sum** of the scores divided by the **number** of scores being averaged) are compared. Similarly, volunteers' attitudes to certain forms of conduct and behaviour are compared with those of the rest of the population using the average scores of the two groups on a series of ten point scales. The mean scores of the volunteer group differ consistently, in both instances, from the rest of the sample and it is necessary to test whether these differences are statistically significant or not. To do so it is essential to have some estimate of the accuracy of the average scores of the two samples we are comparing as a reflection of the average score which would be obtained if **all** volunteers and **all** the rest of the population had been studied. In each sample the scores of the individual volunteers (or the non-volunteers) may be quite close to the mean score for the overall group or they may vary considerably from it. The **variance** and its square-root the **standard deviation** provide summary measures of the spread of individual scores around the sample mean. Similarly, the means of a series of samples will also vary from the true mean of the population which is being sampled. The **standard error of the mean** can be calculated which provides a measure of the likely discrepancy between the sample mean available from the survey data and the true mean for the population being studied. When comparing two samples or groups their respective means and the standard errors relevant to each mean, can be used to calculate a coefficient ('z'), the value of which indicates whether statistically significant differences exist between the samples or not.

Multiple regression is a technique which facilitates the analysis of the relationship between a **dependent** (or **criterion**) variable and a set of **independent** (or **predictor**) variables. It has a number of important applications. For example the technique may be used to describe the structure of the relationship between key variables, according to a causal theory proposed, *a priori*, by the researcher.

'The causal theory specifies an "ordering" among the variables that reflects a presumed structure of cause–effect linkages. Multiple regression techniques are then used to determine the magnitude of direct and indirect influence that each variation has on other variables that follow it in the presumed causal order' (Nie *et al.*, 1975).

In addition to specifying the causal links between the variables, and the effect of a marginal change in an independent variable on a dependent variable, multiple regression also yields a statistic (R^2) which provides a measure of the **amount of variation** in the dependent variable which can be **explained by** the joint influence of the independent variables. When the independent (or predictor) variables are measured in different units (for instance pounds and years) it is difficult to compare their relative effects on the dependent variable. This difficulty is overcome by standardising the units of measurement for the variables used in the regression. These standard regression coefficients are termed **Beta Weights** and provide a useful method of comparing the relative effects of each of the individual independent variables on the dependent variable.

The regression technique used is based on the assumption that most of the relationships of interest to social scientists are **linear**, that is they can be described adequately by an equation for a straight line (of the form $Y = a + bX$) and modifications to it. In its simple two variable form, Y is the dependent variable and X is the independent variable. Plotted as a graph of a straight line showing the value of Y for each specified value of X, the coefficient 'b' gives the slope of the line (thus measuring the amount of change in Y for each unit change in X) and 'a' is a constant, indicating the point at which the line crosses the Y axis. Multiple regression extends the technique to take account of two or more independent variables (i.e. X_1, X_2 etc.) e.g. $Y = A + B_1 X_1 + B_2 X_2$. The 'B' values in this case indicate the change in Y, following a unit change in X when X is held constant or controlled for. It similarly shows how two samples will differ on Y, if they differ on X_1 by one unit but are the same on X_2.

Discriminant analysis distinguishes statistically between two or more groups of cases, such as volunteers and non-volunteers. On the basis of selected **discriminating variables** the analysis provides one (in a two group case) or more linear combinations of the variables. The **discriminant functions** are formed in such a way as to maximise the separation of the groups on a continuum with, for example, volunteers clustered at one end and non-volunteers at the other. The technique provides not only tests of the success with which the discriminating variables actually do discriminate when combined into the discriminating function, but also a means for classifying new cases into one of the two (or more) groups. The classification technique uses a separate linear combination of the discriminating variables for each group. These indicate the probability of membership of the particular group and each case is assigned to the group with the higher (or highest) probability.

Each individual **case** is located on the (volunteer-non-volunteer) continuum on the basis of its **discriminant score.** These scores are always in standard form with a mean of zero and standard deviation of one. Any single score indicates the number of standard deviations that score is away from the mean for all cases on the discriminant function. This score is obtained by multiplying the relevant **discriminant coefficient** for each variable by the value achieved by that case on that variable, summing up the results and adding a constant. The overall results for the sample can be plotted on a histogram. The zero point on the continuum is the grand mean of all classified cases. Each group's location can be plotted on the basis of the mean discriminant scores for the group on the various functions. This location is plotted as a point (centroid) on the continuum.

The standardised discriminant function coefficients are analagous to beta coefficients obtained using multiple regression techniques. They indicate the relative contribution of the associated variable to the discriminant function.

Importantly, the technique of discriminant analysis provides a means of assessing the accuracy of discriminant function by indicating the percentage of the grouped cases correctly classified – on the basis of observed and predicted outcomes.

Factor analysis is a statistical procedure for simplifying and reducing data by identifying a limited number of basic **components** or **factors** which can be regarded as **source variables** forming an underlying pattern of relationships which account for the observed associations among a larger number of variables. The technique involves the preparation of a **correlation matrix**, the search for inter-relationships which will enable the researcher to identify **initial** factors by creating new **composite variables**, and the **rotation** of initial factors to achieve the most illuminating pattern of factors. The **factor loading** measures the extent to which a test measures a given factor and is expressed as a number varying from +1 to −1.

Smallest space analysis (SSA–1) is one of a group of programs from the 'Guttman-Lingoes Series' which portray the relationships between a number of variables (Lingoes, 1974). It does so by transforming measures of association, such as correlation coefficients, into **distances** between points in space. The program produces a plot of points, each denoting one variable, and the closer two points are in the space, the stronger the association between the two variables they represent. Such a plot permits the study of relations betwen all variables at the same time. The procedure by which this transformation is carried out is as follows:- each variable is correlated with every other variable and the variable pairs are ranked in order of the size of the correlation between them. This rank order is then matched to a rank of distances between variable points so that, if the correlation between the variables V1 and V2 is greater than that between V1 and V3, then variable V2 must be represented as closer to V1 than V3 is to V1. As it is usually impossible to represent the distances between more than three points in two-dimensions, the best solution possible is computed and the **goodness of fit** between the original association measures and the computed distances is given. The goodness of fit is measured by the **coefficient of alienation**. An acceptable fit is given by a coefficient of alienation of 0.15 or less (Guttman, 1968).

In constructing the scale to measure respondents' views on the attributes of successful and unsuccessful marriages, items were selected on the basis of the grouping of attributes found in the SSA. **The Guttman scaling technique** permits the unambiguous selection of items which form a **unidimensional scale** in which successive questions measure how extreme the respondent's attitude is to one single issue. In other words it is possible to identify that item which will predict responses to others. Thus with three groups of attributes, a respondent endorsing an item in the first group is expected to endorse items in groups 2 and 3 as well. A respondent not endorsing an item in group 1 may or may not endorse an item in group 2, but if they do then they should endorse an item in group 3 also. There are, in fact, four possible combinations of answers:-

Group 1	Group 2	Group 3
Yes	Yes	Yes
No	Yes	Yes
No	No	Yes
No	No	No

Unfortunately, such scales do not always work perfectly; the answer to one question does not predict the answer to another in quite the way assumed in the theory. Consequently, certain statistical measures of the acceptable errors (respondents answering 'no' to a question when the expected answer is 'yes' and vice versa) have been devised. These include the **coefficient of reproducibility**, a measurement of the extent to which a respondent's scale score is a predictor of the pattern of response; and the **coefficient of scalability**, which measures the extent to which the scale is truly undimensional and cumulative. These coefficients should be at least 0.9 and 0.6 respectively.

Finally, in examining survey evidence it is not uncommon to encounter unexpected findings which are statistically significant. Such results, which have not formed part of the original hypotheses or propositions to be tested, could be among many chance occurrences and cannot be treated as valid findings as they stand. The researcher in such cases is faced with the choice of putting them forward as new hypotheses for future investigation or, if fortunate, comparing the results with previous research on the same theme and drawing provisional conclusions. In short, it is essential to specify at the design and pre-analysis stages the hypotheses and propositions to be tested if the conclusions are to be accepted as credible, scientifically. Apparently significant findings, emerging unexpectedly from the data, can nevertheless be framed as new hypotheses for subsequent research.

Bibliography

AAS = *Acta Apostolicae Sedis*, Vatican.

Abrams, M. (1976) *A Review of Subjective Social Indicators Work, 1971–1975* ix, 2 as 1973. (London: Social Science Research Council).

Abrams, M. (1979) *Beyond Three Score Years and Ten* (London: Age Concern).

Abrams, M. (1983) *Education and Elderly People* (London: Age Concern).

Abrams, P. (1978) 'Community Care: Some Research Problems and Priorities' in Barnes J. and Connelly N. (eds) *Social Care Research* (London: Bedford Square Press).

Abrams, P. (1979) 'Altruism and Reciprocity: Altruism as Reciprocity' *Working Paper ii* (Rowntree Research Group, University of Durham).

Abrams, P., S. Abrams, R. Humphrey and R. Snaith (1981) *Action for Care, a Review of Good Neighbour Schemes in England* (London: The Volunteer Centre).

Adams, S. (1980) *Law at Work: Sex Discrimination* (London: Sweet & Maxwell).

Alderfer, C. P. (1969) 'An Empirical Test of a New Theory of Human Needs' *Organisational Behaviour and Human Performance* 4, pp. 142–75.

Ambrose, P., J. Harper and R. Pemberton (1983) *Surviving Divorce: Men Beyond Marriage* (Brighton: Wheatsheaf).

Anderson, S. A., C. S. Russell and W. R. Schumm (1983) 'Perceived Marital Quality and family-life cycle categories – a further analysis' in Szalai and Andrews *Journal of Marriage and the Family* 45. (London: Sage) pp. 127–139.

Andrews, F. M., and S. B. Withey (1976) *Social Indicators of Well Being* (New York: Plenum Press).

ARCIC (1982) Final Report, Anglican – Roman Catholic International Commission (London: CTS/SPCK).

Armstrong, P. (1982) 'If it's only women it doesn't matter so much' in J. West (ed.) *Work, Women and the Labour Market* (London: Routledge & Kegan Paul).

Aronson, E. (1983) *The Social Animal* (San Francisco: Freeman).

Arrow, K. J. (1972) 'Gifts and Exchanges' *Philosophy and Public Affairs* 1 pp. 343–62.

Austin, M., and J. Posnett (1979) 'Charitable Activity in England & Wales' *Institute of Economic and Social Research and Department of Economics* (University of York; April).

Axelrod, M. (1956) 'Urban Structure and Social Participation' *American Sociological Review* pp. 13–18, 21.

Bales, R. F. (1951) *Interaction Process Analysis* (Reading, Mass: Addison Wesley).

Barclay, W. (1962) *Flesh and Spirit: An Examination of Galatians 5 : 19–23* (London: S.C.M. Press Ltd.).

Barclay, W. (1971) *Ethics in a Permissive Society* (London: Fontana Books).

Barker, D., and S. Allen (1976) *Dependence and Exploitation in Work and Marriage* (London: Tavistock).

Barron, R., and G. Norris (1976) 'Sexual Divisions and the Dual Labour Market' in D. Barker and S. Allen (eds) *Dependence and Exploitation in Work and Marriage* (London: Tavistock).

Barth, K. (1958) *Church Dogmatics* Vol. iv, Part 2. (Edinburgh: Clark).

Bavelas, A. (1956) 'Communication Patterns in Task-Oriented Groups', in D. Cartwright and A. Zander (eds) *Group Dynamics* (New York: Row Peterson).

Bell, D. (1980) 'The Return of the Sacred' in *The Winding Passage* (Cambridge, Mass: ABT Books).

Bellah, R.N. (1964) 'Religious Evolution', *American Sociological Review* 29 pp. 358–74.

Bellah, R. N. (1967) 'Civil Religion in America' *Daedalus* 96(1) pp. 1–21.

Belsky, J., G. B. Spanier and M. Rovine (1983) 'Stability and Change in Marriage across the Transition to Parenthood', *Journal of Marriage and the Family* 45 pp. 567–77.

Benn, S. I., and R. S. Peters (1959) *Social Principles and the Democratic State* (London: Allen & Unwin).

Berger, P. (1961) *The Noise of Solemn Assemblies: Christian Commitment and the Religious Establishment in America* (New York: Doubleday & Company).

Berger, P. (1967) *The Sacred Canopy: Elements of a Sociological Theory of Religion* (New York: Doubleday & Company).

Berger, P. (1969) *A Rumor of Angels, Modern Society and the Rediscovery of the Supernatural* (New York: Doubleday & Company).

Berger, P., and H. Kellner (1964) 'Marriage and the Construction of Reality', *Diogenes*, pp. 1–23.

Bernard, J. (1982) *The Future of Marriage* (New Haven: Yale University Press).

Bessant, J. (1982) *Microprocessors in Production Processes* (London: Policy Studies Institute).

Blalock, H. M. (1960) *Social Statistics* (London: McGraw-Hill).

Blau, P. M. (1964) *Exchange and Power in Social Life* (Chichester: John Wiley & Sons).

Bloom, B. L., S. J. Asher and S. W. White (1978) 'Marital Disruption as a Stressor: a review and analysis', *Psychological Bulletin* 85 pp. 867–94.

Booth, A., and L. White (1980) 'Thinking about Divorce' *Journal of Marriage and The Family* 42 pp. 605–16.

Bowker, J. (1983) *Worlds of Faith* (London: BBC Ariel Books).

Bradburn, N. M. (1969) *The Structure of Psychological Well-being* (Chicago: Aldine).

Brannen, J., and J. Collard (1982) *Marriages in Trouble* (London: Tavistock Publications).

Bromley, D. B. (1974) *The Psychology of Human Ageing* (Harmondsworth: Penguin Books).

Brown, A., and K. Kiernan (1981) 'Cohabitation in Great Britain: Evidence from the G.H.S.' *Population Trends* 25 pp. 4–10.

Bruegel, I. (1979) 'Women as a Reserve Army of Labour: a Note on Recent British Experience' *Feminist Review* 3 pp. 12–23.

Burchinal, L. G. (1964) 'Characteristics of Adolescents from Unbroken Homes and Reconstituted Families' *Journal of Marriage and the Family* 26 pp. 44–5.

Burdas, A. (1977) *You Don't Know Me: A Survey of Youth in Great Britain* (see refs. page 30) (London: McCann Erikson Advertising).

Busfield, J., and M. Paddon (1977) *Thinking about Children: Sociology and Sterility in Post-war England* (Cambridge University Press).

Butler, D., and D. Stokes (1971) *Political Change in Britain* (Harmondsworth: Penguin).

Butler, E. W. (1979) *Traditional Marriage and Emerging Alternatives* (New York: Harper & Row).

Campbell, A. (1976) 'Subjective measures of well-being' *American Psychologist, 31*, pp. 117–24.

Campbell, A., P. E. Converse and W. L. Rodgers (1976) *The Quality of American Life: Perceptions, Evaluations and Satisfactions* (New York: Russell Sage).

Chancellor, L., and T. P. Monhan (1955) 'Religious Preferences and Interreligious Mixtures in Marriages and Divorces in Iowa' *American Journal of Sociology* 61 pp. 233–9.

Chester, R. (1971) 'Health and Marriage Breakdown: Experience of a Sample of Divorced Women' *British Journal of Preventative Social Medicine.* 25 pp.231–5.

Chester, R. (1972) 'Current Incidence and Trends in Marital Breakdown, *Postgraduate Medical Journal* 48 pp. 529–41.

Chesterman, M. (1979) *Charities Trusts and Social Welfare* (London: Weidenfeld & Nicolson).

Chiplin, B., and P. Sloane (1976) *Sex Discrimination in the Labour Market* (London: Macmillan).

Chisolm, G. B. (1946) 'The Re-Establishment of a Peace-Time Society', *Psychiatry* 6.

CIO = Church Information Office, Church House, London.

Collard, D. (1978) *Altruism and Economy* (Oxford: Martin Robertson).

Commager, H. S. (1962) 'Foreword' in *McGuffey's Fifth Eclectic Reader* Reprint (New York: Signet Classics).

Converse, P. E. (1964) 'The Nature of Belief Systems in Mass Publics' in David Apter (ed.) *Ideology & Discontent* (New York: Free Press) pp. 202–61.

Costa, P. T., and R. R. McCrae (1980) 'Influence of Extraversion and Neuroticism on Subjective Well-being: happy and unhappy people' *Journal of Personality & Social Psychology,* 38 pp. 668–78.

Cotgrove, S., and A. Duff (1981) 'Environmentalism, Values and Social Change' *British Journal of Sociology* 1, pp. 92–110.

Crago, M. A. (1972) 'Psychopathology in Married Couples' *Psychological Bulletin* 77 pp. 114–28.

Crook, J. H. (1980) *The Evolution of Human Consciousness* (Oxford: Clarendon Press).

Csikszentmihalyi, M. (1975) *Beyond Boredom and Anxiety: the experience of play in work and games* (San Francisco: Josey-Bass).

Currie, R., A. Gilbert and L. Horsley (1977) *Churches and Church-Goers* (Oxford: Clarendon Press).

Cutright, P. (1971) 'Income and Family Events: marital stability' *Journal of Marriage and the Family* 33 p. 296.

Daniel, W. W. (1981) *The Unemployed Flow* (London: Policy Studies Institute).

Davies, C. (1975) *Permissive Britain* (London: Pitman).

de Moor, R. (1983) 'Nederland binnen de Europese Cultuur: Een studie naar waarden' in: Becker, J. W. (ed.) *Normen en Waarden. Verandering of verschuiving?* ('s-Gravenhage: VUGA-uitgeverij).

Department of Employment (1982) *New Earnings Survey* (London: HMSO).

Dobbelaere, K. (1981) 'Secularization: A Multi-Dimensional Concept' *Current Sociology* 29 (London: Sage Publications) pp. 3–213.

Dobbelaere, K. (1984 i) 'Godsdienste in Belgie' in *De Stille Ommekeer* (Lannoo: Tielt and Weesp).

Dobbelaere, K. (1984 ii) 'The Secularization of Man's Conception of God' *Papers Presented at the 1983–84 'God Conference'* San-Juan, Puerto Rico 30 Dec 1983 – 4 Jan 1984.

Dominion, J. (1968) *Marital Breakdown* (Harmondsworth: Penguin).

Dominion, J. (1980) *Marriage in Britain 1945–1980* (London: Study Commission on the Family).

Dominion, J. (1982) 'Families in Divorce' in R.N. Rapoport, M. P. Fogerty, and R. Rapoport (eds) *Families in Britain* (London: Routledge & Kegan Paul).

Douglas, J. W. B., J. M. Ross and H. R. Simpson (1968) *All Our Futures* (London: Peter Davies).

Downie, R. S. (1971) *Roles and Values. An Introduction to Social Ethics* (London: Methuen).

Dulles, A. (1978) *The Resilient Church: The Necessity and Limits of Adaptation* (Dublin: Gill & Macmillan).

Dunnell, K. (1979) *Family Formation 1976* OPCS Social Survey Division (London: HMSO).

Durkheim, E. (1964) *The Division of Labour in Society* (trans. G. Simpson) (New York: The Free Press).

Economist Intelligence Unit (1982) *Coping with Unemployment: The Effects*

338 *Bibliography*

on the Unemployed Themselves (London: EIU).

Edgell, S. (1980) *Middle Class Couples: A Study of Segregation, Domination and Inequality in Marriage* (London: Allen & Unwin).

Edwards, J. N., and J. M. Saunders (1981) 'Coming Apart: A Model of the Marital Dissolution Decision' *Journal of Marriage and the Family* 43 pp. 379–89.

Elkins, S. M. (1959) *Slavery: A problem in American Institutional and Intellectual Life* (New York: Universal Library).

European Values System Study Group (1980) *The Presentation Documents* (Amsterdam: EVSSG).

Falk, G. (1975) 'Mate Selection' *American International Behavioral Scientist* 7 pp. 68–80.

Fenn, R. K. (1978) *Towards a Theory of Secularization* (Storrs, Connecticut: Society for the Scientific Study of Religion, Monograph No. 1).

Fiegehen, G., P. Lansley and A. Smith (1977) *Poverty and Progress in Britain 1953–1973* National Institute of Economic and Social Research.

Finer, M. (ed.) (1974) *Report of the Committee on One Parent Families* Cmnd. 5629 (London: HMSO).

Fogarty, M. P. (1982) 'Public Opinion on Industrial Relations', Working Paper, Policy Studies Institute, Industrial Relations Project.

Fogarty, M. P. (1983 i) 'Industrial Relations and the British Economy in Recent Years', Working Paper, Policy Studies Institute, Industrial Relations Project.

Fogarty, M. P. (1983 ii) *What have Other Countries to Offer?* 'Working Paper, Policy Studies Institute, Industrial Relations Project'.

Fogarty, M., and R. Rapoport (1971) *Sex, Career and Family* (London: Allen & Unwin).

Fox, A. (1979) *Corporatism and Industrial Democracy: The Social Origins of Present Forms and Methods in Britain and Germany* (University of Oxford, Dept. of Social and Administrative Studies).

Francis, L. J.(1984) *Teenagers and The Church: A Profile of Church–Going Youth in the 1980s* (London: Collins Liturgical Publications).

Fromm, E. (1955) *The Sane Society* (New York: Rinehart & Co.).

Geertz, C. (1968) 'Religion as a Cultural System' in *Anthropological Approach to The Study of Religion* Banton M. (ed.) (London: Tavistock).

Geiger, T. (1969) 'The Bonds of Large Scale Society' in *Social Order and Mass Society* (Chicago: University of Chicago Press).

Gerard, D. (1983) *Charity and Change: A Profile of the Voluntary Sector.* microfiche (London: Bedford Square Press). Summarised in:

Gerard, D. (1983) *Charities in Britain* (London: Bedford Square Press).

Gibson, K. (1983) 'Working Mothers: An examination of women in secondary sector employment' Unpublished MSc. Thesis, University of Surrey, Guildford.

Gilbert, A. D. (1980) *The Making of Post-Christian Britain: A History of the Secularization of Modern Society* (Harlow: Longman).

Glock, C. Y., B. B. Ringer and E. R. Babbie (1967) *To Comfort and To Challenge: A Dilemma of the Contemporary Church* (Berkeley: University of California Press).

Glock, C. Y., and R. Stark (1965) *Religion and Society in Tension* (Chicago:

Rand McNally & Co.).

Gouldner, A. V. (1973) *For Sociology* Essays 8 and 9 (New York: Basic Books).

Greeley, A. M. (1972) *Unsecular Man: The Persistence of Religion* (New York: Schocken Books).

Greer, S., J. Gunn and K. Koller (1966) 'Actiological Factors in Attempted Suicide', *British Medical Journal* 2 pp. 1352–5.

Gurin, G., J. Veroff and S. Feld (1966) *Americans View Their Mental Health* (New York: Basic Books).

Guttman, L. (1968) 'A General Nonmetric Technique for Finding the Smallest Co-ordinate Space for a Configuration' *Psychometrika* 33 pp. 469–506.

Hakim, C. (1978) 'Sexual Divisions within the Labour Force: occupational segregation' *Employment Gazette* pp. 1264–8.

Hakim, C. (1979) 'Occupational Segregation' Dept. of Employment Research Papers No. 9 (London: HMSO).

Halifax, Lord (ed.) (1930) *The Conversations at Malines, 1921–25* (London: Philip Allan).

Hall, D., and K. E. Nougaim (1968) 'An Examination of Maslow's Need Hierarchy in an Organisational Setting' *Organisational Behaviour and Human Performance* 3.

Hall, J. F., and A. J. Ring (1974) *Indicators of Environmental Quality and Life Satisfaction: a Subjective Approach* (London: SSRC Survey Unit).

Halsey, A. H. (1981) *Change in British Society*, 2nd ed. (Oxford University Press).

Halsey, A. H., (1983 i) 'The State of Welfare' *The Listener*, 6 Jan.

Halsey, A. H., (1983 ii) 'To be a Pilgrim' *The Listener*, 20 Jan.

Halsey, A. H., A. F. Heath and J. M. Ridge (1980) *Origins and Destinations* (Oxford University Press).

Hampshire, S., (ed.) (1978) *Public and Private Morality* (Cambridge University Press).

Harding, S. D. (1982) 'Psychological Well-being in Great Britain: an Evaluation of the Bradburn Affect Balance Scale' *Personality & Individual Differences* 3, pp. 167–75.

Harding, S. D., and D. Phillips (1985) *Values in Europe. A Cross National Survey.* (London: Macmillan).

Harding, S. D., and C. George (1979) *European Values Pilot Survey: Comments on the British Data* (Brussels: European Values Systems Study Group).

Harrison, J. (1983) *Attitude to Bible, God, Church: Research Report* June (Swindon: Bible Society).

Hart, H. L. (1961) *The Concept of Law* (Oxford University Press).

Hart, N. (1976) *When Marriage Ends: A Study in Status Passage* (London: Tavistock Publications).

Hatch, S., and I. Mocroft (1977) 'Voluntary Workers' *New Society* 7 April, vol. 40, p. 24.

Hay, D. (1982) *Exploring Inner Space: Scientists and Religious Experience* (Harmondsworth: Penguin Books).

Heald, G., M. James and S. D. Harding (1981) 'Cross-national Research of

People's Values: A New Approach' in *Collected Papers of the 24th Annual Conference* (London: Market Research Society) pp. 229–33.

Herberg, W. (1967) 'Religion in a Secularized Society: The New Shape of Religion in America' in Knudten R. (ed.) *The Sociology of Religion: An Anthology* (New York: Appleton Century Crofts).

Hessert, P. (1968) *New Directions in Theology Today Vol. V. Christian Life* (Guildford: Lutterworth).

Hicks, M., and M. Platt (1970) 'Marital Happiness and Stability: A Review of the Research in the Sixties', *Journal of Marriage and the Family*, 32, pp. 553–74.

Hill, C., Z. Rubin and L. Peplan (1976) 'Breakups before Marriage: the end of 103 Affairs', *Journal of Social Issues* 32 pp. 147–68.

Himmelweit, H. (1982) *Common Market Survey*, London School of Economics.

Hirsch, F. (1977) *The Social Limits to Growth* (London: Routledge & Kegan Paul).

Hobhouse, L. T. (1951) *Morals in Evolution: A Study in Comparative Ethics (1906)* (London: Chapman & Hall).

Hoge, D. R., and D. A. Roozen (eds) (1979) *Understanding Church Growth and Decline 1950–1978* (Derby: Pilgrim Press).

Homans, G. C. (1962) *Social Behaviour: Its Elementary Forms* (London: Routledge & Kegan Paul).

Hornsby-Smith, M., and E. Cordingley (1984) 'Catholic Elites: A Study of Delegates to the National Pastoral Congress', Department of Sociology, Unversity of Surrey.

Houseknecht, S. K. (1979) 'Childlessness and Marital Adjustment' *Journal of Marriage and The Family* 41 pp. 259–65.

Humble, S. (1982) *Voluntary Action in the 1980's: A Summary of the Findings of A National Survey* (Berkhampstead: The Volunteer Centre).

Hurstfield, J. (1978) *The Part-time Trap* (London: Low Pay Unit).

Inglehart, R. (1977) *The Silent Revolution: Changing Values and Political Styles among Western Publics* (Princeton University Press).

Inglehart, R. (1981) 'Post-materialism in an environment of insecurity' *American Political Science Review* 75 pp. 880–900.

Jacobs, E., S. Orwell, P. Paterson and F. Weltz (1978) *The Approach to Industrial Change in Britain and Germany* (Anglo-German Foundation).

Jahoda, M. (1958) *Current Concepts of Mental Health* (New York: Basic Books).

Jenness, L. (1975) *Last Hired: First Fired* (New York: Pathfinder).

Jorgenson, S. R., and A. C. Johnson (1980) 'Correlates of Divorce Liberality' *Journal of Marriage and the Family* 40 pp. 617–26.

Keeton, G., and L. Sheridan (1971) *The Modern Law of Charities* Northern Ireland Legal Quarterly, 2nd ed.

Kerkhofs, J. (1983) 'God in West Europa', *Streven*, Nov.

Kiernan, K. (1983) 'The Structure of Families Today: Continuity or Change?' OPCS Occasional Paper 31.

Kinnard, J., J. Brotherston and J. Williamson (1981) *The Provision of Care for the Elderly* (Edinburgh: Churchill Livingstone).

Klingemann, H., and R. Inglehart (1975) 'Party Identification, Ideological

Preference and the Left-Right Dimension among Western Publics' in I. Budge and I. Crewe (eds) *Party Identification and Beyond* (New York: John Wiley & Sons).

Knupfer, G., W. Clark and R. Room (1966) 'The Mental Health of the Unmarried' *American Journal of Psychiatry* 122 p. 842.

Komarovsky, M. (1964) *Blue Collar Marriage* (New York: Random House).

Kramer, R. M. (1981) *Voluntary Agencies in the Welfare State* (Berkeley University of California Press).

Krebs, D. (1970) 'Altruism – an examination of the concept and a review of the literature' *Psychological Bulletin*, 73, pp. 258–302.

Landis, J. T. (1960) 'The Trauma of children whose parents divorce' *Marriage and Family Living*, 22, pp. 7–13.

Landis, J. T. (1962) 'Marriages of mixed and non-mixed religious faith' in *Selected Studies in Marriage and Family* (New York: Holt Rinehart & Winston).

Leach, E. (1967) *A Runaway World* (London: BBC Publications).

Lee, T. (1975) *Psychology and the Environment* (London: Methuen).

Leete, R., and S. Anthony (1979) 'Divorce and Remarriage: a record linkage study' *Population Trends* 16 (London: HMSO).

Levitt, T. (1973) *The Third Sector: New Tactics for a Responsive Society* (London: Allen and Unwin/Amacom).

Lewis, R. A., and G. B. Spanier (1979) 'Theorising about the quality and stability of marriage' in W. R. Burr, R. Hill, F. I. Nye and I. L. Reiss (eds) *Contemporary Theories about the Family* (New York: The Free Press).

Lingoes, J. (1974) *The Guttman – Lingoes Program Series* (Ann Arbor, Michigan: Mathesis).

Locke, H. J. (1951) *Predicting adjustment in marriage: a comparison of a divorced and happily married group* (New York: Holt).

Luckmann, T. (1967) *The Invisible Religion: The Problem of Religion in Modern Society* (London: Macmillan).

Luhmann, N. (1977) *Funktion der Religion* (Frankfurt am main: Suhrkamp Verlag).

MacIntyre, A. (1981) *After Virtue: A Study in Moral Theory* (London: Duckworth).

Macquarrie, J. (1978) *The Humility of God* (London: SCM).

Mahoney, J. (1981) *Seeking the Spirit: Essays in Moral and Pastoral Theology* (London: Sheed & Ward).

Mansfield, P. (1982 i) 'A Portrait of Contemporary Marriage: equal partners or just good companions' *Change in Marriage: A Collection of Papers presented at the National Marriage Guidance Study Days* (Rugby: NMGC).

Mansfield, P. (1982 ii) 'Getting Ready for Parenthood: attitudes to and expectations of having children of a group of newly-weds' *International Journal of Sociology and Social Policy* 2 pp. 28–39.

Marriage and Divorce Statistics, Office of Population Census Surveys Series FM2 (London: HMSO, Annual).

Marriage Guidance Council (1981) 'Marriage in the Eighties', personal communication.

Marsh, A. (1977) *Protest and Political Consciousness* (Beverly Hills, California: Sage Publications).

Marsh, A., M. Hackmann and D. Miller (1981) *Workplace Industrial Relations in the Engineering Industry in the U.K. and the Federal Republic of Germany* (Anglo German Foundation).

Martin, D. (1967) *A Sociology of English Religion* (London: SCM Press).

Martin, D. (1969) *The Religious and the Secular Studies in Secularization* (London: Routledge & Kegan Paul).

Martin, D. (1978) *A General Theory of Secularization* (Oxford: Basil Blackwell).

Maslow, A. H. (1970) *Motivation and Personality*, 2nd ed. (London: Harper & Row).

Maslow, A. H. (1973) *The Further Reaches of Human Nature* (Harmondsworth: Penguin Books).

McCready, W. C., and A. M. Greeley (1976) *The Ultimate Values of the American Population* Vol. 23, Sage Library of Social Research (Sage).

McCready, W. C. (1981) 'A Researcher's View' *Towards More Effective Research in the Church: A National Catholic Symposium* (FADICA).

McGregor, O. *et al.* (1970) *Separated Spouses* (London: Duckworth).

McKenell, A. C. and F. M. Andrews (1980) 'Models of Cognition and Affect in Perceptions of Well-being' *Social Indicators Research* 8 pp. 257–298.

McMillan, E. L. (1969) 'The Problem Build-up: A description of couples in marriage counselling' *The Family Coordinator* 18 pp. 260–7.

McMullen, D., S. Maurice and D. Parker (1967) *Tudor on Charities* (London: Sweet & Maxwell).

McMurray, L. (1970) 'Emotional Stress and Driving Performance: the effect of divorce' *Behavioural Research in Highway Safety* 1 pp. 100–14.

McQuillan, J. (ed.) (1983) *Charity Statistics 1982–83* (Charities Aid Foundation) p. 9.

Melden, A. I. (1959) *Rights and Right Conduct* (Oxford: Basil Blackwell).

Money-Kyrle, R. E. (1932) *Aspasia: the Future of Amorality* (London: Kegan Paul, Trench Trubner & Co. Ltd.).

Montague, A. (1976) *The Nature of Human Agression* (Oxford University Press).

Moore, R. (1979) 'What Shop Stewards Really Think' *Management Today* July pp. 58–61.

More, T. (1965) *Utopia* (1516) (Harmondsworth: Penguin Books).

Morgan, J., R. Dye and J. Hybels (1977) 'Results from Two National Surveys of Philanthropic Activity' in *Research Papers Volume 1: History, Trends and Current Magnitudes*, Commission on Private Philanthropy & Public Needs. (Washington: Dept. of the Treasury).

Mostyn, B. (1983) 'The meaning of voluntary work: a qualitative investigation', in *Volunteers: Patterns, Meanings and Motives* S. Hatch (ed.) (Berkhampstead: The Volunteer Centre).

Murchison, N. (1974) 'Illustration of the Difficulties of Some Children of One Parent Families', in M. Finer (ed.) *Report of the Committee on One Parent Families* Cmnd 5629 (London: HMSO).

Nagel, T. (1970) *The Possibility of Altruism* (Oxford: Clarendon Press).

Nelson, H. H., and R. F. Everett (1976) 'A Test of Yinger's Measure of Non-Doctrinal Religion: Implications for Invisible Religion as a Belief

System' *Journal for the Scientific Study of Religion* 15 pp. 263–7.

Nelson, E. E., D. Baker and E. N. Nelson (1978) 'Correlates of Voluntary Associational Membership: A Stratification Approach'. Paper presented to the Pacific Sociological Association 1978 Meeting.

Neugarten, B. L. (1968) *Middle Age and Ageing* (Chicago: University Press).

Newton, K. (1976) *Second City Politics* (Oxford: Clarendon Press).

Niebuhr, R. (1963) *Moral Man and Immoral Society* (London: SCM).

Nie, N. H., C. H. Hull, J. G. Jenkins, K. Steinbreuner and D. H. Brent (1975) *SPSS Statistical Package For The Social Sciences*, 2nd ed. (New York: McGraw-Hill).

Northcott, J., and P. Rogers (1982) *Microelectronics in Industry* (London: Policy Studies Institute).

Nye, F. I. (1957) 'Child Adjustment in Broken Homes' *Marriage and the Family* 19 pp. 356–61.

Oakley, A. (1974) *Housewife* (London: Allen & Lane).

Oakley, A. (1976) *The Sociology of Housework* (London: Tavistock Publications).

Office of Population Censuses and Surveys (OPCS) (1983) *General Household Survey 1981* Series GHS No. 11 (London: HMSO).

Office of Population Censuses and Surveys (Annual) *General Household Survey* (London: HMSO).

Ollerstrom, E. (1952) 'The Social Outlook for the Children of Divorcees' *Acta Genetica et Statistica Medica* 3, p.72.

Orwell, G. (1970) 'The Lion and The Unicorn' in *Collective Essays, Journalism and Letters of George Orwell* Vol. 2 (London: Penguin Books).

Parkes, C. M. (1972) *Bereavement* (London: Tavistock).

Parkin, F. (1968) *Middle Class Radicalism* (Manchester University Press).

Parsons, T. (1967) 'Christianity and Modern Industrial Society' in *Sociological Theory, Values and Sociocultural change, Essays in Honour of Pitrim A. Sorokin*, ed. E. A. Tiryakin (London: Harper and Row).

Peters, R. S. (1959) *The Concept of Motivation* (London: Routledge and Kegan Paul).

Phillips, D. L. (1967) 'Social Participation and Happiness' *American Journal of Sociology* 72, pp. 479–88.

Phillips, D. Z., and H. O. Mounce (1969) *Moral Practices* (London: Routledge & Kegan Paul).

Qureshi, H., D. Challis and B. Davies (1983) 'Motivations and Rewards of Helpers in the Kent Community Care Scheme' *Volunteers: Patterns Meanings and Motives*, S. Hatch (ed.) (Berkhampstead: The Volunteer Centre).

Rahner, K. (1963) *Mission and Grace Vol. I* (London: Sheed & Ward).

Rahner, K. (1974) *The Shape of the Church to Come* (London: SCM).

Rapoport, T., and M. Sierakowski (1982) *Recent Social Trends in Family and Work in Britain* (London: Policy Studies Institute).

Raven, J. (1982) *Competence in Modern Society* Draft report available from the author, 30, Gt. King Street, Edinburgh. Chapter 14.

Report of the EVSSG Pilot Study (1981) *The European Value System* October (Paris: Faits et Opinion).

Report of the Wolfenden Committee (1978) *The Future of Voluntary*

Organisations (London: Croom Helm).

Research and Forecasts (1982) A Survey for the Connecticut Mutual Life Insurance Company, September – November 1980 reported in 'Americans Volunteer: A Profile', *Public Opinion* Feb/Mar pp. 5, 21–31.

Robinson, J. (1960) *On Being The Church in the World* (London: SCM).

Rollins, B. C., and R. Galligan (1978) 'The developing child and marital satisfaction of parents' in R. M. Lerner and G. B. Spanier (eds) *Child Influences on Marital and Family Interaction* (New York: Academic Press).

Roof, W. C., and D. R. Hoge (1980) 'Church Involvement in America: Social Factors Affecting Membership and Participation' *Review of Religious Research* 21, pp. 405–26.

Roof, W. C. (1976) 'Traditional Religion in Contemporary Society: A Theory of Local – Cosmopolitan Plausibility' *American Sociological Review* 41, pp. 195–208.

Roof, W. C. (1978) 'Social Correlates of Religious Involvement: Review of Recent Research in the United States' *The Annual Review of the Social Sciences of Religion*, p. 2.

Roof, W. C. (1979) 'Concepts and Indicators of Religious Commitment', in *The Religious Dimensions: New Directions in Quantitative Research* R. Wuthnow (ed.) (London: Academic Press).

Roof, W. C. *et al.* (1977) 'Yinger's Measure of Non-Doctrinal Religion: A Northeastern Test' *Journal for the Scientific Study of Religion* 16, pp. 403–8.

Rokeach, M. (1973) *The Nature of Human Values* (New York: The Free Press).

Roper Organisation (1982) A Survey in conjunction with the Roper Center for Public Opinion Research for the American Enterprise Institute, November 1981, reported in 'Americans Volunteer, A Profile', *Public Opinion*, Feb/Mar 5, pp. 21–31.

Rose, R. (1980) *Politics in England: An Interpretation for the 1980s*, 3rd ed. (London: Faber & Faber).

Rose, R. (1984) 'Proud to be British', *New Society* 7 June.

Rosenberg, M. (1968) *The Logic of Survey Analysis* (New York: Basic Books).

Rossiter, C., and M. Wicks (1982) *Crisis or Challenge: Family Care, Elderly People and Social Policy* (London: Study Commission on the Family).

Russell, C. S. (1974) 'Transition to Parenthood: problems and gratifications' *Journal of Marriage and the Family* 36 pp. 294–302.

Rutter, M., and N. Madge (1976) *Cycles of Disadvantage* (London: Heinemann).

Rutter, M. (1979) 'Separation, Loss and Family Relationships' in M. Rutter and L. Hersov (eds) *Child psychiatry: Modern Approaches* (Oxford: Blackwell).

Sahlins, M. (1972) *Stone Age Economics* (Hawthorne N.Y.: Aldine).

Särlvik, B., and I. Crewe (1983) *Decade of Dealignment: The Conservative Victory of 1979 and Electoral Trends in the 1970's* (Cambridge University Press).

Schmidtchen, G. (1972) *Zwischen Kirche und Gesellschaft. Forschungsber-*

icht uber die Umfragen zur Gemeinsamen Synode der Bistumer in der Bundesrepublik Deutschland (Herder).

Schram, R. W. (1979) 'Marital satisfaction over the family life cycle: a critique and proposal' *Journal of Marriage and the Family* 41, pp. 7–13.

Sen, A., and B. Williams, (eds) (1982) *Utilitarianism and Beyond* (Cambridge University Press).

Sheppard, D. (1984) 'The poverty that imprisons the spirit' The 1984 Richard Dimbleby Lecture *The Listener* 19 April.

Shiner, L. (1967) 'The Concept of Secularization in Empirical Research' *Journal for the Scientific Study of Religion* 6, pp. 207–20.

Sills, D. (1968) 'Voluntary Association: Sociological Aspect', in *International Encyclopedia of the Social Sciences*, vol. 16, Sills D. (ed.) (London and Dallas: Macmillan & Free Press).

Singer, P. (1973) 'Altruism and Commerce: a defence of Titmuss against Arrow', *Philosophy and Public Affairs* 2, pp. 312–20.

Social and Community Planning Research (1984) SSRC Sponsored Survey of Volunteering in association with The Volunteer Centre. Final Report to be published in 1984 (London).

Sorokin P. (1966) 'The Western Religion and Morality of Today', in *International Yearbook of the Sociology of Religion* 2 (Westdeutscher Verlag).

Spanier, G. B., and R. A. Lewis (1980) 'Marital Quality: a review of the 1970s' *Journal of Marriage and the Family* 42, pp. 825–39.

Spanier, G. B., R. A. Lewis and C. L. Cole (1975) 'Marital adjustment over the family life cycle: The issue of curvilinearity' *Journal of Marriage and The Family* 37, pp. 263–275.

Stark, R. (1972) 'The Economics of Piety: Religious Commitment and Social Class', in Thielbar C. and Feldman A. (eds) *Issues in Social Inequality* (Harpers Ferry: Little, Brown).

Stevenson, C. L. (1944) *Ethics and Language* (New Haven: Yale University Press).

Stoetzel, J. (1983) *Les Valeurs du temps present* (Paris: Presse Universitaire de France) Trans. available by Meril James from EVSSG under the title *Europe at the Crossroads*.

Szalai, A., and F. M. Andrews (1983) *The Quality of Life: Comparative Studies* (London: Sage).

The Sun (1980) 'What do teenagers really think?', the *Sun*, 25 October.

Tawney, R. H. (1921) *The Aquisitive Society* (London: G. Bell & Sons) (Reprinted by Fontana Books 1961).

Tawney, R. H. (1965) *Equality* (London: Allen & Unwin).

Thomas, M. M. (1968) 'Children with absent fathers' *Journal of Marriage and The Family* 30, pp. 89–96.

Thornes, B. and J. Collard (1979) *Who Divorces?* (London: Routledge & Kegan Paul).

Thorpe, W. H. (1974) *Animal Nature and Human Nature* VIII, 14. (London: Methuen).

Tiller, J. (1983) *A Strategy for the Church's Ministry* (London: CIO).

Titmuss, R.M. (1970) *The Gift Relationship* (London: Allen & Unwin).

Urmson, J. O. (1968) *The Emotive Theory of Ethics* (London: Hutchinson).

Wallace, G., and A. D. M. Walker (1970) *The Definition of Morality* (London: Methuen).

Wahba, M., and L. Bridwell (1976) 'Maslow Reconsidered: A Review of the Need Hierarchy Theory' in *Organisational Behaviour and Human Performance* 15, pp. 212–40.

Warnock, G. J. (1971) *The Object of Morality* (London: Methuen).

Warr, P. B. (1978) 'A study of psychological well-being' *British Journal of Psychology*, 69, pp. 111–21.

Warr, P. B. (1983) 'Work, Jobs and Unemployment', *Bulletin of the British Psychological Society*, 36, pp. 305–11.

Watson, D. (1983) 'Making Reality Intelligible' *Journal of Social Policy* 12, pp. 491–514.

Weber, M. (1977) *The Protestant Ethic and the Spirit of Capitalism* (Trans. Parsons, T.) (London: Allen & Unwin).

Wermer, B. (1982) 'Recent Trends in Illegitimate Births and Extra-marital Conceptions' *Population Trends* 30, pp. 9–15.

West, J. (1982) *Work, Women and the Labour Market* (London: Routledge & Kegan Paul).

White, M., and M. Trevor (1983) *Under Japanese Management* (London: Heinemann).

Willcocks, D., S. M. Peace and L. Kellaher (1981) *The Residential Life of Old People* (Polytechnic of North London: Survey Research Unit).

Williams, B. (1972) *Morality* (Harmondsworth: Penguin).

Wilson, B. (1982) *Religion in Sociological Perspective* (Oxford University Press).

Wilson, D. C. *et al.* (1982) 'The Limits of Trade Union Power in Organisational Decision Making'. *British Journal of Industrial Relations* pp. 322–41.

Winch, R. F. (1971) *The Modern Family* (New York: Holt Rinehart & Winston).

Wright, D. (1978) *The Psychology of Moral Behaviour* (Harmondsworth: Penguin).

Wuthnow, R. (1976 i) 'Recent Patterns of Secularization: A problem of generations?' *American Sociological Review* 41(5), pp. 850–67.

Wuthnow, R. (1976 ii) *The Consciousness Reformation* (Berkeley: University of California Press).

Yinger, J. M. (1962) *Sociology Looks at Religion* (London: Macmillan).

Yinger, J. M. (1977) 'A Comparative Study of the Substructures of Religion' *Journal for the Scientific Study of Religion* 16, pp. 68–86.

Young, M., and P. Willmott (1973) *The Symmetrical Family* (London: Routledge & Kegan Paul).

Zurcher, L., R. Kirkpatrick, R. Cushing and C. Bowman (1973) 'Ad Hoc Anti-Pornography Organisations and Their Active Members: A Research Summary' *Journal of Social Issues* 29, pp. 69–94.

Zurcher, L., and G. Kirkpatrick (1976) *Citizens for Decency: Anti-Pornography Crusades as Status Defence* (Austin: University of Texas Press).

Index